Psychological Drivers of Herding and Market Overreaction

Ooi Kok Loang
University of Malaya, Malaysia

Published in the United States of America by
    IGI Global Scientific Publishing
    701 East Chocolate Avenue
    Hershey, PA, 17033, USA
    Tel: 717-533-8845
    Fax: 717-533-8661
    E-mail: cust@igi-global.com
    Website: https://www.igi-global.com

Copyright © 2025 by IGI Global Scientific Publishing. All rights reserved. No part of this publication may be reproduced, stored or distributed in any form or by any means, electronic or mechanical, including photocopying, without written permission from the publisher.
Product or company names used in this set are for identification purposes only. Inclusion of the names of the products or companies does not indicate a claim of ownership by IGI Global Scientific Publishing of the trademark or registered trademark.

Library of Congress Cataloging-in-Publication Data

CIP PENDING

ISBN13: 9798369378274
Isbn13Softcover: 9798369378281
EISBN13: 9798369378298

Vice President of Editorial: Melissa Wagner
Managing Editor of Acquisitions: Mikaela Felty
Managing Editor of Book Development: Jocelynn Hessler
Production Manager: Mike Brehm
Cover Design: Phillip Shickler

British Cataloguing in Publication Data
A Cataloguing in Publication record for this book is available from the British Library.

All work contributed to this book is new, previously-unpublished material.
The views expressed in this book are those of the authors, but not necessarily of the publisher.
This book contains information sourced from authentic and highly regarded references, with reasonable efforts made to ensure the reliability of the data and information presented. The authors, editors, and publisher believe the information in this book to be accurate and true as of the date of publication. Every effort has been made to trace and credit the copyright holders of all materials included. However, the authors, editors, and publisher cannot assume responsibility for the validity of all materials or the consequences of their use. Should any copyright material be found unacknowledged, please inform the publisher so that corrections may be made in future reprints.

Table of Contents

Preface xiii

Chapter 1
Artificial Intelligence in Detecting Herding and Market Overreaction:
Specifying Impact of Behaviors on Market Dynamics 1
    Bhupinder Singh, Sharda University, India
    Christian Kaunert, Dublin City University, Ireland
    Ritu Gautam, Sharda University, India

Chapter 2
Availability Cascade and Herd Behavior in Financial Markets 23
    Eren Kırmızıaltın, Sinop University, Turkey
    Duygu Çeri, Sinop University, Turkey

Chapter 3
Breaking the Herd Leveraging Financial Mindfulness to Combat Investor
Herding Behavior 53
    J. Manjusha, Christ University, India
    Lakshmi Bhooshetty, Christ University, India

Chapter 4
Emotional Contagion and Financial Markets: The Interplay of Fear, Greed,
and Herding 79
    Ooi Kok Loang, Universiti Malaya, Malaysia

Chapter 5
Herding in Crisis: Financial Contagion and Collective Panic During
Economic Turmoil 101
    Xiong Xu, Chengdu International Studies University, China

Chapter 6
Herding Through the Ages: Historical Perspectives and Modern Implications 123
    Ooi Kok Loang, Universiti Malaya, Malaysia

Chapter 7
Role of Artificial Intelligence in Detecting Herding 145
    Partap Singh, Lovely Professional University, India

Chapter 8
Share Repurchase: Importance and Measuring Its Effect on the Stock Price.... 173
    Lingli Lyu, Peter the Great Saint-Petersburg Polytechnic University,
        Russia
    Liudmila A. Guzikova, Peter the Great Saint-Petersburg Polytechnic
        University, Russia

Chapter 9
The Emotional Rollercoaster of Market Overreaction: Understanding the
Psychological Drivers of Irrational Market Behaviour 221
    Sushil Kumar Gupta, Pune Institute of Business Management, Pune,
        India
    Varsha Shriram Nerlekar, School of Business, Dr. Vishwanath Karad
        MIT World Peace University, India
    Anjali Sane, Dr. Vishwanath Karad MIT World Peace University, India
    Manjiri Gadekar, School of Business, Dr. Vishwanath Karad MIT World
        Peace University, Pune, India
    Shrikant Waghulkar, RIMS, India

Chapter 10
The Herd Mentality Understanding the Theories and Models of Herding
Behavior in Financial Markets 255
    Varsha Shriram Nerlekar, School of Business, Dr. Vishwanath Karad
        MIT World Peace University, India
    Anjali Sane, Dr. Vishwanath Karad MIT World Peace University, India
    Manjiri Gadekar, School of Business, Dr. Vishwanath Karad MIT World
        Peace University, Pune, India
    Sushil Kumar Gupta, Pune Institute of Business Management, Pune,
        India
    Shrikant Waghulkar, RIMS, India

Chapter 11
The Paradox of Crowd Wisdom: When Collective Intelligence Fails in
Financial Markets 291
    Xiong Xu, Chengdu International Studies University, China

Compilation of References 311

About the Contributors 357

Index 363

Detailed Table of Contents

Preface... xiii

Chapter 1
Artificial Intelligence in Detecting Herding and Market Overreaction:
Specifying Impact of Behaviors on Market Dynamics 1
    Bhupinder Singh, Sharda University, India
    Christian Kaunert, Dublin City University, Ireland
    Ritu Gautam, Sharda University, India

Herding behavior, where individuals in a group act collectively without centralized direction, is a phenomenon observed in various domains, including financial markets, consumer behavior and social media trends. Detecting herding behavior is crucial for understanding market dynamics, predicting economic crises, and managing risks. Artificial Intelligence (AI) has emerged as a powerful tool in identifying and analyzing herding patterns due to its ability to process vast amounts of data and uncover complex patterns that are not easily visible through traditional methods. The future of AI in this industry is optimistic, with continued developments promising even higher efficiency and accuracy, despite the limitations. AI will grow more sophisticated in its application to herding behavior detection as it develops, enabling more informed risk management and decision-making. This chapter explores the role of AI in detecting herding, highlighting its applications, benefits, challenges and future prospects.

Chapter 2

Availability Cascade and Herd Behavior in Financial Markets 23

Eren Kırmızıaltın, Sinop University, Turkey
Duygu Çeri, Sinop University, Turkey

Herd behavior is important topics in behavioral finance. In financial markets, herd behavior occurs when investors follow the crowd, making decisions based on current trends or the actions of others rather than conducting their own thorough analysis. This behavior, combined with market overreaction plays a significant role in price volatility and financial instability. To analyze these behaviors effectively, it's essential to understand the underlying mechanisms, particularly the psychological and cognitive factors that drive them. This study focuses on the connection between herd behavior and the availability cascade. Given the focus of this study, the analysis has been tailored to explore this relationship specifically. Consequently, the study not only focuses on the psychological and cognitive factors that cause herding behavior in financial markets but also tries to explain the relationship between the psychological and cognitive factors that cause herding behavior and the availability cascade.

Chapter 3

Breaking the Herd Leveraging Financial Mindfulness to Combat Investor
Herding Behavior 53

J. Manjusha, Christ University, India
Lakshmi Bhooshetty, Christ University, India

This chapter examines herding behaviour in investors that affect the financial market. Herding involves investors mimicking others' actions due to factors like limited information, market sentiments, and psychological biases. Individual investors, less informed and more susceptible to emotions, herd more. Drawing from Buddhist economics, financial mindfulness emerges as a crucial intervention to mitigate herding. It promotes awareness of one's financial situation, enhancing independent decision-making and reducing impulsive behaviour. Empirical evidence supports mindfulness-based interventions in improving financial decisions and managing debt effectively. By cultivating a thoughtful approach to finance, financial mindfulness empowers investors to resist herd behaviour, fostering stability in financial markets.

Chapter 4

Emotional Contagion and Financial Markets: The Interplay of Fear, Greed, and Herding.. 79

Ooi Kok Loang, Universiti Malaya, Malaysia

The study investigates the complex dynamics that drive market overreaction in financial markets. This research focuses on the impact of emotional states (fear and greed), market news and rumors, peer influence, market volatility, and investor experience on market overreaction. The study employs the concepts of emotional contagion as a mediating variable and social proof as a moderating variable to understand how these factors interact and influence market behaviour. The findings highlight the significant role of emotional states and social dynamics in driving market inefficiencies. Emotional contagion is shown to amplify the impact of fear and greed, market news and rumors, peer influence, and market volatility on market overreaction. Conversely, social proof moderates these relationships, often intensifying the effect of emotions and social influences on market behaviour. The study's results underscore the importance of considering psychological and social factors in financial market analysis and regulatory frameworks.

Chapter 5

Herding in Crisis: Financial Contagion and Collective Panic During Economic Turmoil 101

Xiong Xu, Chengdu International Studies University, China

This study investigates the impact of media coverage intensity, market volatility, investor sentiment, institutional investor activity, and regulatory announcements on market stability, incorporating the moderating effect of social network influence and the mediating effect of financial contagion. Using panel data regression and structural equation modeling, the research aims to provide a nuanced understanding of the dynamics influencing market stability. The findings reveal that media coverage intensity, investor sentiment, and regulatory announcements positively impact market stability, while market volatility negatively impacts it. Institutional investor activity also contributes positively to market stability. Furthermore, social network influence moderates these relationships, either amplifying or mitigating the impacts, and financial contagion mediates the effects, weakening the positive impacts.

Chapter 6
Herding Through the Ages: Historical Perspectives and Modern Implications 123
  Ooi Kok Loang, Universiti Malaya, Malaysia

This study investigates the multifaceted influences on herding behaviour in financial markets, focusing on the impact of historical market events, regulatory changes, economic indicators, social and political events, and technological advancements. Utilizing market structure as a moderating variable and investor learning as a mediating variable, the research provides a comprehensive analysis of the dynamics that drive herding behaviour. The study employs panel data regression and structural equation modeling to analyze the interactions between these variables and their collective impact on herding behaviour. The findings indicate that historical market events, regulatory changes, economic indicators, social and political events, and technological advancements significantly influence herding behaviour. Market structure moderates these relationships, with certain structures either amplifying or dampening the effects. Additionally, investor learning mediates the impact of these factors, with higher levels of financial literacy and education mitigating herding behaviour.

Chapter 7
Role of Artificial Intelligence in Detecting Herding 145
  Partap Singh, Lovely Professional University, India

This research investigates the role of Artificial Intelligence (AI) in detecting herding behavior in financial markets. Herding, a phenomenon where investors follow the majority, can lead to market inefficiencies and increased volatility. By leveraging AI techniques, including machine learning and deep learning, this study aims to improve the detection and understanding of herding patterns. The research explores how AI models can analyze large datasets, recognize non-linear relationships, and identify subtle patterns indicative of herding. It gives the picture of Factors Affecting Herd-Behavior, Impact of Herd-Behavior, Sources for data analysis for detecting Herding with AI, Navigating Herding with AI, Challenges and threats in Detecting Herding with AI. The findings suggest that AI provides more accurate and timely detection of herding behavior compared to traditional methods, offering significant implications for market stability and investor strategies.

Chapter 8

Share Repurchase: Importance and Measuring Its Effect on the Stock Price.... 173

*Lingli Lyu, Peter the Great Saint-Petersburg Polytechnic University,
Russia*

*Liudmila A. Guzikova, Peter the Great Saint-Petersburg Polytechnic
University, Russia*

Share repurchase refers to the behavior of listed companies to repurchase their own shares from the stock market for stabilizing the share price and improving the governance structure. The empirical evidence of share repurchase of Chinese A-share listed companies during the period from 2021.1.1 to 2024.1.1 is collected to construct a model, and an empirical study is conducted based on the event study method in STATA. The top four industries with the highest percentage in the sample are selected for comparative analysis. The results of the study show that for the effect of share repurchase on share price, China's stock market also behaves in the same way as the western capital market, and share repurchase has a significant positive promotion effect on listed companies' stock price, but the promotion effect is short-lived. It is also found that listed firms with share repurchases have significant positive excess stock returns before the repurchase announcement, reflecting the fact that there is indeed an early leakage of repurchase information in the Chinese share repurchase market.

Chapter 9
The Emotional Rollercoaster of Market Overreaction: Understanding the
Psychological Drivers of Irrational Market Behaviour 221
Sushil Kumar Gupta, Pune Institute of Business Management, Pune,
India
Varsha Shriram Nerlekar, School of Business, Dr. Vishwanath Karad
MIT World Peace University, India
Anjali Sane, Dr. Vishwanath Karad MIT World Peace University, India
Manjiri Gadekar, School of Business, Dr. Vishwanath Karad MIT World
Peace University, Pune, India
Shrikant Waghulkar, RIMS, India

Market overreactions, driven by psychological and cognitive factors, have significant economic consequences, impacting individual investors and broader financial systems. This chapter explores how emotions like fear, anxiety, greed, and euphoria contribute to market volatility, alongside cognitive biases such as confirmation and anchoring. It also examines herding behavior, the influence of authority figures, and the role of media in shaping market sentiment. Additionally, it considers neurological and physiological factors like stress and dopamine responses in investor behavior. Through case studies, the chapter illustrates these drivers' real-world impacts and offers strategies for mitigating emotional and cognitive biases. Emphasizing diversification, risk management, and regulatory measures, it provides insights for investors and policymakers to navigate and stabilize market overreactions.

Chapter 10
The Herd Mentality Understanding the Theories and Models of Herding
Behavior in Financial Markets 255
 Varsha Shriram Nerlekar, School of Business, Dr. Vishwanath Karad
  MIT World Peace University, India
 Anjali Sane, Dr. Vishwanath Karad MIT World Peace University, India
 Manjiri Gadekar, School of Business, Dr. Vishwanath Karad MIT World
  Peace University, Pune, India
 Sushil Kumar Gupta, Pune Institute of Business Management, Pune,
  India
 Shrikant Waghulkar, RIMS, India

This chapter explores herding behavior in financial markets, where individuals follow the actions of a larger group, impacting market dynamics and asset prices. It covers key theories and models, such as social influence, behavioral finance, and empirical studies, to explain why herding occurs. Psychological biases like overconfidence, fear, and greed are highlighted as drivers of this behavior. Models such as rational expectations, noise traders, and information cascades are discussed, along with methods to measure herding. Case studies like the dot-com bubble and the 2008 financial crisis demonstrate its effects on market volatility and efficiency. The chapter also addresses regulatory implications and future research on the influence of technology and social media in shaping herding.

Chapter 11
The Paradox of Crowd Wisdom: When Collective Intelligence Fails in
Financial Markets 291
Xiong Xu, Chengdu International Studies University, China

The notion of "wisdom of crowds" postulates that collective decision-making often outperforms individual judgements. However, in financial markets, this collective intelligence can falter, leading to inefficiencies and anomalies. This study investigates the factors contributing to the failure of collective intelligence in financial markets, specifically examining information cascades, cognitive biases, market sentiment, herding behaviour, and market performance. Using the Adaptive Market Hypothesis (AMH) as a theoretical framework, the research explores how these factors interact and impact market efficiency. Employing panel data regression and quantile regression, the study provides a comprehensive analysis of market dynamics across different conditions. The findings underscore the crucial roles of investor education and regulatory environment in moderating and mediating these relationships, offering valuable insights for policymakers, financial managers, and investors in enhancing market stability and efficiency.

Compilation of References 311

About the Contributors 357

Index 363

Preface

In the world of finance, the allure of quick profits and the fear of potential losses often drive investors to act in ways that defy logic, resulting in phenomena such as herding and market overreaction. However, what if these behaviours, which are often dismissed as irrational, are actually driven by deep-seated psychological patterns? *Psychological Drivers of Herding and Market Overreaction* dive into a fascinating intersection of psychology and financial markets, unravelling the hidden forces that shape investor behaviour.

This book serves as both a comprehensive guide and a fresh exploration of why investors frequently follow the crowd, make impulsive decisions, and succumb to waves of collective emotion. Each chapter offers readers a window into the psychological and emotional triggers that underpin market dynamics, shedding light on everything from the *Availability Cascade* and *Emotional Contagion* to the paradoxical *Wisdom of the Crowd*. We explore how, during times of crisis, herding intensifies, as fear and uncertainty spread through markets like wildfires, leading to amplified risks and unexpected outcomes.

However, this was not merely a theoretical exploration. With the rise of *Artificial Intelligence*, new tools are now available to detect and predict herding and overreaction patterns in real time. This book also examines how AI-driven analysis transforms our understanding of these behaviours by equipping investors and regulators with strategies to mitigate the impact of collective irrationality. For instance, chapters on "AI in Detecting Herding and Market Overreaction" and "Breaking the Herd with Financial Mindfulness" offer actionable insights into how data-driven approaches and psychological awareness can help counteract market biases.

Each topic was chosen to resonate with the modern reader, particularly as we confront the volatility and unpredictability of today's financial world. Whether it's understanding the *Emotional Rollercoaster* of market overreaction or analyzing the real-world impacts of *Share Repurchase* on stock prices, this book offers a deep dive into the psychological drivers that shape financial landscapes. We also tackle how specific triggers—such as *Availability Cascades* and *Fear of Missing Out*

(FOMO)—can sway even the most seasoned investors, leading them down paths they would normally avoid.

Psychological Drivers of Herding and Market Overreaction are crafted to appeal to diverse audiences. Whether you are a financial professional looking to better understand market psychology, a researcher exploring behavioral finance, or simply a curious reader, this book will provide you with fresh perspectives and a deeper appreciation for the forces shaping today's markets. In each chapter, we dissect the theories, present historical and modern examples, and offer forward-looking insights into how to navigate the complex psychology of finance.

Prepare to uncover the psychological currents that drive markets and discover how these insights can empower people to make better, more informed decisions in a world driven by the powerful dynamics of crowd behaviour and emotional overreaction.

Chapter 1
Artificial Intelligence in Detecting Herding and Market Overreaction:
Specifying Impact of Behaviors on Market Dynamics

Bhupinder Singh
https://orcid.org/0009-0006-4779-2553
Sharda University, India

Christian Kaunert
https://orcid.org/0000-0002-4493-2235
Dublin City University, Ireland

Ritu Gautam
Sharda University, India

ABSTRACT

Herding behavior, where individuals in a group act collectively without centralized direction, is a phenomenon observed in various domains, including financial markets, consumer behavior and social media trends. Detecting herding behavior is crucial for understanding market dynamics, predicting economic crises, and managing risks. Artificial Intelligence (AI) has emerged as a powerful tool in identifying and analyzing herding patterns due to its ability to process vast amounts of data and uncover complex patterns that are not easily visible through traditional methods. The future of AI in this industry is optimistic, with continued developments promising even higher efficiency and accuracy, despite the limitations. AI will grow more sophisticated in its application to herding behavior detection as it develops, enabling

DOI: 10.4018/979-8-3693-7827-4.ch001

Copyright © 2025, IGI Global Scientific Publishing. Copying or distributing in print or electronic forms without written permission of IGI Global is prohibited.

more informed risk management and decision-making. This chapter explores the role of AI in detecting herding, highlighting its applications, benefits, challenges and future prospects.

1. INTRODUCTION

Herd behavior occurs when individuals in a group follow the actions of others instead of relying on their own information or analysis. This can lead to significant market movements, asset bubbles, and crashes. Key areas where herd behavior is observed include Financial Markets: Investors often mimic the trades of others, creating market trends that can result in bubbles or crashes; Consumer Behavior: Buyers purchase products that are popular or trending, often influenced by social proof and peer recommendations; Social Media: Viral trends and the rapid spread of information or misinformation can be attributed to herd behavior among users. In many different sectors, artificial intelligence is essential for identifying herding behavior. It is a priceless tool for social media monitoring, consumer behavior analysis, and the financial markets because to its capacity to handle massive information, reveal intricate patterns, and generate predictive insights. A phenomenon known as "herd behavior" occurs when people behave collectively as members of a group, often coming to conclusions as a group that they would not have individually (Hussain & Alaya, 2024).

Herd behavior may be explained by one of two commonly recognized theories as to begin with, people are driven by social pressure to fit in by imitating the behaviors of others, even when such behaviors go against their innermost desires. Secondly, people often find it hard to accept that a sizable group may be erroneous and end up adopting the group's actions because they mistakenly think that the collective knows something that the individual does not. When a large number of people adopt the same conduct mostly because that is what everyone else is doing, it is known as herding. This phenomenon may happen in a variety of settings, including investing, shopping and sports (Jagirdar & Gupta, 2024).

Figure 1. The Dimensions of Introduction Split Sections (Source- Original)

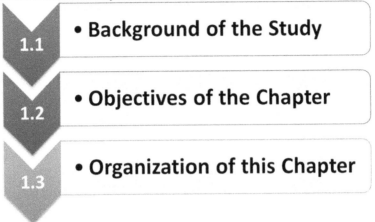

1.1 Background of the Study

Herding behavior refers to how individual decisions are influenced by the actions of a group. It originates from the observation that if a herd of animals begin moving in one direction, all the animals tend to follow. Introduced in the middle of the 1960s, the Efficient Market Hypothesis (EMH) is a well recognized financial hypothesis. According to this theory, significant price swings are the outcome of markets responding to fresh information from outside sources or shifting fundamentals. Financial markets are unable to produce internal forces that would upset equilibrium. The Efficient Market Hypothesis holds that asset values do not rise or fall.

The EMH's capacity to explain phenomena in financial markets is called into question by statistics and historical occurrences. Bubbles and crashes have happened and will continue to happen, as evidenced by events like the Dutch tulip bubble in 1626, the South Sea bubble in the UK, the French Mississippi bubble in the early 1700s, the Japanese bubble in the 1980s, and the recent US subprime mortgage crisis and the 2008 financial crisis. More and more individuals are of the opinion that conventional economic theories are unable to account for these financial booms, collapses, and associated crises. As a result, interest in agent-based models (ABMs) has increased as a substitute approach to comprehending the intricate dynamics of financial markets. This "following the crowd" phenomenon is also seen in economics. For instance, if individuals notice a popular interest in purchasing a particular asset, they may interpret this popularity as a cue to follow suit. Because people consciously or unconsciously mimic others' actions, the market can exhibit collective irrationality, challenging the efficient market hypothesis. If a mortgage advisor recommends taking out a subprime mortgage, people often assume—either consciously or unconsciously that the advisor knows what they're doing, given their professional experience in the industry. A strong aspect of human psychology is the desire not to miss out. This can drive people to follow prevailing market sentiments (Singh & Kaunert, 2024).

John Maynard Keynes noted in "The General Theory" (1936)" Worldly wisdom teaches that it is better for reputation to fail conventionally than to succeed unconventionally. This quote illustrates Keynes' point that failing in line with the majority can protect one from criticism. If everyone makes the same mistake, blame is less likely to fall on an individual. Conversely, taking a contrarian stance makes one a target for majority opinion. If the majority is correct and you are not, you are isolated and embarrassed. Even if the majority is wrong, proving them wrong may not earn you any friends. Hence, following the crowd aligns you with your peers, preventing you from being seen as a "loose cannon," which can also drive herding behavior. In financial markets, herding behavior is especially prevalent in finance and asset investment, areas where people often lack specific expertise and emotions play a significant role. For example, most individuals are not housing market experts. If house prices are raising and many experts advocate buying, people may follow this trend, assuming others have knowledge they don't possess (Lo & Zhang, 2024).

1.2 Objectives of the Chapter

This chapter has the following objectives to-

- scrutinize the fundamental processes and components that lead to herding behavior and market overreaction in financial markets in order to analyze the processes of Herding and Market Overreaction.
- determine how well different AI methods, such machine learning and neural networks, operate in real-time to identify herding behavior and market overreaction.
- look at how found cases of herding and overreaction affect the general dynamics of the market, such as price changes, volatility, and stability.
- enhance the precision and dependability of identifying behavioral abnormalities, a thorough framework for integrating AI into conventional financial market analysis must be developed.
- make recommendations for useful uses of AI-driven insights for investors and market regulators. These uses should improve decision-making procedures and put policies in place to lessen the negative effects of herding and market overreaction.

Figure 2. The Objectives of the Chapter (Source- Original)

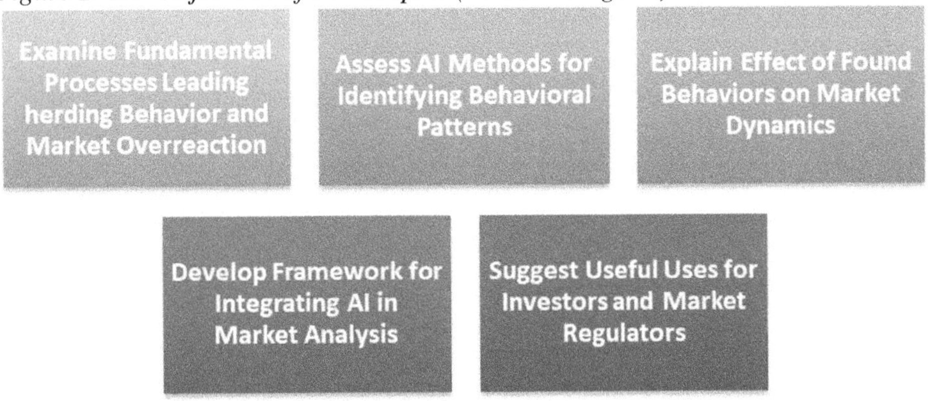

Examine Fundamental Processes Leading herding Behavior and Market Overreaction

Assess AI Methods for Identifying Behavioral Patterns

Explain Effect of Found Behaviors on Market Dynamics

Develop Framework for Integrating AI in Market Analysis

Suggest Useful Uses for Investors and Market Regulators

1.3 Organization of this Chapter

This chapter deeply dives into the diverse arena of Artificial Intelligence in Detecting Herding and Market Overreaction: Specifying Impact of Behaviors on Market Dynamics. Section 2 elaborates the Herding Behavior and Market Overreaction in Financial Markets. Section 3 specifies the Artificial Intelligence (AI) in Financial Market Analysis. Section 4 lays down the AI Techniques for Detecting Herding Behavior. Section 5 conveys the Detection of Market Overreaction. Section 6 explores the Impact of Herding and Overreaction on Market Dynamics. Section 7 Conclude the Chapter with Future Scope.

Figure 3. The Flow of this Chapter (Source- Original)

2. HERDING BEHAVIOR AND MARKET OVERREACTION IN FINANCIAL MARKETS

The rational or illogical conduct is influenced by an individual's degree of self-confidence. Personal conditions and factors which may originate from a variety of motivations have an impact on overconfidence. Three categories of overconfidence were distinguished as overestimation of one's own talents, overplacement of one's own beliefs and overprecision of one's statements on their correctness. . Herding behavior has characteristics with other behavioral biases such the illusion of control, self-serving bias, hindsight bias, and cognitive dissonance. Evolutionary origins may be found in overconfidence behavior, which is shown in many forms. Human language, memory, and mental processes are consistently skewed toward positivity. The self-deception has a long history stemming from the development of the brain. Positive illusions were advantageous for hunter-gatherer communities in warfare, interpersonal fighting, disputes, bargaining, enticing friends, and discouraging competitors (Singh et al., 2024).

These delusions have serious repercussions for chances for reproduction, resource availability, and survival. Investors who are driven by self-righteousness or a sense of superiority tend to become overconfident, which is often shown in "overtrading" in an attempt to maximize gains. The causal relationship between returns and trading volume is acknowledged in the empirical literature as proof of overconfidence. Overconfidence may sometimes be beneficial since it can be reinforced by favorable results, such as large gains from overtrading. Therefore, it is essential to look at the situations in which having too much confidence might be advantageous. The Efficient Markets Hypothesis (EMH), which maintains that market prices accurately represent all available information, has long dominated theories of finance and economics. EMH holds that without taking on above-average risks, investors cannot generate above-average returns. This theory has been extensively used in theoretical models and empirical research on the pricing of financial assets, leading to a great deal of debate and offering important new understandings of the process of price discovery. The representative agent framework which portrays a person as a utility maximizer who acts in accordance with their preferences and restrictions while upholding the principles of rational choice theory has served as the foundation for many financial theories and models. However, the validity of expected utility theory, Bayesian learning, and rational expectations as descriptive theories of decision-making has been called into question by psychologists and behavioral scientists over the past few decades due to systematic and consistent violations of these concepts. It also highlighted the idea of bounded rationality, which takes into account humans' limited ability to adapt to complicated surroundings in an optimum or even satisfactory way (Saltik, 2024).

Figure 4. The Points on Herding Behavior and Market Overreaction in Financial Markets (Source- Original)

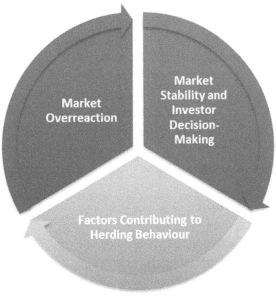

2.1 Market Stability and Investor Decision-Making

Understanding the many facets and variables that might affect decision-making is essential to making the best financial choices. Our study takes a holistic approach by taking into account a number of aspects, in contrast to earlier studies that usually only looked at one. The purpose of this research was to determine the factors that financial firms listed on the Iraqi stock exchanges (ISX) consider when making investment choices. Six businesses from the study's sample were the subject of the investigation. A standardized questionnaire of eight questions was delivered to each responder individually in order to gather data. The split-half technique and test-retest method were used to examine the questionnaire's variables for normal distribution, multicollinearity, content and face validity, and stability. This represents a good and almost comprehensive interpretation of the influence of the extracted dimensions on investment choices. The indications for the coefficients of the five variables were positive, suggesting that the factors had a direct influence on investment choices, even if the regression coefficients for all variables showed a little reduction (Kabir et al., 2024).

2.2 Factors Contributing to Herding Behaviour

Herding behavior is influenced psychologically by heuristics, emotions, motivational variables, social conventions, and personality features. These factors have the potential to produce systematic judgment mistakes, which might result in illogical or poor judgments being made by investors. Compliant and aggressive personality qualities are known to considerably increase herding behavior, whereas detached personality traits significantly decrease it. Herding behavior is also significantly influenced by motivational elements such as emotional factors, social influences, and cognitive abilities. Herding behavior may be influenced by a variety of demographic variables, including age, gender, and marital status, as well as by word-of-mouth financial information sources. Furthermore, the presence of financial crises and speculative booms might affect investors' tendency to herd. In developing and emerging markets, herding behavior is more prevalent, especially in bullish or negative market situations (Silver, 2024).

2.3 Market Overreaction

An excessive emotional reaction to fresh knowledge is known as an overreaction. In the context of finance and investing, it describes a fear- or greed-driven emotional reaction to a security, such a stock or other investment. When investors respond excessively to news, the asset either overbought or oversold until it reaches its inherent value again. When stocks become overly overbought or oversold for psychological rather than fundamental reasons, the financial markets experience an overreaction. Overreactions to the upside and downside are best shown by bubbles and crashes, respectively. Overreactions should not happen, according to the efficient markets hypothesis, but behavioral finance indicates that they do, offering possibilities for astute investors to profit from them. The investors do not always make sense and emotions influence a lot of people's choices to purchase and sell. Having quick access to news and information around-the-clock may cause investors to behave irrationally. Investors are typically swayed by cognitive and emotional biases, rather than correctly and instantaneously valuing all publicly available information as the efficient market theory predicts. Funds that seek to profit from overreactions search for businesses whose stock has dropped due to unfavorable earnings reports, but where the drop is probably transitory (Raja & Messaoudi, 2024). Value stocks, or low price-to-book stocks, are one kind of investment that offers such prospects. On the other hand, underreaction to fresh information is often more irreversible. Anchoring, or the tendency for individuals to hold to outdated knowledge, particularly when it confirms their preexisting worldview, is a common source of underreaction also known as a hermeneutic. Anchoring beliefs like "brick and mortar retail stores are dead" might lead to investors missing out on profitable possibilities and cheap firms (Singh & Kaunert, 2024).

3. ARTIFICIAL INTELLIGENCE (AI) IN FINANCIAL MARKET ANALYSIS

All businesses, including the financial sector, are changing due to the AI surge. AI is becoming more and more common in the financial services industry, changing established organizations by developing more effective operational models. The potential AI gives to financial markets and the difficulties it poses to different stakeholders are examined. AI technologies provide fast and effective process execution for businesses. To make wise choices and precise forecasts, traders need to take into account a number of variables, including the market, economics, and strategy. AI may help by making up for conventional financial models' shortcomings (Ni, 2024).

Machine Learning and Big Data

Large volumes of data, including stock prices, news stories, macroeconomic indicators, and sentiment analysis, are analyzed by AI systems using machine learning. Artificial intelligence (AI) can handle millions of data points in seconds, in contrast to human analysis, which may be constrained by missing data, delay, or errors. It is capable of mobilizing several data sources, analyzing multiple data kinds at once market prices, news, social media postings, satellite photos, etc. and seeing intricate connections and patterns between numerous factors that human traders could overlook. Large amounts of historical and current data are analyzed by computers using statistical techniques to find patterns, which enables more precise forecasts of future market movements. In addition, these AI systems are capable of autonomously deriving rules and continually learning to become better decision makers (Singh et al., 2024)

Quants and High-frequency Trading

More than half of all US equities trading is done by quants and high-frequency traders. In high-frequency trading (HFT), where there is a race to maximize automation and reduce execution and reaction times to nanoseconds, artificial intelligence (AI) algorithms play a critical role. AI shortens execution times by allowing HFT players to profit from an autonomous value chain. At a speed only robots could be able to match, these technologies can quickly identify signals, formulate plans, and place trades in order to seize chances and profit from small fluctuations in the market (Zhu et al., 2024).

Effectiveness of Operations

Businesses in a variety of sectors have been able to lower operating costs and boost productivity thanks to automation and computerized company processes, which has enhanced operational efficiency and profitability. Financial organizations also show this tendency. Because to automated trading algorithms, the number of traders on Goldman Sachs' U.S. cash equities trading desk in New York has decreased significantly over the previous 20 years from 600 in 2000 to only two in 2017. Using neural networks to create its software, Goldman Sachs has extended the usage of AI-driven programs beyond the stocks to the FX and derivatives markets. AI is automating back-office and front-office tasks. The new AI-powered order type on Nasdaq decreased markouts by 11.4% and increased fill rates by 20.3%. AI also reduces costs brought on by operational risks like fraud and human mistake. BlackRock introduced Aladdin, an AI-based tool for risk assessment and portfolio management, to turn its risk management division into a source of income (Singh et al., 2024).

Difficulties

Financial institutions may be at danger from both traditional and generative AI since many cutting-edge solutions come from outside providers. The implementation of these technologies may have significant repercussions for data privacy if these organizations fail to do appropriate due diligence. There are hazards associated with AI technology since it relies on information from all users to improve its skills, identify trends, and make conclusions. It's critical to reduce the likelihood of data leaks since they may have a negative effect on investors and companies, particularly when it comes to sensitive information (Cervellati et al., 2024). A manipulated photo of an explosion outside causes market movements, demonstrating the potential danger of AI-generated material. This incident made clear how players may take advantage of the weaknesses in the financial markets. Fraud schemes may use voice cloning or other forms of spoofing to further influence markets. In order to safeguard cybersecurity and stop false information from inciting investor fear and upsetting the market, closer examination of new technologies is necessary (Othman, 2024).

3.1 Techniques used in AI for Market Analysis: Machine Learning and Neural Networks

The propensity of traders or investors to follow the lead of their peers instead of making their own conclusions based on research and analysis is known as herding behavior. Essentially, investors do not do fundamental analysis or market research they just purchase or sell assets because others are doing so. Herd mentality may cause prices to increase or fall swiftly and unexpectedly, which can result in market bubbles or collapses. Herding behavior is typically motivated by emotions like fear, greed, and panic (Saltik et al., 2024). The availability of real-time information and social media, which magnify the activities of the herd, may exacerbate these emotions even more. In a number of financial markets, such as stocks, bonds, and commodities, herding behavior may be seen. Investors must be able to identify this tendency and refrain from basing their judgments only on what other people have done (Singh et al., 2024).

4. AI TECHNIQUES FOR DETECTING HERDING BEHAVIOR

Artificial intelligence (AI) describes computer programs that can do activities like voice recognition, image interpretation, and decision making that normally needs human intellect. AI technologies are improving banking, investing, insurance, and other financial operations and providing new insights. Computers may learn from data without explicit programming thanks to machine learning (ML), a subset of artificial intelligence. Regression, random forests, and neural networks are examples of machine learning (ML) methods used in finance that find patterns in data to automate tasks or forecast fraud, pricing, risks, and other variables. A specific kind of machine learning called deep learning (DL) makes use of multi-layered artificial neural networks to extract knowledge from very large datasets, such financial transaction histories (Dimitriadou, 2024). Credit scoring, chatbots, algorithmic trading, and anti-money laundering technologies are all driven by DL. Understanding human languages is the main goal of natural language processing, or NLP. In order to automate procedures or gain insights into risks, sentiment, and compliance, NLP is used in the banking industry to evaluate earnings calls, news, regulations, client inquiries, and other texts. Computers can now read and comprehend digital photos and movies thanks to computer vision (CV). In the financial industry, CV is used for duties like as checking checks, keeping an eye on tangible assets, examining face expressions, and thwarting fraud (Shukla et al., 2024).

Artificial intelligence (AI) promises to provide new capabilities and efficiency to financial institutions, improving their capacity to serve clients by automating repetitive processes and uncovering hidden patterns. Banking procedures are being quickly transformed by AI to become more economical and efficient. AI systems automate manual activities by analyzing large data sets, freeing up workers to concentrate on higher-value work. Routine customer support inquiries are handled by AI chatbots, which speed up response times and free up contact center employees. AI also improves fraud prevention and detection by examining millions of transactions to find minute patterns that point to fraud faster and more precisely than humans (Singh & Kaunert, 2024). With using these techniques, banks may reduce fraud losses by identifying fraudulent transactions in real time. With adding an extra layer of verification and guaranteeing that only authorized users may access financial transactions and services, digital identity can help lower AI-based fraud (Abdullah et al., 2024).

Compared to conventional approaches, AI systems provide more accurate and equitable evaluations by generating credit risk ratings from a variety of client data. In order to enhance client satisfaction and increase conversion rates, banks may also use AI to provide tailored product suggestions based on past transactions and spending trends. Because AI can handle enormous volumes of data more quickly than humans and can identify dangers and fraudulent activity that could otherwise go undetected, it is revolutionizing risk management and compliance in the banking industry (Ncube et al., 2024). Artificial intelligence (AI) techniques are used for anti-money laundering (AML) surveillance and know-your-customer (KYC) checks, flagging suspect activities for further examination. With finding connections in big datasets, AI improves predictive analytics, scenario planning, and risk assessments, allowing for more sophisticated financial analysis and risk models. As a result, lending, insurance underwriting, and investment choices are made with more knowledge (Singh, 2024).

Artificial Intelligence (AI) improves digital financial transaction security in decentralized finance (DeFi). AI-powered smart contract audits defend against complex financial crimes by identifying weaknesses and preventing fraud. Even though AI has numerous advantages, there are still concerns about bias, explainability, and ethical dilemmas. In order to guarantee that AI systems improve speed, accuracy, and efficiency while people set corporate objectives, risk tolerance, and ethical standards, governance structures and human supervision are crucial (Talbi et al., 2024).

Figure 5. The AI Techniques for Detecting Herding Behavior (Source- Original)

5. DETECTION OF MARKET OVERREACTION AND AI

To decide what to buy, banks, brokers, trading companies, and hedge funds examine a tonne of data. It costs a lot of money and time to examine alternative data—data assets used to get insights into the investing process. As a result, a distinct market where information is gathered, vetted, and sold to trading firms has emerged (Singh, 2024). The investing community relies heavily on the optimization of data analysis and financial projections; hence, the application of AI to finance and trading represents a critical answer. Forecasts of market trends are anticipated to be significantly impacted by artificial intelligence software for stock trading. Banking, investing, and insurance are just a few of the financial industry sectors that artificial intelligence (AI) is poised to transform (Su & Debg, 2024). Finance will be easier to access, more efficient, and less prone to prejudice or human mistake thanks to artificial intelligence and machine learning. Like any quickly developing technology, artificial intelligence (AI) brings with it new difficulties and worries. It will be necessary to handle important concerns including ethics, regulations, and changes to the workforce. Regulators and governments will need to strike a balance between promoting innovation and shielding customers from possible exploitation or unforeseen repercussions (Ahmed et al., 2024).

To gain the confidence of end users, the banking sector must also prioritize quality control and the explainability of intricate machine learning models. In general, AI has a lot to offer society and the banking sector—that is, assuming the right legislative frameworks are put in place. Improved fraud detection, tailored asset management, and more accurate underwriting might all be advantageous to consumers. AI signals the start of a fascinating new age in the financial sector (Singh & Kaunert, 2024). Over the course of the next 10 years and beyond, however, concerted efforts by corporations, consumers, civil society, and politicians will be needed to realize its full potential while controlling risks and transition costs. DataCamp can assist with practical data and AI training for your finance staff. Developing the data skills of staff can- Increase income by using machine learning to provide more individualized client interactions; Cut expenses by mechanizing tedious task; Enhance the precision and dependability of reporting - Reduce risk by using the most recent analytical methods in portfolio management and credit risk modeling (Singh, 2024).

6. IMPACT OF HERDING AND OVERREACTION ON MARKET DYNAMICS

AI is revolutionizing the financial services sector's operations and improving client satisfaction. From an operational perspective, artificial intelligence automates procedures and saves money. Robotic process automation expedites and lowers human error in repetitive, high-volume jobs like claims management and loan processing. Massive volumes of organized and unstructured data are analyzed by AI to find insights that people would overlook (Persakis & Koutoupis, 2024). Banks use artificial intelligence (AI) algorithms to evaluate social media, news, and market data in order to inform trading and investing choices. AI is used by insurance firms to better forecast risk, identify fraud early, and determine more precise rates. AI chatbots and virtual assistants can interpret natural language, retrieve client data, and respond to frequently asked questions while offering 24/7 customer care at a fraction of the cost of human workers. Handling more complicated problems to human personnel goes more easily, saving a lot of money and increasing customer satisfaction (Vidani, 2024).

Finance-related AI system implementation presents logistical and regulatory issues. AI initiatives need to be carefully managed by financial institutions to guarantee data security, quality, and compliance with regulations. To train AI models, it is essential to have clean, representative data. Financial institutions need to have strong data governance procedures in place and make sure that private client information is secure and anonymised. Financial rules must be followed by AI systems, and businesses need to have model risk management processes in place to keep an eye on AI performance, identify biases, and handle unexpected consequences (Singh & Kaunert, 2024). For AI workloads, storage and processing infrastructure may be costly. Financial companies often use cloud infrastructure, however there are obstacles due to legal obligations for data protection and domicile. There are difficulties in integrating contemporary AI techniques with antiquated IT infrastructure. Since laws and ethical standards are changing quickly, managing regulatory expectations surrounding AI is difficult. Financial firms need to keep an eye on changes in regulations and have adaptable procedures. They are capable of overcoming these obstacles with rigorous project governance and scoping (Manahov, 2024).

When integrating AI into finance, ethical concerns like prejudice and justice are crucial. Biases in training data may be strengthened or perpetuated by AI systems. Fairness-aware machine learning methods are being used by financial organizations to guarantee that AI judgments do not unfairly affect any one group (Singh, 2023). Decision-making procedures using AI may be made more transparent and responsible with the support of ethical committees and other measures. Experts believe artificial intelligence will keep changing the financial sector. AI will be used in sophisticated ways to data analysis, pattern recognition, process automation, and recommendation making. AI may develop to the point where it can execute complex trading strategies and make precise market forecasts in the investing and trading domains, maximizing profits. However, as AI becomes increasingly involved in financial decision-making, proper oversight will be required (Brini & Lenz, 2024).

With data analysis, artificial intelligence (AI) can help banks better understand their consumers and provide more individualized services. Advanced chatbots and robo-advisors will get more human-like. Complex AI systems will automate manual operations like fraud detection and loan application screening, but human supervision and control will always be essential (Affah et al., 2024). AI is also revolutionizing the regulation and evaluation of financial risk. In order to help regulators with supervision, machine learning can evaluate alternative data and identify hazards or occurrences that people would overlook. Accountability, however, will depend on

AI systems' explanations and openness. Even though AI greatly improves efficiency, intelligence, and creativity, human engagement in finance is essential. We need hybrid intelligence systems, which integrate AI with human knowledge, morality, and feelings. This human-AI partnership is where finance is headed (Nia et al., 2024).

7. CONCLUSION AND FUTURE SCOPE

Herding may have an impact on your financial judgments and t is helpful to comprehend how it functions, such as the herd effect happens when a large number of individuals follow suit mostly due to peer pressure. The bandwagon effect and herding are some names for this phenomenon. The primary emphasis of finance has always been on data analysis to forecast returns and risks. However, human analysis has its limitations given the massive volumes of digital data available today. Finding the needles in the financial data haystacks is where artificial intelligence (AI) comes in. AI is automating repetitive operations and seeing intricate patterns, changing the financial industry. It can provide insights beyond human capacity by analyzing millions of data points, documents, and news items. Significantly better forecasting, real-time risk assessment, and more intelligent investment choices are among the possible advantages. But it goes beyond financial gain. AI in finance has the potential to increase access to credit and financial instruments when used responsibly. AI may be the answer to improved financial management in a world where complexity is rising, from Wall Street to community banks and even household budgets. Thus may not always be aware of how behavioral biases like the herd effect affect your financial choices. With concentrating on your long-term objectives and developing a personalized financial strategy with the assistance of a certified financial counselor, it may lessen the influence of the herd effect.

REFERENCES

Abdullah, M., Sulong, Z., & Chowdhury, M. A. F. (2024). Explainable deep learning model for stock price forecasting using textual analysis. *Expert Systems with Applications*, 249, 123740. DOI: 10.1016/j.eswa.2024.123740

Afifah, N., Nugraha, N., Purnamasari, I., Supriatna, Y., Rahayu, A., & Wibowo, L. A. (2024, June). Strategic Role of Climate Finance: A Bibliometric Analysis. In *8th Global Conference on Business, Management, and Entrepreneurship (GCBME 2023)* (pp. 141-146). Atlantis Press. DOI: 10.2991/978-94-6463-443-3_21

Ahmed, M. S., El-Masry, A. A., Al-Maghyereh, A. I., & Kumar, S. (2024). Cryptocurrency Volatility: A Review, Synthesis, and Research Agenda. *Research in International Business and Finance*, 71, 102472. DOI: 10.1016/j.ribaf.2024.102472

Brini, A., & Lenz, J. (2024). A comparison of cryptocurrency volatility-benchmarking new and mature asset classes. *Financial Innovation*, 10(1), 122. DOI: 10.1186/s40854-024-00646-y

Cervellati, E. M., Angelini, N., & Stella, G. P. (2024). Behavioral finance and wealth management: Market anomalies, investors' behavior and the role of financial advisors.

Dimitriadou, A. T. H. A. N. A. S. I. A. (2024). *The influence of news and investor sentiment on exchange rate determination: new evidence using panel data in the banking sector* (Doctoral dissertation, College of Business, Law and Social Sciences, University of Derby).

Hussain, S. M., & Alaya, A. (2024). Investor response to financial news in the digital transformation era: The impact of accounting disclosures and herding behavior as indirect effect. *Journal of Financial Reporting and Accounting*, 22(2), 254–273. DOI: 10.1108/JFRA-05-2023-0287

Jagirdar, S. S., & Gupta, P. K. (2024). *Charting the financial odyssey: a literature review on history and evolution of investment strategies in the stock market (1900–2022)*. China Accounting and Finance Review.

Kabir, A. I., Vyas, S., Mitra, S., Uddin, M. M., & Jakowan, J. (2024, March). Evaluating the machine learning based momentum stock trading strategies with back-testing: An emerging market perspective. In *AIP Conference Proceedings* (Vol. 2919, No. 1). AIP Publishing.

Lo, A. W., & Zhang, R. (2024). *The Adaptive Markets Hypothesis: An Evolutionary Approach to Understanding Financial System Dynamics*. Oxford University Press. DOI: 10.1093/oso/9780199681143.001.0001

Manahov, V. (2024). The great crypto crash in September 2018: Why did the cryptocurrency market collapse? *Annals of Operations Research*, 332(1), 579–616. DOI: 10.1007/s10479-023-05575-0

Ncube, M., Sibanda, M., & Matenda, F. R. (2024). Application of Explainable Artificial Intelligence to model the influence of firm-specific factors on stock performance in sub-Saharan Africa during. *COVID*, ●●●, 19.

Ni, Y. (2024). Navigating Energy and Financial Markets: A Review of Technical Analysis Used and Further Investigation from Various Perspectives. *Energies*, 17(12), 2942. DOI: 10.3390/en17122942

Nia, V. M., Siregar, H., Sembel, R., & Zulbainarmi, N. (2024). Behavioral Finance in Psycho-Social Approaches: A Literature Review. In *International Conference on Business and Technology* (pp. 311-329). Springer, Cham. DOI: 10.1007/978-3-031-53998-5_27

Othman, N. N. (2024). Mind Games in the Market: Unraveling the Impact of Psychological Biases on Your Stock Portfolio. *Available atSSRN* 4844961. DOI: 10.2139/ssrn.4844961

Persakis, A., & Koutoupis, A. (2024). Synchronicity and Sentiment: Decoding Earnings Quality and Market Returns in EU under Economic Policy Uncertainty. *Journal of Behavioral Finance*, ●●●, 1–21. DOI: 10.1080/15427560.2024.2345342

Raja, E. L., & MESSAOUDI, A. (2024). Behavioral biases influencing investment decision making in emergent markets: A systematic literature review. *International Journal of Accounting, Finance, Auditing. Management and Economics*, 5(6), 18–39.

Saltık, Ö. (2024). Navigating the Stock Market: Modeling Wealth Exchange and Network Interaction with Loss Aversion, Disposition Effect and Anchoring and Adjustment Bias. *Ekonomi Politika ve Finans Araştırmaları Dergisi*, 9(1), 88–122. DOI: 10.30784/epfad.1435009

Saltik, O., Jalil, F., & Degirmen, S. (2024). Viral decisions: Unmasking the impact of COVID-19 info and behavioral quirks on investment choices. *Humanities & Social Sciences Communications*, 11(1), 1–20.

Shukla, A., Dadhich, M., & Dipesh Vaya, A. G. (2024). Impact of Behavioral Biases on Investors' Stock Trading Decisions: A Comparehensive Quantitative Analysis. *Indian Journal of Science and Technology*, 17(8), 670–678. DOI: 10.17485/IJST/v17i8.2845

Silver, S. D. (2024). Agent expectations and news sentiment in the dynamics of price in a financial market. *Review of Behavioral Finance*, 16(5), 836–859. DOI: 10.1108/RBF-09-2023-0237

Singh, B. (2023). Blockchain Technology in Renovating Healthcare: Legal and Future Perspectives. In Kaushik, K., Dahiya, S., Aggarwal, S., & Dwivedi, A. (Eds.), *Revolutionizing Healthcare Through Artificial Intelligence and Internet of Things Applications* (pp. 177–186). IGI Global., DOI: 10.4018/978-1-6684-5422-0.ch012

Singh, B. (2024). Lensing Legal Dynamics for Examining Responsibility and Deliberation of Generative AI-Tethered Technological Privacy Concerns: Infringements and Use of Personal Data by Nefarious Actors. In Ara, A., & Ara, A. (Eds.), *Exploring the Ethical Implications of Generative AI* (pp. 146–167). IGI Global., DOI: 10.4018/979-8-3693-1565-1.ch009

Singh, B. (2024). Social Cognition of Incarcerated Women and Children: Addressing Exposure to Infectious Diseases and Legal Outcomes. In Reddy, K. (Ed.), *Principles and Clinical Interventions in Social Cognition* (pp. 236–251). IGI Global., DOI: 10.4018/979-8-3693-1265-0.ch014

Singh, B. (2024). Evolutionary Global Neuroscience for Cognition and Brain Health: Strengthening Innovation in Brain Science. In Prabhakar, P. (Ed.), *Biomedical Research Developments for Improved Healthcare* (pp. 246–272). IGI Global., DOI: 10.4018/979-8-3693-1922-2.ch012

Singh, B., Dutta, P. K., & Kaunert, C. (2024). Replenish Artificial Intelligence in Renewable Energy for Sustainable Development: Lensing SDG 7 Affordable and Clean Energy and SDG 13 Climate Actions With Legal-Financial Advisory. In Derbali, A. (Ed.), *Social and Ethical Implications of AI in Finance for Sustainability* (pp. 198–227). IGI Global., DOI: 10.4018/979-8-3693-2881-1.ch009

Singh, B., Jain, V., Kaunert, C., Dutta, P. K., & Singh, G. (2024). Privacy Matters: Espousing Blockchain and Artificial Intelligence (AI) for Consumer Data Protection on E-Commerce Platforms in Ethical Marketing. In Saluja, S., Nayyar, V., Rojhe, K., & Sharma, S. (Eds.), *Ethical Marketing Through Data Governance Standards and Effective Technology* (pp. 167–184). IGI Global., DOI: 10.4018/979-8-3693-2215-4.ch015

Singh, B., & Kaunert, C. (2024). Computational Thinking for Innovative Solutions and Problem-Solving Techniques: Transforming Conventional Education to Futuristic Interdisciplinary Higher Education. In Fonkam, M., & Vajjhala, N. (Eds.), *Revolutionizing Curricula Through Computational Thinking, Logic, and Problem Solving* (pp. 60–82). IGI Global., DOI: 10.4018/979-8-3693-1974-1.ch004

Singh, B., & Kaunert, C. (2024). Wind and Solar Energy as Renewable Energy for Sustainable Global Future: Projecting Future Multi-Sector Sustainable Policies and Innovation. In Ara, A., & Thakore, R. (Eds.), *Promoting Multi-Sector Sustainability With Policy and Innovation* (pp. 210–245). IGI Global., DOI: 10.4018/979-8-3693-2113-3.ch009

Singh, B., & Kaunert, C. (2024). Aroma of Highly Smart Internet of Medical Things (IoMT) and Lightweight Edge Trust Expansion Medical Care Facilities for Electronic Healthcare Systems: Fortified-Chain Architecture for Remote Patient Monitoring and Privacy Protection Beyond Imagination. In Hassan, A., Bhattacharya, P., Tikadar, S., Dutta, P., & Sagayam, M. (Eds.), *Lightweight Digital Trust Architectures in the Internet of Medical Things (IoMT)* (pp. 196–212). IGI Global., DOI: 10.4018/979-8-3693-2109-6.ch011

Singh, B., & Kaunert, C. (2024). Augmented Reality and Virtual Reality Modules for Mindfulness: Boosting Emotional Intelligence and Mental Wellness. In Hiran, K., Doshi, R., & Patel, M. (Eds.), *Applications of Virtual and Augmented Reality for Health and Wellbeing* (pp. 111–128). IGI Global., DOI: 10.4018/979-8-3693-1123-3.ch007

Singh, B., & Kaunert, C. (2024). Salvaging Responsible Consumption and Production of Food in the Hospitality Industry: Harnessing Machine Learning and Deep Learning for Zero Food Waste. In Singh, A., Tyagi, P., & Garg, A. (Eds.), *Sustainable Disposal Methods of Food Wastes in Hospitality Operations* (pp. 176–192). IGI Global., DOI: 10.4018/979-8-3693-2181-2.ch012

Singh, B., & Kaunert, C. (2024). Revealing Green Finance Mobilization: Harnessing FinTech and Blockchain Innovations to Surmount Barriers and Foster New Investment Avenues. In Jafar, S., Rodriguez, R., Kannan, H., Akhtar, S., & Plugmann, P. (Eds.), *Harnessing Blockchain-Digital Twin Fusion for Sustainable Investments* (pp. 265–286). IGI Global., DOI: 10.4018/979-8-3693-1878-2.ch011

Singh, B., & Kaunert, C. (2024). Harnessing Sustainable Agriculture Through Climate-Smart Technologies: Artificial Intelligence for Climate Preservation and Futuristic Trends. In Kannan, H., Rodriguez, R., Paprika, Z., & Ade-Ibijola, A. (Eds.), *Exploring Ethical Dimensions of Environmental Sustainability and Use of AI* (pp. 214–239). IGI Global., DOI: 10.4018/979-8-3693-0892-9.ch011

Singh, B., & Kaunert, C. Reinventing Artificial Intelligence and Blockchain for Preserving Medical Data. In *Ethical Artificial Intelligence in Power Electronics* (pp. 77–91). CRC Press. DOI: 10.1201/9781032648323-6

Singh, B., Vig, K., Dutta, P. K., & Kaunert, C. (2024). Unraveling Agile Transformation for Customer Satisfaction in Changing Market Conditions: Roadmap for Industry Embracing Change in Project Management. In Misra, S., Jadeja, R., & Mittal, M. (Eds.), *Practical Approaches to Agile Project Management* (pp. 305–321). IGI Global., DOI: 10.4018/979-8-3693-3318-1.ch017

Singh, D., Malik, G., Jain, P., & Abouraia, M. (2024). A systematic review and research agenda on the causes and consequences of financial overconfidence. *Cogent Economics & Finance*, 12(1), 2348543. DOI: 10.1080/23322039.2024.2348543

Su, Q., & Deng, Y. (2024). Tax Avoidance News, Investor Behavior, and Stock Market Performance. *Finance Research Letters*, 67, 105834. DOI: 10.1016/j.frl.2024.105834

Talbi, M., Ferchichi, M., Ismaalia, F., & Samil, S. (2024). Resilience Amidst Turbulence: Unraveling COVID-19's Impact on Financial Stability through Price Dynamics and Investor Behavior in GCC Markets. *International Journal of Economics and Finance*, 16(4), 22. DOI: 10.5539/ijef.v16n4p22

Vidani, J. (2024). Why 90% of Stock Market Traders are in Loss? *Available at SSRN* 4849875.

Vukovic, D. B., Kurbonov, O. O., Maiti, M., Özer, M., & Radovanovic, M. (2024). Outperforming the market: A comparison of Star and NonStar analysts' investment strategies and recommendations. *Humanities & Social Sciences Communications*, 11(1), 1–15. DOI: 10.1057/s41599-023-02527-8

Zhu, X., Li, S., Srinivasan, K., & Lash, M. T. (2024). Impact of the COVID-19 pandemic on the stock market and investor online word of mouth. *Decision Support Systems*, 176, 114074. DOI: 10.1016/j.dss.2023.114074

Chapter 2
Availability Cascade and Herd Behavior in Financial Markets

Eren Kırmızıaltın
https://orcid.org/0009-0009-4165-7379
Sinop University, Turkey

Duygu Çeri
https://orcid.org/0000-0002-9035-1183
Sinop University, Turkey

ABSTRACT

Herd behavior is important topics in behavioral finance. In financial markets, herd behavior occurs when investors follow the crowd, making decisions based on current trends or the actions of others rather than conducting their own thorough analysis. This behavior, combined with market overreaction plays a significant role in price volatility and financial instability. To analyze these behaviors effectively, it's essential to understand the underlying mechanisms, particularly the psychological and cognitive factors that drive them. This study focuses on the connection between herd behavior and the availability cascade. Given the focus of this study, the analysis has been tailored to explore this relationship specifically. Consequently, the study not only focuses on the psychological and cognitive factors that cause herding behavior in financial markets but also tries to explain the relationship between the psychological and cognitive factors that cause herding behavior and the availability cascade.

DOI: 10.4018/979-8-3693-7827-4.ch002

Copyright © 2025, IGI Global Scientific Publishing. Copying or distributing in print or electronic forms without written permission of IGI Global is prohibited.

INTRODUCTION

Herd behavior and market overreactions are important topics in behavioral finance. These behaviors, which are driven by psychological, social and cognitive factors, affect market efficiency and investors' decision-making processes. In financial markets, herd behavior occurs when investors follow the crowd, making decisions based on current trends or the actions of others rather than conducting their own thorough analysis. This behavior, combined with market overreaction—characterized by disproportionate responses to new information—plays a significant role in price volatility and financial instability. To analyze these behaviors effectively, it's essential to understand the underlying mechanisms, particularly the psychological and cognitive factors that drive them. By examining these factors and their relationship to these behaviors in detail, we can gain a comprehensive understanding of the associated patterns of behavior.

This study focuses on the connection between herd behavior and the availability cascade. Given the focus of this study, the analysis has been tailored to explore this relationship specifically. Consequently, the study not only focuses on the psychological and cognitive factors that cause herding behavior in financial markets but also tries to explain the relationship between the psychological and cognitive factors that cause herding behavior and the availability cascade.

Ultimately, the availability cascade -a self-reinforcing process that shapes collective belief formation- provides a valuable theoretical framework for understanding herd behavior in financial markets. The availability cascade is the result of decision-makers basing their decisions on the influence of the information they repeatedly confront rather than on a comprehensive analysis. It occurs when a particular piece of information gains traction through repetition and social reinforcement, leading decision-makers to overestimate its importance and accuracy. This process can trigger herd behavior as investors collectively respond to perceived trends or popular sentiments.

In this study, we aim to provide a comprehensive theoretical analysis of how the availability cascade contributes to herd behavior in financial markets. In this context, in the first section, the availability cascade concept will be explained in detail, including its definition, mechanisms, and effects on collective belief formation. This explanation will begin with a description of the availability heuristic that underlies the availability cascade concept. Then, the content of the availability cascade will be addressed and the two components of the availability cascade, the informational component and the reputational component, will be defined. In the second section, the concept of herd behavior will first be defined. Then, the psychological ("emotional contagion and mimicry"; "social norms, conformity and docility" and "stories") and cognitive ("conformity and information cascades"; "representativeness heuristic" and "mirror neurons") factors underlying this behavior will be examined. In the third section, the theoretical background on the availability cascade and herd behavior will be used to examine the relationship between the availability cascade and herd behavior and how the availability cascade contributes to market overreaction and price volatility. In the fourth section, based on the analysis, we will propose strategies for financial market investors and regulators to mitigate the adverse effects of herd behavior and contribute to market stability by avoiding erroneous or incorrect inferences that may be caused by the availability cascade.

AVAILABILITY CASCADE: DEFINITION AND PROCESS

Before analysing the definition of the availability cascade, its mechanisms, and its impact on collective belief formation, we will first examine the definition of the availability heuristic and its effect on the decision-making process. Then we will define the availability cascade concept and emphasize its components.

Availability Heuristic

A. Tversky and D. Kahneman, who are important thinkers of behavioral economics, have conducted studies on the heuristics that people use when making decisions. In their study, Tversky and Kahneman (1974) showed that people use heuristics (and the biases caused by these heuristics) when making decisions under uncertainty and that these heuristics can lead to systematic and predictable errors in decision-making (and that decision-makers may not be able to take instrumental rational[1] action for this reason). Heuristics typically work through a process of "attribute substitution", where people answer a difficult question by replacing it with an easier one (Sunstein, 2005: 4). Here, it is not about answering the question in the most accurate way, but about answering it quickly or answering it by inference in case of uncertainty where complete information is not accessible. Tversky and Kahneman's approach to heuristics can be analyzed under three headings: representativeness, availability, adjustment, and anchoring. One of these heuristics, availability, which we will focus on in this section within the scope of this study, was first discussed in Tversky and Kahneman (1973).[2]

Tversky and Kahneman treat availability as a mediating variable rather than a dependent variable as, is typical in memory studies. Availability is an ecologically valid guide to frequency judgments because, in general, frequent events are easier to remember or imagine than infrequent ones (Tversky & Kahneman, 1973: 209). Accordingly, the more easily people remember a situation, the more they tend to estimate the probability of that situation, and ease of remembering can result from personal experience or information from the environment (Du, 2022: 154). However, availability is also influenced by various factors unrelated to the actual frequency. The availability heuristic is realized if people estimate probabilities based on the ease with which relevant examples or associations are brought to mind, and hence the weight of available information, rather than processing all relevant information. In other words, the availability heuristic is a cognitive shortcut in which decision-makers assess the frequency or probability of events based on how easily examples come to mind.

The use of the availability heuristic leads to systematic biases (Tversky & Kahneman, 1973: 209). In Tversky and Kahneman's (1973) and (1974) studies on the availability heuristic, the data obtained as a result of various experiments were interpreted. For example, the following experiment was conducted:

The subjects were made to listen to a list of famous people of both sexes and were asked whether there were more men or women in the list in question. In the experiment, different lists were played to different groups of subjects. In some of the lists, men were relatively more famous than women, while in others, women were relatively more famous than men. As a result, the subjects erroneously rated the gender category with relatively more famous people in each list as more (Tversky & Kahneman, 1974: 1127).

Here, it should be noted that the situations we encounter in our environment or one-on-one can also cause availability heuristics. We take our own experiences more seriously and pay more attention to them. Let us consider two scenarios about a house fire. In the first scenario, we see the house on fire with our own eyes, and in the second scenario, we read about a house fire in the newspaper. If we take into account that the situations we encounter one-on-one affect us more, we can say that the effect of seeing the fire will be greater than the effect of reading the news about the fire. In this case, the impact of having a real experience of a house fire on our decision to insure the house against fire risk will be greater than the effect of the information obtained from the newspaper news (Tversky & Kahneman, 1974: 1127).[3]

Availability Cascade

T. Kuran and C. R. Sunstein (1999) introduce the concept of "availability cascade" based on Kahneman and Tversky's work on heuristics and biases and prospect theory[4]. In their study, they argue that availability affects the framing effect defined by Kahneman and Tversky (the change in the decision-maker's preference as a result of a different formulation of the decision problem, i.e. a different design [Tversky & Kahneman 1981: 453; 1986: 257]) and the reference point (the current asset possessed; for the decision-maker, an increase in the current asset is a gain and a decrease in the current asset is a loss [Kahneman & Tversky, 1979: 274]), and therefore it is more important than these two. They give the following example: if public discourse codifies any kind of pollution as a loss depending on the imagined environmental purity, this imagined environmental purity becomes the reference point and the easy availability of this codification affects how people frame their pollution judgments (Kuran & Sunstein, 1999: 711-712). In other words, as a result of the availability of an argument on an issue, this argument determines the reference point of the relevant issue and people's judgments about the relevant issue. Availability cascade has two components: informational cascade and reputational cascade.

"An informational cascade occurs when people with incomplete personal information on a particular matter base their own beliefs on the apparent beliefs of others" (Kuran & Sunstein, 1999: 685-686). For example, if individuals A, B and C are convinced that the water canal spreads disease, individual D may believe this claim without considering it much, thinking that not all of his friends can be wrong; he may believe this claim by considering the fact that many people think that this claim is true as a compensation for the lack of reliable personal information on this subject, and in this case the informational cascade is active (Kuran & Sunstein, 1999,p. 714).

"In the case of reputational cascade, individuals do not subject themselves to social influences because others may be more knowledgeable. Rather, the motivation is simply to earn social approval and avoid disapproval." (Kuran & Sunstein, 1999: 686). For example, if Individuals A and B think that the water channel is heavily polluted, Individual C, despite not believing this claim, may refrain from expressing his/her reservations in order not to be accused of insensitivity or stupidity and may support the position that causes panic. In this case, the reputation cascade is active (Kuran & Sunstein, 1999, p. 714).

Kuran and Sunstein provide the following explanation of the availability cascade consisting of informational and reputational components:

"Risk judgments and preferences are formed through a circular social process. *Identifiable social mechanisms govern the availability of information; and through the mediation of the availability heuristic, this availability shapes, on the one hand, judgments about the magnitudes of various risks and, on the other, the acceptability of these risks. Simultaneously, the consequent individual actions and expressions affect the availability of information.* There are thus two-way relations between social outcomes and individual cognitive processes. These relations form an *availability cascade* whenever individual uses of the availability heuristic increase the public availability of data pointing to a particular interpretation or conclusion, and this increase in availability then triggers reinforcing individual responses." (Kuran & Sunstein, 1999, p.712).

In this sense, we can say that the availability cascade occurs when a certain information becomes highly salient due to repeated exposure, leading decision-makers to base their decisions on this readily available information, either because of the reputational component or the informational component, rather than a thorough analysis. This process is driven by social and psychological mechanisms, such as social proof and cognitive convenience, which reinforce the salience and perceived accuracy of information.

The process by which collective beliefs are formed and diffused in a population through a cascade of availability can be divided into four stages:

i.   Inception: The availability of information, whether accurate or not, is the primary determinant. Presentation of information in mass media (written, visual or social media) increases the accessibility of information.
ii. Dissemination: Information is reinforced through repetition and social validation. Individuals share, comment on, and discuss information within their social networks without thoroughly analyzing it or questioning its accuracy, thus increasing its perceived importance of information.
iii. Normalization: As more individuals accept the information as true, it becomes a widely accepted norm, influencing the behavior of others who may be undecided or skeptical.
iv. Entrenchment: The belief in the information's accuracy becomes ingrained in the group, which in turn shapes collective decision-making and behavior. At this stage, contradictionary information or evidence that contradicts the information presented is often ignored or rejected, reinforcing the dominant narrative.

Availability and availability cascade are important in financial markets where investors are constantly overloaded with information. Due to cognitive limitations, investors rely on the availability heuristic by overweighting new or salient information. They base their decisions on information that they are repeatedly exposed to rather than on a comprehensive analysis. This is because repeated exposure to specific information leads investors to overestimate its importance and accuracy. In this context, both informational and reputational components may influence an investor's decision. For instance, the investor may make an investment decision based on the information of others due to incomplete information, in which case the informational component is effective. Or, an investor may conform to the general investment trend in their environment, even if skeptical, making the reputational component effective. In both cases, the investor does not need empirical evidence or detailed questioning when making an investment decision; the information cascade or the reputational cascade is sufficient for the investor. This contributes to herd behavior in the financial market.

HERD BEHAVIOR: DEFINITION AND PSYCHOLOGICAL AND COGNITIVE FACTORS AFFECTING THIS BEHAVIOR

Herd behavior, where individuals in a group align their actions and decisions with the majority, is a complex phenomenon influenced by various psychological and cognitive factors, with a rich history across multiple disciplines, including psychology, sociology, and economics. It can be defined as follows: "Herding can be broadly defined as the alignment of thoughts or behaviors of individuals in a group (herd) through local relations rather than centralized coordination." (Raafat, Chater, & Frith, 2009: 420). As can be understood from this definition, herd behavior results from local relations rather than top-down directives. The lack of central coordination and reliance on local relations distinguish herd behavior from other forms of collective action. This phenomenon can be seen in various fields ranging from economic and financial markets to social and political movements. In this sense, understanding the mechanisms that drive herd behavior is important for interpreting collective human action and its implications for financial markets, consumer behavior, political movements and even everyday social relations.

We can examine the mechanisms that drive herd behavior under two headings: psychological and cognitive factors. In this study, we will examine the psychological factors that cause herd behavior under three headings, drawing on the content presented in Kameda and Hastie (2015: 4-7) and Raafat, Chater and Frith (2009, pp. 421-423): "emotional contagion and mimicry"; "social norms, conformity and docility" and "stories". Likewise, we will examine the cognitive factors that cause herd behavior under three headings: "conformity and information cascade"; "representativeness heuristic" and "mirror neurons".[5]

Psychological Factors[6]

The psychological factors driving herd behavior are explored under three main categories in this study. These are "emotional contagion and mimicry"; "social norms, conformity and docility" and "stories".

Emotional Contagion and Mimicry

Emotional contagion is defined as "the tendency to automatically mimic and synchronize expressions, vocalizations, postures, and movements with those of another person and, consequently, to converge emotionally" (Hatfield, Cacioppo, and Rapson, 1992: 153). It involves an observer experiencing emotions that are congruent with the emotions displayed by another individual. For instance, seeing someone smile may lead one to feel happy, while observing someone frown might induce feelings of sadness or concern.

Mimicry, on the other hand, is "the imitation of others' non-verbal displays by an observer" (Hess and Blairy, 2001, p. 129). It is typically an automatic, reflex-like process where the observer's facial expression matches the observed facial expression.

Hess and Blairy (2001) note that while mimicry involves the physical imitation of another's expressions, emotional contagion encompasses the resulting emotional state that aligns with the observed emotion. This relationship is not merely one of cause and effect but rather a complex relation where mimicry can lead to emotional contagion, which in turn can reinforce mimicry.

Emotional contagion and mimicry can lead to herd behavior by influencing how emotions spread through groups. When individuals in a group mimic each other's expressions and emotions, it can lead to a rapid and widespread alignment of emotions within the group. This alignment can facilitate coordinated actions and collective decision-making, often without explicit communication.

Social Norms, Conformity and Docility

Social norms defined as "customs, traditions, standards, rules, values, fashions, and all other criteria of conduct which are standardized as a consequence of the contact of individuals" (Sherif, 1936 Cited in Chung and Rimal, 2016: 3). Norms may also be understood as "social behavior that is more characteristic of some sociocultural collective unit than of individuals observed at random" (Pepitone, 1976, Cited in Chung and Rimal, 2016: 3). These norms dictate acceptable behavior within a group and are reinforced through social approval and disapproval. S. Asch's (1955) conformity experiments demonstrated how individuals often conform to group opinions even when those opinions are obviously incorrect, highlighting the powerful influence of social norms on individual behavior. In the experiments conducted in Asch's studies, individuals conformed to the wrong majority views due to the social pressure exerted by the group, showing the effect of social norms on behavior (Asch, 1955: 33)[7]

Docility, on the other hand, as described by H. Simon (1990: 1665), refers to "the human tendency to learn from others (more accurately, the tendency to accept social influence)". It is characterized by an individual's propensity to be taught and to accept social norms and behaviors from their surroundings. Simon further explains that docility enhances fitness by facilitating the acquisition of beneficial knowledge and skills through social learning (Simon, 1990, p.1666).

The relationship between social norms and docility is inherently intertwined. Docile individuals are more likely to adhere to social norms because they are predisposed to accepting and internalizing the behaviors and standards prevalent in their social environment. This acceptance is not always critically evaluated but is often adopted due to the social pressures and the benefits of conformity.

Asch's experiments illustrate this relationship. In these experiments, individuals conformed to incorrect majority opinions due to the social pressure exerted by the group, demonstrating the influence of social norms on behavior (Asch, 1955, p. 33). Similarly, Simon argues that docility leads to the acceptance of social norms, even when such norms may not be directly advantageous to the individual (Simon, 1990: 1666). This relationship underscores how docility can amplify the effects of social norms, leading to widespread conformity within groups.

Social norms and docility influence herd behavior by promoting conformity and reducing individual critical thinking. When individuals in a group exhibit high levels of docility, they are more likely to conform to the group's norms and behaviors, leading to a collective movement or action that characterizes herd behavior.

Stories

Humans are storytellers by nature. There are even studies claiming that the feature that best distinguishes us from animals is creating and telling stories (Shiller, 2017: 9), because the human mind thinks in terms of narratives and stories and is influenced by them (Kameda & Hestie, 2015:5). "The human mind is built to think in terms of narratives, of sequences of events with an internal logic and dynamic that appear as a unified whole. In turn, much of human motivation comes from living through a story of our lives, a story that we tell to ourselves and that creates a framework for motivation." (Akerlof & Shiller, 2009: 51)

Stories are, in a sense, a way of constructing meaning and understanding. Events, experiences or phenomena gain meaning by being structured in a story. Thus, stories help individuals to make sense of complex information and provide a framework for interpreting reality.

The impact of stories on decision-making is analyzed in detail by Akerlof and Shiller (2009). In this study, the power of stories in shaping economic and political behavior is evaluated through various examples. They show how a story can lead to collective action. Stories are powerful because they shape perceptions, attitudes, and behaviors, often serving as a heuristic for decision-making. In this sense, stories influence herd behavior by creating a shared perspective that can guide collective actions and decisions.

Cognitive Factors

The cognitive factors driving herd behavior are explored under three main categories. These are "conformity and information cascades"; "representativeness heuristic" and "mirror neurons".

Conformity and Information Cascade

Bikhchandani, Hirshleifer and Welch (1992: 994) define informational cascade as follows: "An informational cascade occurs when it is optimal for an individual, having observed the actions of those ahead of him, to follow the behavior of the preceding individual without regard to his own information." In this case, people proceed by observing the "crowd" and imitating their decisions (Anderson and Holt, 2000). There is no punishment underlying people's conformity to the decisions of the crowd, rather it happens spontaneously (Bikhchandani, Hirshleifer & Welch, 1992: 1016).

Various experiments have been conducted on the informational cascade. The results obtained from the experiments can be summarized under three headings (Easley & Kleinberg, 2010:503):

(i) Cascades can be wrong: For instance, if choosing an option is actually a bad decision but the first two individuals receive strong positive signals, a cascade of acceptances will immediately begin, even though it is the incorrect choice for the group.

(ii) Cascades can be based on little information: Once a cascade begins, people disregard their private information, so only the information available before the cascade influences the group's behavior. This implies that if a cascade starts quickly in a large group, most of the private information that individuals possess is not utilized.

(iii) Cascades are fragile: The fact that cascades can start with very little information makes them easy to initiate, but also easy to disrupt. One example of this is that individuals with slightly better information can overturn even long-standing cascades.

Informational cascades are linked to social environments and have an impact on economic, political and other decisions. In this sense, it may seem to be the same as herd behavior, but it is not. There are many factors that can cause herd behavior. That is, informational cascade causes herd behavior, but not every herd behavior is caused by informational cascade (Tuominen, 2017:12).

Representativeness Heuristic[8]

The representativeness heuristic is one of the important issues affecting the decision-making behavior of individuals, which is discussed in the works of D. Kahneman and A. Tversky. Representativeness, which causes herding, is related to insensitivity to prior probability of outcomes and insensitivity to predictability.

One factor that has no effect on representativeness but should have a significant effect on probability is prior probability or base-rate frequency of outcomes. If people evaluate probability according to representativeness, prior probability will be neglected (Tversky & Kahneman, 1974: 1124). For example, suppose that a player makes five successful shots in a basketball match. It is assumed that the player will not miss the other shots. However, each shot has a success probability independent of the other shot. However, the a priori probability is neglected here. This is called the hot hand fallacy. "The exaggerated belief in hot hands seems partly explained by the misperception that purely random streaks are too long to be purely random" (Rabin, 1998:26).

This situation encourages herding, especially in financial markets. This is because investors' decisions are surrounded by uncertainty, not only because of the information limitations of the markets themselves but also because of the cognitive limitations of individuals. There is uncertainty not only about the true value of the securities traded but also about the quality of the information available (Fernández et al. 2009: 5). Under conditions of uncertainty, the investor observing various trading transactions in the market thinks that the trend will continue and decides to trade in the same way as his predecessors. He/she ignores the a priori probability in his/her investment decision (Fernández et al. 2009: 8).

Another representativeness that causes herding is insensitivity to predictability. Representativeness is often used when making a numerical prediction about the future value of a stock or the outcome of a football match. For example, suppose you are given a description of a company and asked to make a prediction about its future profits. If the description of the company is very positive, a prediction that the company will make high profits in the future would seem to be the best representation of the current description. If the description is average, a prediction that the company's future profits will be average would seem to be the best representation of the current description. The degree to which the description is favorable is not affected by the reliability of the description or the degree to which it allows an accurate prediction. If they make predictions based only on the positive (or negative) description, their predictions will be insensitive to the reliability of the evidence (Tversky & Kahneman, 1974: 1126). Therefore, the person who does not question the reliability of the description, together with other people with a similar behavioral pattern, makes an investment decision by thinking that the future profit of the company will be high (or average) depending on the content of the description.

Mirror Neurons

Mirror neurons were discovered in research with monkeys. The mirror neuron is a specific class of visuomotor neurons discovered in the F5 region of the monkey premotor cortex that discharges both when the monkey performs a specific action and when it observes another individual (monkey or human) performing a similar action (Rizzolatti et al. 1996; Rizzolatti et al. 2008; Rizzolatti et al. 2009). In other words, the mirror neuron discharges not only during the performance of the action but also when observing another person performing the same or a similar action (Lacoboni, 2009:659). Although mirror neurons were discovered in the monkey brain, research on the human brain has revealed that mirror neurons also exist in the human brain. The results obtained in studies using transcranial magnetic stimulation (TMS) and functional magnetic resonance imaging (fMRI) were interpreted as evidence that humans also have mirror neurons (Rizzolatti et al., 2008:181-182; Heyes, 2010: 578).

As explained in detail in Rizzolatti and Craighero (2004), mirror neurons are active in gestural communication, speech evolution, and auditory modality. Ramachandran (2000) also argues that mirror neurons have an important role in understanding people's intentions, as well as in empathy, learning, and the rapid transmission of culture. In this sense, it is an important element in the relation between individuals and between individuals and groups and can affect various social cognitive functions, including understanding people's actions, predicting people's actions, language processing, and cognition (Hayes, 2010: 581).

Mirror neurons may contribute to herd behavior due to the above-mentioned features. This is because mirror neurons triggered both when an individual performs an action and when he/she observes another individual performing the same action, creating a neural basis for imitation and social learning. (However, in our opinion, it does not affect herd behavior in the context of financial markets as much as other factors examined in this section).

In conclusion, herd behavior is an important concept for understanding not only individual but also group dynamics and collective decision making. Understanding herd behavior allows us to make more accurate predictions in areas such as financial markets, consumer behavior and political movements[9]

THE RELATION BETWEEN THE AVAILABILITY CASCADE & HERD BEHAVIOR & THE IMPACT OF THE AVAILABILITY CASCADE ON MARKET DYNAMICS

The availability cascade concept provides a theoretical framework for understanding how information diffusion affects investor behavior. The availability heuristic explains how individuals assess the frequency or probability of events based on the ease with which examples come to mind. This cognitive heuristic leads to systematic biases, and these biases become stronger when information is presented repeatedly, creating a cascade of availability. This process affects investors' decisions. When investors are repeatedly exposed to certain information, whether accurate or not, they begin to overestimate its importance. This overemphasis on the information presented rather than a comprehensive analysis can significantly affect market dynamics. For example, if media reports repeatedly about the rising potential of a particular stock, investors may disproportionately invest in that stock and drive its price up regardless of its fundamental value.

The concept of herd behavior refers to individuals harmonizing their actions with the majority, guided by local relations rather than central coordination. There are various psychological and cognitive reasons for this behavior. In financial markets, herd behavior occurs when investors follow the actions of the majority instead of conducting independent analysis. As a result, for instance, investors may act collectively to move prices away from their true value, leading to bubbles and crashes.

In this section, we will explain the mechanisms through which the availability cascade and herd behavior interact and manifest in financial markets. By examining these relations in detail, we aim to explain how the availability cascade can drive herd behavior and how this can affect market dynamics.

Impact of the Relation between Availability Cascade and Herd Behavior on Financial Markets

The relationship between the availability cascade and herding behavior can be understood through the psychological and cognitive mechanisms driving these concepts. Availability sets the stage for heuristic information to become salient, and a gradual process ensures that this information gains traction within the investor community. Once the information is widely accepted, herd behavior is triggered as investors align their actions with the majority. How the availability cascade can trigger herd behavior in financial markets can be revealed by separately examining the relationship between the psychological and cognitive factors that cause herd behavior and the availability cascade.

Relations between Psychological Mechanisms Causing Herd Behavior and Availability Cascade

Emotional contagion & mimicry: Emotional contagion occurs when individuals in a group synchronize their emotions, while mimicry involves imitating the non-verbal behavior of others. In the context of the availability cascade, repeated exposure to emotionally charged information may increase investors' emotional responses, leading to herding behavior. For example, suppose that positive news about a company's performance is repeatedly presented in the media. This may create a wave of optimism among the company's current investors, and this optimism may influence investors who are not currently investors in the company. As a result, non-investors may also be influenced by the wave of optimism and invest in the company. More investors investing in the company may trigger mimicry in investment behavior and this may lead to an increase in the company's stock price.

Social norms & docility: Social norms determine acceptable behavior within a group and conformity refers to the tendency to accept social influences. The availability cascade can reinforce certain social norms by making certain information more salient and acceptable within the investor community. For instance, if investors perceive that others act on specific information, they are more likely to conform to this behavior due to social pressure and the desire for social approval. This can lead to herd behavior, where individuals follow the actions of the majority without critically evaluating the information.

Stories: Stories provide a framework for interpreting complex information. In this sense, they have a strong influence on decision-making. In an availability cascade, the repeated presentation of a compelling narrative can shape investors' perceptions and drive collective behavior. For example, suppose a story is being created about the potential of a technology startup to revolutionize an industry. If this story is well prepared and repeatedly told in the media, investors may believe it without thoroughly questioning its accuracy. As more investors believe the story, they may invest in the startup, leading to an increase in investment.

Relations Between Cognitive Mechanisms Causing Herd Behavior and the Availability Cascade

Conformity and Information Cascades: Information cascades occur when individuals follow the majority's actions due to incomplete personal information. In the context of an availability cascade, suppose that information about an industry or a company is repeatedly presented in various media. Investors may disregard their private information and follow the actions of the majority by relying on this information that is repeatedly presented in various media. This behavioral conformity leads investors to over-rely on information provided by others rather than conducting independent analysis. As a result of this overconfidence, investors may follow the investment decisions of others without questioning them.

Representativeness Heuristic: Insensitivity to the a priori probability of outcomes can lead to herding in financial markets. In this case, decisions are made by ignoring probability calculations. For instance, if it is repeatedly emphasized that a particular type of investment is successful, investors may assume that similar investments will also be successful, which may lead to herding behavior when investing in them.

Another representation that causes herding is insensitivity to predictability. When inferring a company's future value, herding behavior may occur if the description of the company is adhered to and the reliability of what is presented in the description is not questioned. This is because the person who does not question the reliability of the description, together with other people with similar behavioral patterns, may make an investment decision by thinking that the future profit of the company will be high (or average) depending on the content of the description. This may lead to the formation of herd behavior in investing in the mentioned company.

Mirror Neurons: Mirror neurons facilitate social learning by being activated both when performing an action and when observing others performing the same action. For example, information repeated by "influential people" in mass media can activate mirror neurons and lead investors to follow each other's behavior. This is because mirror neurons are triggered when a person observes another person, creating a neural basis for imitation and social learning.

The relations between the psychological and cognitive factors that cause herd behavior and the availability cascade shows that repeated information significantly impacts herd behavior. Repetition of information is more important than its accuracy. Individual or a groups with a high capacity to manage information may cause investors to engage in herding behavior and create a certain investment pattern. This means that the managers of information, not the quality of information, drive herding behavior in investments. In other words, those who manages the availability cascade lead the herd.

Implications for Market Dynamics

The relationship between the availability cascade and herd behavior has significant implications for market dynamics: it can lead to price volatility, market bubbles and crashes, as well as distortions in asset pricing and resource allocation.

Price Volatility: The availability cascade can increase the visibility of specific information, leading to exaggerated market reactions. Price volatility increases as investors collectively react to the same information, regardless of its accuracy. For instance, repeated news about economic instability may lead to panic selling, causing sharp falls in asset prices.

Distortions in Asset Pricing: Overemphasis on specific information may lead to asset mispricing. Investors may overvalue assets frequently discussed in the media while undervaluing assets with less attention.

Resource Allocation: Herd behavior influenced by the availability cascade can cause capital misallocation. During a market bubble, overinvestment may occur in overvalued sectors, while underinvestment occurs in sectors with sound fundamentals but less media coverage. This misallocation can hinder the growth of well-established sectors with high value-added potential and lead to inefficient resource allocation, negatively impacting overall economic growth.

Market Bubbles & Crashes: If herd behavior driven by the availability cascade leads to unfounded optimism about asset prices, it can create market bubbles. When the optimism-fueling cascade ends or conflicting information emerges, the bubble bursts, and the market crashes. The dot-com bubble is a prime example. During the dot-com bubble, repeated narratives about the transformative potential of internet companies created a cascade of positive availability. Investors, constantly confronted with positive news and success stories, collectively overestimated these companies' potential and invested heavily. This led to large investments and inflated valuations. Herd behavior driven by both information and reputation cascades further inflated the bubble. When the bubble burst, the same mechanisms led to a rapid and violent market crash.[10] Another significant example is the 2008 financial crisis. Initially, constant and repeated assurances about the stability and profitability of mortgage-backed securities created an availability cascade. Investors, including large financial institutions, reinforced the belief that these investments were safe. Herd behavior driven by cognitive heuristics and social influences led to the widespread adoption of these high-risk financial products. When the risks of mortgage-backed securities materialized, the market's collective overreaction to negative news created a financial crisis.[11]

STRATEGIC RECOMMENDATIONS FOR REDUCING HERD BEHAVIOR

In the previous section, we focused on the positive relationship between the availability cascade and herd behavior and their combined impact on market dynamics. It examined the psychological and cognitive mechanisms driving these phenomena and how they contribute to market volatility, asset mispricing, and financial instability. This section will provide strategic recommendations for financial market investors and regulators to mitigate the negative effects of herd behavior and thus promote market stability and efficient resource allocation.

Improving Financial Literacy and Critical Thinking

One of the main steps to reduce herd behavior is to enhance the financial literacy of investors. Educating investors about cognitive biases and psychological factors influencing their decisions can help counter these effects. Training programs should teach investors about common cognitive biases, such as the availability heuristic, representativeness heuristic, emotional contagion, and mimicry. Understanding these biases can help investors recognize when they are likely to be susceptible to them. Training should also focus on developing investors' critical thinking skills, encouraging them to question information critically and consider multiple sources before making investment decisions. This approach can help develop a skeptical mindset towards repetitive narratives that can create an availability cascade. Using real-world examples, such as the dot-com bubble and the 2008 financial crisis, can increase attention to training by demonstrating the importance of financial literacy and critical thinking.

Developing the Regulatory Framework

Regulatory measures that increase transparency and improve the quality of information available to investors can reduce reliance on the availability cascade and mitigate herding behavior. An effective regulatory measure could be for regulators to require financial institutions to provide detailed and accurate disclosures about financial products. This could help investors make more informed decisions and reduce the tendency to rely on narratives that are not based on facts. Another regulatory measure could be taken in financial reporting. Ensuring accurate and timely publication of financial reports and penalizing irregularities in the reports can prevent a cascade of misleading availability. For example, auditing standards could be set to detect irregularities. Another regulatory measure can be taken in oversight mechanisms. Regulators can increase market surveillance to detect and prevent manipulative practices that may lead to herd behavior. For example, unusual behavior can be monitored and potential market manipulations can be investigated. Such regulatory measures may enhance the regulatory framework. Thus, the reliability of the information provided can be increased and the possibility of investors being misled by repeated but inaccurate narratives can be reduced.

Utilization of Technology and Data Analytics

Advances in technology and data analytics can be leveraged to better understand and mitigate herd behavior. For example, real-time data monitoring systems can help detect herd behavior and the availability cascade by analyzing large volumes of market data to identify patterns indicative of collective behavior. Behavioral analytics can also provide insights into investor behavior, helping financial institutions develop strategies for rational decision-making.

Creating an Ethical Investment Culture

Promoting ethical investment practices can help mitigate the negative effects of herd behavior and the availability cascade. In this context, the establishment of ethical investment standards places responsibility on investors. These standards can be environmental, social and governance related. In the case of governance, for example, corporate governance standards could be set to ensure that companies adhere to ethical practices and provide accurate information to investors. These standards can increase transparency and accountability in financial markets.

Promoting Diverse Investment Strategies

Encouraging diverse investment strategies can reduce the effects of herd behavior by discouraging investors from following a single trend. Portfolio diversification is an important tool in this regard, allowing investors to spread their investments across different asset classes and sectors, reducing the impact of any market trend or bubble.

Encouraging Collaborative Research and Policy Development

Collaboration between researchers, policy makers and industry stakeholders can lead to the development of more effective strategies to reduce herding behavior. In this context, fostering collaborative research initiatives that examine the interplay between cognitive biases, social influences and market dynamics can provide valuable information. These initiatives could involve interdisciplinary teams of economists, psychologists and data scientists. It is also important to seek input from all stakeholders in the investment market when formulating policy implications. Facilitating policy dialogues that bring together regulators, industry leaders and academics can lead to the development of comprehensive strategies to reduce herding behavior.

These dialogues can focus on identifying best practices and developing regulatory frameworks that promote market stability.

The recommendations summarized in this section aim to address the complex relationship between the availability cascade and herd behavior in financial markets. By enhancing financial literacy, promoting diverse investment strategies, and leveraging technology, we can mitigate the adverse effects of these factors. Additionally, promoting an ethical investment culture and encouraging collaborative research and policy development can contribute to market stability and investors' rational decision-making. Implementation of these recommendations requires a concerted effort by financial institutions, regulators, and investors, creating a financial market environment less susceptible to fluctuations and distortions caused by herd behavior and availability cascades.

CONCLUSION

The concepts of herd behavior and availability cascade in financial markets are complex, interactive processes that significantly affect investment market dynamics. This study examines the relationship between herd behavior and the availability cascade in financial markets, aiming to understand how these phenomena impact market dynamics. The study focuses on the psychological and cognitive factors shaping these behaviors and their effects on market stability.

The study argues that the relations between the availability cascade and herd behavior can trigger non-rational behavior in the markets and lead to excessive fluctuations in asset prices. As a result, investors may overreact to repetitive information, overestimating its accuracy and importance. The analyses in this study help us understand the psychological and cognitive dynamics behind market price fluctuations, asset pricing distortions, and market bubbles and crashes.

The efficient functioning of investment markets can therefore be achieved through strategies to reduce herd behavior and the availability cascade. For example, increasing financial literacy, raising investors' awareness of cognitive biases and psychological effects, and developing critical thinking skills can prevent non-rational investment behavior. Improving the regulatory framework, increasing transparency and preventing manipulative practices are important steps to ensure market stability. Additionally, leveraging technology and data analytics is important for early detection and prevention of herd behavior. Creating an ethical investment culture and adopting diverse investment strategies can contribute to the effective functioning of the financial system by enabling market participants to make more responsible and informed decisions. Finally, collaborative research and policy development processes can generate effective solutions against inefficiencies in financial markets by increasing knowledge in this field.

REFERENCES

Akerlof, G. A., & Shiller, J. R. (2009). *Animal Spirits How Human Psychology Drives The Economy, and Why It Matters for Global Capitalism*. Princeton University Press.

Anderson, R. L. And Holt, A. C. (2000) Information Cascades and Rational Conformity *Encyclopedia of Cognitive Science*, Macmillan Reference Ltd.

Ariely, D. (2008). *Predictably Irrational*. Harper Collins.

Asch, S. E. (1955). Opinions and social pressure. *Scientific American*, 193(5), 31–35. DOI: 10.1038/scientificamerican1155-31

Barr, R., & William, R. (2013). An Evidence Based Approach to Sports Concussion: Confronting the Availability Cascade. *Neuropsychology Review*, 23(4), 271–272. DOI: 10.1007/s11065-013-9244-3 PMID: 24281980

Barros, G. (2010). Herbert A. Simon and The Concept of Rationality: Boundaries and Procedures *Brazilian. Journal of Political Economy*, 30(3), 455–472.

Bikhchandani, S., Hirshleifer, D., & Welch, I. (1992). A Theory of Fads, Fashion, Custom, and Cultural Change as Informational Cascades. *Journal of Political Economy*, 100(5), 992–1026. DOI: 10.1086/261849

Chung, A., & Rimal, R. N. (2016). Social Norms: A Review. *Review of Communication Research*, 4, 1–28. DOI: 10.12840/issn.2255-4165.2016.04.01.008

Du, R. (2022). Availability Heuristic: An Overview and Applications, *Highlights in Business. Economics and Management*, 1, 153–159.

Easley, D. And Kleinberg, J. (2010) *Networks, Crowds, and Markets: Reasoning about a Highly Connected World* Cambridge University Press

Fernández, B., Garcia-Merino, T., Mayoral, R., Santos, V., & Vallelado, E. (2009). The role of the interaction between information and behavioral bias in explaining herding. *Behavioral finance working group. London.*

Goodnight, G. T., & Green, S. (2010). Rhetoric, Risk, and Markets: The Dot-Com Bubble. *The Quarterly Journal of Speech*, 96(2), 115–140. DOI: 10.1080/00335631003796669

Hargreaves Heap, S. (1989). *Rationality in Economics*. Basil Blackwell.

Hatfield, E., Cacioppo, J. T., & Rapson, R. L. (1992). Primitive Emotional Contagion. In Clark, M. S. (Ed.), *Emotion and social behavior* (pp. 151–177). Sage Publications, Inc.

Hayes, C. (2010). Where Do Mirro Neurons Come From? *Neuroscience and Biobehavioral Reviews*, 34(4), 575–583. DOI: 10.1016/j.neubiorev.2009.11.007 PMID: 19914284

Hess, U., & Blairy, S. (2001).. . *Facial Mimicry and Emotional Contagion to Dynamic Emotional Facial Expressions and Their Influence on Decoding Accuracy International Journal of Psychophysicology*, 40, 129–141.

Kahneman, D., & Tversky, A. (1979). Prospect Theory: An Analysis of Decision under Risk *Econometrica,* vol. 47, no. 2, ss. 263-292.

Kameda, T., & Hastie, R. (2015) Herd Behavior *in Emerging Trends in the Social and Behavioral Sciences.* Edited by Robert Scott John Wiley & Sons, Inc. 1-14.

Kuran, T., & Sunstein, C. R. (1999). Availability Cascades and Risk Regulation. *Stanford Law Review*, 51(4), 683–768. DOI: 10.2307/1229439

Lacoboni, M. (2009). Imitation, Emphaty, and Mirror Neurons. *Annual Review of Psychology*, 60(1), 653–670. DOI: 10.1146/annurev.psych.60.110707.163604 PMID: 18793090

Leibenstein, H. (1950). Bandwagon, Snob, and Veblen Effects in the Theory of Consumers' Demand. *The Quarterly Journal of Economics*, 64(2), 183–207. DOI: 10.2307/1882692

Morris, J. J., & Alam, P. Analysis of the Dot-Com Bubble of the 1990s (June 27, 2008). Available at *SSRN*: https://ssrn.com/abstract=1152412 or http://dx.doi.org/ DOI: 10.2139/ssrn.1152412

Murphy, J. Austin, An Analysis of the Financial Crisis of 2008: Causes and Solutions (November 4, 2008). Available at *SSRN*: https://ssrn.com/abstract=1295344 or http://dx.doi.org/DOI: 10.2139/ssrn.1295344

Ospina, J., & Uhling, H. (2018) Mortgage-Backed Securities and the Financial Crisis of 2008: a Post Mortem, NBER Working Paper, 24509

Pallier, G., Wilkinson, R., Danthiir, V., Kleitman, S., Knezevic, G., Stankov, L., & Roberts, R. D. (2002). The Role of Individual Differences in The Accuracy of Confidence Judgments. *The Journal of General Psychology*, 129(3), 257–299. DOI: 10.1080/00221300209602099 PMID: 12224810

Pepitone, A. (1976). Toward a normative and comparative biocultural social psychology. *Journal of Personality and Social Psychology*, 34(4), 641–653. DOI: 10.1037/0022-3514.34.4.641

Pikulina, E., Renneboog, L., & And Tobler, P. N. (2017). Overconfidence and Investment: An Experimental Approach. *Journal of Corporate Finance*, 43, 175–192. DOI: 10.1016/j.jcorpfin.2017.01.002

Raafat, R. M., Chater, N., & Frith, C. (2009). Herding in Humans. *Trends in Cognitive Sciences*, 13(10), 420–428. DOI: 10.1016/j.tics.2009.08.002 PMID: 19748818

Rabin, M. (1998). Psychology and Economics. *Journal of Economic Literature*, 36(1), 11–46.

Ramachandran, V.S. (2000) Mirror Neurons and Imitation Learning as the Driving Force Behind 'the Great Leap Forward' in Human Evolution, *Edge,* No. 69

Rizzolatti, G., & Craighero, L. (2004). The Mirror-Neuron System. *Annual Review of Neuroscience*, 27(1), 169–192. DOI: 10.1146/annurev.neuro.27.070203.144230 PMID: 15217330

Rizzolatti, G., & Fabbri-Destro, M. (2008). The Mirror System and Its Role in Social Cognition. *Current Opinion in Neurobiology*, 18(2), 179–184. DOI: 10.1016/j.conb.2008.08.001 PMID: 18706501

Rizzolatti, G., Fabbri-Destro, M., & And Cattaneo, L. (2009). Mirror neurons and their clinical relevance. *Nature Clinical Practice. Neurology*, 5(1), 24–34. DOI: 10.1038/ncpneuro0990 PMID: 19129788

Rizzolatti, G., Fadiga, L., Fogassi, L., & Gallese, V. (1996). Premotor Cortex and the Recognition of Motor Actions. *Brain Research. Cognitive Brain Research*, 3(2), 131–141. DOI: 10.1016/0926-6410(95)00038-0 PMID: 8713554

Robin, R., & Angelina, V. (2020). Analysis of The Impact of Anchoring, Herding Bias. *Overconfidence and Ethical Consideration Towards Investment Decision JIMFE*, 6(2), 253–264.

Sanders, A. (2008). The subprime crisis and its role in the financial crisis. *Journal of Housing Economics*, 17(4), 254–261. DOI: 10.1016/j.jhe.2008.10.001

Sherif, M. (1936). *The psychology of social norms*. Harper.

Shiller, J. R. (2017) Narrative Economics *NBER Working Paper Series* no. 23075

Simon, H. A. (1957). *Models of Man, Social and Rational: Mathematical Essays on Rational Human Behavior in a Social Setting*. John Wiley and Sons.

Simon, H. A. (1990). A mechanism for social selection and successful altruism. *Science*, 250(4988), 1665–1668. DOI: 10.1126/science.2270480 PMID: 2270480

Stanovich, K. E. (2010). *Decision Making and Rationality in the Modern World*. Oxford University Press.

Sunstein, C. R. (2005). The Availability Heuristic, Intuitive Cost-Benefit Analysis, and Climate Change *Chicago John M. Olin Law and Economics Working Paper no. 263*

Tong, H., & Wei, S. (2008) Real Effects of the Subprime Mortgage Crisis: Is it a Demand or a Finance Shock? NBER Working Papers, 14205.

Tuominen, N. (2017) *A Basic Theory of Rational Herd Behavior and Informational Cascades Does It Apply to Financial Markets,* Bachelor's Thesis in Economics, Aalto University's School of Business.

Tversky, A., & Kahneman, D. (1973). Availability: A Heuristic for Judging Frequency and Probability. *Cognitive Psychology*, 5(2), 207–232. DOI: 10.1016/0010-0285(73)90033-9

Tversky, A., & Kahneman, D. (1974). Judgement Under Uncertainity: Heuristics and Biases. *Science*, 185(4157), 1124–1131. DOI: 10.1126/science.185.4157.1124 PMID: 17835457

Tversky, A., & Kahneman, D. (1981). The Framing of Decisions and the Psychology of Choice. *Science*, 211(4481), 453–458. DOI: 10.1126/science.7455683 PMID: 7455683

Tversky A. and Kahneman D. (1986). Rational Choice and the Framing of Decisions *The Journal of Business*, vol. 39, no. 4, part. 2, 251-278.

Wheale, P. R., & Amin, L. H. (2003). Bursting the dot.com "Bubble': A Case Study in Investor Behaviour. *Technology Analysis and Strategic Management*, 15(1), 117–136. DOI: 10.1080/0953732032000046097

Endnotes

[1]   Instrumental rationality can be defined as the optimal fulfillment of an individual's objective (goal) (Stanovich, 2010: 1 and 8) or the selection of the means that best fulfil the given set of objectives (Hargreaves Heap, 1989: 39). Being consistent in choice and choosing what is best for oneself without making any mistakes (without making systematic errors) can also be added to the definition of instrumental rationality.

[2] The part of the representativeness heuristic that is relevant to the study is examined in the section on herd behavior under the heading of cognitive factors that cause herd behavior.

[3] The examples given here are related to biases due to retrievability of instances. There are other biases due to the availability heuristic. For example, biases due to the effectiveness of a search set. Suppose a word (of three or more letters) is randomly selected from an English text. Is it more likely that the word starts with "r" or that "r" is the third letter of the word? It is more common for "r" to be the third letter of the word rather than the first letter. However, since it is much easier to search for words according to their first letter, this question is usually answered by saying that the probability of the word starting with the letter "r" is higher (Tversky & Kahneman, 1974: 1127). Another bias is related to imaginability. "Sometimes one has to assess the frequency of a class whose instances are not stored in memory but can be generated according to a given rule. In such situations, one typically generates several instances and evaluates frequency or probability by the ease with which the relevant instances can be constructed. However, the case of constructing instances does not always reflect their actual frequency, and this mode of evaluation is prone to biases" (Tversky & Kahneman, 1974: 1127). For example, when the risk involved in an expedition is assessed by imagining the difficulties that may be encountered on the expedition and the availability of equipment that can be used in the face of these difficulties, the expedition may be seen as extremely dangerous even if the frequency of these difficulties is low (Tversky & Kahneman, 1974: 1128).

[4] Prospect Theory was identified in the study of Kahneman and Tversky (1979). Prospect theory identified by Tversky and Kahneman is related to the principles of perception and judgment that limit the rationality of decision-makers. In this sense, prospect theory argues that individuals make decisions with bounded rationality, not with instrumental rationality, as explained in footnote 1. Bounded rationality was first defined by H. Simon. Simon says that people depend on limited information and calculation capability. Therefore, when making decisions, people act based on bounded rationality, not instrumental rationality. "The alternative approach employed in these papers is based on what I shall call the principle of bounded rationality: The capacity of the human mind for formulating and solving complex problems is very small compared with the size of the problems whose solution is required for objectively rational behavior in the real world - or even for a reasonable approximation to such objective rationality" ((Simon, 1957: 198, see also p. 202, cited in Barros, 2010: 459). Accordingly, human beings cannot optimally fulfill their objectives as

assumed in instrumental rationality because he does not have the information capacity and calculation capability to make this possible. "Global rationality, the rationality of neoclassical theory [instrumental rationality], assumes that the decision-maker has a comprehensive, consistent utility function, knows all the alternatives that are available for choice, can compute the expected value of utility associated with each alternative, and chooses the alternative that maximizes expected utility. Bounded rationality, a rationality that is consistent with our knowledge of actual human choice behavior, assumes that the decision-maker must search for alternatives, has egregiously incomplete and inaccurate knowledge about the consequences of actions, and chooses actions that are expected to be satisfactory (attain goals while satisfying constraints)." (Simon, 1997:17, cited in Barros, 2010: 460)) Tversky and Kahneman's bounded rationality is similar to Simon's bounded rationality, but the factors that cause bounded rationality are defined differently. While Simon defines bounded rationality based on limited human knowledge and calculation capability, Tversky and Kahneman define bounded rationality based on heuristics, heuristic-related biases and Prospect theory's value and weighting functions. According to Tversky and Kahneman, the values and decision weights that people use when making decisions are not linear (Tversky & Kahneman, 1981: 457). People make decisions based on these two non-linear functions due to cognitive influences and limited judgement. Therefore, people have bounded rationality.

[5] One more factor causing herding should be mentioned here: Bandwagon effect. The bandwagon effect, as an effect related to the willingness to buy the good, is defined by Leibenstein (1950: 189) as follows: "By the bandwagon effect, we refer to the extent to which the demand for a commodity is increased due to the fact that others are also consuming the same commodity. It represents the desire of people to purchase a commodity in order to get into 'the swim of things'; in order to conform with the people they wish to be associated with; in order to be fashionable or stylish; or, in order to appear to be 'one of the boys'" Accordingly, the person buys the good in order to be accepted in his/her environment in some way. Although it is defined in the context of consumption, the bandwagon effect does not only shape the consumption demand. It can be expressed as the individual taking into account the decisions of the group he/she wants to be a part of in any action and harmonizing his/her preferences with the preferences of the group. In this sense, it is one of the most important reasons for herding. However, it is not included in the flow of the study.

6   Within the scope of the study, the factors that cause herding behavior are discussed. However, there are also psychological factors that are likely to prevent herding from occurring. For example, the overconfidence effect. Overconfidence occurs when a person overestimates his/her own abilities and knowledge. The subjective confidence in one's own ability and knowledge is greater than the objective situation (Pallier et al. 2002, Pikulina, 2017). Investors with overconfidence tend to overestimate their skills and knowledge and underestimate risk. When the stock they invest in rises, investors become overconfident. They are sure that they have more knowledge and are more competent than others (Robin & Angelina, 2020: 254). When there is a herd behavior towards selling the relevant stock, the overconfident investor may not participate in this behavior and continue to maintain his/her position.

7   Asch conducted experiments that examined the effect of the person's inclusion in the group on his/her decision. For example, the following experiment was conducted: Participants are shown two white cards. On one of them, there is a single vertical black line, and on the other, there are three black lines of different sizes. The participants are asked to determine which of the different lines on the second card is the same length as the single black line on the first card. This matching is repeated with other cards. The first and second pairings are unanimous, but the following pairings are not unanimous. The line chosen by the main participant (there is one participant, the rest of those present follow Asch's instructions) differs from the line chosen unanimously by those following Asch's instructions. This difference continues and the participant remains between what his/her perceptions say is right and the group's view, and a certain proportion of the participants begin to choose the line chosen by the group (which their perceptions say is wrong) as the experiment progresses (Asch, 1955: 32-34).

8   In this context, it is necessary to mention one more situation, which is analyzed under the heading of representativeness heuristic and is likely to prevent herding from occurring: gambler fallacy, which can be analyzed under the heading of the misconception of chance. For example, suppose you are playing roulette. If you observe a long succession of reds, you believe that it is time for black because there is a sequence of representations that you expect in accordance with the basic characteristic of the random process. According to this representation sequence, if it has been red for a long time, this cannot continue any longer, it is time for black (Tversky & Kahneman, 1974: 1125). In financial markets, this misconception may lead, for instance, to the belief that a stock whose price has been increasing for a long time will not increase further and

therefore to take an investment position separate from and even against those who invest in the stock.

[9] Within the scope of the study, the relationship between individual characteristics and herd behavior is discussed. However, cultural characteristics also affect herd behavior. Studies have been conducted on this subject. The experiments in the studies have shown that cultural differences affect people's behavior and therefore should be included in the examination of decision-making processes. As an example, the experiment in Ariely's (2008: 233-8) study can be given. In the experiment, the tables sitting in the pub were divided into two groups. The tables forming the first group were asked to choose one of 4 different beers out loud. The tables forming the second group were asked to choose one of the same 4 different beers in writing. In other words, those in the first group made their decisions openly to the environment and those in the second group made their decisions secretly. Afterward, they were given a questionnaire and asked how much they liked that beer and whether they regretted choosing that beer. The same experiment was conducted both in the USA, where being authentic is coded positively in the culture of the country, and in Hong Kong, where being authentic is coded negatively in the culture of the country. In the experiment conducted in the USA, those in the first group tended to choose a beer that was different from the beer chosen by the others at the table, and they made a choice that reflected "being authentic" even though it was not the beer they initially wanted. Their enjoyment of the beer they chose in the name of "being authentic" was less than that of those who made their choice in secret. This result suggests that people in the US may sacrifice the enjoyment of consumption for the sake of an image of "authenticity" (not being part of the general trend of the group). In the experiment conducted in Hong Kong, where the characteristic of being unique is coded negatively, opposite results were obtained from those in the USA. In the culture where the trait of being authentic was coded negatively, in contrast to the culture where it was coded positively, in vocal choices, people conformed to the general tendency of the group in order to show that they belonged to the group.

[10] For more information on the dot.com buble see Goodnight, G. T., & Green, S. (2010). Rhetoric, Risk, and Markets: The Dot-Com Bubble. *Quarterly Journal of Speech*, *96*(2), 115–140; Wheale, P. R., & Amin, L. H. (2003). Bursting the dot.com "Bubble': A Case Study in Investor Behaviour. *Technology Analysis & Strategic Management*, *15*(1), 117–136; Morris, John J. and Alam, Pervaiz, Analysis of the Dot-Com Bubble of the 1990s (June 27, 2008). Available at SSRN: https://ssrn.com/abstract=1152412 or https://dx.doi.org/10.2139/ssrn .1152412

[11] For more information: Murphy, J. Austin, An Analysis of the Financial Crisis of 2008: Causes and Solutions (November 4, 2008). Available at SSRN: https://ssrn.com/abstract=1295344 or https://dx.doi.org/10.2139/ssrn.1295344; Ospina, J. & Uhling, H. (2018) Mortgage-Backed Securities and the Financial Crisis of 2008: a Post Mortem, NBER Working Paper, 24509; Sanders, A. (2008) The subprime crisis and its role in the financial crisis, Journal of Hausing Economics, 17, 254-261; Tong H. & Wei, S. (2008) Real Effects of the Subprime Mortgage Crisis: Is it a Demand or a Finance Shock?, NBER Working Papers, 14205

Chapter 3
Breaking the Herd Leveraging Financial Mindfulness to Combat Investor Herding Behavior

J. Manjusha
https://orcid.org/0000-0002-1635-1046
Christ University, India

Lakshmi Bhooshetty
https://orcid.org/0000-0001-7152-1055
Christ University, India

ABSTRACT

This chapter examines herding behaviour in investors that affect the financial market. Herding involves investors mimicking others' actions due to factors like limited information, market sentiments, and psychological biases. Individual investors, less informed and more susceptible to emotions, herd more. Drawing from Buddhist economics, financial mindfulness emerges as a crucial intervention to mitigate herding. It promotes awareness of one's financial situation, enhancing independent decision-making and reducing impulsive behaviour. Empirical evidence supports mindfulness-based interventions in improving financial decisions and managing debt effectively. By cultivating a thoughtful approach to finance, financial mindfulness empowers investors to resist herd behaviour, fostering stability in financial markets.

DOI: 10.4018/979-8-3693-7827-4.ch003

Copyright © 2025, IGI Global Scientific Publishing. Copying or distributing in print or electronic forms without written permission of IGI Global is prohibited.

INTRODUCTION TO KEY TERMS

Financial Mindfulness: Mindfulness, originating from Buddhist philosophy, emphasizes being attentive and aware of the present moment. Research indicates that applying mindfulness in finance aids in achieving clarity of perspective and impartiality in financial decision-making (Faugere, 2016). Dr. Dan Stone introduced the term "financial mindfulness" in his book chapter in 2011, defining it as "openness and attention to, and awareness of, present financial events and experiences(Pandith-arathne & Chen, 2021; Stone, 2012). Essentially, financial mindfulness refers to the heightened awareness and attention one gives to one's financial matters. The practice of financial mindfulness cultivates a healthy attitude towards money, encouraging both financial planning and management. This quality empowers individuals to approach their finances with a balanced mindset, reducing anxiety and promoting better financial health. By maintaining this rational approach, individuals can act ethically and avoid fraudulent practices. (Pereira & Coelho, 2019). Financial mindfulness enhances financial stability and overall well-being by promoting financial planning and management (Faugere, 2016; Panditharathne & Chen, 2021; Pereira & Coelho, 2019; Stone, 2012). In sum, financial mindfulness is a valuable practice that can transform how individuals interact with their finances, leading to more ethical, rational, and effective financial decision-making (Iram et al., 2022b, 2022a).

Herding Behavior: Herding is defined as how investors imitate the actions of other investors (Merli & Roger, 2013). Intuitively, an individual can be considered to be herding if she would have invested without knowledge of other investors' decisions but decides to withdraw it upon discovering that others have chosen not to invest (Bikhchandani & Sharma, 2000). In the herd effect, while an individual's behaviour may be rational, it can result in collective irrational behaviour. (Liu et al., 2019). Investors herd mainly due to the unavailability of accurate information, reputational concerns and sometimes for speculative motives. Different behavioural theories have been applied to study herding behaviour. Herding occurs among both institutional and individual investors (Li et al., 2017). Herding has to be differentiated from spurious herding where a group of investors react similarly to a publicly available information(Bikhchandani & Sharma, 2000). In the case of spurious herding, there is no blind imitation of other investors.

Behavioural Bias: In simple terms, bias is a prejudice that affects financial decisions, influenced by underlying beliefs (Chira et al., 2008). According to Hersh Shefrin, behavioural bias means "predisposition towards error"(Shefrin, 2001). The behaviour of investors in the financial market is driven by behavioural bias (Agrawal, 2012). There are many types of bias that affect the individual's decision-making process. Each bias exists in a person due to different reasons. Gender, cultural traits, educational background, personality types etc., will contribute towards the development of behavioral bias (Tekçe et al., 2016). The most common types of biases are excessive optimism, overconfidence, illusion of control and familiarity bias (Bashir et al., 2013; Dervishaj, 2021; Sarin & Chowdhury, 2018).

Institutional investors: Institutional investors are legal entities and not physical persons. Institutional investors can take different legal forms, such as joint stock companies, limited liability partnerships, or incorporation by special statute. Institutional investors sometimes operate independently, but they also act on behalf of large companies (Çelik & Isaksson, 2013). This group consists of all investors in financial markets who are neither private households nor public institutions. It includes mutual funds, pension funds, banks, insurance companies, and similar private entities (Menkhoff, 2002). The rise of institutional investors has resulted in a higher concentration of equity ownership, with a significant portion of shares in most public corporations now being held by a small number of these investors (Bebchuk et al., 2017).

Individual investors: Individual investors are private investors who invest their money in different types of assets like stocks, bonds, mutual funds, etc. They have different financial goals. Unlike institutional investors, individual investors have fewer resources to acquire superior information. Individual investors manage their equity portfolios (Lovric et al., 2008).

INTRODUCTION

The herding phenomenon is not a recent concept. In the financial world, it may be prevalent (Devenow & Welch, 1996). The phenomenon of herding was first discussed by Keynes in 1936 (Keynes, 1937). He observed a pattern of conspicuous consumption among leisure-class individuals. He pointed out that strange group behaviours or irrational emotions can affect the whole market and change investment returns. However, the term "herding" did not come into existence. Herding term became popular in the 1990s when (Banerjee, 1992) published his article on herding behaviour. In this article, he defined herding as the act of trying to use information in the decisions made by others. After this study, several other empirical researches were published on herding, analyzing its effects on financial market transactions.

Herding, in layman's terms, means imitation of others. Herding is a way in which an investor imitates the actions of the other investor (Merli & Roger, 2013). For an investor to mimic others, she must be aware of their actions, and those actions must also influence her (Bikhchandani & Sharma, 2000). From a perspective of wealth management, herding behaviour is mainly caused because investors facing difficulty in making accurate forecasts due to insufficient information. Therefore, they are forced to follow the crowd's decision(Liu et al., 2019). Herding occurs among both institutional and individual investors, but there are differences. Individual investors are generally less informed and more susceptible to psychological biases, market sentiments, and attention-grabbing events like market return shocks when compared to institutional investors (Barber & Odean, 2008; Li et al., 2017). Institutional investors are more skilled and sophisticated compared to individual investors. Therefore, in most cases, institutional investors herd because of security features or trends or how information spreads in the market. On the other hand, individual investors herd due to their irrational mentality, market sentiments or psychological bias(Li et al., 2017; Nofsinger & Sias, 1999). Since individual investors have less access to accurate information, they herd more, leading to excess volatility and instability in financial markets. Hence it is necessary to help the individual investors overcome their herding behavior. It was identified in research that financial decisions that are affected by behavioural issues require a behavioural intervention to tackle the same (Pitthan & De Witte, 2023).

Financial Mindfulness is a behavioural intervention that can help individual investors overcome herding behaviour. Financial mindfulness, a concept recently developed from Buddhist economics, is based on the principles of mindfulness(Stone, 2012). Financial mindfulness involves a heightened awareness of one's economic situation and overall life circumstances. (Garbinsky et al., 2023; Iram et al., 2022b). Financial mindfulness is essential in financial planning and managing investment portfolios, helping individuals make better financial decisions (Panditharathne & Chen, 2021). There are several pieces of research that have proven that mindfulness-based interventions in financial matters have helped people overcome their impulsive decisions and unethical monetary intentions and improved their debt management(-Celsi et al., 2017; Gentina et al., 2021; Schomburgk & Hoffmann, 2023). Practising financial mindfulness helps individuals become aware of their financial position and transactions. This awareness enables them to make better decisions independently, without following others' patterns. Understanding one's financial position aids in making an informed investment choices. This analytical mind, as a result of financial mindfulness, helps investors to avoid herding behaviour.

This book chapter examines the concept of herding behaviour and delves into its psychological underpinnings. The latter part provides a critical assessment of how financial mindfulness can serve as an effective behavioural intervention to address herding behaviour.

The Basics of Herding Behavior

Cognitive Psychology considers humans as the primary unit of analysis (Goldstone & Janssen, 2005; Raafat et al., 2009). Humans exist within a complex social structure system that shapes and organises much of their behaviour, from national identity to religious affiliation (Raafat et al., 2009). Imitation and mimicry are fundamental human instincts (Devenow & Welch, 1996) .As social beings, people tend to follow group behaviour, influencing their actions and decisions across various contexts and fostering a sense of belonging (Baddeley, 2010). Herding can be understood as aligning an individual's thoughts or behaviours within a group through local interactions (Raafat et al., 2009). There are numerous forms of herding behaviour exhibited by human beings, who are considered to be the most socially interdependent species on Earth. According to Kameda & Hastie (2015), herding refers to "an alignment of thoughts or behaviours of individuals in a group through local interactions among individuals rather than through some purposeful coordination by a central authority in the group". Herding behaviour is evident in various aspects of human life, from daily social interactions to economic bubbles and political movements. In everyday interactions, people often think and act similarly, which can lead to irrational behaviour (Shiller, 1995). This phenomenon is not limited to social contexts; it also extends to economic and political spheres. During economic bubbles, for instance, investors may follow the crowd, ignoring fundamental valuations and contributing to market inefficiencies. Similarly, in political movements, individuals may adopt the prevailing attitudes and actions of the group, sometimes leading to unreasoned and impulsive decisions. Herding behaviour can be observed even in trends and fads (Devenow & Welch, 1996). Herding, thus, plays a significant role in shaping human behavior across different domains (Akerlof & Shiller, 2010; Kameda & Hastie, 2015). Therefore, herding behavior cannot be studied from a single perspective or discipline. The concept of herding dates back to the early 1950s when Harvey Leibenstein introduced the social psychological bandwagon metaphor in economics (Rook, 2006). Leibenstein defined a bandwagon as "the extent to which demand for a commodity is increased due to the fact that others are also consuming the same commodity"(Leibenstein, 1950). This explains the fundamental aspect of herding, where individuals attempt to align their actions with those of the crowd. In the mid-1980s, the bandwagon theory of herding started to be linked to economic studies. Here bandwagon theory was used to study the consumption patterns in the economy (Rook, 2006). In 1992, Abhijit Banerjee published research demonstrating that people might follow others even when their private information suggests doing otherwise (Banerjee, 1992). This marked the beginning of understanding herd behavior within an economic context.

Herding is a significant aspect of human behavior in economics and finance (Raafat et al., 2009; Shiller, 2002). Examples of phenomena associated with herd behavior include stock market bubbles financial speculation etc. (Raafat et al., 2009). Herding behavior in financial markets refers to phenomenon where investors tend to follow the actions of other investors blindly rather than making an independent decision. This behavior of investors often leads to market inefficiency, instability and other issues.

The theoretical base of herding lies in theory published by J M Keynes (1930). This theory explains the motivation behind the individual behavior of mimicking others. According to Keynes uncertainty and their own perception of ignorance compel people to mimic others. Investors often exhibit herding behavior by underestimating their own private and relevant information. They think that rest of the crowd have superior information. J M Keynes again in 1936 highlighted the presence of unusual group dynamics or even irrational emotions that resulted in fluctuations in market returns. He subtly indicated the herding behavior of investors in this context (Keynes, 1937). The underlying cause of herding behavior is explained by conformity theory (Komalasari et al., 2022). Conformity as defined by theory is change in behavior or opinion of person due to pressure from a group. It makes the person follow the group norms with expectation of reward or in fear of punishment (Bernheim, 1994). It is normal for an individual to feel anxious or embarrassed when his behavior is different from the majority. To avoid that feeling, individuals frequently adjust their behaviors, attitudes, and opinions to align with group norms. This leads to herding behavior (Chen et al., 2022; Komalasari et al., 2022). In social psychology, the theory of herding behavior is also referred to as crowd or mob psychology (Kameda & Hastie, 2015; Komalasari et al., 2022; Raafat et al., 2009). In simpler terms, in a crowd, people are influenced to follow others without much thought. The collective mentality of the crowd can significantly change how individuals behave. The other theory that is used to explain herding behavior is Agency theory. This perspective from agency theory is highly applicable in explaining the herding behavior of fund managers or institutional investors (Komalasari et al., 2022). From an agency theory perspective, herding behavior occurs due to the agency or contractual relationship between investment managers and investors. Investment managers have to maintain their reputation and compensation which depends upon their investment performance. Herding behavior originates when an investment manager with low ability blindly imitate the decision of senior managers ignoring their private information since they feel that their senior managers have superior information (Scharfstein & Stein, 1990).

Defining herding is a difficult task. There is no single definition which every researcher could agree upon (Devenow & Welch, 1996; Komalasari et al., 2022) . Merli and Roger (2013) presumed herding as the "fact of irrationally imitating oth-ers". Whereas several others researchers defined herding as the form of correlated behavior that occurs when investors imitate or follow other investors decision while discarding their own private information and belief (Li et al., 2017). Nofsinger and Sias (1999) defined herding as the group of investors trading in the same direction over a period of time. Banerjee (1992) states that herding occurs when everyone does what others do, even when their information suggests doing something entirely different. The author gave this definition on the assumption that every individual is rational. Although definitions of herding vary, they all share the common idea of imitating others. An individual is said to herd when she initially decides to invest in an asset, but refrains from doing so upon learning that others are not investing in it (Bikhchandani & Sharma, 2000). There are two opposing views on herding: non-rational and rational. Non-rational view focuses on investor psychology, and it focuses on the blind imitation of others, ignoring rational analysis. Whereas the rational view focuses on external factors that affect the optimum decision making (Devenow & Welch, 1996). This rational view can be connected to spurious herding. Spurious herding occurs when a group of investors react to commonly known public information (Bikhchandani & Sharma, 2000). For example, due to fluctuations in interest rates, stocks become less attractive, and investors may hold only a small percentage in their portfolio. This is not blindly following other investors. It is a rational decision taken by the investors. Spurious herding occurs when investors face similar information and problems and make the same decision without necessarily observing others. This is different from irrational or intentional herding, where investors consciously imitate the decisions of others (Fernández et al., 2011). Investors who do intentional herding do not know either the quality of information other investors possess or the market trends. Hence, it cannot be considered rational (Parker & Prechter, 2005).

Herding occurs due to many reasons. One of the major reasons is the lack of accurate information (Avery & Zemsky, 1998; Bikhchandani et al., 1992; Fernández et al., 2011; Liu et al., 2019; Merli & Roger, 2013; Wang, 2008). Information that is accurate and timely helps investors obtain higher profits or avoid major economic losses. Different investors have different capabilities of processing the information and different access to information (Liu et al., 2019). Investors are not fully skilled in processing the large quantity of information in the market (Hirshleifer & Teoh, 2003; Simon, 1957). Therefore, individuals with limited processing ability use vague rules to understand the company valuations and estimates of cashflows (Fernández et al., 2011). Investors then do major portions of their analysis under the influence of behavioral bias (Daniel & Titman, 1999; Fernández et al., 2011). When many investors adopt imitation to cope with the informational limitation, it results in herding behaviour. And this herding behavior arise from the obvious intent of investors to copy the behavior of other investors (Fernández et al., 2011).

Another major reason for herding is reputational concerns (Dasgupta & Prat, 2008; Fernández et al., 2011; Liu et al., 2019; Roider & Voskort, 2016). Dasgupta and Prat'(2008) theory on reputational herding explains the herding that is caused by the reputational reasons of investors. This article introduced a large group of traders, known as fund managers, who trade for other investors and are concerned with maintaining their reputations. Again, these fund managers are of two types:

smart and dump. Smart fund managers find their path of investments, whereas dump fund managers blindly imitate the smart fund managers. If an investor has a piece of private information that contradicts the actions of earlier investors, following their information might harm their reputation (Fernández et al., 2011). Thus, they choose herding as the safer option. If many investors have bought an asset, going against the trend based on personal information can make an investor feel that they will lose their reputation. Consequently, investors follow the crowd (Roider & Voskort, 2016).

Another reason for herding could be the speculative mentality of investors (Liu et al., 2019). Many investors want to increase their wealth and to improve their financial status. Therefore, they change their mentality to speculative. A speculative mentality is often concerned with taking high risks to earn profits. When investors have such a mindset, they are easily influenced by market comments, actions of other investors and media information. As a result, they tend to follow the strategies of fellow investors without any critical analysis.

Herding occurs among institutional and individual investors (Li et al., 2017). Several researchers have discussed the occurrence of herding in institutional investors (Choi & Sias, 2009; Choi & Skiba, 2015; Sias, 2004). For institutional investors, it is often driven by information cascades, reputational concerns, and habit investing. Information cascades happen when these investors prioritize collective wisdom over their private information. Habit investing refers to the tendency to follow established patterns in decision-making. Additionally, institutional investors engage in herding to safeguard their reputation, as aligning with the crowd can reduce the risk of being seen as outliers. When it comes to individual investors, they engage in herd behaviour due to Payoff externalities, Reputational Concerns and Informational Externalities (Merli & Roger, 2013; Nofsinger & Sias, 1999). Payoff externalities refer to a situation where the more people engage in an action, the more the benefits of that action. Here, in the case of investments, investors try to align their actions with the majority group in the hope that it will lead to more benefits. Individual investors often lack the resources to obtain reliable market information, so they tend to rely on the actions of other investors and follow their lead. Like institutional investors, individual investors also care about their reputation. To protect it, they often follow the majority.

Comparative studies show that institutional investors herd less than individual investors(Li et al., 2017). Institutional investors trade more selectively, while individual investors follow public information more closely. This difference highlights the distinct behaviours and decision-making processes between these two types of investors in the market. Research has shown that institutional investors tend to earn positive returns through herding, whereas individual investors often incur losses (Hsieh, 2013). This discrepancy arises because individual herding is typically driven by emotions, such as overconfidence, the thrill of trading, and regret aversion, rather than rational decision-making principles. In contrast, institutional investors make more calculated decisions, which can lead to better outcomes in the market. Researchers have revealed that individuals are more likely to herd during market downturns, while there is less evidence of imitative trading behavior in bullish markets (Goodfellow et al., 2009). This is mainly driven by the fear of economic losses in individuals' minds. As prospect theory suggests, people tend to prioritize avoiding losses over seeking gains (Kahneman, 1979).

A major issue for individual investors is their limited access to resources, such as superior information and advanced software for analysis, unlike institutional investors. The ability to process available information is also constrained, making it difficult to make well-informed decisions. Consequently, many individual investors rely on emotions and personal judgments when making investment choices. This emotional decision-making frequently leads to herding behaviour, where investors mimic the actions of others in an attempt to sustain themselves in the financial markets. Herding, while seemingly a safe strategy, can have significant downsides. By following the crowd, individual investors may reinforce market inefficiencies, contribute to asset bubbles, and increase exposure to market volatility. Unfortunately, many investors are unaware of these negative aspects of herding, leading to repeated patterns of poor decision-making and financial losses. To address this issue, it is crucial to introduce behavioural interventions to help individual investors overcome herding behaviour.

Psychological Reason Behind Herding Behaviour

Herding is a behavioural issue influenced by various psychological drivers. Understanding these underlying psychological factors is essential before developing effective solutions to address herding behaviour. By analyzing these motivations, we can create targeted interventions that help individuals make more independent financial choices and reduce the tendency to follow the crowd. This deeper understanding is crucial for fostering healthier financial behaviours and promoting informed decision-making among investors.

Social influence: It is common that during uncertainty, people tend to follow the actions of others since they assume that the crowd has more knowledge than them. It has been proven by several studies that social influence have great influence in creating herding behavior (Baddeley, 2010, 2013). It is a common practice for the investor to rely on expert opinion before taking any investment decision. It is a general belief that expert opinions are rational. But in reality, even the experts can rely on heuristics and rules of thumb to guide their interpretation of events, which, in turn, makes a group follow a decision that is not completely rational. This creates herding behaviour.

Conformity: Individuals often want acceptance from their peers. This is known as conformity. Resisting peer pressure may result in awkwardness. However, conformity with the crowd generates satisfaction and gives psychological reassurance(Baddeley, 2013). It has been proven that the need for conformity among peers in individuals leads to herding behaviour (Bobe & Piefke, 2019).

Loss Aversion: Loss aversion is a situation where an investor tries to avoid economic losses. Investors fear economic losses from their investments. Loss aversion and herding behaviour occur together, and they have an impact on the investment decisions of individuals (Aprilianti et al., 2023). People who want to avoid loss tend to prefer herding (Arlen & Tontrup, 2015; Fernández et al., 2011). They believe that following the majority leads to economic gain, based on the assumption that the majority has superior information.

Behavioral Bias: It has been proved that the existence of behavioural bias leads to herding behaviour(Din et al., 2021). When behavioural bias exists in investor, their rationality is affected. An investor influenced by behavioural biases may struggle to analyze current market conditions logically. Consequently, they are likely to engage in herding behaviour, following the crowd believing it is the right decision. Individuals with bias often feel that they can completely control random events and underestimate the role of luck. In such social situations, these individuals feel that other investors are influenced by the same factors. Therefore, they assume that others' decisions are based on relevant information, not random choices, and use these decisions to guide their own(Fernández et al., 2011; Wyer Jr & Carlston, 2018). This creates herding.

Herding and Portfolio Diversification

Diversifying a portfolio is a vital financial strategy for managing investment risk and improving long-term performance. According to Markowitz's 1952 finance theory, portfolio diversification involves reducing overall risk by combining different assets in a portfolio that are not strongly correlated (Markowitz, 1959). Most rational models of portfolio choice suggest that investors hold a diversified portfolio to reduce the risk(Goetzmann & Kumar, 2008). Portfolio diversification helps investors reduce overall losses by spreading investments across various assets that react differently to changing market conditions (De Winne & Petkeviciute, 2021; Nevins, 2004). The core idea of diversification is to spread the investment across various assets to mitigate the impact of poor performance in any single asset (French & Poterba, 1991). When investors are not overly dependent on the performance of one asset, this helps to reduce the possibility of huge economic loss. The principle of "not putting all your eggs in one basket applies in the case of portfolio diversification

(Baker et al., 2020; Whitehouse, 2002). A diversified portfolio often acts as a hedge during inflationary periods (Dabara et al., 2015)

It has been revealed that individual investors hold under diversified portfolio due to the existence of cognitive issues. This tendency towards under-diversification is more pronounced among younger, low-income, less-educated, and less-sophisticated investors. Cognitive issues can impact the portfolio diversification decisions of investors (Goetzmann & Kumar, 2004).

It has been proven in studies that herding has a significant impact on the portfolio diversification decisions of investors (Aharon, 2021). Expert discussions with high-ranking bank managers conducted as a part of research revealed that one of the possible reasons for sub-optimal diversification is by observing the investment choices of other investors [herding](Filiz et al., 2018). There are two forms of herding that occur here. One investor follows the majority of investors. The other is investors following the most successful investor. Both of these can generate negative outcomes for the investors since their personal circumstances and financial position differ. When investors blindly follow the behaviour of others, ignoring their relevant personal information, they may end up selecting an under-diversified portfolio to align with the majority. Under diversified portfolio is not beneficial in generating good returns (Goetzmann & Kumar, 2008; Phan et al., 2018).

From General Mindfulness to Financial Mindfulness: A Transition

The term mindfulness is the English translation of the Pali word Sati. Sati means awareness, attention, and remembering. The fundamental definition of mindfulness is "moment-by-moment awareness" (Germer, 2004). Brown and Ryan, (2003) defined mindfulness as the "state of being attentive to and aware of what is occurring in the present". General mindfulness is about the awareness and attention a person can provide for his daily activities. This helps the person to have a clear idea of his daily activities. This allows the person to avoid unnecessary stress and tension. Mindfulness fosters daily discipline in a person's life. This improves the overall focus on life. As a result, a person will be able to achieve satisfaction and well-being in life.

When it comes to financial mindfulness, it involves applying the principles of mindfulness to financial matters. Managing financial matters is an important aspect of a person's life. Therefore, cultivating financial mindfulness helps the person know his financial habits and practices. This awareness enables a person to recognize and promptly avoid habits or practices that have negative effects. A person with financial mindfulness will be more attentive towards his financial transactions. Also, financial mindfulness helps the person to develop an open mindset towards financial matters. An open mindset enables the individual to identify and avoid different behavioural biases that affect rational decisions. Financial mindfulness helps to cultivate a financial discipline. It also helps to develop a healthy mindset towards money.

Financial mindfulness is greatly influenced by mindfulness. Yet financial mindfulness is more into understanding the core aspects of financial management and regulating financial habits and thoughts. However, financial mindfulness and financial literacy should not be considered synonymous. Financial literacy means knowledge and understanding of financial concepts and principles that enable individuals to make informed decisions regarding financial matters. Financial literacy is often regarded as the ability of people to make financial decisions (Lusardi, 2019). The Organization for Economic Co-operation and Development (OECD) defined financial literacy as the knowledge and understanding of financial concepts and risks and the skills, motivation, and confidence to apply this knowledge. Financial mindfulness focuses on enhancing the behavioural aspects of personal financial management. It aims to improve individuals' perspectives on their financial matters. Only with the right mindset can individuals effectively apply their financial knowledge. Therefore, it is clear that financial mindfulness is essential to achieve the best outcomes from financial literacy training.

Understanding Financial Mindfulness

Financial Mindfulness is a transformative approach that is adopted to bring changes in the financial behavior. Mindfulness has been originated from Buddhist philosophy which refers to attention and awareness given to the present moment (Faugere, 2016). In the recent times, concept of mindfulness has been applied in financial matters. The major reason for this is that mindfulness has an inverse relationship with materialism which leads to lesser financial anxiety and more financial well-being in individuals (Sinha et al., 2021). According to Faugere, (2016), one needs to have an open and non-judgmental mind while making financial decisions. This is to ensure that a person is not making financial decisions under the influence of emotions. Such decisions that are not based on emotions will be rational and practical. Mindfulness when applied to financial matters, helps in developing a healthy attitude towards money (Pereira & Coelho, 2019; Riaz et al., 2022). It also boosts the financial self-efficacy of individuals (Pereira & Coelho, 2019). The application of mindfulness in finance helps to create a responsible attitude towards money.

Financial mindfulness, a recently developed concept derived from Buddhist economics, is based on the principles of mindfulness (Stone, 2012). According to Stone (2012), financial mindfulness is a balance point between impulsivity and thoughtfulness. Making effective financial decisions requires critically analysing financial matters while avoiding impulsive actions. However over thinking on financial matters can lead to confusion. Therefore, a financially mindful person is able to maintain the balance between overthinking and impulsive decisions. Iram et.el (2022b) defined financial mindfulness as effectively managing an individual's personal life. Panditharathne and Chen, (2021) defined financial mindfulness as the openness and awareness one can give to financial matters. A recent research on financial mindfulness defined it as "the inclination to maintain a heightened awareness of one's actual financial situation while simultaneously embracing it without passing judgment" (Garbinsky et al., 2023). It is said that unethical practices like embezzlement, fraud, and theft are less common in people with financial mindfulness (Stone, 2012). This is because they have better impulse control. They critically analyse decisions before making the decisions. Financial Mindfulness is important in financial planning and portfolio management (Panditharathne & Chen, 2021; Serowik et al., 2013). There are several reasons for this. Financial mindfulness enhances individuals' awareness of their spending habits, prompting them to create and adhere to budgets. People can develop better savings skills by prioritising expenditures, leading to fewer financial discrepancies. This practice helps manage unnecessary wants and enables more effective financial management. As a result, individuals are better equipped to handle their finances. Moreover, financial mindfulness has been proven to help investors adopt a more analytical approach to decision-making (Iram et al., 2022b). By fostering a mindful attitude towards money, individuals can improve their financial stability and make more informed investment choices (Serowik et al., 2013). Overall, cultivating financial mindfulness leads to better financial health and decision-making.

It has been proven that financial mindfulness is able to control emotional bias in individuals(Iram et al., 2022b, 2022a). When people develop financial mindfulness, they gain a heightened awareness of their financial position and transactions. This increased awareness allows them to control impulsive actions and make more deliberate choices regarding spending and saving. By taking the time to understand various financial requirements, individuals can better align their actions with their long-term goals. This mindset enables them to identify and address emotional biases that may influence their decision-making. Individuals can make more rational and informed choices by recognizing these biases and adopting a nonjudgmental approach to financial matters. Ultimately, financial mindfulness fosters a more thoughtful relationship with money, empowering individuals to achieve greater financial stability and make decisions that align with their values and objectives. This holistic understanding of personal finance contributes to healthier financial behaviours and improved overall well-being.

Based on existing research on financial mindfulness, three key aspects emerge. First, financial mindfulness significantly promotes financial awareness. This involves clearly understanding one's assets, liabilities, and overall financial position. Individuals can make informed decisions that align with their financial goals by cultivating this awareness. Second, financial mindfulness encourages individuals to be more attentive to their financial matters. When people actively engage with their financial situations, they are less likely to make impulsive or unwanted decisions. This heightened attention helps them avoid pitfalls and promotes healthier financial habits. Third, financial mindfulness enables individuals to recognize the biases influencing their financial decision-making. By understanding their own behavioural biases—such as overconfidence or loss aversion—individuals can develop strategies to counteract these tendencies. This awareness fosters a more rational approach to financial choices, leading to better outcomes in investment and spending behaviours. These aspects of financial mindfulness enhance personal financial management and contribute to overall financial well-being, empowering individuals to navigate their financial journeys with greater confidence and clarity.

Numerous experimental studies have demonstrated that mindfulness in finance can lead to positive outcomes. A study in Australia looked at the link between mindfulness, Buy Now, Pay Later (BNPL) schemes, and consumer well-being (Schomburgk & Hoffmann, 2023). It found that using BNPL is connected to lower feelings of overall well-being, mainly because it negatively affects how people view their financial situation. The study suggests that adding mindfulness to financial decision-making and offering mindfulness training along with financial literacy programs can improve financial well-being and help reduce impulsive spending. An experimental study conducted in the USA found that relying solely on financial literacy is not enough to produce significant changes in debt management programs (Celsi et al., 2017). Participants shared their experiences of weekly temptations while in the program, defined as the urge to spend on items beyond their budget. The study identified three response patterns related to these temptations. It concluded that individuals who practice mindfulness tend to have higher self-efficacy, which leads to greater self-control and reduced levels of temptation. As a result, the research indicated that mindfulness-based interventions could lead to significant behavioural changes in individuals. A study with 523 participants found that mindfulness-based interventions effectively managed unethical monetary intentions (Gentina et al., 2021). The survey targeted individuals who had completed the Mindfulness-Based Stress Reduction (MBSR) program and assessed traits such as mindfulness, materialistic attitudes, and consumer ethics using validated scales. The findings revealed that mindfulness reduced materialistic thinking by fostering values like compassion, generosity, and kindness. It promotes ethical consumer beliefs by increasing awareness of thoughts, feelings, and behaviours, leading to healthier attitudes toward money. The study strongly advocates developing training programs incorporating mindfulness to help individuals better regulate their attitudes and intentions regarding finances.

Hence, it is evident that mindfulness-based training can significantly impact people's financial management and money attitudes. Financial mindfulness allows individuals to effectively use their financial knowledge and make more rational decisions. By developing financial mindfulness, individuals can reduce unethical intentions related to money. Awareness of one's financial position and giving sufficient attention to financial matters helps avoid unethical thoughts and greed. Therefore, necessary steps should be taken to incorporate financial mindfulness into individuals' daily lives.

Incorporating Financial Mindfulness in Daily Life

To achieve financial mindfulness, individuals must adopt specific steps. Below is a consolidated list based on recommendations from money coaches and financial well-being experts:

Track your daily spending: To become financially mindful, one has to track his daily spending. The person should not neglect even the smallest amount. This tracking can help individuals to understand the areas where they overspend and make changes accordingly. This fosters money discipline and creates financial awareness regarding one's financial situation. It also promotes financial attention towards one's position and financial matters.

Create a financial budget: To be financially mindful, one needs to create a clear budget for his expenses. While spending, the person has to stick to the budget as much as possible. If there are any deviations in the budget, one has to analyze the reason for such deviations critically. This fosters a sense of responsibility towards financial matters. A well-planned budget serves as a financial roadmap, guiding them through their spending and helping them avoid unnecessary debt

Schedule regular financial reviews: To be financially mindful, one has to conduct regular financial reviews. Individuals can conduct these reviews either quarterly, monthly or weekly based on convenience. This is done in order to track your income, savings, expenses and investments. This gives an idea of the current financial position. Financial reviews help track your progress towards financial goals and allow you to reassess those goals based on your current financial position.

Continue to Learn About Financial Management: Managing finances requires continuous learning. As the financial sector evolves, new and innovative policies emerge, necessitating individuals to understand and adapt their financial plans accordingly. A financially mindful person is prepared to learn and embrace these changes, enhancing financial management skills. Staying informed about new developments ensures they can make well-informed decisions, optimize their financial strategies, and remain resilient in a dynamic financial landscape.

Set Clear Financial Goals: Before setting financial goals, analysing an individual's financial position is essential. This analysis should critically evaluate assets and debts to ensure that the goals set are realistic and achievable. Understanding one's financial status helps in formulating practical and attainable financial objectives. Setting goals is essential to help individuals stay disciplined in managing their financial matters.

Monitor Thoughts About Money: Individuals must be aware of their thoughts and attitudes towards money. Thoughts, such as fear of financial failure or greed, can negatively influence financial decisions. One can identify and address your thoughts associated with money and its management by keeping a close watch. If managing such thoughts is beyond an individual's control, it is advisable to seek professional help. Developing a positive and healthy attitude towards money promotes better financial behaviour and decision-making. It helps foster a balanced approach to earning, saving, spending, and investing money.

Role Of Financial Mindfulness in Controlling Herd Behavior

Herd behaviour is caused in individual investors due to psychological issues like social influence, reputational concerns, conformity, loss aversion and other behavioural biases. This herd behaviour causes individuals to follow the actions of other investors, leading them to make irrational decisions, which can result in economic losses. Here comes the importance of financial mindfulness. By practising financial mindfulness, a person becomes aware of their financial position, which enables them to rationally evaluate whether other investors' actions will benefit them. Financial mindfulness helps to create a sense of self-awareness in individuals. This helps them to critically evaluate the thoughts and emotions that lead to herd behaviour. When individuals become more aware of these thoughts and emotions, it helps them to ignore it. This mindset helps them to avoid following the path of other investors. Instead, they will try to critically analyze their own investment paths. Financial mindfulness encourages people to seek and process information before making financial decisions. Financial mindfulness promotes research and personal evaluation in investors. This helps them to make independent decisions. Financial mindfulness promotes budgeting and setting financial goals. This allows investors to gain insight into their long-term objectives. When they have a clear understanding of these goals, they can critically assess various investment strategies and select the most suitable one. Financial mindfulness encourages continuous learning and self-reflection. This helps the individuals to trust their judgements and capabilities. Hence, they start giving more importance to their private information and intuition. When individuals feel confident in their financial knowledge and decision-making skills, they are less likely to follow the crowd out of fear or uncertainty. Financial mindfulness fosters ethical behaviour, enabling investors to recognize legitimate ways to earn returns while avoiding fraudulent practices. By promoting awareness and responsible decision-making, individuals are encouraged to align their financial actions with ethical standards, contributing to a healthier financial environment and sustainable investing practices. Emotional bias significantly influences individuals to follow the crowd. However, incorporating financial mindfulness has been shown to greatly reduce behavioural biases. By cultivating financial mindfulness, a person can minimize emotional biases and their impact on financial decision-making, leading to more rational and informed choices.

Financial Mindfulness presents a transformative method for handling personal finances. Financial mindfulness offers a comprehensive approach to addressing herd behaviour in financial decision-making. By cultivating a mindful attitude towards finance, individuals can break free from the constraints of herd behaviour, leading to more rational and responsible financial outcomes. Financial mindfulness encourages individuals to gather and analyze information, promoting research and self-evaluation for independent decision-making.

CONCLUSION

This book chapter mainly dealt with herding behaviour. Herding behaviour means the blind imitation of other investors. This is considered irrational because investors often overlook their private information when following the actions of other investors. Investors often feel that they lack the ability, knowledge and information to plan their investments effectively. This makes them believe that others have superior knowledge and ability when compared to them. This thought compels them to align their investment actions with the majority of investors. This is also an indirect way of saving their reputation and seeking acceptance among the other investors. Often, investors engage in herding behaviour due to their speculative motives. Major psychological reasons for herding behaviour are social influence, conformity, loss aversion and behavioural bias. Financial mindfulness is one of the best behavioural interventions that can be introduced to reduce herd behaviour. Financial mindfulness refers to the increased awareness and attention one gives to financial matters. It encourages an open-minded approach to financial issues and helps individuals avoid emotional biases when making financial decisions. Financial mindfulness fosters self-awareness, allowing individuals to critically evaluate their thoughts and emotions contributing to herd behaviour. This mindset enables individuals to prioritize their information and insights while developing investment strategies, effectively breaking away from herd behaviour

REFERENCES

Agrawal, K. (2012). *A Conceptual Framework of Behavioral Biases in Finance.* IUP Journal of Behavioral Finance.

Aharon, D. Y. (2021). Uncertainty, fear and herding behavior: Evidence from size-ranked portfolios. *Journal of Behavioral Finance*, 22(3), 320–337. DOI: 10.1080/15427560.2020.1774887

Akerlof, G. A., & Shiller, R. J. (2010). *Animal spirits: How human psychology drives the economy, and why it matters for global capitalism.* Princeton university press.

Aprilianti, A. A., Tanzil, N. D., & Pratama, A. (2023). Herding Behavior, Loss Aversion Bias, Financial Literacy, and Investment Decisions (a Study on Millennial Generation in Indonesia in the Digital Era). *JASa (Jurnal Akuntansi, Audit Dan Sistem Informasi Akuntansi), 7*(3), 555–565.

Arlen, J., & Tontrup, S. (2015). Strategic bias shifting: Herding as a behaviorally rational response to regret aversion. *The Journal of Legal Analysis*, 7(2), 517–560. DOI: 10.1093/jla/lav014

Avery, C., & Zemsky, P. (1998). Multidimensional uncertainty and herd behavior in financial markets. *The American Economic Review*, ●●●, 724–748.

Baddeley, M. (2010). Herding, social influence and economic decision-making: Socio-psychological and neuroscientific analyses. *Philosophical Transactions of the Royal Society of London. Series B, Biological Sciences*, 365(1538), 281–290. DOI: 10.1098/rstb.2009.0169 PMID: 20026466

Baddeley, M. (2013). Herding, social influence and expert opinion. *Journal of Economic Methodology*, 20(1), 35–44. DOI: 10.1080/1350178X.2013.774845

Baker, H. K., Nofsinger, J. R., & Puttonen, V. (2020). Common Investing Pitfalls that Can Separate You from Financial Security and Success. In *The Savvy Investor's Guide to Avoiding Pitfalls, Frauds, and Scams* (pp. 5–34). Emerald Publishing Limited. DOI: 10.1108/978-1-78973-559-820201003

Banerjee, A. V. (1992). A simple model of herd behavior. *The Quarterly Journal of Economics*, 107(3), 797–817. DOI: 10.2307/2118364

Barber, B. M., & Odean, T. (2008). All that glitters: The effect of attention and news on the buying behavior of individual and institutional investors. *Review of Financial Studies*, 21(2), 785–818. DOI: 10.1093/rfs/hhm079

Bashir, T., Rasheed, S., Raftar, S., Fatima, S., & Maqsood, S. (2013). Impact of behavioral biases on investor decision making: Male vs female. *Journal of Business and Management*, 10(3), 60–68.

Bebchuk, L. A., Cohen, A., & Hirst, S. (2017). The agency problems of institutional investors. *The Journal of Economic Perspectives*, 31(3), 89–112. DOI: 10.1257/jep.31.3.89

Bernheim, B. D. (1994). A theory of conformity. *Journal of Political Economy*, 102(5), 841–877. DOI: 10.1086/261957

Bikhchandani, S., Hirshleifer, D., & Welch, I. (1992). A theory of fads, fashion, custom, and cultural change as informational cascades. *Journal of Political Economy*, 100(5), 992–1026. DOI: 10.1086/261849

Bikhchandani, S., & Sharma, S. (2000). Herd behavior in financial markets. *IMF Staff Papers*, 47(3), 279–310. DOI: 10.2307/3867650

Bobe, M. C., & Piefke, M. (2019). Why do we herd in financial contexts? *Journal of Neuroscience, Psychology, and Economics*, 12(2), 116–140. DOI: 10.1037/npe0000108

Brown, K. W., & Ryan, R. M. (2003). The benefits of being present: Mindfulness and its role in psychological well-being. *Journal of Personality and Social Psychology*, 84(4), 822–848. DOI: 10.1037/0022-3514.84.4.822 PMID: 12703651

Carlos Medina, J. (2024, May 7). *8 Ways To Use Financial Mindfulness To Enhance Your Life.* https://www.forbes.com/sites/financialfinesse/2024/05/07/financial-mindfulness-the-key-to-enhancing-your-financial-life/

Çelik, S., & Isaksson, M. (2013). *Institutional investors as owners: Who are they and what do they do?* Celsi, M. W., Nelson, R. P., Dellande, S., & Gilly, M. C. (2017). Temptation's itch: Mindlessness, acceptance, and mindfulness in a debt management program. *Journal of Business Research*, 77, 81–94. DOI: 10.1016/j.jbusres.2017.03.002

Chen, X., Li, S., Zhang, Y., Zhai, Y., Zhang, Z., & Feng, C. (2022). Different drives of herding: An exploratory study of motivations underlying social conformity. *PsyCh Journal*, 11(2), 247–258. DOI: 10.1002/pchj.515 PMID: 35080146

Chira, I., Adams, M., & Thornton, B. (2008). *Behavioral bias within the decision making process.*

Choi, N., & Sias, R. W. (2009). Institutional industry herding. *Journal of Financial Economics*, 94(3), 469–491. DOI: 10.1016/j.jfineco.2008.12.009

Choi, N., & Skiba, H. (2015). Institutional herding in international markets. *Journal of Banking & Finance*, 55, 246–259. DOI: 10.1016/j.jbankfin.2015.02.002

Dabara, I. D., Ogunba, A. O., & Araloyin, F. M. (2015). The diversification and inflation-hedging potentials of direct and indirect real estate investments in Nigeria. *Proceedings of the 15th African Real Estate Society (AFRES) Annual Conference, 31st August–3rd September*, 169–185. DOI: 10.15396/afres2015_117

Daniel, K., & Titman, S. (1999). Market efficiency in an irrational world. *Financial Analysts Journal*, 55(6), 28–40. DOI: 10.2469/faj.v55.n6.2312

Dasgupta, A., & Prat, A. (2008). Information aggregation in financial markets with career concerns. *Journal of Economic Theory*, 143(1), 83–113. DOI: 10.1016/j.jet.2008.01.005

De Winne, R., & Petkeviciute, A. (2021). *Financial Literacy and Multi-Asset Portfolio Diversification. International Conference of the French Finance Association (AFFI)*.

Dervishaj, B. (2021). Psychological biases, main factors of financial behaviour-A literature review. *European Journal of Medicine and Natural Sciences*, 4(1), 27–44.

Devenow, A., & Welch, I. (1996). Rational herding in financial economics. *European Economic Review*, 40(3–5), 603–615. DOI: 10.1016/0014-2921(95)00073-9

Din, S. M. U., Mehmood, S. K., Shahzad, A., Ahmad, I., Davidyants, A., & Abu-Rumman, A. (2021). The impact of behavioral biases on herding behavior of investors in Islamic financial products. *Frontiers in Psychology*, 11, 600570. DOI: 10.3389/fpsyg.2020.600570 PMID: 33613358

Faugere, C. (2016). Applying mindfulness and compassion in finance. *Critical Studies on Corporate Responsibility. Governance and Sustainability*, 10(May), 299–319. DOI: 10.1108/S2043-905920160000010032

Fernández, B., Garcia-Merino, T., Mayoral, R., Santos, V., & Vallelado, E. (2011). Herding, information uncertainty and investors' cognitive profile. *Qualitative Research in Financial Markets*, 3(1), 7–33. DOI: 10.1108/17554171111124595

Filiz, I., Nahmer, T., Spiwoks, M., & Bizer, K. (2018). Portfolio diversification: The influence of herding, status-quo bias, and the gambler's fallacy. *Financial Markets and Portfolio Management*, 32(2), 167–205. DOI: 10.1007/s11408-018-0311-x

French, K. R., & Poterba, J. (1991). *Investor diversification and international equity markets*.

Garbinsky, E., Blanchard, S. J., & Kim, L. (2023). FINANCIAL MINDFULNESS. *Georgetown McDonough School of Business Research Paper Forthcoming*.

Gentina, E., Daniel, C., & Tang, T. L.-P. (2021). Mindfulness reduces avaricious monetary attitudes and enhances ethical consumer beliefs: Mindfulness training, timing, and practicing matter. *Journal of Business Ethics*, 173(2), 301–323. DOI: 10.1007/s10551-020-04559-5

Germer, C. (2004). What is mindfulness. *The Insight Journal*, 22(3), 24–29.

Goetzmann, W. N., & Kumar, A. (2004). Diversification decisions of individual investors and asset prices. *Yale School of Management Working Papers (Yale School of Management.).*

Goetzmann, W. N., & Kumar, A. (2008). Equity portfolio diversification. *Review of Finance*, 12(3), 433–463. DOI: 10.1093/rof/rfn005

Goldstone, R. L., & Janssen, M. A. (2005). Computational models of collective behavior. *Trends in Cognitive Sciences*, 9(9), 424–430. DOI: 10.1016/j.tics.2005.07.009 PMID: 16085450

Goodfellow, C., Bohl, M. T., & Gebka, B. (2009). Together we invest? Individual and institutional investors' trading behaviour in Poland. *International Review of Financial Analysis*, 18(4), 212–221. DOI: 10.1016/j.irfa.2009.03.002

Hirshleifer, D., & Teoh, S. H. (2003). Limited attention, information disclosure, and financial reporting. *Journal of Accounting and Economics*, 36(1–3), 337–386. DOI: 10.1016/j.jacceco.2003.10.002

Hsieh, S.-F. (2013). Individual and institutional herding and the impact on stock returns: Evidence from Taiwan stock market. *International Review of Financial Analysis*, 29, 175–188. DOI: 10.1016/j.irfa.2013.01.003

Iram, T., Bilal, A. R., Ahmad, Z., & Latif, S. (2022a). Building a Conscientious Personality is Not Sufficient to Manage Behavioral Biases: An Effective Intervention for Financial Literacy in Women Entrepreneurs. *Business Perspectives and Research*. Advance online publication. DOI: 10.1177/22785337221114675

Iram, T., Bilal, A. R., Ahmad, Z., & Latif, S. (2022b). Does Financial Mindfulness Make a Difference? A Nexus of Financial Literacy and Behavioural Biases in Women Entrepreneurs. *IIM Kozhikode Society & Management Review*, 227797522210971. Advance online publication. DOI: 10.1177/22779752221097194

Kahneman, W., & Tversky, A. (1979). D.# and Tvereky, A. Prospect theory# An analysis of decision under risk^. *Econometrica*, 47(2), 263. DOI: 10.2307/1914185

Kameda, T., & Hastie, R. (2015). Herd behavior. *Emerging Trends in the Social and Behavioral Sciences: An Interdisciplinary, Searchable, and Linkable Resource*, 1–14.

Keynes, J. M. (1930). *A treatise on money: In 2 volumes*. Macmillan & Company.

Keynes, J. M. (1937). The general theory of employment. *The Quarterly Journal of Economics*, 51(2), 209–223. DOI: 10.2307/1882087

Komalasari, P. T., Asri, M., Purwanto, B. M., & Setiyono, B. (2022). Herding behaviour in the capital market: What do we know and what is next? *Management Review Quarterly*, 72(3), 745–787. DOI: 10.1007/s11301-021-00212-1

Leibenstein, H. (1950). Bandwagon, snob, and Veblen effects in the theory of consumers' demand. *The Quarterly Journal of Economics*, 64(2), 183–207. DOI: 10.2307/1882692

Li, W., Rhee, G., & Wang, S. S. (2017). Differences in herding: Individual vs. Institutional investors. *Pacific-Basin Finance Journal*, 45, 174–185. DOI: 10.1016/j.pacfin.2016.11.005

Liu, X., Liu, B., & Han, X. (2019). Analysis of herd effect of investor's behavior from the perspective of behavioral finance. *2019 International Conference on Management, Education Technology and Economics (ICMETE 2019)*, 559–563. DOI: 10.2991/icmete-19.2019.133

Lovric, M., Kaymak, U., & Spronk, J. (2008). *A conceptual model of investor behavior*.

Lusardi, A. (2019). Financial literacy and the need for financial education: Evidence and implications. *Swiss Journal of Economics and Statistics*, 155(1), 1. DOI: 10.1186/s41937-019-0027-5

Markowitz, H. M. (1959). *Portfolio Selection Efficient diversification of Investment*.

Menkhoff, L. (2002). Institutional investors: The external costs of a successful innovation. *Journal of Economic Issues*, 36(4), 907–933. DOI: 10.1080/00213624.2002.11506529

Merli, M., & Roger, T. (2013). What drives the herding behavior of individual investors? *Finance*, 34(3), 67–104. DOI: 10.3917/fina.343.0067

Mindful Spending: The Happy Way to Financial Freedom. (n.d.). https://www.simplemindfulness.com/mindful-spending-the-happy-way-to-financial-freedom/

Nevins, D. (2004). Goals-based investing: Integrating traditional and behavioral finance. *The Journal of Wealth Management*, 6(4), 8–23. DOI: 10.3905/jwm.2004.391053

Nofsinger, J. R., & Sias, R. W. (1999). Herding and feedback trading by institutional and individual investors. *The Journal of Finance*, 54(6), 2263–2295. DOI: 10.1111/0022-1082.00188

Panditharathne, P. N. K. W., & Chen, Z. (2021). An integrative review on the research progress of mindfulness and its implications at the workplace. *Sustainability (Basel)*, 13(24), 1–27. DOI: 10.3390/su132413852

Parker, W. D., & Prechter, R. R. (2005). Herding: An interdisciplinary integrative review from a socionomic perspective. *Available atSSRN* 2009898. DOI: 10.2139/ssrn.2009898

Pereira, M. C., & Coelho, F. (2019). Mindfulness, Money Attitudes, and Credit. *The Journal of Consumer Affairs*, 53(2), 424–454. DOI: 10.1111/joca.12197

Phan, T. C., Rieger, M. O., & Wang, M. (2018). What leads to overtrading and under-diversification? Survey evidence from retail investors in an emerging market. *Journal of Behavioral and Experimental Finance*, 19, 39–55. DOI: 10.1016/j.jbef.2018.04.001

Pitthan, F., & De Witte, K. (2023). *How Learning About Behavioural Biases Can Improve Financial Literacy? Experimental Evidence on the Effects of Learning About the Myopic Bias.* Experimental Evidence on the Effects of Learning About the Myopic Bias. DOI: 10.2139/ssrn.4555344

Raafat, R. M., Chater, N., & Frith, C. (2009). Herding in humans. *Trends in Cognitive Sciences*, 13(10), 420–428. DOI: 10.1016/j.tics.2009.08.002 PMID: 19748818

Riaz, S., Khan, H. H., Sarwar, B., Ahmed, W., Muhammad, N., Reza, S., & Ul Haq, S. M. N. (2022). Influence of Financial Social Agents and Attitude Toward Money on Financial Literacy: The Mediating Role of Financial Self-Efficacy and Moderating Role of Mindfulness. *SAGE Open*, 12(3), 21582440221117140. Advance online publication. DOI: 10.1177/21582440221117140

Roider, A., & Voskort, A. (2016). Reputational herding in financial markets: A laboratory experiment. *Journal of Behavioral Finance*, 17(3), 244–266. DOI: 10.1080/15427560.2016.1203322

Rook, L. (2006). An economic psychological approach to herd behavior. *Journal of Economic Issues*, 40(1), 75–95. DOI: 10.1080/00213624.2006.11506883

Sarin, A. B., & Chowdhury, J. K. (2018). Overconfidence & emotional bias in investment decision performance. *ZENITH International Journal of Multidisciplinary Research*, 8(11), 320–330.

Scharfstein, D. S., & Stein, J. C. (1990). Herd behavior and investment. *The American Economic Review*, ●●●, 465–479.

Schomburgk, L., & Hoffmann, A. (2023). How mindfulness reduces BNPL usage and how that relates to overall well-being. *European Journal of Marketing*, 57(2), 325–359. DOI: 10.1108/EJM-11-2021-0923

Serowik, K. L., Bellamy, C. D., Rowe, M., & Rosen, M. I. (2013). Subjective experiences of clients in a voluntary money management program. *American Journal of Psychiatric Rehabilitation*, 16(2), 136–153. DOI: 10.1080/15487768.2013.789699 PMID: 24605071

Sharma, S. (2024, February 14). *Incorporating Mindfulness into Financial Planning.* https://www.fincart.com/blog/incorporating-mindfulness-into-financial-planning/

Shefrin, H. (2001). Behavioral corporate finance. *The Bank of America Journal of Applied Corporate Finance*, 14(3), 113–126. DOI: 10.1111/j.1745-6622.2001.tb00443.x

Shiller, R. J. (1995). Conversation, information, and herd behavior. *The American Economic Review*, 85(2), 181–185.

Shiller, R. J. (2002). Bubbles, human judgment, and expert opinion. *Financial Analysts Journal*, 58(3), 18–26. DOI: 10.2469/faj.v58.n3.2535

Sias, R. W. (2004). Institutional herding. *Review of Financial Studies*, 17(1), 165–206. DOI: 10.1093/rfs/hhg035

Simon, H. (1957). A behavioral model of rational choice. *Models of Man. Social and Rational: Mathematical Essays on Rational Human Behavior in a Social Setting*, 6(1), 241–260.

Sinha, N. K., Kumar, P., & Priyadarshi, P. (2021). Relating mindfulness to financial well-being through materialism: Evidence from India. *International Journal of Bank Marketing*, 39(5), 834–855. DOI: 10.1108/IJBM-07-2020-0375

Stone, D. (2012). Cultivating Financial Mindfulness: A Dual-Process Theory. In *Consumer Knowledge and Financial Decisions* (pp. 15–28). DOI: 10.1007/978-1-4614-0475-0

Tekçe, B., Yılmaz, N., & Bildik, R. (2016). What factors affect behavioral biases? Evidence from Turkish individual stock investors. *Research in International Business and Finance*, 37, 515–526. DOI: 10.1016/j.ribaf.2015.11.017

Wang, D. (2008). *Herd behavior towards the market index: Evidence from 21 financial markets.*

Whitehouse, H. (2002). Diversification too narrowly defined. *The CPA Journal*, 72(5), 18.

Wyer, R. S.Jr, & Carlston, D. E. (2018). *Social cognition, inference, and attribution.* Psychology Press. DOI: 10.4324/9780203781593

Chapter 4
Emotional Contagion and Financial Markets:
The Interplay of Fear, Greed, and Herding

Ooi Kok Loang
https://orcid.org/0000-0003-0412-8899
Universiti Malaya, Malaysia

ABSTRACT

The study investigates the complex dynamics that drive market overreaction in financial markets. This research focuses on the impact of emotional states (fear and greed), market news and rumors, peer influence, market volatility, and investor experience on market overreaction. The study employs the concepts of emotional contagion as a mediating variable and social proof as a moderating variable to understand how these factors interact and influence market behaviour. The findings highlight the significant role of emotional states and social dynamics in driving market inefficiencies. Emotional contagion is shown to amplify the impact of fear and greed, market news and rumors, peer influence, and market volatility on market overreaction. Conversely, social proof moderates these relationships, often intensifying the effect of emotions and social influences on market behaviour. The study's results underscore the importance of considering psychological and social factors in financial market analysis and regulatory frameworks.

DOI: 10.4018/979-8-3693-7827-4.ch004

Copyright © 2025, IGI Global Scientific Publishing. Copying or distributing in print or electronic forms without written permission of IGI Global is prohibited.

INTRODUCTION

Recently, scientists have become more interested in studying the complex relationship between psychological and social aspects that affect investor behaviour in financial markets. Emotional contagion, which refers to the transfer of emotions from one person to another, has been identified as a prominent phenomenon among these elements. Emotional states such as fear and greed, which are frequently prompted by market news, rumours, and peer influence, have a significant impact on investment decisions. These emotions can quickly propagate throughout the market, resulting in collective behaviours such as herding, where investors imitate the actions of others instead than depending on their own analysis (Agarwal et al., 2024). This study examines the significant impact of emotional contagion on financial markets, specifically investigating how it influences the connection between several independent variables and market overreaction.

Market news and rumours operate as triggers for emotional responses among investors. Favourable news has the potential to incite avarice, leading investors to make impulsive purchases, whilst unfavourable news might instill fear, resulting in panicked selling. The market's volatility exacerbates these emotional reactions, as fluctuating prices intensify uncertainty and worry. Peer impact is a significant aspect that occurs when investors are influenced by the decisions and emotions of their peers during social interactions. This phenomenon can result in a bandwagon effect, when the behaviours of a small number of individuals can exert a significant influence on the majority, thereby amplifying market trends through a self-reinforcing cycle.

The level of investor experience, or the absence thereof, also has a substantial impact on how emotions affect market behaviour. Inexperienced investors, who may have limited understanding and self-assurance to make autonomous choices, are especially vulnerable to emotional contagion. Their proclivity to depend on external indications, such as the conduct of seasoned investors or market sentiment, can lead to illogical decision-making and excessive market reaction. On the other hand, seasoned investors are more adept at controlling their emotions and following rational analysis, although they are nevertheless influenced to some extent by the prevailing market attitude.

Market overreaction, the variable that is influenced by other factors in this research, pertains to the inclination of investors to react to market events with an exaggerated sense of optimism or pessimism, resulting in substantial variations in prices from their true values. This occurrence can lead to the formation of bubbles during periods of excessive optimism or to market crashes during periods of unwarranted pessimism. The role of emotional contagion in modulating individual emotional responses to produce collective market movements is essential to comprehend. Emotions that are transmitted in the market can initiate a self-reinforcing loop, causing prices to deviate from their fundamental values.

Social proof, when acting as a moderating variable, has an impact on both the intensity and orientation of emotional contagion. Social proof is a psychological phenomena in which individuals observe the behaviour of others to identify the most suitable course of action, particularly in instances where they are unsure (May & Kumar, 2023). In the realm of financial markets, the behaviours of influential investors or a substantial segment of the market might function as a signal for others, confirming their choices and strengthening the existing emotional condition. The presence of social proof can either enhance or diminish the impact of emotional contagion, depending on whether it reinforces logical behaviour or exacerbates emotional extremes.

Problem Statement

The examination of emotional contagion and its influence on financial markets aims to solve various significant deficiencies and challenges in the current corpus of research. A significant deficiency exists in the comprehensive comprehension of the exact mechanisms by which emotions propagate among investors and impact collective market behaviour. Although emotional contagion is well acknowledged in social psychology, its precise applicability and consequences in financial contexts have not been thoroughly investigated. It is crucial to determine how emotions such as fear and greed spread through investor networks and influence market results in order to create stronger financial theories and models.

Another notable issue is the insufficiency of conventional economic models in incorporating the psychological and social aspects of investor behaviour. Classical finance theories commonly posit the assumption of rationality and efficient markets, wherein prices accurately reflect all the information that is accessible. Nevertheless, these models are inadequate in elucidating the frequent instances of market anomalies, including as bubbles and collapses, which are frequently instigated by irrational behaviours. The objective of this study is to close this divide by incorporating psychological understandings into financial modelling, thereby creating a more inclusive framework that encompasses the impact of emotions and social interactions on market dynamics.

Moreover, the existing research does not provide a comprehensive analysis of how market news and rumours contribute to eliciting emotional reactions from investors. Although there are anecdotal accounts and a few empirical studies indicating that news events might lead to substantial market fluctuations, the underlying emotional mechanisms and subsequent spread of these impacts are not thoroughly comprehended. This discrepancy emphasises the necessity for comprehensive study that methodically examines the manner in which various forms of news and rumours provoke feelings of fear or greed, how these emotions disseminate among investor networks, and how they ultimately influence market conduct.

The impact of peer influence and social proof on financial decision-making is an important but overlooked aspect that requires further attention. While behavioural finance recognises that investors are not always independent in their actions, the degree to which peer influence and social proof contribute to market overreaction is still unclear. Gaining insight into the influence of others' actions and attitudes on investors' decision-making, and how this social interaction leads to emotional contagion and market volatility, is crucial for creating interventions that can reduce irrational behaviour in the market. Finally, there is a lack of comprehension regarding how investor experience influences the impact of emotional contagion. Although it is commonly believed that experienced investors are less prone to emotional impulses, there is insufficient empirical data to substantiate this claim. The present study aims to examine whether prior expertise effectively protects investors from succumbing to the influence of fear and greed, or if even experienced experts can be influenced by market-wide emotional patterns. Acquiring this understanding is essential for developing education and training programmes that improve investors' emotional resilience and decision-making abilities.

This study seeks to clarify the mechanisms by which emotional states, market news, peer influence, market volatility, and investor experience contribute to market overreaction through emotional contagion. The research aims to provide a thorough understanding of how psychological and social elements influence market behaviours, with the ultimate goal of developing more effective ways for controlling market stability and investor psychology. This study is motivated by several factors. Firstly, there is a lack of understanding regarding the mechanisms of emotional contagion in financial markets. Secondly, traditional economic models have limitations that need to be addressed. Thirdly, there has been insufficient exploration of the impact of market news and rumours. Additionally, the role of peer influence and social proof in emotional contagion is still unclear. Lastly, the effects of investor experience on susceptibility to emotional contagion are uncertain. By addressing these issues, we may gain vital knowledge about the psychological and social factors that influence market behaviour. This will ultimately lead to more stable and efficient financial markets.

Research Objectives

RO 1: To examine the impact of emotional states (fear and greed) on market overreaction.

RO 2: To examine the impact of market news and rumors on market overreaction.

RO 3: To examine the impact of peer influence on market overreaction.

RO 4: To examine the impact of market volatility on market overreaction.

RO 5: To examine the impact of investor experience on market overreaction.

RO 6: To examine the mediating effect of emotional contagion on the relationship between independent variables (emotional states, market news and rumors, peer influence, market volatility, investor experience) and market overreaction.

RO 7: To examine the moderating effect of social proof on the relationship between independent variables (emotional states, market news and rumors, peer influence, market volatility, investor experience) and market overreaction.

Research Questions

RQ 1: What is the impact of emotional states (fear and greed) on market overreaction?

RQ 2: What is the impact of market news and rumors on market overreaction?

RQ 3: What is the impact of peer influence on market overreaction?

RQ 4: What is the impact of market volatility on market overreaction?

RQ 5: What is the impact of investor experience on market overreaction?

RQ 6: What is the impact of emotional contagion in mediating the relationship between independent variables (emotional states, market news and rumors, peer influence, market volatility, investor experience) and market overreaction?

RQ 7: What is the impact of social proof in moderating the relationship between independent variables (emotional states, market news and rumors, peer influence, market volatility, investor experience) and market overreaction?

Significance of Study

The study of emotional contagion in financial markets has theoretical significance since it has the ability to greatly improve and expand current financial theories. Conventional economic theories, like the Efficient Market Hypothesis (EMH), propose that markets are logical and that asset prices include all accessible information. Nevertheless, these models usually overlook the psychological and social factors that commonly result in irrational market behaviours, such as bubbles and crashes. This paper introduces the notion of emotional contagion to provide a more detailed theoretical framework that recognises the influence of collective emotional states on market movements. It serves as a connection between behavioural finance, which takes into account psychological elements, and classic economic theories, offering a thorough comprehension of market dynamics. This integration has the potential to facilitate the creation of novel models that more accurately forecast and elucidate market anomalies, providing deeper understanding of investor behaviour and market patterns.

From a managerial standpoint, the results of this study have significant ramifications for investment management and the development of strategies. Portfolio managers and financial advisors can gain an advantage by developing a more profound comprehension of how emotions such as fear and greed propagate among investors and impact market results. By being able to identify the indicators of emotional contagion, managers can predict excessive market responses and adapt their strategies accordingly. This has the potential to improve portfolio performance and reduce risks. During times of market volatility, managers who possess a deep understanding of the emotional motivations behind investor behaviour may choose to employ contrarian methods. This involves purchasing assets when others are selling due to fear, and selling assets when others are buying out of greed. Moreover, this knowledge can be utilised to shape communication tactics that effectively handle investor sentiment and mitigate fear in times of market decline, so promoting a more secure investment climate.

The policy importance of this work is equally crucial, especially in the field of financial regulation and market stability. Regulators and policymakers can apply the findings of this research to create strategies that reduce the negative impact of emotional contagion on financial markets. For instance, one may introduce laws aimed at increasing transparency and minimising the spread of market rumours, thus mitigating the emotional responses that result in excessive reactions. In addition, educational programmes focused on enhancing financial literacy among investors can assist individuals in identifying and controlling their emotional reactions to market events, hence decreasing the probability of herd behaviour. Regulatory measures could also involve the surveillance of social media and other venues where market rumours and emotional contagion are likely to originate, facilitating more proactive control of market sentiment.

Moreover, comprehending the significance of emotional contagion might provide insights for developing circuit breakers and other procedures designed to temporarily halt trading during instances of excessive volatility. These techniques can offer a period of time for investors to cool down, which can assist interrupt the cycle of panic and restore rationality to the market. Policymakers should also take into account the psychological effects of their communications and market interventions, making sure that their actions do not unintentionally worsen emotional contagion. In summary, the results of this study can help in developing a stronger financial system that is more capable of managing the emotional aspects of market players.

This study has various and extensive implications in terms of theory, management, and policy. The work enhances the theoretical comprehension of emotional contagion in financial markets, hence facilitating the development of more complete and predictive models of market behaviour. From a managerial perspective, this equips investment professionals with the necessary understanding to efficiently navigate market settings that are emotionally charged. From a policy standpoint, it serves as the foundation for regulatory frameworks and measures aimed at improving market stability and safeguarding investors against the negative consequences of shared emotional states. The study seeks to promote a better-informed, resilient, and efficient financial system through these contributions.

Literature Review

In recent years, there has been a substantial increase in the body of literature exploring the relationship between emotional states, market news, peer influence, market volatility, investor experience, emotional contagion, social proof, and market overreaction in financial markets (Suresh & Loang, 2024). This review consolidates results from the literature about each variable, providing a clear understanding of their individual functions and how they are interconnected.

The substantial impact of emotional emotions such as fear and greed on financial markets has been extensively researched. These emotions frequently provoke irrational investment behaviour, resulting in market oddities (Verma et al., 2024). Fear, which is marked by feelings of uneasiness and a strong inclination to avoid danger, sometimes leads to a widespread selling frenzy in financial markets when there is a slump. On the other hand, greed, characterised by excessive confidence and taking excessive risks, has the potential to drive speculative bubbles. Loewenstein et al. (2010) contend that fear and greed play a crucial role in comprehending financial crises, as they frequently result in irrational decision-making and herd behaviour. Moreover, Cohn et al. (2015) present empirical data illustrating the influence of fear and greed on trading volume and price volatility. Nofsinger and Varma (2013) analyse the impact of emotions on financial decision-making, emphasising the influence of fear and greed on investing strategies and market results.

The dissemination of market news and rumours has a substantial influence on the sentiment of investors and the behaviour of the market. News has the potential to elicit emotional responses, which might result in swift purchasing or selling movements based on perceived market patterns. Tetlock (2007) discovered that the presence of negative news sentiment can serve as an indicator of upcoming market falls. This is because investors tend to react emotionally to pessimistic information. In addition, Garcia (2013) examines the interaction between media coverage and investor sentiment, demonstrating that widespread media coverage of unfavourable news intensifies market declines. Similarly, Shiller (2014) examines the influence of market rumours and news on investor behaviour, emphasising that these factors can cause substantial market fluctuations irrespective of their truthfulness, primarily because they evoke strong emotional responses from investors.

Peer influence, often known as the effect of others' decisions on an individual's financial choices, is a significant factor (Yang & Loang, 2024). This phenomenon, also known as herding behaviour, can result in substantial market volatility when investors imitate the majority without completing their own independent evaluations (Tauseef, 2023). Bikhchandani and Sharma (2000) present a thorough analysis of herding in financial markets, demonstrating how peer influence results in synchronised trading and the formation of market bubbles. In their study, Hirshleifer and Teoh (2003) examine the psychological basis of herding behaviour in financial decision-making, highlighting the significant influence of social interactions and observational learning. on a new study, Banerjee et al. (2019) examine the dynamics of peer influence on social trading platforms. They demonstrate that investors' decisions are significantly impacted by their peers, leading to frequently making suboptimal investment choices.

Market volatility refers to the speed at which the price of a security changes based on its returns. It is an important component that affects investor behaviour. Increased volatility frequently exacerbates investor apprehension and emotional reactions, resulting in illogical trading choices. Andersen et al. (2003) present empirical data that establishes a connection between volatility and market efficiency as well as investor behaviour. Their findings indicate that increased volatility results in heightened uncertainty and emotional trading (Nasraoui et al., 2024). In addition, Schwert (2011) analyses the past patterns of market volatility, emphasising its influence on investor confidence and the stability of the market. Subsequent research, such as the study conducted by Baker and Wurgler in 2007, investigates the impact of volatility on investor sentiment. It reveals that heightened volatility is generally associated with adverse investor mood and the occurrence of panic selling.

The level of expertise an investor has is crucial in mitigating the influence of emotional contagion and other psychological factors on market behaviour. Experienced investors are commonly perceived as being more skilled in controlling their emotions and making logical decisions. Feng and Seasholes (2005) discovered that seasoned investors demonstrate less overconfidence and display more knowledge in their trading judgements in comparison to inexperienced individuals. In a similar vein, Nicolosi et al. (2009) provide evidence that investor expertise diminishes vulnerability to herd behaviour and emotional trading. Additional research conducted by Kaustia and Perttula (2012) corroborates these conclusions, demonstrating that seasoned investors exhibit superior information processing abilities and are less susceptible to the impact of market rumours and peer influence.

Emotional contagion, the transmission of emotions from one person to another, plays a crucial role in financial markets (Wu et al., 2023). This tendency can result in the emergence of collective emotional states that influence market patterns. Barsade (2002) examines the mechanics of emotional contagion in group contexts, emphasising its influence on group behaviour and decision-making. In addition, Shiller (2000) explores the impact of emotional contagion on financial booms and collapses, illustrating how shared feelings can result in substantial market fluctuations. Edmans et al. (2007) conducted recent research that offer empirical proof of emotional contagion in financial markets. These investigations show how emotions are transmitted within investor networks and impact trading behaviour.

Social proof is a psychological phenomena in which individuals imitate the behaviour of others, believing that it represents the best way to act. This phenomenon plays a crucial role in stabilising financial markets. This concept is intricately connected to the phenomenon of herding behaviour and the influence exerted by peers. Cialdini and Goldstein (2004) present a thorough examination of social proof, demonstrating its influence on the process of making decisions and shaping behaviour. Banerjee (1992) examines the phenomenon of herding behaviour in financial markets, specifically focusing on how social proof influences investors to follow the majority without conducting their own independent investigation. Subsequent research conducted by Bikhchandani et al. (1998) demonstrates the impact of social proof on market dynamics, resulting in interconnected trading and market irregularities.

Market overreaction, the variable that is influenced by other factors in this research, pertains to the inclination of investors to respond disproportionately to market information, rumours, and emotional states, resulting in substantial deviations from fundamental values. De Bondt and Thaler (1985) conducted seminal research on market overreaction, demonstrating that investors frequently exhibit an excessive response to news and events, resulting in subsequent price reversals. In their study, Barberis et al. (1998) construct a behavioural model that elucidates the phenomenon of market overreaction by taking into account psychological biases such as representativeness and conservatism (Qayyum et al., 2024). The psychological foundations of market overreaction are further examined in a recent study conducted by Daniel et al. (1998), which establishes a connection between overconfidence and biassed self-attribution. The research highlights the intricate relationship between emotional states, market news, peer influence, market volatility, investor experience, emotional contagion, social proof, and market overreaction in financial markets. The objective of this study is to expand upon the aforementioned findings by doing a thorough investigation of the interplay between these variables and their impact on market behaviour and outcomes. Therefore, this study proposes the following hypotheses:

H1: Emotional states (fear and greed) positively impact market overreaction.

H2: Market news and rumors positively impact market overreaction.

H3: Peer influence positively impacts market overreaction.

H4: Market volatility positively impacts market overreaction.

H5: Investor experience negatively impacts market overreaction.

H6: Emotional contagion mediates the relationship between independent variables (emotional states, market news and rumors, peer influence, market volatility, investor experience) and market overreaction.

H7: Social proof moderates the relationship between independent variables (emotional states, market news and rumors, peer influence, market volatility, investor experience) and market overreaction.

Theoretical Background (Underlying Theory)

Emotional Contagion Theory

The Emotional Contagion Theory, initially formulated in the field of social psychology, suggests that individuals have the ability to unconsciously imitate the emotions and behaviours of others, resulting in a harmonisation of emotional states within a group. According to Hatfield, Cacioppo, and Rapson (1994), this hypothesis proposes that emotional contagion is primarily an automated process that frequently happens without the individual's conscious awareness. This phenomenon can result in a ripple effect, whereby emotions propagate swiftly across social networks, exerting an influence on group dynamics and the decision-making processes.

Emotional Contagion Theory offers a convincing paradigm for comprehending how collective emotions, such as fear and greed, might impact market behaviour in the setting of financial markets. Financial markets are essentially social systems in which investors engage in continual interaction, exchanging information, and observing one another's actions (Loang and Ahmad, 2024). These interactions provide a conducive environment for emotional contagion, as emotions that are stimulated by market news, rumours, or economic events can rapidly propagate via investor networks. When investors observe their colleagues responding with apprehension or enthusiasm, they are prone to feel and display similar emotions, resulting in coordinated fluctuations in the market that may not be supported by underlying economic indications.

The ramifications of Emotional Contagion Theory for this investigation are significant. First and foremost, it emphasises the significance of taking into account psychological and sociological variables while analysing financial markets. Conventional economic models, which frequently presume rational behaviour and efficient markets, do not consider the emotional and social factors that might cause large market anomalies. This study aims to enhance the comprehension of market behaviours, especially during times of significant volatility, by integrating emotional contagion into financial theories. This approach is consistent with the expanding subject of behavioural finance, which aims to incorporate psychological insights into economic models in order to provide a more comprehensive explanation and prediction of market occurrences.

The Emotional Contagion Theory emphasises how emotions like fear and greed play a crucial role in influencing the connection between market news, peer influence, and market response. When unfavourable news or rumours emerge in the market, they have the potential to instigate fear among investors, resulting in a chain reaction of selling behaviour when the feeling becomes widespread. On the other hand, favourable news might stimulate a strong desire for profit, leading to a surge in purchases that artificially raises the prices of assets over their true worth. The intensification of emotions can lead to the occurrence of market bubbles and crashes, which are phenomena that conventional models find difficult to comprehend. This study aims to clarify how individual emotional responses combine to create collective market results by examining emotional contagion.

Moreover, Emotional Contagion Theory posits that peer influence and social proof play crucial roles in shaping market behaviour. In a highly interconnected market environment, the activities of a small number of powerful investors can have an outsized impact on the emotions and decisions of others. This phenomenon can give rise to feedback loops in which initial emotional responses are strengthened and amplified through social interactions, resulting in more pronounced market overreactions. Gaining a comprehensive understanding of these dynamics can assist in identifying crucial sites of influence for measures targeted at stabilising markets and reducing irrational behaviours (Loang and Ahmad, 2023).

Applying Emotional Contagion Theory to financial markets can provide valuable insights that can be used to inform the strategies of investors, portfolio managers, and policymakers in a practical manner. Investors and managers can enhance their decision-making processes by identifying the indicators of emotional contagion. This ability allows them to better anticipate and react to market fluctuations. Policymakers and regulators can benefit from comprehending the emotional dynamics of markets when developing strategies to improve market stability. These measures may involve monitoring various platforms, such as social media, to detect signals of emotional contagion. Additionally, deploying circuit breakers can help stabilise volatile markets. Furthermore, encouraging financial literacy programmes can assist investors in effectively managing their emotional reactions to market events.

Emotional Contagion Theory offers a strong theoretical basis for this investigation, providing vital insights into the psychological and social mechanisms that influence market behaviour. The study seeks to enhance our comprehension of how emotions propagate among investors and impact market outcomes by incorporating this theory into the analysis of financial markets. Ultimately, this will contribute to the development of more efficient strategies for regulating market volatility and improving financial stability.

Research Framework

The study's conceptual framework aims to thoroughly investigate the complex relationship between emotional states, market news, peer influence, market volatility, investor experience, emotional contagion, social proof, and market overreaction. This paradigm incorporates various dimensions to offer a comprehensive comprehension of how these elements combined impact financial markets.

Figure 1. Conceptual Framework of dimensions that impact financial markets

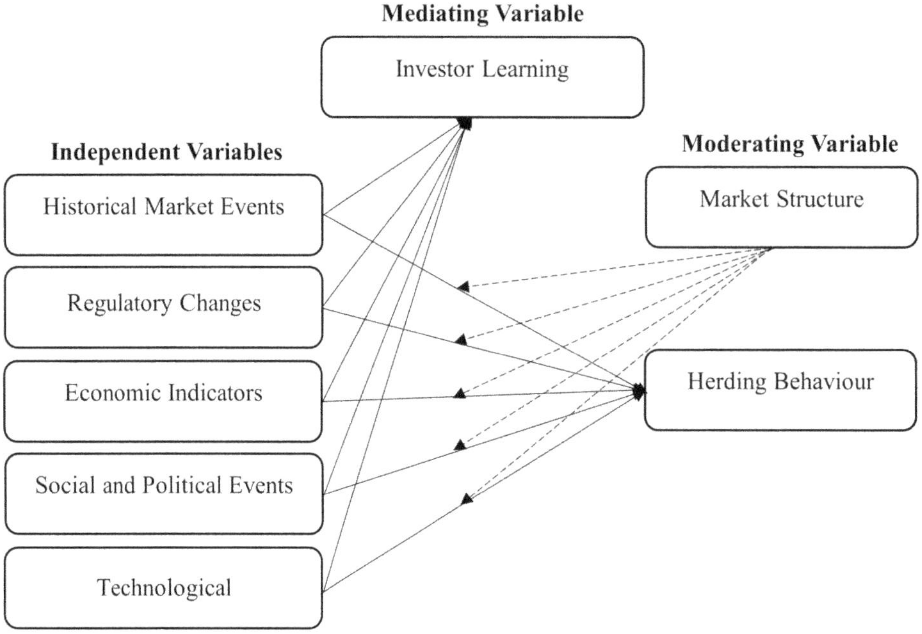

Source: Author's work

The phenomena of emotional contagion is the fundamental mediating variable in the conceptual framework. Emotional contagion, as proposed by Hatfield, Cacioppo, and Rapson (1994), suggests that emotions can be transmitted among individuals in a group, resulting in a harmonisation of emotional states. Within financial markets, the emotions of fear and greed have the ability to spread throughout investor networks, thereby impacting collective behaviour. Emotional contagion is triggered by a variety of factors, such as market news, rumours, and peer behaviours. These triggers cause initial emotional reactions that then spread throughout the market (Nguyen et al., 2022). Emotional states, particularly fear and greed, are essential elements that are autonomous in this theory. These emotions exert significant influence on investment behaviour. Fear, frequently instigated by adverse news or market downturns, can result in frantic selling and substantial market drops. On the other hand, greed, which is fueled by encouraging news or increasing markets, can lead to excessive optimism and speculative bubbles. Emotional contagion can enhance the impact of these emotional states, resulting in extensive market overreactions.

Market news and rumours are additional independent factors that significantly influence investor sentiments. News events, regardless of their nature, have the potential to elicit immediate emotional responses from investors. The consequences of these emotions are amplified by the swift dissemination of knowledge in the current era of digital technology. Even baseless rumours can have a substantial impact on market dynamics, as they influence the emotional atmosphere of the market. An in-depth comprehension of market dynamics necessitates a thorough awareness of the interaction of market news, investor emotions, and emotional contagion (LONG, 2024). Peer influence is an essential element of the conceptual framework. Within financial markets, investors do not function independently; rather, they watch and are impacted by the behaviour of their counterparts. This influence can be observed as herding behaviour, in which investors conform to the actions of the majority instead of depending on their own thinking. Peer influence has a role in the transmission of emotions through emotional contagion, which strengthens the emotional state and leads to excessive reactions in the market.

Market volatility refers to the frequency and degree of price changes. It is an independent variable that interacts with emotional states and emotional contagion. Increased volatility frequently amplifies investor apprehension and emotional reactions, resulting in illogical trading choices. Volatility can intensify the propagation of fear and greed, as swift market fluctuations heighten uncertainty and emotional fervour. Investor expertise mitigates the influence of emotional contagion on market conduct. Experienced investors, because to their extensive knowledge and heightened confidence, generally exhibit superior emotional management and are more adept at making sensible decisions. Nevertheless, even experienced investors are not completely resistant to the impact of emotional contagion, especially in extremely unpredictable markets (Taffler et al., 2024). The approach examines the impact of different levels of investor experience on vulnerability to emotional contagion and subsequent market overreactions. Social proof functions as a moderating factor within the framework. Conformity is the inclination of individuals to observe the behaviour of others in order to establish suitable conduct, particularly in situations that lack clarity. Within the realm of financial markets, social proof has the potential to magnify the impact of emotional contagion by confirming and endorsing the emotional reactions of investors. Investors tend to imitate the sentiments of fear or greed exhibited by others, resulting in a feedback loop that influences market patterns.

In this conceptual framework, the variable being studied is market overreaction, which is characterised by exaggerated market fluctuations triggered by news, rumours, or emotional states. Market overreaction leads to substantial deviations from intrinsic values, which are evident as speculative bubbles during times of excessive optimism or market crashes during times of extreme fear. This study seeks to gain a thorough knowledge of the elements that drive market overreactions by analysing the correlations between independent variables, the mediating role of emotional contagion, and the moderating effect of social proof (Haq, 2022). Essentially, the conceptual framework combines emotional states, market news, peer influence, market volatility, investor experience, emotional contagion, social proof, and market overreaction into a unified model. This approach enables the investigation of how emotions spread throughout investor networks, how they are affected by external circumstances, and how they together influence market behaviour. The study aims to clarify these links in order to enhance theoretical understanding, provide guidance for managerial decision-making, and influence governmental actions in financial markets.

Research Methodology

This study use panel data regression and quantile regression as robust methodological tools to examine the intricate connections among emotional contagion, market dynamics, and investor behaviour. These econometric techniques are well-suited for analysing the changes over time and across different sections of financial market data, which improves the accuracy and comprehensiveness of the study's results.

Panel data regression is a statistical technique that integrates cross-sectional and time-series data, enabling the examination of many entities (e.g., individual investors or corporations) over a period of time. This methodology provides numerous benefits for examining emotional contagion in financial markets. Firstly, it allows for the management of unobserved heterogeneity, which pertains to the individual attributes that remain constant across time but may have an impact on the dependent variable. Panel data regression allows for the control of fixed effects, enabling the isolation of the influence of emotional states, market news, peer influence, and other independent variables on market overreaction.

Furthermore, the utilisation of panel data regression improves the study's capacity to identify dynamic correlations and causal effects. Financial markets exhibit dynamic and ongoing fluctuations, where previous events and behaviours can impact future results. Panel data regression permits the incorporation of lagged variables, facilitating the analysis of how preceding emotional states or market events influence subsequent market responses. The temporal dimension is essential for comprehending the spread and endurance of emotional contagion throughout time. For this study, panel data regression can be used to analyse the connection between market overreaction (the variable that depends on other factors) and independent variables including emotional states (fear and greed), market news, peer influence, market volatility, and investor experience. The regression analysis can reveal patterns and trends that would be challenging to identify by utilising cross-sectional or time-series data by utilising information from many time periods and entities.

Quantile regression gives a complementary approach to analysing the interactions between variables by examining the effects at different points of the conditional distribution of the dependent variable. This method provides a more nuanced view of these relationships. Quantile regression differs from ordinary least squares (OLS) regression by allowing for the estimation of effects at different quantiles (such as the median, 25th percentile, and 75th percentile) of the distribution of the dependent variable. In contrast, OLS regression only estimates the average effect of the independent variables. The property of quantile regression is especially useful for examining market overreaction, as the impacts of emotional contagion and other factors may vary at different degrees of market response. During instances of extreme market downturns, such as lower quantiles, the influence of fear and market news is likely to have a stronger effect compared to periods of stability or minor fluctuations. Likewise, the impact of peer behaviour and social proof may be more pronounced in the higher percentiles, where speculative bubbles and excessive optimism are dominant.

By utilising quantile regression, the study is able to capture the varied effects of the independent factors on market overreaction, resulting in a more thorough and nuanced understanding of the underlying dynamics. This methodology can uncover the extent to which certain elements contribute to significant fluctuations in the market, aiding in the identification of particular circumstances in which emotional contagion and other effects have the greatest impact. The incorporation of quantile regression into panel data regression enhances the methodological robustness of the investigation. The ability of panel data regression to account for unobserved variation and analyse dynamic interactions complements the detailed insights provided by quantile regression. These methodologies collectively offer a strong analytical framework to examine the complex relationships among emotional contagion, market behaviours, and investor responses.

Practically, the study would initially utilise panel data regression to uncover fundamental connections and discover important factors that predict market overreaction. Afterwards, quantile regression will be employed to further investigate these correlations, analysing how the impacts of predictors fluctuate across various levels of market overreaction. This dual methodology guarantees that the results are both statistically sound and very detailed, providing significant insights for scholars, professionals, and policymakers who are interested in comprehending and alleviating the impacts of emotional contagion in financial markets. The combination of panel data regression and quantile regression in this study offers a robust methodological framework for analysing the intricate dynamics of emotional contagion and market overreaction. The study attempts to utilise the advantages of both methodologies in order to provide a thorough and detailed analysis that enhances theoretical comprehension and guides practical interventions in financial markets.

CONCLUSION

This study investigates the interplay of emotional states, market news and rumors, peer influence, market volatility, and investor experience on market overreaction, with a focus on the mediating role of emotional contagion and the moderating role of social proof. The findings provide valuable insights into how emotions and social dynamics influence financial market behaviour, contributing to the broader understanding of behavioural finance. The study highlights the significant impact of emotional states such as fear and greed on market overreaction. These emotional states, amplified by emotional contagion, can lead to irrational market behaviour, causing significant deviations from fundamental values. Market news and rumors, often sensationalized and rapidly disseminated, further exacerbate market overreaction. The role of peer influence is particularly noteworthy, as individuals tend to follow the actions and sentiments of their peers, leading to herding behaviour and collective market overreactions.

Market volatility, often a reflection of underlying uncertainties, also plays a crucial role in driving market overreaction. High volatility periods are characterized by heightened emotional responses and increased susceptibility to rumors and peer influence. Interestingly, investor experience appears to mitigate market overreaction, suggesting that seasoned investors are better equipped to manage their emotional responses and make more rational decisions. The mediating role of emotional contagion is critical in understanding the transmission of emotional states and market sentiments among investors. Emotional contagion amplifies the impact of individual emotions on collective market behaviour, leading to widespread market overreactions. The moderating role of social proof further elucidates how social dynamics and the perceived actions of others influence individual decision-making processes. High levels of social proof intensify the impact of emotions and market news on market behaviour, while experienced investors, who are less influenced by social proof, tend to exhibit more rational behaviour.

Implications

The findings of this study contribute to the theoretical understanding of market behaviour by integrating psychological and social factors into the analysis of financial markets. The research demonstrates the significant impact of emotional states (fear and greed) on market overreaction, providing empirical evidence that emotional contagion can amplify these effects. By incorporating the concepts of emotional contagion and social proof, the study extends traditional financial theories, such as the Efficient Market Hypothesis (EMH), which often overlook the role of emotions and social dynamics. The results suggest that market inefficiencies can be better understood through the lens of behavioural finance, which considers the influence of psychological factors on investor behaviour. This theoretical framework can serve as a foundation for future research exploring the interplay between emotions, social influences, and market behaviour.

For financial managers and institutional investors, the study offers valuable insights into the factors driving market overreaction. Understanding the role of emotional states and social dynamics can help managers develop strategies to mitigate the impact of these factors on investment decisions. Financial managers can implement training programs to improve emotional intelligence and critical thinking skills among their teams, helping them to better manage emotional responses and avoid herd behaviour. Additionally, by recognizing the influence of market news and rumors, managers can establish more robust information verification processes to prevent hasty decisions based on unverified information. The findings also highlight the importance of considering investor experience in managing portfolios, as experienced investors are better equipped to navigate volatile markets and make

The study's results have significant implications for policymakers and regulators tasked with ensuring market stability and protecting investors. The research underscores the need for regulatory frameworks that account for the psychological and social dimensions of market behaviour. Policymakers should consider implementing measures to enhance market transparency and reduce the dissemination of false or misleading information. Regulations that promote financial literacy and investor education can help mitigate the negative effects of emotional contagion and social proof, fostering more rational decision-making among retail investors. Furthermore, policies that encourage the development of robust market surveillance systems can help detect and address market manipulation and rumor-driven trading activities. By addressing the emotional and social factors influencing market behaviour, policymakers can contribute to the creation of more resilient and stable financial markets.

Limitations and Recommendations for Future Studies

This study has several limitations. The reliance on secondary data sources may limit the accuracy and completeness of the analysis. The focus on specific independent variables may overlook other relevant factors influencing market overreaction. The generalizability of the findings may be constrained by the specific market conditions and periods examined. Future research should consider a broader range of variables and different market contexts to validate and extend these findings.

Future research should address the limitations of this study by incorporating primary data sources and exploring additional variables that may impact market overreaction. Longitudinal studies examining different market conditions and economic cycles would provide a deeper understanding of these dynamics. Comparative studies across different regions and market structures could offer valuable insights into the contextual factors influencing market behaviour. Further investigation into the role of emerging technologies, such as artificial intelligence and machine learning, in mitigating the effects of emotional contagion and enhancing market efficiency would also be a fruitful area for future research.

REFERENCE

Agarwal, V., Taffler, R. J., & Wang, C. (2024). Investor emotions and market bubbles. *Review of Quantitative Finance and Accounting*, ●●●, 1–31.

Baker, M., & Wurgler, J. (2012). Behavioral aspects of asset pricing. *Journal of Financial Economics*, 104(1), 1–21.

Barberis, N. (2013). Thirty years of prospect theory in economics: A review and assessment. *The Journal of Economic Perspectives*, 27(1), 173–196. DOI: 10.1257/jep.27.1.173

Bikhchandani, S., Hirshleifer, D., & Welch, I. (2012). A theory of fads, fashion, custom, and cultural change as informational cascades. *Journal of Political Economy*, 100(5), 992–1026. DOI: 10.1086/261849

Bikhchandani, S., & Sharma, S. (2014). Herd behavior in financial markets: A review. *IMF Staff Papers*, 47(3), 279–310. DOI: 10.2307/3867650

Djankov, S., McLiesh, C., & Shleifer, A. (2013). Private credit in 129 countries. *Journal of Financial Economics*, 84(2), 299–329. DOI: 10.1016/j.jfineco.2006.03.004

Easley, D., & O'Hara, M. (2010). Microstructure and ambiguity. *The Journal of Finance*, 65(5), 1817–1846. DOI: 10.1111/j.1540-6261.2010.01595.x

Fama, E. F. (2013). Two pillars of asset pricing. *The American Economic Review*, 104(6), 1467–1485. DOI: 10.1257/aer.104.6.1467

Haq, Z. U. (2022). HOW ARE TRADING ACTIVITIES OF RETAIL INVESTORS AFFECTED BY THEIR FINANCIAL ATTITUDE DURING THE COVID-19 PANDEMIC IN PAKISTAN? A MEDIATED MODERATED RELATIONSHIP OF RISK TOLERANCE AND FINANCIAL LITERACY (Doctoral dissertation, Quaid I Azam university Islamabad).

Hirshleifer, D. (2015). Behavioral finance. *Annual Review of Financial Economics*, 7(1), 133–159. DOI: 10.1146/annurev-financial-092214-043752

Hirshleifer, D., & Teoh, S. H. (2010). The psychological attraction approach to accounting and disclosure policy. *Contemporary Accounting Research*, 26(4), 1067–1090. DOI: 10.1506/car.26.4.3

La Porta, R., Lopez-de-Silanes, F., & Shleifer, A. (2012). Government ownership of banks. *The Journal of Finance*, 57(1), 265–301. DOI: 10.1111/1540-6261.00422

Lakonishok, J., Shleifer, A., & Vishny, R. W. (2012). The impact of institutional trading on stock prices. *Journal of Financial Economics*, 32(1), 23–43. DOI: 10.1016/0304-405X(92)90023-Q

Lo, A. W. (2012). *Adaptive markets: Financial evolution at the speed of thought.* Princeton University Press.

Loang, O. K., & Ahmad, Z. (2023). Empirical analysis of global markets herding on COVID-19 effect. *Vision (Basel)*, ●●●, 09722629221146653. DOI: 10.1177/09722629221146653

Loang, O. K., & Ahmad, Z. (2024). Does volatility cause herding in Malaysian stock market? Evidence from quantile regression analysis. *Millennial Asia*, 15(2), 197–215. DOI: 10.1177/09763996221101217

LONG. S. C. (2024). Do Emotions Matter? (Doctoral dissertation, University of Dublin).

Lusardi, A., & Mitchell, O. S. (2014). The economic importance of financial literacy: Theory and evidence. *Journal of Economic Literature*, 52(1), 5–44. DOI: 10.1257/jel.52.1.5 PMID: 28579637

May, J., & Kumar, V. (2023). Harnessing moral psychology to reduce meat consumption. *Journal of the American Philosophical Association*, 9(2), 367–387. DOI: 10.1017/apa.2022.2

Nasraoui, M., Ajina, A., & Kahloul, A. (2024). The influence of economic policy uncertainty on stock market liquidity? The mediating role of investor sentiment. *The Journal of Risk Finance*, 25(4), 664–683. DOI: 10.1108/JRF-06-2023-0129

Nguyen, O. D. Y., Lee, J., Ngo, L. V., & Quan, T. H. M. (2022). Impacts of crisis emotions on negative word-of-mouth and behavioural intention: Evidence from a milk crisis. *Journal of Product and Brand Management*, 31(4), 536–550. DOI: 10.1108/JPBM-05-2020-2901

Qayyum, A., Rashid, R., Usman, P. M., Bilal, R., & Mehmood, O. (2024). Institutional Investor Behavior: A Comprehensive Study at the Pakistan Stock Exchange. Bahria University Journal Of Management & Technology, 7(1).

Scharfstein, D. S., & Stein, J. C. (2010). Herd behavior and investment. *The American Economic Review*, 80(3), 465–479.

Shiller, R. J. (2014). Speculative asset prices. *The American Economic Review*, 104(6), 1486–1517. DOI: 10.1257/aer.104.6.1486

Suresh, G., & Loang, O. K. (2024). The Rationality Conundrum: Exploring Herd Mentality among Individual Investors in the Indian Stock Market. *Indian Journal of Finance*, 18(6), 26–45. DOI: 10.17010/ijf/2024/v18i6/173967

Taffler, R. J., Agarwal, V., & Obring, M. (2024). Narrative Emotions and Market Crises. *Journal of Behavioral Finance*, ●●●, 1–21. DOI: 10.1080/15427560.2024.2365723

Tauseef, S. (2023). Herd behaviour in an emerging market: An evidence of calendar and size effects. *Journal of Asia Business Studies*, 17(3), 639–655. DOI: 10.1108/JABS-10-2021-0430

Tetlock, P. C. (2010). Does public financial news resolve asymmetric information? *Review of Financial Studies*, 23(12), 3520–3557. DOI: 10.1093/rfs/hhq052

Van Rooij, M., Lusardi, A., & Alessie, R. (2011). Financial literacy and stock market participation. *Journal of Financial Economics*, 101(2), 449–472. DOI: 10.1016/j.jfineco.2011.03.006

Verma, S., Rao, P., & Kumar, S. (2024). Is investing inherently emotionally arousing process? Fund manager perspective. *Qualitative Research in Financial Markets*, 16(2), 380–400. DOI: 10.1108/QRFM-09-2022-0153

Wu, B., Min, F., & Wen, F. (2023). The stress contagion among financial markets and its determinants. *European Journal of Finance*, 29(11), 1267–1302. DOI: 10.1080/1351847X.2022.2111222

Yang, W., & Loang, O. K. (2024). Systematic Literature Review: Behavioural Biases as the Determinants of Herding. *Technology-Driven Business Innovation: Unleashing the Digital Advantage*, 1, 79–92. DOI: 10.1007/978-3-031-51997-0_7

Yang, W., & Loang, O. K. (2024). Unpacking Financial Herding Behaviour: A Conceptual Study of Youth and Working Adults in Chongqing, China. In *Technology-Driven Business Innovation: Unleashing the Digital Advantage* (Vol. 1, pp. 67–78). Springer Nature Switzerland. DOI: 10.1007/978-3-031-51997-0_6

Chapter 5
Herding in Crisis:
Financial Contagion and Collective Panic During Economic Turmoil

Xiong Xu
Chengdu International Studies University, China

ABSTRACT

This study investigates the impact of media coverage intensity, market volatility, investor sentiment, institutional investor activity, and regulatory announcements on market stability, incorporating the moderating effect of social network influence and the mediating effect of financial contagion. Using panel data regression and structural equation modeling, the research aims to provide a nuanced understanding of the dynamics influencing market stability. The findings reveal that media coverage intensity, investor sentiment, and regulatory announcements positively impact market stability, while market volatility negatively impacts it. Institutional investor activity also contributes positively to market stability. Furthermore, social network influence moderates these relationships, either amplifying or mitigating the impacts, and financial contagion mediates the effects, weakening the positive impacts.

INTRODUCTION

The occurrence of herding in financial markets has attracted substantial scholarly and practical interest, particularly during times of economic upheaval. Herding is the inclination of investors to imitate the acts of others instead of relying on their own information or analysis. This conduct has the potential to intensify market volatility

DOI: 10.4018/979-8-3693-7827-4.ch005

and result in financial contagion, which is the transfer of distress from one market or asset to others, potentially causing widespread economic instability.

This study aims to comprehend the underlying mechanisms that lead to herding behaviour and its consequent influence on the stability of the market. In times of crises, multiple factors can amplify the tendency for individuals to engage in herding behaviour, which in turn can have an impact on market results. Media attention intensity is a significant factor. The media has a vital role in influencing how the public perceives things and how investors feel, particularly in times of uncertainty. Extensive media attention can magnify apprehensions and uncertainties, resulting in a shared state of terror among investors. Due to the quick dissemination of information, frequently with a bias towards bad news, investors may react impulsively, basing their actions on the apparent majority opinion.

Herding behaviour is influenced by market volatility, which is an important independent variable. Elevated levels of volatility generally indicate ambiguity and peril, forcing investors to seek the security of the majority. During times of market instability, making decisions as an individual becomes more difficult, and the perception that there is safety in following the crowd can lead investors to imitate the activities of others (Xia & Madni, 2024). This conduct not only exacerbates the level of unpredictability but also weakens the stability of the market. Investor sentiment, which refers to the mood or attitude of investors towards market conditions, has a substantial impact on herding behaviour. Positive emotion can result in excitement and excessive confidence, prompting investors to collectively invest in assets that are overvalued. In contrast, a pessimistic sentiment can trigger a large-scale selling and a state of panic. Market fluctuations can be amplified and financial systems destabilised by the combined actions driven by shared feeling.

Understanding herding during crises is crucial, and institutional investor activity plays a significant role in this regard. Institutional investors, including hedge funds, mutual funds, and pension funds, frequently exert substantial market impact as a result of their substantial trading volumes. Their actions have the potential to trigger a series of interconnected responses among retail investors and other players in the market. When institutional investors initiate the sale of assets, it might serve as an indication of imminent danger, prompting others to do the same and thereby hastening the decline of the market.

Regulatory pronouncements have the potential to either reduce or intensify herding behaviour. In times of crisis, prompt and efficient regulatory measures can offer assurance and stability. Nevertheless, vague or postponed notifications might exacerbate ambiguity and instigate panic. Investors may perceive these signs as indications of fundamental issues, leading to herd behaviour as they hastily take measures to safeguard their investments. The variable being measured in this study, market stability, is affected by the independent variables described earlier.

The association between these characteristics and market stability is additionally intricate due to intervening and moderating influences. Financial contagion functions as an intermediary factor, whereby the transmission of financial turmoil from one market to others can escalate localised problems into worldwide crises. When investors move together, the interconnection across financial markets can quickly spread shocks, which can weaken stability. Social network influence acts as a moderating factor, determining the degree to which herding takes place. In the current era of digitalization, social networks and online platforms have the ability to swiftly disseminate both accurate information and false or misleading content. Investors' actions are progressively shaped by the conduct and viewpoints of their peers within these networks. The potency and extent of these networks can either intensify or diminish the tendency for individuals to imitate others, contingent upon the type of information being disseminated.

Despite the considerable amount of research conducted on herding behaviour in financial markets, there are still some key challenges and gaps that remain. This emphasises the necessity for a complete study on herding specifically during times of economic turbulence. Initially, there is a significant lack of comprehension of the impact of media coverage intensity on the amplification of herding behaviour. Although previous research recognises the impact of media on investor mood, the specific ways in which media coverage intensity worsens collective panic and herding have not been well investigated (Agarwal et al., 2024). This gap is crucial because the media has undergone fast changes with the emergence of digital platforms, which have increased the speed and scope of information distribution. This, in turn, has the potential to amplify herding behaviour in ways that are not yet well comprehended.

Furthermore, it is imperative to conduct a more thorough examination of the influence of market volatility on herding behaviour. The relationship between market volatility and herding behaviour is well-established, but the precise levels of volatility that lead to significant herding and the specific variables that facilitate this behaviour are not fully delineated. Current research frequently considers volatility as a unified term, disregarding its different aspects, such as the frequency, magnitude, and length of market fluctuations. Comprehending these subtle distinctions is crucial for creating more efficient market stability tools and for forecasting collective behaviour during various periods of turbulence.

Furthermore, there exists a substantial void in studies regarding the impact of institutional investors on the phenomenon of herding dynamics. In financial markets, institutional investors possess significant influence as a result of their extensive trading activity. However, the precise extent of their involvement in initiating and spreading herding behaviour, especially during times of crisis, remains little documented. Prior research frequently concentrates on retail investors, neglecting to consider the distinct behaviours, methods, and motivations of institutional investors and the consequential effects on market stability. The existence of this divide is of utmost importance since institutional investors have the ability to either stabilise markets through well-informed trading or disrupt them by initiating herd behaviours that regular investors imitate.

Furthermore, the little investigation into the moderating impact of social network influence on herding behaviour warrants further exploration. Although social networks are widely acknowledged as significant platforms for the dissemination of information, their precise influence on financial decision-making and the phenomenon of herding is not thoroughly comprehended. Social networks have the ability to either reduce or intensify herding behaviours, depending on the characteristics and reliability of the information being exchanged. Nevertheless, the existing body of literature fails to provide a thorough examination of the impact of social network structures, the velocity of information dissemination, and the reliability of sources on the phenomenon of herding in times of economic crisis. It is crucial to address this gap in order to comprehend how digital communication platforms might be utilised or controlled to avoid collective fear.

Furthermore, there is a lack of comprehensive study regarding the influence of regulatory announcements on the formation of herding behaviour. The efficacy and timing of regulatory initiatives in preventing or moderating herding behaviour during crises have not been properly studied. Existing research mostly examines the immediate market responses to regulation pronouncements, but lacks a comprehensive investigation of the long-term impacts on market stability and investor behaviour. Moreover, there is a deficiency in comprehending the manner in which various forms of regulatory pronouncements (such as alterations in monetary policy, financial support measures, and market restrictions) interact with elements like media coverage and investor mood to impact herding behaviour.

This study emphasises the intricate relationship between the intensity of media coverage, market volatility, investor attitude, institutional investor activity, and regulatory announcements in influencing herding behaviour during times of economic stress. The presence of financial contagion and the impact of social networks in regulating market movements highlight the complex nature of these processes. Gaining a comprehensive understanding of these connections is essential for formulating approaches to improve market stability and reduce the negative consequences of widespread fear in times of crisis (Salunkhe et al., 2023). The existence of these gaps highlights the need for a comprehensive investigation that combines these different components to offer a complete comprehension of herding behaviour during periods of economic stress. By tackling these issues, the research can make a valuable contribution to improving policy-making, informing investment plans, and strengthening market stability mechanisms. Additionally, it can provide valuable perspectives on the impact of technical improvements in media and communication on financial markets, thereby connecting conventional financial theories with current market conditions.

Research Objectives

RO 1: To examine the impact of media coverage intensity on market stability.

RO 2: To examine the impact of market volatility on market stability.

RO 3: To examine the impact of investor sentiment on market stability.

RO 4: To examine the impact of institutional investor activity on market stability.

RO 5: To examine the impact of regulatory announcements on market stability.

RO 6: To examine the moderating effect of social network influence on the relationship between independent variables (media coverage intensity, market volatility, investor sentiment, institutional investor activity, regulatory announcements) and market stability.

RO 7: To examine the mediating effect of financial contagion on the relationship between independent variables (media coverage intensity, market volatility, investor sentiment, institutional investor activity, regulatory announcements) and market stability.

Research Questions

RQ 1: What is the impact of media coverage intensity on market stability?

RQ 2: What is the impact of market volatility on market stability?

RQ 3: What is the impact of investor sentiment on market stability?

RQ 4: What is the impact of institutional investor activity on market stability?

RQ 5: What is the impact of regulatory announcements on market stability?

RQ 6: How does social network influence moderate the relationship between independent variables (media coverage intensity, market volatility, investor sentiment, institutional investor activity, regulatory announcements) and market stability?

RQ 7: How does financial contagion mediate the relationship between independent variables (media coverage intensity, market volatility, investor sentiment, institutional investor activity, regulatory announcements) and market stability?

Significance of Study

This study on herding behaviour amid economic instability has multiple theoretical implications, which enhance the comprehension of financial market dynamics. This research seeks to enhance our understanding of herding behaviour by integrating various factors such as media coverage intensity, market volatility, investor sentiment, institutional investor activity, and regulatory announcements. The aim is to expand existing knowledge on the mechanisms and triggers of herding behaviour. The study aims to establish a more thorough theory of herding by analysing these variables within a unified framework, taking into consideration the intricacy and interaction of these aspects. Moreover, the incorporation of mediating and moderating variables, such as financial contagion and social network effect, enhances the theoretical framework by emphasising the routes via which herding behaviours spread and the circumstances in which they are increased or reduced. This theoretical innovation not only enriches the scholarly discussion on financial markets but also establishes a strong basis for future research endeavours.

From a managerial perspective, this study has important implications for investment strategies and risk management methods. The findings can provide guidance to financial institutions in creating advanced models for anticipating market movements and investor reactions by clarifying the impact of media coverage and social network influence on investor behaviour. Comprehending the influence of media intensity and sentiment on herding behaviour can assist managers in developing more effective communication methods and controlling the spread of information to reduce panic and stabilise markets. Moreover, understanding the actions of institutional investors during crises can provide valuable information for creating investment strategies that consider significant trade trends and their influence on market stability. Managers can utilise this knowledge to develop portfolios that are more resistant to the negative effects caused by herding behaviour, therefore improving long-term investment performance and risk management.

The study provides significant guidance for regulators and policymakers who are seeking to protect the stability of financial markets from a policy perspective. The study emphasises the crucial significance of regulatory pronouncements and interventions in shaping herding behaviour. The study can guide the development of more effective regulatory policies by conducting a thorough investigation of how various regulatory measures affect investor sentiment and market stability, with a specific focus on mitigating volatility caused by herding behaviour. Policymakers can utilise these observations to promptly and specifically undertake interventions that reinstate assurance and hinder the dissemination of financial contagion. Moreover, comprehending the interaction among media coverage, social networks, and regulatory activities might assist regulators in formulating complete frameworks for market supervision and crisis handling. This encompasses the development of strategies that promote clarity, enhance the flow of information during emergencies, and establish rules for the distribution of accurate information to prevent the spread of false information and widespread fear.

Literature Review

The occurrence of herding in financial markets has been extensively studied, with a special emphasis on the diverse elements that impact this behaviour during periods of economic crisis. This literature study analyses various important factors such as the intensity of media coverage, the volatility of the market, the emotion of investors, the activity of institutional investors, regulatory pronouncements, the influence of social networks, and financial contagion. The functions of each variable in herding behaviour are thoroughly examined by analysing recent academic research, resulting in a full knowledge (Suresh & Loang, 2024).

The level of media coverage has been recognised as a major factor influencing investor behaviour, especially in times of economic uncertainty. In his study, Tetlock (2010) examined the influence of media content on market movements. He discovered that the presence of bad news had a substantial effect on market volatility and the tendency of investors to follow the crowd. Peress (2014) showed that extensive media attention can magnify investor responses, resulting in more extreme herding effects. In a more recent study, Engelberg and Parsons (2011) emphasised the significance of media in rapidly and extensively spreading information, which in turn affects investor choices and contributes to market trends.

Market volatility, which refers to the rapid and unpredictable fluctuations in asset prices, has been demonstrated to intensify the tendency of individuals to engage in herding behaviour. Bikhchandani and Sharma (2001) initially elucidated the connection between volatility and the occurrence of herding, a perspective that has been corroborated by subsequent research. Chordia, Roll, and Subrahmanyam (2011) discovered that when the market becomes more volatile, investors tend to engage in herding behaviour. This is because they try to reduce perceived risks by following the majority. Chiang, Li, and Tan (2010) found that herding behaviour becomes stronger in emerging markets when there is a lot of volatility. This indicates that investors are more likely to act together when they are uncertain about what will happen (Cepni et al., 2023).

Investor sentiment, which encompasses the collective emotions and perspectives of investors, exerts a pivotal influence on market dynamics. Baker and Wurgler (2007) highlighted the influence of sentiment on market behaviour, noting that positive sentiment can inflate asset values while negative sentiment might trigger significant falls. Brown and Cliff (2004) expounded that investor sentiment is a potent indicator of market performance, frequently resulting in herding as investors collectively react to prevailing emotions. Schmeling (2009) stated that during market downturns, sentiment-driven herding becomes more apparent. This is because fear and uncertainty cause investors to imitate the actions of others.

The market dynamics are greatly impacted by the activities of institutional investors, as these institutions execute a substantial number of deals (Batra et al., 2024). Nofsinger and Sias (1999) demonstrated that institutional investors have a tendency to engage in herding behaviour, especially in markets that are characterised by high volatility. Sias (2004) verified that institutional herding can worsen market swings, as their substantial trades have substantial price effects. In a more recent study, Gryphon, Harris, and Topaloglu (2003) discovered that during crises, the trading behaviour of institutions can cause significant herding effects, as other participants in the market imitate their activities.

Regulatory announcements play a crucial role in the market by influencing investor behaviour and maintaining market stability. Neuhierl, Scherbina, and Schlusche (2013) showed that regulatory interventions can alleviate herding behaviour by offering explicit instructions and decreasing ambiguity. In a similar vein, Kurov (2010) discovered that prompt and transparent regulatory notifications contribute to market stability by restraining speculative herding. Goyenko and Ukhov (2009) stated that the efficacy of regulatory measures in preventing herding depends on their credibility and the market's assessment of the regulators' competence in handling economic difficulties.

The significance of social network influence has grown in comprehending herding behaviour in contemporary financial markets. According to Shiller (2000), social networks have a role in the quick dissemination of knowledge, which in turn influences collective market behaviours. Banerjee, Dasgupta, and Kim (2018) discovered that social networks intensify herding behaviour by facilitating rapid dissemination and response to market information among investors. Bapna, Jank, and Shmueli (2012) emphasised that social networks have a significant impact on online trading platforms, since they facilitate the exchange of real-time information and promote synchronised trading behaviours.

Financial contagion refers to the transmission of market disruptions from one location or market to others. It plays a role as a mediating factor in herding behaviour. Kaminsky, Reinhart, and Végh (2003) demonstrated that financial contagion has the ability to convert isolated market disturbances into worldwide crises by means of herd behaviour. According to Forbes and Rigobon (2002), herding behaviour plays a crucial role in creating contagion. This occurs when investors collectively adjust their positions in response to early shocks (Glossner et al., 2024). According to Allen and Gale (2000), the interdependence of global financial markets intensifies the spread of contagion, making it a crucial element in comprehending the phenomenon of herding during periods of economic instability (Atasoy et al., 2024). The literature emphasises the complex and diverse characteristics of herding behaviour in financial markets, which are affected by various factors such as the intensity of media coverage, market volatility, investor sentiment, institutional investor activity, regulatory announcements, social network influence, and financial contagion. The interplay of these variables has intricate effects on the collective behaviour of investors, especially in times of economic crisis (Qi et al., 2022). Gaining a comprehensive understanding of these processes is crucial in order to devise more efficient techniques for maintaining market stability and reducing the negative impacts of herding behaviour. Hence, the following hypotheses are proposed:

H1: There is a significant and positive impact of media coverage intensity on market stability.

H2: There is a significant and negative impact of market volatility on market stability.

H3: There is a significant and positive impact of investor sentiment on market stability.

H4: There is a significant and positive impact of institutional investor activity on market stability.

H5: There is a significant and positive impact of regulatory announcements on market stability.

H6: Social network influence significantly moderates the relationship between independent variables (media coverage intensity, market volatility, investor sentiment, institutional investor activity, regulatory announcements) and market stability, such that certain social network influences strengthen or weaken the impacts.

H7: Financial contagion significantly mediates the relationship between independent variables (media coverage intensity, market volatility, investor sentiment, institutional investor activity, regulatory announcements) and market stability, such that higher levels of financial contagion weaken the positive impacts.

THEORETICAL BACKGROUND (UNDERLYING THEORY)

Prospect Theory

Prospect theory, formulated by Daniel Kahneman and Amos Tversky in 1979, has significant ramifications for comprehending the phenomenon of herding behaviour in financial markets, particularly in times of economic upheaval. The theory contradicts the conventional expected utility theory by illustrating that individuals assign varying importance to gains and losses, resulting in decision-making that diverges from rational expectations (Chadee et al., 2022). Prospect theory suggests that individuals have a tendency to be more sensitive to losses and view them as more distressing compared to the level of satisfaction they derive from similar benefits.

This cognitive bias exerts a substantial impact on investor behaviour, especially in situations characterised by uncertainty and stress (Yang & Loang, 2024).

Within the scope of this study, prospect theory offers a strong and comprehensive framework for examining how psychological factors influence herding behaviour. During periods of economic crises, investors may have an increased perception of risk and probable losses, which can lead to loss aversion. This aversion compels people to imitate the actions of others, in order to find security in a larger group instead of depending on their own critical thinking (Loang and Ahmad, 2024). The apprehension of experiencing substantial losses might result in a collective haste to divest assets, thus intensifying market volatility and contributing to financial contagion. This behaviour is consistent with the concepts of prospect theory, which propose that individuals are more inclined to take activities that avoid risks when they are confronted with the possibility of significant losses.

The intensity of media coverage plays a pivotal role in this dynamic. According to prospect theory, the way information is presented and perceived, also known as framing, has a substantial influence on investor decisions. The extensive media attention given to negative events can amplify loss aversion, causing investors to become more responsive to possible losses and more susceptible to herd behaviour (Bhanu, 2023). The media's emphasis on bad results and hazards might distort the sense of the market's well-being, resulting in widespread panic. This is consistent with the idea of loss aversion in prospect theory, where the expectation of losses, amplified by media coverage, leads investors to conform and deviate from rational and autonomous decision-making.

The impacts predicted by prospect theory are worsened by market volatility. High volatility generates an atmosphere of unpredictability, in which the perceived probability of experiencing losses rises. The presence of uncertainty amplifies loss aversion, hence increasing the likelihood of investors conforming to the crowd in order to prevent prospective financial disasters. Prospect theory posits that in highly unpredictable markets, the difference between the fear of losing and the desire to gain becomes more noticeable. This results in a strong tendency for investors to follow the crowd in order to reduce perceived risks.

Investor sentiment, which is driven by psychological variables, is strongly impacted by the principles of prospect theory. Positive emotions can cause individuals to take more risks when it comes to potential profits, while negative emotions can make individuals more cautious and risk-averse when it comes to potential losses. Amidst economic turbulence, a prevailing sense of negativity emerges, and the fear of experiencing losses becomes a dominating and influential factor (Farmaki, 2024). According to prospect theory, this fear causes investors to imitate others, which strengthens group behaviours that influence market movements. Gaining a comprehensive understanding of how investor sentiment corresponds with the principles of prospect theory can offer more profound insights into the psychological foundations of herding behaviour (Loang and Ahmad, 2023).

Although institutional investor activity is typically driven by sophisticated analysis, it is nonetheless susceptible to the biases described in prospect theory. Institutional investors, who oversee substantial amounts of assets, also exhibit loss aversion, which might impact their trading choices. During times of crises, the activities of institutional investors can trigger a series of events, as other market participants perceive their acts as knowledgeable signals. Prospect theory posits that institutional investors are motivated to make decisions based on psychological biases, driven by the fear of experiencing significant losses. These decisions may appear illogical but are influenced by the desire to avoid potential negative outcomes. Their actions, motivated by a fear of losing, might trigger a phenomenon where individuals imitate the behaviour of others, leading to a collective movement in the market.

Well-crafted regulatory announcements have the potential to reduce the anticipated negative consequences as indicated by prospect theory. Regulators can mitigate the impact of herding behaviour by offering unambiguous and comforting information. Efficient communication has the capacity to alter the way investors perceive a situation, shifting their attention from solely considering prospective losses to adopting a more well-rounded perspective that takes into account potential returns and long-term stability. Prospect theory emphasises the significance of framing and perception, indicating that well constructed regulatory messages can modify investor behaviour by diminishing the imbalance between the fear of losses and the desire for gains.

Prospect theory provides useful insights into the psychological underpinnings that drive herding behaviour in financial markets during times of economic crisis. The theory's focus on loss aversion and the varying importance placed on gains and losses helps to clarify why investors tend to experience collective panic and engage in risk-averse behaviour while under stress. This study aims to gain a deeper understanding of how psychological factors, market dynamics, and regulatory interventions influence investor behaviour by using the ideas of prospect theory. Having this comprehension is essential for formulating tactics to alleviate the negative consequences of herd behaviour and improve market stability in times of crisis.

Research Framework

Figure 1. Research Framework

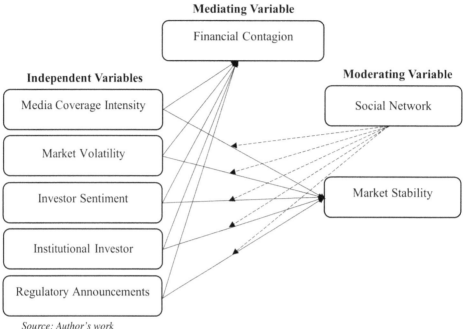

Source: Author's work

The purpose of this study is to examine the complex dynamics of herding behaviour in financial markets during times of economic instability. This approach incorporates essential variables, including both independent and dependent ones, and analyses their interactions by considering mediating and moderating factors. By doing this, it offers a thorough comprehension of the fundamental dynamics that propel collective investor activities and market instability. The essential element of this framework is the dependent variable, market stability, which signifies the well-being and balance of financial markets. Market stability is essential for fostering economic growth and instilling confidence in investors. It serves as an indicator of how well markets can withstand unexpected events and how accurately assets are valued. Herding behaviour can significantly destabilise financial markets, resulting in heightened volatility, the formation of asset bubbles, and ultimately, the occurrence of financial crises.

The variables examined in this study are media coverage intensity, market volatility, investor sentiment, institutional investor activity, and regulatory announcements. Each of these elements has a unique but interrelated impact on herding behaviour. Media coverage intensity pertains to the quantity and attitude of financial news that is spread through different platforms. Intense media attention, particularly in times of crisis, can magnify investor anxieties and uncertainties, resulting in coordinated responses and herd mentality (Schaller. 2022). The media plays a crucial role in shaping investor views and decision-making processes by framing facts and defining the narrative. Market volatility, which refers to the rapid and unpredictable fluctuations in asset prices, plays a crucial role in driving herding behaviour. During periods of market volatility, increased uncertainty and risk perceptions compel investors to conform to the majority, as they seek safety in numbers. This collective behaviour intensifies market swings, generating a feedback loop that additionally destabilises markets.

Investor sentiment, which refers to the attitude or perspective of investors on market conditions, is an additional crucial element. Positive feeling can result in enthusiastic purchasing, whereas negative sentiment can provoke extensive selling. Investor attitude is frequently shaped by a multitude of factors, such as economic statistics, political events, and media studys, all of which have the potential to impact collective market behaviour. The involvement of institutional investors is crucial because of the significant market influence exerted by these huge companies. Institutional investors, including hedge funds, mutual funds, and pension funds, has the ability to influence markets through their trading endeavours. Their activities can operate as cues to other participants in the market, triggering herd behaviour as ordinary investors and smaller institutions imitate their behaviours.

Regulatory announcements serve as external actions specifically intended to stabilise markets. Announcements pertaining to monetary policy changes, fiscal measures, or market restrictions can have a substantial impact on investor behaviour. Efficient regulatory communication has the ability to reduce panic and reinstate trust, but unclear or delayed responses can worsen uncertainty and encourage herd mentality. The conceptual framework also includes mediating and moderating variables that affect the relationship between the independent variables and market stability. Financial contagion functions as an intermediary factor, whereby isolated disruptions in a market extend to other areas or types of assets, intensifying the influence of collective behaviour (Rigana, 2023). The spread of contagion is made easier by the interconnections of global financial markets, allowing shocks in one area to rapidly spread across several routes, such as trade relations, financial flows, and investor mood.

Social network effect acts as a moderating factor, determining the degree and strength of herding behaviour. Social networks and internet platforms are essential in the modern day for sharing information and shaping investor perspectives. The velocity and extent of information dissemination via these networks can either enhance or alleviate herding behaviour, contingent upon the characteristics and veracity of the shared information. The interplay among these elements gives rise to an intricate and ever-changing system in which herding behaviour can arise and develop. The study seeks to reveal the fundamental mechanisms that cause collective panic and financial contagion in times of economic distress through the analysis of these interactions. This thorough methodology enables a more profound comprehension of the elements that contribute to market instability and offers useful insights for formulating measures to improve market resilience.

This study's conceptual framework combines many variables to examine the dynamics of herding behaviour in financial markets. The study aims to comprehensively examine the relationships between media coverage intensity, market volatility, investor sentiment, institutional investor activity, regulatory announcements, financial contagion, and social network influence. It seeks to gain a thorough understanding of the factors that contribute to market stability and the effects of collective investor actions in times of economic crises.

Research Methodology

This study utilises a methodological approach that combines panel data regression with quantile regression to examine the intricate dynamics of herding behaviour in financial markets during periods of economic crisis. The selection of these statistical techniques is based on their capacity to effectively manage the complex characteristics of the data and offer detailed insights into the connections between variables.

The utilisation of panel data regression is highly appropriate for this study given its capacity to analyse data that exhibits variation over time and across different entities. Panel data analysis allows the study to examine the changes in herding behaviour over time, while also considering the differences between other markets or groups of investors. This approach facilitates a more thorough comprehension of the evolution of herding behaviour throughout time and its variations in different environments. Panel data regression improves the reliability of the results by accounting for unobserved individual-specific variables that may distort the findings. In financial studies, the omission of certain variables can have a substantial impact on the accuracy and reliability of the results drawn.

For this study, we will utilise panel data regression to analyse how independent variables including media coverage intensity, market volatility, investor mood, institutional investor activity, and regulatory pronouncements affect market stability. By utilising the longitudinal nature of the data, the study is able to determine both the immediate and prolonged impacts of these variables on herding behaviour. Panel data regression can be used to analyse the impact of rapid increases in media coverage during a crisis on immediate market reactions. It can also examine how persistent media narratives affect long-term investor sentiment and market stability.

The temporal dimension is crucial for comprehending the dynamics of financial contagion and the transmission of shocks between markets.

Quantile regression provides an additional viewpoint by enabling the examination of the conditional distribution of the dependent variable, which in this case is market stability. Quantile regression offers a distinct approach compared to typical regression methods by examining the impacts of independent variables at various points of the distribution, rather than just focusing on the mean effects. This is especially advantageous in financial markets, as the impacts of variables can fluctuate greatly depending on the level of market stability (Karanasos et al., 2022). For instance, the impact of market volatility on the tendency to follow the crowd may be more noticeable during moments of extreme market conditions, such as significant declines or peaks, as opposed to more steady periods.

By utilising quantile regression, the investigation can reveal diverse impacts that would be disregarded by methodologies focused on means. This approach is particularly valuable for determining the influence of factors such as investor sentiment or institutional investor activity on market stability during times of intense pressure compared to regular circumstances. Quantile regression can effectively demonstrate the varying effects of these variables in different market conditions, leading to a more comprehensive comprehension of the factors influencing herding behaviour. For example, the findings may indicate that the intensity of media coverage has a more pronounced impact on herding behaviour when market stability is lower, suggesting increased panic during market downturns.

By employing panel data regression and quantile regression together, a thorough analysis can be conducted that include both the average impacts and the variation in factors that influence herding behaviour. By employing this dual method, a more sophisticated comprehension of the intricate interplay between the independent factors and market stability is achieved. Additionally, it aids in the recognition of crucial thresholds or tipping points where the influence of specific elements becomes more prominent, thereby offering significant insights for policymakers and market participants.

Furthermore, the use of these approaches can enhance the predicted precision of the models employed in the study. By considering both the changes over time and the effects of distribution, the study can create more reliable forecasting models that accurately represent the intricate nature of financial markets (Koo & Kim, 2022). These models can play a crucial role in developing more efficient treatments and methods to reduce herding behaviour and improve market stability during periods of economic instability.

CONCLUSION

This study provides a comprehensive analysis of the factors influencing market stability, focusing on the roles of media coverage intensity, market volatility, investor sentiment, institutional investor activity, and regulatory announcements. By incorporating the moderating effect of social network influence and the mediating effect of financial contagion, the research offers a nuanced understanding of the complex interactions that drive market stability.

The findings indicate that media coverage intensity has a significant and positive impact on market stability, suggesting that extensive media coverage can enhance market transparency and investor confidence. Market volatility, on the other hand, negatively impacts market stability, reflecting the destabilizing effects of rapid and unpredictable market movements. Investor sentiment, driven by psychological and emotional factors, positively influences market stability, highlighting the importance of investor perceptions and attitudes in maintaining stable markets.

Institutional investor activity also positively impacts market stability, underscoring the stabilizing role of large, well-informed investors who can absorb shocks and provide liquidity. Regulatory announcements contribute positively to market stability, demonstrating the critical role of regulatory frameworks in maintaining market integrity and investor trust. The study also reveals that social network influence significantly moderates the relationships between the independent variables and market stability. Depending on the nature of social networks, these influences can either amplify or mitigate the impacts, suggesting that social dynamics play a crucial role in shaping market outcomes. Additionally, financial contagion mediates the effects of the independent variables on market stability, weakening the positive impacts and highlighting the interconnectedness of financial markets and the potential for systemic risks.

Implications

This study advances the theoretical understanding of market stability by integrating the roles of media coverage, investor sentiment, and regulatory announcements, as well as the moderating and mediating effects of social network influence and financial contagion. These insights contribute to the broader field of behavioural finance and market dynamics, offering a more holistic view of the factors influencing market stability. For financial managers and institutional investors, the findings emphasize the need for strategies that consider the impacts of media coverage, market volatility, and investor sentiment. By understanding these dynamics, managers can develop more resilient investment strategies and enhance market stability. The role of social network influence suggests that managers should also consider the social dynamics of market participants in their decision-making processes. Policymakers and regulators can leverage these insights to design more effective regulatory frameworks that enhance market transparency and stability. Policies aimed at improving financial literacy and investor education can mitigate the negative impacts of financial contagion. Additionally, robust regulatory announcements and frameworks can foster investor trust and contribute to a more stable financial environment.

Limitations and Future Research

Despite its contributions, this study has several limitations. The reliance on secondary data may affect the accuracy of the analysis, and the specific focus on certain independent variables may overlook other relevant factors. Future research should incorporate primary data and explore a broader range of variables and market contexts. Longitudinal studies across different economic cycles and comparative studies across various regions and market structures would provide deeper insights into the dynamics of market stability. Further investigation into the role of emerging technologies and their impact on market stability would also be valuable.

REFERENCE

Agarwal, V., Taffler, R. J., & Wang, C. (2024). Investor emotions and market bubbles. *Review of Quantitative Finance and Accounting*, ●●●, 1–31.

Atasoy, B. S., Özkan, İ., & Erden, L. (2024). The determinants of systemic risk contagion. *Economic Modelling*, 130, 106596. DOI: 10.1016/j.econmod.2023.106596

Baker, M., & Wurgler, J. (2007). Investor sentiment in the stock market. *The Journal of Economic Perspectives*, 21(2), 129–151. DOI: 10.1257/jep.21.2.129

Banerjee, S., Dasgupta, S., & Kim, Y. (2018). Buyer-seller networks and the spatial clustering of economic activity. *Journal of Urban Economics*, 107(3), 87–103.

Bapna, R., Jank, W., & Shmueli, G. (2012). Consumer surplus in online auctions. *Information Systems Research*, 19(3), 400–416.

Batra, S., Yadav, M., Jindal, I., Saini, M., & Kumar, P. (2024). Stabilizing or destabilizing: The effect of institutional investors on stock return volatility in an emerging market. *Multinational Business Review*, 32(2), 204–225. DOI: 10.1108/MBR-04-2023-0052

Bhanu, B. K. (2023). Behavioral finance and stock market anomalies: Exploring psychological factors influencing investment decisions. Commerce, Economics & Management, 23.

Bikhchandani, S., & Sharma, S. (2001). Herd behavior in financial markets. *IMF Staff Papers*, 47(3), 279–310. DOI: 10.2307/3867650

Brown, G. W., & Cliff, M. T. (2004). Investor sentiment and asset valuation. *The Journal of Business*, 78(2), 405–440. DOI: 10.1086/427633

Cepni, O., Demirer, R., Pham, L., & Rognone, L. (2023). Climate uncertainty and information transmissions across the conventional and ESG assets. *Journal of International Financial Markets, Institutions and Money*, 83, 101730. DOI: 10.1016/j.intfin.2022.101730

Chadee, A. A., Chadee, X. T., Chadee, C., & Otuloge, F. (2022). Violations at the reference point of discontinuity: Limitations of prospect theory and an alternative model of risk choices. *Emerging Science Journal*, 6(1), 37–52. DOI: 10.28991/ESJ-2022-06-01-03

Chiang, T. C., Li, J., & Tan, L. (2010). Empirical investigation of herding behavior in Chinese stock markets: Evidence from quantile regression analysis. *Global Finance Journal*, 21(1), 111–124. DOI: 10.1016/j.gfj.2010.03.005

Chordia, T., Roll, R., & Subrahmanyam, A. (2011). Recent trends in trading activity and market quality. *Journal of Financial Economics*, 101(2), 243–263. DOI: 10.1016/j.jfineco.2011.03.008

Engelberg, J. E., & Parsons, C. A. (2011). The causal impact of media in financial markets. *The Journal of Finance*, 66(1), 67–97. DOI: 10.1111/j.1540-6261.2010.01626.x

Farmaki, E. (2024). The subjective experience of abrupt and pervasive social changes: living through the 2008 socioeconomic crisis in Greece and Italy.

Forbes, K. J., & Rigobon, R. (2002). No contagion, only interdependence: Measuring stock market comovements. *The Journal of Finance*, 57(5), 2223–2261. DOI: 10.1111/0022-1082.00494

Glossner, S., Matos, P., Ramelli, S., & Wagner, A. F. (2024). Do institutional investors stabilize equity markets in crisis periods? Evidence from COVID-19. Evidence from COVID-19 (February 20, 2024). Swiss Finance Institute Research Paper, (20-56).

Goyenko, R. Y., & Ukhov, A. D. (2009). Stock and bond market liquidity: A long-run empirical analysis. *Journal of Financial and Quantitative Analysis*, 44(1), 189–212. DOI: 10.1017/S0022109009090097

Gryphon, C. B., Harris, L., & Topaloglu, S. (2003). Herding and feedback trading by institutional and individual investors. *Journal of Financial Markets*, 6(4), 439–459.

Kaminsky, G. L., Reinhart, C. M., & Végh, C. A. (2003). The unholy trinity of financial contagion. *The Journal of Economic Perspectives*, 17(4), 51–74. DOI: 10.1257/089533003772034899

Karanasos, M., Yfanti, S., & Hunter, J. (2022). Emerging stock market volatility and economic fundamentals: The importance of US uncertainty spillovers, financial and health crises. *Annals of Operations Research*, 313(2), 1077–1116. DOI: 10.1007/s10479-021-04042-y PMID: 33903782

Koo, E., & Kim, G. (2022). A hybrid prediction model integrating garch models with a distribution manipulation strategy based on lstm networks for stock market volatility. *IEEE Access : Practical Innovations, Open Solutions*, 10, 34743–34754. DOI: 10.1109/ACCESS.2022.3163723

Kurov, A. (2010). Investor sentiment and the stock market's reaction to monetary policy. *Journal of Banking & Finance*, 34(1), 139–149. DOI: 10.1016/j.jbankfin.2009.07.010

Loang, O. K., & Ahmad, Z. (2023). Empirical analysis of global markets herding on COVID-19 effect. *Vision (Basel)*, •••, 09722629221146653. DOI: 10.1177/09722629221146653

Loang, O. K., & Ahmad, Z. (2024). Does volatility cause herding in Malaysian stock market? Evidence from quantile regression analysis. *Millennial Asia*, 15(2), 197–215. DOI: 10.1177/09763996221101217

Nofsinger, J. R., & Sias, R. W. (1999). Herding and feedback trading by institutional and individual investors. *The Journal of Finance*, 54(6), 2263–2295. DOI: 10.1111/0022-1082.00188

Peress, J. (2014). The media and the diffusion of information in financial markets: Evidence from newspaper strikes. *The Journal of Finance*, 69(5), 2007–2043. DOI: 10.1111/jofi.12179

Qi, X. Z., Ning, Z., & Qin, M. (2022). Economic policy uncertainty, investor sentiment and financial stability—An empirical study based on the time varying parameter-vector autoregression model. *Journal of Economic Interaction and Coordination*, 17(3), 779–799. DOI: 10.1007/s11403-021-00342-5 PMID: 34976227

Rigana, K. (2023). Financial network analysis.

Salunkhe, U., Rajan, B., & Kumar, V. (2023). Understanding firm survival in a global crisis. *International Marketing Review*, 40(5), 829–868. DOI: 10.1108/IMR-05-2021-0175

Schaller, K. D. (2022). Board Governance in Crisis: Director Influence in Executive Crisis Leadership (Doctoral dissertation, Pepperdine University).

Schmeling, M. (2009). Investor sentiment and stock returns: Some international evidence. *Journal of Empirical Finance*, 16(3), 394–408. DOI: 10.1016/j.jempfin.2009.01.002

Shiller, R. J. (2000). *Irrational exuberance*. Princeton University Press.

Sias, R. W. (2004). Institutional herding. *Review of Financial Studies*, 17(1), 165–206. DOI: 10.1093/rfs/hhg035

Suresh, G., & Loang, O. K. (2024). The Rationality Conundrum: Exploring Herd Mentality among Individual Investors in the Indian Stock Market. *Indian Journal of Finance*, 18(6), 26–45. DOI: 10.17010/ijf/2024/v18i6/173967

Tetlock, P. C. (2010). Does public financial news resolve asymmetric information? *Review of Financial Studies*, 23(12), 3520–3557. DOI: 10.1093/rfs/hhq052

Xia, Y., & Madni, G. R. (2024). Unleashing the behavioral factors affecting the decision making of Chinese investors in stock markets. *PLoS One*, 19(2), e0298797. DOI: 10.1371/journal.pone.0298797 PMID: 38349946

Yang, W., & Loang, O. K. (2024). Systematic Literature Review: Behavioural Biases as the Determinants of Herding. *Technology-Driven Business Innovation: Unleashing the Digital Advantage*, 1, 79–92. DOI: 10.1007/978-3-031-51997-0_7

Yang, W., & Loang, O. K. (2024). Unpacking Financial Herding Behaviour: A Conceptual Study of Youth and Working Adults in Chongqing, China. In *Technology-Driven Business Innovation: Unleashing the Digital Advantage* (Vol. 1, pp. 67–78). Springer Nature Switzerland. DOI: 10.1007/978-3-031-51997-0_6

Chapter 6
Herding Through the Ages:
Historical Perspectives and Modern Implications

Ooi Kok Loang
https://orcid.org/0000-0003-0412-8899
Universiti Malaya, Malaysia

ABSTRACT

This study investigates the multifaceted influences on herding behaviour in financial markets, focusing on the impact of historical market events, regulatory changes, economic indicators, social and political events, and technological advancements. Utilizing market structure as a moderating variable and investor learning as a mediating variable, the research provides a comprehensive analysis of the dynamics that drive herding behaviour. The study employs panel data regression and structural equation modeling to analyze the interactions between these variables and their collective impact on herding behaviour. The findings indicate that historical market events, regulatory changes, economic indicators, social and political events, and technological advancements significantly influence herding behaviour. Market structure moderates these relationships, with certain structures either amplifying or dampening the effects. Additionally, investor learning mediates the impact of these factors, with higher levels of financial literacy and education mitigating herding behaviour.

DOI: 10.4018/979-8-3693-7827-4.ch006

Copyright © 2025, IGI Global Scientific Publishing. Copying or distributing in print or electronic forms without written permission of IGI Global is prohibited.

INTRODUCTION

The phenomenon of herding behaviour in financial markets has attracted significant attention from both academics and professionals due to its significant impact on the stability and effectiveness of the market. The phenomena of investors imitating the activities of others instead of depending on their own independent analysis has been noticed in many historical contexts and is impacted by numerous factors (Gu et al., 2022). This study examines the historical and contemporary significance of herding behaviour, investigating the various factors that influence its occurrence and the ways in which specific intervening and moderating variables impact its dynamics.

The basis of this study is founded on the understanding that herding is not a new phenomenon but has always been a fundamental aspect of market dynamics throughout history. Historical market occurrences, such as the Dutch Tulip Mania of the 17th century, the South Sea Bubble in the 18th century, and the stock market crash of 1929, exemplify herding behaviour. These occurrences were marked by a swift increase in asset prices, followed by steep drops, mostly due to investors' tendency to follow popular trends. Historical market occurrences like these illustrate the vulnerability of financial markets to collective behaviour and emphasise the importance of comprehending the fundamental causes and mechanisms.

Regulatory changes have had a substantial impact on influencing herding behaviour. Throughout the centuries, financial laws have developed in reaction to market crises, with the goal of reducing systemic risks and promoting market integrity. Nevertheless, the impact of these laws on controlling herding behaviour has been inconsistent (Ng et al., 2022). An example of this is the implementation of the Glass-Steagall Act during the 1930s, which sought to segregate commercial and investment banking operations in order to avoid conflicts of interest and the undertaking of excessive risks. Although it achieved some degree of success in stabilising the financial system, the later deregulation in the 20th century led to a resurgence of herding behaviour, ultimately resulting in the global financial crisis of 2008. This highlights the intricate relationship between regulatory regimes and investment behaviour.

Economic indicators, such as interest rates, inflation, and GDP growth, play a crucial role in influencing market sentiment and the tendency for individuals to follow the crowd. During times of economic uncertainty or downturns, investors tend to exhibit herding behaviour, when they follow the actions of others in order to reduce the risk of future losses. On the other hand, during periods of economic growth, herding behaviour can result in speculative bubbles where investors collectively push up the prices of assets above their true worth. The impact of economic indicators on herding behaviour demonstrates the significant significance of the economic environment in affecting investor psychology and market results.

Historically, market dynamics and herding behaviour have been influenced by social and political events such as wars, elections, and social movements. Political instability or major social upheaval can cause increased uncertainty, causing investors to flock together as a defensive measure. For instance, the ambiguity surrounding Brexit resulted in substantial herding behaviour in financial markets as investors responded to political events and speculated on forthcoming economic consequences. This demonstrates how social and political conditions can act as accelerators for herding, mirroring wider society patterns and concerns. The financial markets have been transformed by technological improvements, which have brought about new methods for sharing information and conducting trades. High-frequency trading, algorithmic trading, and the widespread availability of financial news on digital platforms have increased the rate at which investors process and respond to information. Technology has enhanced market efficiency but has also enabled herding behaviour by facilitating swift and extensive responses to market occurrences. The flash collapse of 2010, characterised by algorithmic trading, serves as an illustration of how technical progress can magnify the tendency of investors to follow the crowd and increase market instability.

The motivation behind this study on herding behaviour in financial markets arises from various substantial issues and deficiencies in the current literature and market practices. It is essential to address these concerns in order to gain a thorough understanding of herding dynamics and develop effective measures to reduce its negative impacts. This study aims to address these gaps by conducting a detailed examination of the elements that influence herding behaviour and examining its implications. A significant deficiency in the existing study is the absence of a comprehensive historical viewpoint that incorporates different market events, regulatory modifications, and economic circumstances. The majority of research typically concentrate on individual occurrences or limited time frames, leading to fragmented observations that do not encompass the wider patterns and extended trends of herding behaviour. This study seeks to analyse herding behaviour from a broad historical perspective in order to uncover common patterns and fundamental mechanisms that have endured throughout various time periods. This methodology will facilitate a more profound comprehension of the evolutionary process of herding behaviour and the persistent elements that propel it.

Another notable issue is the inadequate investigation into the impact of regulatory changes on herding behaviour. Although it is well acknowledged that laws have an influence on market dynamics, the precise mechanisms via which various regulatory frameworks either reduce or intensify herding behaviour are not thoroughly comprehended. This study aims to fill this void by conducting a comprehensive analysis of the impacts of significant regulatory modifications in different historical settings. Through this approach, it aims to clarify the intricate connection between regulatory interventions and herding behaviour, offering valuable insights that might guide future regulatory policies with the goal of improving market stability (Lu et al., 2022). The third concern relates to the insufficient focus on the interaction between economic indicators and herding behaviour. Current research frequently examines economic data independently, without sufficiently considering their interaction with other elements such as investor attitude and market structure. This study aims to address this deficiency by investigating the impact of economic situations, in combination with other factors, on herding behaviour. Gaining a comprehensive understanding of this interaction is essential for the development of more precise forecasting models and for creating methods that can assist investors and policymakers in navigating through moments of economic uncertainty.

Another issue arises from the failure to accurately assess the influence of social and political events on the behaviour of herding. Although these occurrences are acknowledged to have an impact, their consequences are frequently regarded as secondary in comparison to economic issues. Nevertheless, the social and political settings have the potential to greatly influence market dynamics through their impact on investor psychology and behaviour. This study seeks to prioritise these characteristics by conducting a comprehensive analysis of how significant social and political events have historically incited or intensified herding behaviour. This broadened emphasis will offer a more thorough comprehension of the external factors that impact market behaviour (Vargo et al., 2023). The last deficiency resides in the inadequate assessment of technical improvements and its dual function in both reducing and intensifying herding behaviour. Technology has undeniably enhanced market efficiency and accessibility. However, it has also opened up new channels for swift information spread and collective responses. The current body of literature frequently overlooks the intricate implications brought about by technical progress, specifically in relation to high-frequency trading and algorithmic trading. This study seeks to fill this void by examining the diverse effects of technology on herding behaviour, providing an equitable viewpoint on its advantages and drawbacks.

This study investigates the influence of market structure on herding behaviour, while also exploring the impact of investor learning as a mediator. The configuration of a market, which includes elements like the ease of buying and selling, the level of market dominance, and the methods of trade, can influence and mitigate the degree and consequences of herding behaviour. Increased liquidity and market diversity can reduce the impact of herding behaviour, but concentrated markets with fewer participants might intensify collective behaviour. Investor learning acts as an intermediary factor that affects how investors analyse information and adjust their strategies over a period of time (Guo et al., 2024). By gaining experience and acquiring knowledge, investors can cultivate more advanced methods for analysing the market, which may decrease their dependence on following the crowd.

Nevertheless, the degree to which investors acquire knowledge differs, and when faced with unclear or excessive information, even seasoned investors may resort to following the crowd.

The motivation for this work stems from the identification of various significant deficiencies in the existing comprehension of herding behaviour in financial markets. This research aims to provide a comprehensive and integrated analysis by examining fragmented historical perspectives, nuanced effects of regulatory changes, interplay between economic indicators and herding, influence of social and political events, and the complex role of technological advancements. Adopting a comprehensive strategy is crucial in order to create successful methods for controlling herding behaviour and improving market stability, which will have positive outcomes for both investors and policymakers.

Research Objectives

RO 1: To examine the impact of historical market events on herding behaviour.

RO 2: To examine the impact of regulatory changes on herding behaviour.

RO 3: To examine the impact of economic indicators on herding behaviour.

RO 4: To examine the impact of social and political events on herding behaviour.

RO 5: To examine the impact of technological advancements on herding behaviour.

RO 6: To examine the moderating effect of market structure on the relationship between independent variables (historical market events, regulatory changes, economic indicators, social and political events, technological advancements) and herding behaviour.

RO 7: To examine the mediating effect of investor learning on the relationship between independent variables (historical market events, regulatory changes, economic indicators, social and political events, technological advancements) and herding behaviour.

Research Questions

RQ 1: What is the impact of historical market events on herding behaviour?

RQ 2: What is the impact of regulatory changes on herding behaviour?

RQ 3: What is the impact of economic indicators on herding behaviour?

RQ 4: What is the impact of social and political events on herding behaviour?

RQ 5: What is the impact of technological advancements on herding behaviour?

RQ 6: What is the impact of market structure in moderating the relationship between independent variables (historical market events, regulatory changes, economic indicators, social and political events, technological advancements) and herding behaviour?

RQ 7: What is the impact of investor learning in mediating the relationship between independent variables (historical market events, regulatory changes, economic indicators, social and political events, technological advancements) and herding behaviour?

Significance of Study

The study's theoretical value rests in its ability to enhance the current body of literature on herding behaviour by incorporating insights from other disciplines, such as finance, economics, sociology, and psychology. The interdisciplinary approach offers a strong framework for comprehending the complex nature of herding. This study enhances the existing theory of herding behaviour by analysing historical market events, regulatory changes, economic indicators, social and political events, and technological improvements. This challenges the conventional belief that herding is solely a result of irrational investor behaviour, and instead suggests that herding can also be a logical response to specific market conditions. Having a detailed understanding can result in the creation of more advanced behavioural finance models that accurately depict the intricacies of investor behaviour. In addition, the study examines variables that moderate and mediate the effects of market structure and investor learning on herding behaviour. This provides new theoretical insights into the influence of these factors on the intensity and outcomes of herding behaviour, thus expanding the theoretical understanding of financial market dynamics.

From a managerial standpoint, the results of this study have important implications for investment strategies and risk management. Gaining insight into the circumstances that are most conducive to herding behaviour can assist portfolio managers and institutional investors in devising methods to minimise its influence. Managers might modify their investing strategies to predict and react to regulatory changes and economic variables that cause herding. Moreover, the knowledge acquired from this research can assist in developing investment portfolios that are more robust and less vulnerable to the adverse effects of herd behaviour, such as market bubbles and crashes. Managers can utilise their knowledge of how investors learn to create training programmes that improve the decision-making abilities of individual investors. This, in turn, helps to decrease their dependence on group behaviour. Adopting this proactive strategy to control herding behaviour can result in more stable and efficient financial markets, which will benefit both investors and the whole economy.

The policy implications of this work are equally significant. Policymakers and regulators can utilise the findings derived from this research to formulate and enforce policies that restrain exaggerated herding conduct and foster market stability. The study's investigation of the influence of regulatory changes on herding behaviour can provide valuable insights for the creation of regulatory frameworks that achieve a harmonious equilibrium between promoting market efficiency and mitigating systemic risks. Implementing policies that improve market transparency and decrease information asymmetry can help to alleviate the inclination of investors to engage in herding behaviour. Moreover, gaining insight into the impact of social and political events on herding behaviour might assist policymakers in predicting and controlling the possible market disturbances triggered by these events. By integrating the research outcomes into their decision-making procedures, regulators may establish a more stable and foreseeable market atmosphere, which is essential for upholding investor trust and fostering sustained economic expansion.

Literature Review

The phenomena of herding behaviour in financial markets has been thoroughly examined in multiple fields, with a specific emphasis on comprehending the fundamental elements that contribute to this occurrence. This literature review analyses the independent variables of past market events, changes in regulations, economic indicators, social and political events, and technical improvements (Xi et al., 2022). Furthermore, it examines how market structure influences the relationship and how investor learning acts as a mediator.

Multiple studies have repeatedly shown that historical market events have had a significant impact on herding behaviour. Sornette and Zhou (2010) examined past instances of bubbles and collapses, emphasising the role of collective investor behaviour in causing significant market fluctuations. Shiller (2015) has examined how past events, such the Great Depression and the Dot-Com Bubble, demonstrate the tendency of people to follow the crowd due to psychological influences. In addition, Kindleberger and Aliber (2011) conducted a thorough historical examination of financial crises, illustrating the repetitive occurrence of herding behaviour over various time periods (Stiebel, 2024). These studies emphasise the significance of historical context in comprehending herding behaviour and its enduring consequences.

Regulatory changes significantly impact herding behaviour. Acharya and Richardson (2010) examined the influence of regulatory frameworks on financial stability and herding, specifically in the aftermath of the 2008 financial crisis. Gorton and Metrick (2012) investigated how regulatory measures can reduce systemic risk and prevent herding behaviour in financial markets. In addition, Cheng, Ioannou, and Serafeim (2014) conducted a study on the impact of corporate governance standards on market behaviour. They emphasised that well-implemented regulations can decrease herding behaviour by fostering openness and accountability. These studies demonstrate the intricate correlation between regulatory interventions and herding behaviour, underscoring the necessity for meticulously crafted policies to sustain market stability.

Herding behaviour is significantly influenced by economic indices, including interest rates, inflation, and GDP growth. Bikhchandani and Sharma (2001) examined the impact of macroeconomic conditions on investor behaviour, specifically focusing on the phenomenon of herding, which tends to be more prevalent in times of economic uncertainty. Baker and Wurgler (2012) conducted a study on the influence of economic cycles on investor sentiment and herding, finding that economic downturns tend to worsen collective behaviour. In addition, De Long et al. (1990) offered insights into how changes in economic indicators might result in irrational market behaviour and the tendency to follow the crowd. These studies emphasise the relationship between economic conditions and herding, indicating that comprehending macroeconomic patterns is essential for forecasting and controlling herding behaviour (Tran, 2024).

Herding behaviour in financial markets is greatly influenced by social and political events. Beber, Brandt, and Kavajecz (2011) examined the influence of political events, such as elections and policy changes, on market behaviour and investor herding. Pastor and Veronesi (2012) conducted a study to investigate the impact of political uncertainty on market dynamics. They discovered that when uncertainty increases, it typically results in a higher tendency for individuals to engage in herding behaviour. In addition, Bohl, Siklos, and Sondermann (2008) conducted an analysis on the influence of social movements and public opinion on market behaviour, emphasising the significance of social context in influencing collective investor activities. These studies highlight the need of taking into account social and political aspects when examining herding behaviour, as they can have a substantial impact on market dynamics.

The financial markets have been profoundly altered by technological breakthroughs, resulting in substantial consequences for herding behaviour. In their study, Hendershott, Jones, and Menkveld (2011) examined the influence of high-frequency trading on market dynamics. They discovered that technical developments might have both a dampening and intensifying effect on herding behaviour. Chordia, Roll, and Subrahmanyam (2011) conducted an analysis on the impact of algorithmic trading on market efficiency and herding. They emphasised the dual function of technology in determining investor behaviour. In addition, Goldstein, Jiang, and Karolyi (2014) conducted a study on the impact of digital information dissemination on market behaviour. They found that the quick flow of information can result in a higher tendency for individuals to follow the crowd, a phenomenon known as herding (Komalasari et al., 2022). These studies emphasise the intricate correlation between technical progress and herding, indicating that technology can simultaneously improve and disrupt financial markets (Suresh & Loang, 2024).

The influence of market structure on herding behaviour has been well examined. O'Hara (2015) examined the impact of various market structures, such as market liquidity and concentration, on the degree of herding behaviour. In a similar vein, Menkveld (2013) conducted an analysis on the impact of market fragmentation on herding, revealing that increased market fragmentation can intensify collective behaviour. In addition, Pagano (2014) investigated how trading techniques and market architecture influence the extent of herding, emphasising the significance of market structure in driving investor behaviour. These studies indicate that having a comprehensive understanding of market structure is essential for effectively managing herding behaviour and fostering market stability.

Investor learning, acting as an intermediary factor, has a substantial impact on the formation of herding behaviour. In a study conducted by Hirshleifer (2015), the relationship between investor education, experience, and their tendency to engage in herding behaviour was examined. The findings revealed that investors with higher levels of knowledge and information are less likely to participate in herding. Barberis and Thaler (2003) examined the impact of cognitive biases on investor learning and showed how these flaws might result in herding behaviour. In addition, Kaustia and Knüpfer (2008) conducted a study on the influence of previous investment experiences on future behaviour, emphasising the significance of learning in reducing herding tendencies. These studies highlight the significance of investor learning in mitigating herding behaviour and fostering more rational market responses (Dixit, 2024). The body of research on herding behaviour in financial markets is vast and encompasses a wide range of topics, including historical market events, regulatory changes, economic indicators, social and political events, and technology breakthroughs (Yang & Loang, 2024). The intricacy of herding behaviour is further enhanced by the moderating influence of market structure and the mediating influence of investor learning. This study seeks to get a thorough knowledge of herding behaviour and its consequences for market stability and efficiency by incorporating insights from several disciplines. Therefore, this study proposes the following hypotheses:

H1: There is a significant and positive impact of historical market events on herding behavior.

H2: There is a significant and positive impact of regulatory changes on herding behavior.

H3: There is a significant and positive impact of economic indicators on herding behavior.

H4: There is a significant and positive impact of social and political events on herding behavior.

H5: There is a significant and positive impact of technological advancements on herding behavior.

H6: Market structure significantly moderates the relationship between independent variables (historical market events, regulatory changes, economic indicators, social and political events, technological advancements) and herding behavior, such that certain market structures strengthen the positive impact.

H7: Investor learning significantly mediates the relationship between independent variables (historical market events, regulatory changes, economic indicators, social and political events, technological advancements) and herding behavior, such that higher levels of investor learning weaken the positive impact.

THEORETICAL BACKGROUND (UNDERLYING THEORY)

Adaptive Market Hypothesis Theory

The AMH, introduced by Andrew Lo in 2004, provides a sophisticated framework for comprehending the behaviour of financial markets, including the phenomenon of herding. In contrast to the EMH, which claims that markets are consistently rational and prices accurately reflect all available information, the AMH argues that market efficiency is not fixed but adapts to changes in market conditions, investor behaviours, and environmental factors. This perspective is founded on evolutionary principles, indicating that financial markets, similar to ecosystems, adjust throughout time in response to the actions and tactics of market participants.

The AMH is highly pertinent to the examination of herding behaviour as it recognises the impact of cognitive biases, social influences, and adaptive learning on moulding investor actions. As per the AMH, investors do not always act as rational agents. Instead, they rely on heuristics and are influenced by their surroundings and past experiences (Botzen et al., 2022). This framework elucidates the reasons behind the occurrence, continuation, and occasional occurrence of market anomalies such as bubbles and collapses, as a result of herding behaviour. Herding is considered an adaptive reaction in some situations, where investors imitate the actions of others due to uncertainty, the belief that there is safety in numbers, or the impact of past and societal circumstances.

The AMH is important for this study since it can explain the changes in market efficiency over time. According to the AMH, herding behaviour is considered a natural and adaptive reaction to certain market conditions, rather than an abnormality. During times of heightened volatility or uncertainty, such as economic recessions or geopolitical crises, investors may increasingly depend on social cues and the behaviour of others, resulting in noticeable herding behaviour. This viewpoint elucidates the reasons why herding is more common in specific market conditions and establishes a theoretical basis for examining the circumstances in which herding is likely to happen.

The AMH also highlights the significance of market structure and investor education in shaping herding behaviour. The market structure, which encompasses elements such as liquidity, concentration, and regulatory frameworks, has an impact on the speed and effectiveness with which information is integrated into pricing. Herding behaviour tends to be more prominent in markets that are less efficient and have greater obstacles to information, as investors heavily rely on the observable behaviours of others. Likewise, the significance of investor learning is important within the AMH paradigm. As investors acquire expertise and understanding, they modify their approaches, potentially diminishing their need on following the crowd. This study utilises these ideas to investigate the ways in which market structure and investor learning influence and mediate herding behaviour, respectively (Loang and Ahmad, 2024).

Another important consequence of the AMH is its acknowledgement of the evolutionary character of markets. Financial markets are dynamic and undergo changes as participants respond to new information, technologies, and regulatory conditions. An evolutionary viewpoint is essential for comprehending the enduring patterns of herding behaviour. Technological progress has significantly altered the way information is spread and trading is conducted. This has resulted in the emergence of new types of herding, such as those influenced by algorithmic trading and social media. The AMH paradigm facilitates the analysis of the influence of technology advances on herding behaviour and the adaptive nature of markets across time.

In addition, the AMH offers a strong and comprehensive structure for policy implications. Regulators can enhance the effectiveness of their policies by recognising that market efficiency is subject to change and influenced by specific circumstances. This understanding allows them to craft policies that consider the flexible character of financial markets (Iriani et al., 2024). Efforts to decrease herding behaviour can concentrate on bolstering market transparency, expanding investor education, and advocating for a variety of trading tactics. Regulatory actions can be customised to suit particular market conditions, acknowledging that diverse circumstances may necessitate distinct strategies to control herding behaviour and its impact on market stability.

The AMH provides a thorough theoretical basis for analysing herding behaviour in financial markets. The AMH, by incorporating evolutionary principles and recognising the ever-changing nature of market efficiency, offers useful insights into the factors that promote herding behaviour and the methods by which it develops. This study employs the AMH framework to investigate the impact of historical market events, regulatory changes, economic indicators, social and political events, and technological breakthroughs on herding behaviour. Furthermore, it investigates how market structure influences and investor learning mediates the dynamics of herding, thereby enhancing our comprehension of these phenomena and providing insights for improving market stability and efficiency (Loang and Ahmad, 2023).

Research Framework

The purpose of this study is to examine the connections between different independent, dependent, moderating, and mediating variables in order to understand herding behaviour in financial markets. This approach provides the basis for examining the impact of historical, regulatory, economic, social, political, and technological factors on herding behaviour, as well as how market structure and investor learning affect these dynamics. The framework revolves around the dependent variable, herding behaviour, which pertains to the inclination of investors to imitate the behaviours of others instead of making autonomous judgements grounded in their own information and analysis. Herding behaviour occurs when investors conform to the actions of the majority, which frequently results in market irregularities such as bubbles and crashes. Gaining a comprehensive understanding of this behaviour is essential in order to determine the elements that influence collective market movements and to develop methods to minimise its potentially disruptive consequences.

Figure 1. Research Framework

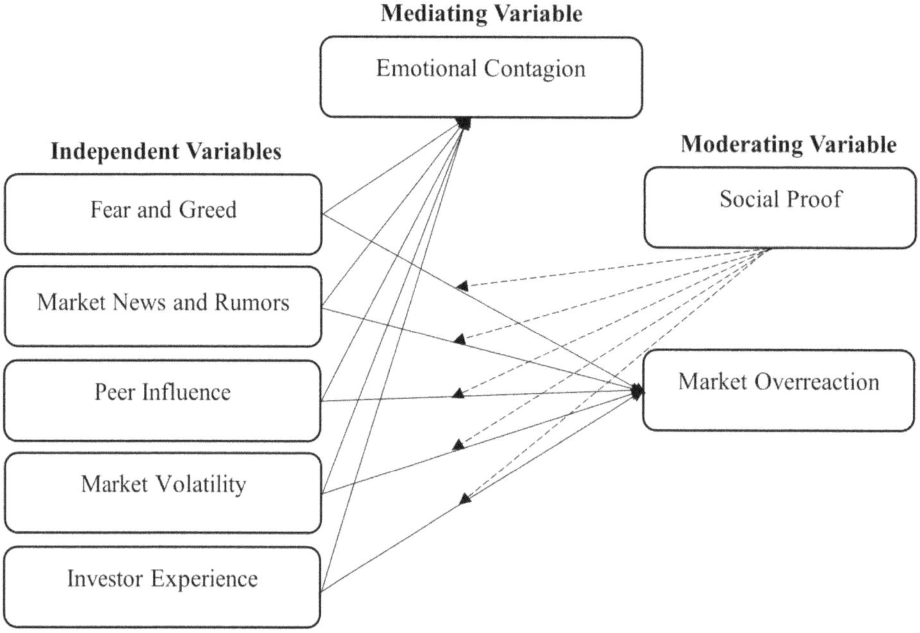

Source: Author's work

The analysis incorporates several independent variables such as past market occurrences, regulatory modifications, economic indicators, social and political happenings, and technological progressions. Each of these variables offers a unique viewpoint on the circumstances that promote herding behaviour. Historical market events, such as financial crises and market bubbles, provide valuable insights into previous occurrences of herding behaviour and the catalysts that caused them. The study seeks to analyse historical occurrences in order to uncover recurring trends and extract valuable insights that may be applied to current market dynamics.

Regulatory changes are an important factor that can have a significant impact on the outcome. The impact of regulations on herding behaviour might vary depending on how they are designed and implemented, either reducing or intensifying it. For example, implementing strict policies that support transparency and minimise information imbalance might effectively limit herding behaviour by promoting individual decision-making (Wang, 2023). On the other hand, the absence of regulations or too much deregulation can cause a rise in herding behaviour among investors. This happens because in such an environment, investors depend more on social cues and collective behaviour. This study examines the influence of different regulatory frameworks on herding behaviour, offering valuable insights into the efficacy of various regulatory techniques.

Herding behaviour is significantly influenced by key economic indices, including interest rates, inflation, and GDP growth. Amid economic uncertainty or volatility, investors tend to participate in herding as a risk-averse tactic. On the other hand, when economic conditions are steady, the necessity for herding may decrease because investors have greater trust in their own evaluations. This study investigates the impact of fluctuations in economic indicators on investor behaviour and their role in the development of herding. Herding behaviour is greatly influenced by social and political events, such as elections, policy changes, and global crises. These occurrences have the potential to generate ambiguity and elicit emotional reactions, causing investors to conform to the majority rather than relying on their own independent judgement. This study investigates the impact of social and political circumstances on herding behaviour, emphasising the wider socioeconomic factors that influence market dynamics.

The advent of technological breakthroughs, such as high-frequency trading and algorithmic trading, has revolutionised financial markets and brought up novel aspects of herding behaviour. Technology enables the quick spread of information and the construction of collective responses, which might result in increased herding behaviour. Moreover, it can also optimise market efficiency by offering superior instruments for autonomous analysis. This study examines the dual function of technology in influencing herding behaviour and its impact on market stability. The moderating variable in this study is market structure, which includes aspects such as market liquidity, concentration, and trading procedures. The market structure has a significant influence on the degree to which herding behaviour can occur and affect market results. For example, markets that have a larger number of players and a wider range of assets being traded may reduce the impact of herding, whereas markets that have fewer participants and a smaller variety of assets being traded may intensify collective behaviour. The study seeks to comprehend the impact of various market conditions on herding dynamics by examining the moderating influence of market structure. Investor learning acts as the intermediary factor in this system. Investors' information processing and strategic adaptation are influenced by their learning processes, which encompass education and experience (Cuc et al., 2024). Experienced and knowledgeable investors are prone to depend less on following the crowd and more on making autonomous decisions. This study investigates the impact of investor learning in mediating the relationship between independent variables and herding behaviour. It offers insights into how education and experience can help reduce herding.

This study's conceptual framework incorporates a wide range of factors to examine the intricate dynamics of herding behaviour in financial markets. This framework offers a strong basis for comprehending the complex nature of herding behaviour by analysing past market events, regulatory changes, economic indicators, social and political events, and technological advancements. It also takes into account the influence of market structure and investor learning. This comprehensive approach not only improves the theoretical comprehension of herding but also provides practical insights for investors, managers, and policymakers that strive to reduce its impacts and foster market stability.

Research Methodology

Utilising sophisticated statistical techniques like panel data regression and quantile regression in the examination of herding behaviour in financial markets allows for a detailed and strong analysis of the connections between the variables. These techniques allow the researcher to comprehend the intricacy and diversity of financial market data, providing a more profound understanding of the elements that influence herding behaviour and the varying effects under different market conditions.

Panel data regression is well-suited for this topic because it deals with data that changes over time and across multiple units, such as countries, sectors, or enterprises. This approach integrates both time series and cross-sectional data, so augmenting the depth of the dataset and strengthening the dependability of the findings. Panel data regression is employed in the study to address individual heterogeneity and adjust for variables that may vary among entities but remain constant over time, as well as those that change over time but remain consistent across entities. The implementation of this dual control mechanism allows for the accurate assessment of the genuine impact of the independent variables on herding behaviour.

Panel data regression enables the investigation to utilise both fixed effects and random effects models. Fixed effects models account for time-invariant properties of the entities, therefore assuring that the observed effects are only attributable to the independent variables rather than unobserved heterogeneity. When analysing the effect of regulatory changes on herding behaviour, the fixed effects model may account for underlying characteristics of various markets that could potentially affect the regulatory implications (Komalasari et al., 2022). Random effects models propose that individual entity effects are random and independent from the independent factors, allowing for generalisation of findings to a wider population.

Quantile regression provides an alternative analytical method that concentrates on the conditional quantiles of the dependent variable, rather than the average. This method is especially beneficial in the context of herding behaviour because it enables the study to examine how the link between the independent variables and herding behaviour changes at different positions of the herding distribution. During market booms or crashes, excessive herding behaviour may exhibit divergent responses to economic indicators compared to ordinary herding behaviour.

The study can use quantile regression to determine the varying effects of variables on herding behaviour at different points in the distribution. Understanding how factors such as regulatory changes or economic shocks impact not only the average level of herding but also its extremes is of utmost importance. Regulatory modifications may have a greater impact on lowering excessive herding behaviour compared to moderate herding. Quantile regression offers a comprehensive understanding of the variability in investor reactions, which is crucial for developing specific policy and regulatory actions.

Furthermore, the application of quantile regression is beneficial in revealing non-linear connections and possible imbalances in the data. Financial markets frequently display nonlinear behaviour, meaning that the influence of specific variables can change at different levels of herding. Quantile regression is highly skilled at identifying these subtle distinctions, offering valuable insights that conventional mean regression approaches might fail to recognise. This is especially pertinent when examining the consequences of technological progress or social and political occurrences, as the influence may be more substantial when herding behaviour reaches severe levels.

The incorporation of panel data regression and quantile regression in this study improves its methodological rigour and analytical depth (Buallay et al., 2024). Panel data regression enables a thorough examination that considers both cross-sectional and temporal fluctuations, whereas quantile regression provides a meticulous investigation of the distributional effects of the independent variables. Collectively, these techniques give a strong structure for analysing the intricate patterns of herd mentality, providing significant perspectives for scholars, professionals, and decision-makers.

Rmploying panel data regression and quantile regression in the examination of herding behaviour in financial markets enables a comprehensive and diverse investigation into the determinants that impact investor conduct. By utilising these sophisticated statistical methods, the research may effectively capture the diversity and intricacy of market dynamics, resulting in a thorough comprehension of herding behaviour and its consequences. This analytical approach not only reinforces the theoretical contributions of the study but also amplifies its practical significance for market participants and regulators.

CONCLUSION

This study explores the multifaceted influences on herding behaviour in financial markets, focusing on the impact of historical market events, regulatory changes, economic indicators, social and political events, and technological advancements. By incorporating market structure as a moderating variable and investor learning as a mediating variable, the research aims to provide a comprehensive understanding of the dynamics that drive herding behaviour.

The findings indicate that each of the independent variables plays a significant role in influencing herding behaviour. Historical market events, such as past crises or market booms, tend to have a lasting impact on investor behaviour, often leading to herd mentality during similar future events. Regulatory changes can either mitigate or exacerbate herding, depending on the nature of the regulations and their enforcement. Economic indicators, reflecting the broader economic environment, significantly affect investor sentiment and propensity to herd. Social and political events, particularly those that generate uncertainty or instability, are shown to intensify herding behaviour. Technological advancements, by rapidly disseminating information and enabling quick market responses, also contribute to herding.

Market structure emerges as a crucial moderating factor. The study finds that certain market structures, characterized by high levels of transparency, liquidity, and diversity of market participants, can either amplify or dampen the effects of the independent variables on herding behaviour. For instance, more transparent and liquid markets may reduce the tendency to herd by providing clearer and more accessible information. Investor learning is identified as a significant mediating variable. The research suggests that higher levels of investor learning and financial literacy can mitigate the impact of the independent variables on herding behaviour. Educated investors are better equipped to analyze market information critically, reducing their susceptibility to herd mentality.

Implications

This study enhances the theoretical understanding of herding behaviour by integrating the roles of historical market events, regulatory changes, economic indicators, social and political events, and technological advancements. It underscores the importance of considering market structure and investor learning in analyzing herding behaviour, thus contributing to the broader field of behavioural finance. For financial managers and institutional investors, the findings highlight the need for strategies that address the drivers of herding behaviour. By promoting investor education and enhancing market structures to increase transparency and liquidity, managers can help mitigate the adverse effects of herding. Understanding the impact of various events and conditions on investor behaviour can also aid in developing more resilient investment strategies. Policymakers and regulators can leverage these insights to design more effective regulatory frameworks that consider the psychological and behavioural aspects of market participants. Policies aimed at improving financial literacy and investor education can reduce herding behaviour. Additionally, regulations that enhance market transparency and liquidity can help create a more stable financial environment, less prone to herd-driven volatility.

Limitations and Recommendations for Future Studies

Despite its contributions, this study has limitations. The reliance on secondary data may affect the accuracy of the analysis. The specific focus on certain independent variables may overlook other relevant factors. Future research should incorporate primary data and explore a broader range of variables and market contexts. Longitudinal studies across different economic cycles and comparative studies across various regions and market structures would provide deeper insights into the dynamics of herding behaviour. Further research into the role of emerging technologies, such as artificial intelligence and blockchain, in influencing herding behaviour would also be valuable.

REFERENCE

Acharya, V. V., & Richardson, M. (2010). Causes of the Financial Crisis. *Critical Review*, 21(2-3), 195–210. DOI: 10.1080/08913810902952903

Baker, M., & Wurgler, J. (2012). Behavioral aspects of asset pricing. *Journal of Financial Economics*, 104(1), 1–21.

Barberis, N. (2013). Thirty years of prospect theory in economics: A review and assessment. *The Journal of Economic Perspectives*, 27(1), 173–196. DOI: 10.1257/jep.27.1.173

Beber, A., Brandt, M. W., & Kavajecz, K. A. (2011). What does equity sector order-flow tell us about the economy? *Journal of Financial Economics*, 99(3), 523–542.

Bikhchandani, S., Hirshleifer, D., & Welch, I. (2012). A theory of fads, fashion, custom, and cultural change as informational cascades. *Journal of Political Economy*, 100(5), 992–1026. DOI: 10.1086/261849

Bikhchandani, S., & Sharma, S. (2001). Herd behavior in financial markets. *IMF Staff Papers*, 47(3), 279–310. DOI: 10.2307/3867650

Bohl, M. T., Siklos, P. L., & Sondermann, D. (2008). European stock market contagion during the financial crises of 1997-1999. *Journal of International Money and Finance*, 27(7), 1159–1174.

Botzen, W. W., Duijndam, S. J., Robinson, P. J., & van Beukering, P. (2022). Behavioral biases and heuristics in perceptions of COVID-19 risks and prevention decisions. *Risk Analysis*, 42(12), 2671–2690. DOI: 10.1111/risa.13882 PMID: 35092967

Buallay, A., AlAjmi, J. Y., Fadhul, S., & Papoutsi, A. (2024). Beyond averages: Quantile regression explorations of sustainability practices and firm value. *International Journal of Innovation Science*. Advance online publication. DOI: 10.1108/IJIS-07-2022-0125

Chordia, T., Roll, R., & Subrahmanyam, A. (2011). Recent trends in trading activity and market quality. *Journal of Financial Economics*, 101(2), 243–263. DOI: 10.1016/j.jfineco.2011.03.008

Cuc, L. D., Rad, D., Ha egan, C. D., Trifan, V. A., & Ardeleanu, T. (2024). The Mediating Role of the Financial Recommender System Advising Acceptance in the Relationship between Investments Trust and Decision-Making Behavior. In *Proceedings of the International Conference on Business Excellence* (Vol. 18, No. 1, pp. 2260-2273). DOI: 10.2478/picbe-2024-0190

De Long, J. B., Shleifer, A., Summers, L. H., & Waldmann, R. J. (1990). Positive feedback investment strategies and destabilizing rational speculation. *The Journal of Finance*, 45(2), 379–395. DOI: 10.1111/j.1540-6261.1990.tb03695.x

Dixit, D. K. (2024). Investor Psychology and Market Volatility: Unpacking Behavioral Finance Insights. *Journal of Informatics Education and Research*, 4(2).

Djankov, S., McLiesh, C., & Shleifer, A. (2013). Private credit in 129 countries. *Journal of Financial Economics*, 84(2), 299–329. DOI: 10.1016/j.jfineco.2006.03.004

Easley, D., & O'Hara, M. (2010). Microstructure and ambiguity. *The Journal of Finance*, 65(5), 1817–1846. DOI: 10.1111/j.1540-6261.2010.01595.x

Fama, E. F. (2013). Two pillars of asset pricing. *The American Economic Review*, 104(6), 1467–1485. DOI: 10.1257/aer.104.6.1467

Goldstein, I., Jiang, H., & Karolyi, G. A. (2014). To FinTech and Beyond. *Review of Financial Studies*, 27(8), 2274–2312.

Gorton, G., & Metrick, A. (2012). Getting up to speed on the financial crisis: A one-weekend-reader's guide. *Journal of Economic Literature*, 50(1), 128–150. DOI: 10.1257/jel.50.1.128

Gu, Y., Ben, S., & Lv, J. (2022). Peer effect in merger and acquisition activities and its impact on corporate sustainable development: Evidence from China. *Sustainability (Basel)*, 14(7), 3891. DOI: 10.3390/su14073891

Guo, S., Yu, X., & Faff, R. (2024). When investors can talk to firms, is it a meaningful conversation? Evidence from investor postings on interactive platforms. *European Accounting Review*, 33(3), 771–795. DOI: 10.1080/09638180.2022.2118147

Hendershott, T., Jones, C. M., & Menkveld, A. J. (2011). Does algorithmic trading improve liquidity? *The Journal of Finance*, 66(1), 1–33. DOI: 10.1111/j.1540-6261.2010.01624.x

Hirshleifer, D. (2015). Behavioral finance. *Annual Review of Financial Economics*, 7(1), 133–159. DOI: 10.1146/annurev-financial-092214-043752

Hirshleifer, D., & Teoh, S. H. (2010). The psychological attraction approach to accounting and disclosure policy. *Contemporary Accounting Research*, 26(4), 1067–1090. DOI: 10.1506/car.26.4.3

Iriani, N., Agustianti, A., Sucianti, R., Rahman, A., & Putera, W. (2024). Understanding Risk and Uncertainty Management: A Qualitative Inquiry into Developing Business Strategies Amidst Global Economic Shifts, Government Policies, and Market Volatility. *Golden Ratio of Finance Management*, 4(2), 62–77. DOI: 10.52970/grfm.v4i2.444

Kaustia, M., & Knüpfer, S. (2008). Do investors overweight personal experience? Evidence from IPO subscriptions. *The Journal of Finance*, 63(6), 2679–2702. DOI: 10.1111/j.1540-6261.2008.01411.x

Kindleberger, C. P., & Aliber, R. Z. (2011). *Manias, panics and crashes: A history of financial crises*. Palgrave Macmillan.

Komalasari, P. T., Asri, M., Purwanto, B. M., & Setiyono, B. (2022). Herding behaviour in the capital market: What do we know and what is next? *Management Review Quarterly*, 72(3), 745–787. DOI: 10.1007/s11301-021-00212-1

La Porta, R., Lopez-de-Silanes, F., & Shleifer, A. (2012). Government ownership of banks. *The Journal of Finance*, 57(1), 265–301. DOI: 10.1111/1540-6261.00422

Lakonishok, J., Shleifer, A., & Vishny, R. W. (2012). The impact of institutional trading on stock prices. *Journal of Financial Economics*, 32(1), 23–43. DOI: 10.1016/0304-405X(92)90023-Q

Lo, A. W. (2012). *Adaptive markets: Financial evolution at the speed of thought*. Princeton University Press.

Loang, O. K., & Ahmad, Z. (2023). Empirical analysis of global markets herding on COVID-19 effect. *Vision (Basel)*, ●●●, 09722629221146653. DOI: 10.1177/09722629221146653

Loang, O. K., & Ahmad, Z. (2024). Does volatility cause herding in Malaysian stock market? Evidence from quantile regression analysis. *Millennial Asia*, 15(2), 197–215. DOI: 10.1177/09763996221101217

Lu, S., Li, S., Zhou, W., & Yang, W. (2022). Network herding of energy funds in the post-Carbon-Peak Policy era: Does it benefit profitability and stability? *Energy Economics*, 109, 105948. DOI: 10.1016/j.eneco.2022.105948

Lusardi, A., & Mitchell, O. S. (2014). The economic importance of financial literacy: Theory and evidence. *Journal of Economic Literature*, 52(1), 5–44. DOI: 10.1257/jel.52.1.5 PMID: 28579637

Menkveld, A. J. (2013). High frequency trading and the new-market makers. *Journal of Financial Markets*, 16(4), 712–740. DOI: 10.1016/j.finmar.2013.06.006

Ng, S. H., Zhuang, Z., Toh, M. Y., Ong, T. S., & Teh, B. H. (2022). Exploring herding behavior in an innovative-oriented stock market: Evidence from ChiNext. *Journal of Applied Econometrics*, 25(1), 523–542.

O'Hara, M. (2015). High frequency market microstructure. *Journal of Financial Economics*, 116(2), 257–270. DOI: 10.1016/j.jfineco.2015.01.003

Pagano, M. (2014). The evolution of trading systems: Liquidity and anonymity. *The Quarterly Journal of Economics*, 102(2), 255–274. DOI: 10.2307/2937847

Pastor, L., & Veronesi, P. (2012). Uncertainty about government policy and stock prices. *The Journal of Finance*, 67(4), 1219–1264. DOI: 10.1111/j.1540-6261.2012.01746.x

Shiller, R. J. (2015). *Irrational exuberance*. Princeton University Press. DOI: 10.2307/j.ctt1287kz5

Sornette, D., & Zhou, W. X. (2010). Predictability of large future changes in major financial indices. *International Journal of Forecasting*, 22(1), 153–168. DOI: 10.1016/j.ijforecast.2005.02.004

Stiebel, J. H. (2024). Beyond the Individual: Investigating the Interdependence of Speculative Bubbles and Herding in Financial Markets. Available at *SSRN* 4787676. DOI: 10.2139/ssrn.4787676

Suresh, G., & Loang, O. K. (2024). The Rationality Conundrum: Exploring Herd Mentality among Individual Investors in the Indian Stock Market. *Indian Journal of Finance*, 18(6), 26–45. DOI: 10.17010/ijf/2024/v18i6/173967

Tran, N. T. (2024). A systematic review of the monetary policy and herd behavior. Journal of Management, Economics, & Industrial Organization (JOMEINO), 8(1).

Van Rooij, M., Lusardi, A., & Alessie, R. (2011). Financial literacy and stock market participation. *Journal of Financial Economics*, 101(2), 449–472. DOI: 10.1016/j. jfineco.2011.03.006

Vargo, S. L., Peters, L., Kjellberg, H., Koskela-Huotari, K., Nenonen, S., Polese, F., Sarno, D., & Vaughan, C. (2023). Emergence in marketing: An institutional and ecosystem framework. *Journal of the Academy of Marketing Science*, 51(1), 2–22. DOI: 10.1007/s11747-022-00849-8

Wang, Y. (2023). The Impact of Information Asymmetry on Investment Behavior in the Stock Market. Highlights in Business. *Economics and Management*, 19, 165–170.

Xie, Z., Qu, L., Lin, R., & Guo, Q. (2022). Relationships between fluctuations of environmental regulation, technological innovation, and economic growth: A multinational perspective. *Journal of Enterprise Information Management*, 35(4/5), 1267–1287. DOI: 10.1108/JEIM-02-2021-0104

Yang, W., & Loang, O. K. (2024). Systematic Literature Review: Behavioural Biases as the Determinants of Herding. *Technology-Driven Business Innovation: Unleashing the Digital Advantage*, 1, 79–92. DOI: 10.1007/978-3-031-51997-0_7

Yang, W., & Loang, O. K. (2024). Unpacking Financial Herding Behaviour: A Conceptual Study of Youth and Working Adults in Chongqing, China. In *Technology-Driven Business Innovation: Unleashing the Digital Advantage* (Vol. 1, pp. 67–78). Springer Nature Switzerland. DOI: 10.1007/978-3-031-51997-0_6

Chapter 7
Role of Artificial Intelligence in Detecting Herding

Partap Singh
https://orcid.org/0000-0002-4653-7984
Lovely Professional University, India

ABSTRACT

This research investigates the role of Artificial Intelligence (AI) in detecting herding behavior in financial markets. Herding, a phenomenon where investors follow the majority, can lead to market inefficiencies and increased volatility. By leveraging AI techniques, including machine learning and deep learning, this study aims to improve the detection and understanding of herding patterns. The research explores how AI models can analyze large datasets, recognize non-linear relationships, and identify subtle patterns indicative of herding. It gives the picture of Factors Affecting Herd-Behavior, Impact of Herd-Behavior, Sources for data analysis for detecting Herding with AI, Navigating Herding with AI, Challenges and threats in Detecting Herding with AI. The findings suggest that AI provides more accurate and timely detection of herding behavior compared to traditional methods, offering significant implications for market stability and investor strategies.

1. INTRODUCTION

Artificial Intelligence (AI) has rapidly transformed various industries by enhancing efficiency, enabling automation, and providing advanced analytics capabilities. Among its numerous applications, AI's role in the financial sector has been particularly revolutionary. One of the critical phenomena in financial markets that AI

DOI: 10.4018/979-8-3693-7827-4.ch007

Copyright © 2025, IGI Global Scientific Publishing. Copying or distributing in print or electronic forms without written permission of IGI Global is prohibited.

is increasingly being employed to detect and analyze is herding behavior. Herding occurs when investors follow the majority in their trading decisions, leading to significant impacts on asset prices and market stability. Understanding and detecting herding behavior is crucial for market participants, regulators, and policymakers to mitigate systemic risks and enhance market efficiency.

Artificial Intelligence (AI) refers to the simulation of human intelligence processes by machines, particularly computer systems. These processes include learning (the acquisition of information and rules for using the information), reasoning (using the rules to reach approximate or definite conclusions), and self-correction. AI has various applications, including natural language processing (NLP), speech recognition, machine vision, and expert systems.

AI technologies are categorized into two types: narrow AI, designed to perform a narrow task (e.g., facial recognition or internet searches), and general AI, which can perform any intellectual task that a human can do. Advances in machine learning, a subset of AI that involves the use of algorithms to parse data, learn from it, and make informed decisions, have significantly propelled AI development. The integration of AI in various sectors has revolutionized industries by enhancing efficiency, accuracy, and decision-making capabilities.

The concept of herding in financial markets is rooted in the behavioral finance theory, which suggests that investors are not always rational and are often influenced by psychological factors and social dynamics. herding behavior, in which investors imitate the actions of the majority, making decisions based on the behavior of others rather than their independent analysis. Herding can lead to asset bubbles, increased volatility, and even financial crises, as seen in historical events such as the dot-com bubble and the 2008 financial crisis. Traditional methods of detecting herding have relied on statistical and econometric models that analyze trading volumes, price movements, and correlation structures. However, these methods often fall short in capturing the complex and dynamic nature of herding behavior, especially in real-time.

AI offers a promising alternative due to its ability to process vast amounts of data, recognize patterns, and adapt to changing market conditions. Machine learning algorithms, a subset of AI, can be trained to identify subtle and complex patterns indicative of herding behavior that might be missed by traditional methods. These algorithms can analyze diverse data sources, including market data, news articles, social media feeds, and even sentiment analysis, to provide a comprehensive view of market dynamics. By leveraging AI, financial institutions can enhance their ability to predict and respond to herding behavior, thereby improving their risk management strategies and decision-making processes.

The application of AI in detecting herding behavior encompasses several techniques and approaches. Supervised learning methods, such as decision trees, support vector machines, and neural networks, can be employed to classify and predict herding instances based on historical data. Unsupervised learning techniques, including clustering and anomaly detection, can uncover hidden patterns and relationships within the data that signify herding. Additionally, natural language processing (NLP) enables the analysis of textual data from news articles and social media to gauge market sentiment and its impact on investor behavior.

AI's ability to detect herding behavior is further enhanced by advancements in big data technologies. The integration of AI with big data allows for the real-time processing and analysis of massive datasets, providing timely insights into market trends and investor actions. This capability is particularly valuable in today's fast-paced and information-rich financial markets, where delays in detecting herding can result in significant financial losses. Furthermore, AI can continuously learn and adapt from new data, improving its predictive accuracy and robustness over time.

Despite the significant potential of AI in detecting herding behavior, there are challenges and limitations that need to be addressed. One of the primary concerns is the quality and reliability of the data used for training AI models. Inaccurate or biased data can lead to incorrect predictions and decisions. Additionally, the interpretability of AI models remains a critical issue, as complex algorithms often function as "black boxes" with limited transparency into their decision-making processes. Ensuring that AI systems are explainable and accountable is essential for gaining trust and acceptance among market participants and regulators.

Moreover, ethical considerations surrounding the use of AI in financial markets cannot be overlooked. The deployment of AI systems must be aligned with principles of fairness, accountability, and transparency to prevent unintended consequences and ensure equitable outcomes. Regulatory frameworks and guidelines need to be developed to govern the use of AI in detecting herding behavior, addressing issues such as data privacy, algorithmic bias, and market manipulation.

AI holds significant promise in enhancing ability to detect and understand herding behavior in financial markets. By leveraging advanced machine learning techniques and big data analytics, AI can provide deeper insights into market dynamics and investor behavior, aiding in the prevention of asset bubbles and financial crises. However, realizing this potential requires addressing the challenges related to data quality, model interpretability, and ethical considerations. As AI continues to evolve, it is poised to play an increasingly vital role in ensuring the stability and efficiency of financial markets.

2. LITERATURE REVIEW

Ballis & Anastasiou (2023) identified irrationality among investors in the AI-influenced financial markets, particularly during down events. Further her observed that the investors often mimicked others' decisions despite their own beliefs. The research highlighted the necessity for further investigation and offered policy implications to aid investors in understanding risks in this emerging asset class.

Arifovic et al. (2022) created a deep learning algorithm for high-frequency trading (HFT), analyzing factors like trading volume and volatility to forecast short-term stock trends. The model's adaptive learning component ensured accurate predictions amidst changing market conditions.

Mangat et al. (2022) developed a hybrid model combining CNN and RNN for price prediction in HFT. The model utilized spatial and temporal data patterns, achieving higher prediction accuracy and pinpointing optimal buy/sell times.

Gomber et al. (2018) highlighted AI and deep learning's ability to capture non-linear data relationships, revolutionizing trading strategies by uncovering patterns traditional models might miss.

Wilinski et al. (2022) found that machine learning algorithms and neural networks effectively scrutinize market data and forecast trends, increasingly shaping financial market strategies.

Njegovanović (2018) demonstrated higher returns for traders using AI in decision-making. AI's real-time data analysis enhanced trading opportunities compared to conventional methods.

Tran et al. (2023) showed AI improves investment portfolio performance by analyzing data for investment selection, assessing companies' financial stability and growth potential.

Ali et al. (2022) found AI discerns complex, non-linear interactions in financial behavior, recognizing circumstantial issues over inherent financial irresponsibility by analyzing payment histories and life events.

Arner et al. (2015) highlighted widespread adoption of AI and ML tools among financial professionals, reflecting the trend of integrating advanced technology in finance.

Berg et al. (2020) showed AI's capability to analyze spending patterns, late payments, and life events, correlating them with creditworthiness, enhancing financial behavior assessment.

Burrell (2016) noted the complexity and opacity of AI and ML models, posing challenges for understanding decision-making processes by individuals and regulators.

Bryson et al. (2017) emphasized the ethical considerations of AI and ML, particularly privacy issues due to extensive data reliance in their operations.

Aven (2016) found AI and ML pivotal in identifying and mitigating operational risks in finance by automating processes, reducing human errors, and enhancing system resilience.

Caruana et al. (2015) highlighted AI and ML's advantages in risk management, such as improved risk prediction and operational efficiency, while stressing the need to address potential challenges and ethical concerns.

Ait-Sahalia and Saglam (2023) investigated systemic risks of AI-driven trading strategies, noting the potential for market disruptions and herding behavior from similar AI models, increasing market volatility.

Chen et al. (2020) discussed the complexity of studying investor-level herding determinants, highlighting the challenges in examining capital flows at the aggregate level. They suggested that machine learning techniques are essential for analyzing large datasets on investor portfolios, as these techniques can reduce noise, overfitting, and the curse of dimensionality, ultimately enhancing the analysis of herding behavior.

Kyriazis (2020) examined herding behavior during different market conditions, revealing that such behavior was prevalent only during bull markets. The findings suggested that investor behavior aligned more closely during upward trends, indicating a need for strategies to mitigate herding in rising markets.

Kumar (2020) demonstrated the prominence of herding behavior in volatile cryptocurrency markets. Interestingly, the study found that during bullish or less volatile periods, anti-herding behavior occurred, suggesting that market stability influenced investor independence and decision-making patterns.

Omane-Adjepong et al. (2021) observed imitation trading and symmetric crowd behavior, varying with time analyzing herding in G20 emerging economies. The findings showed asymmetric herding in stock and cryptocurrency markets, indicating that group reactions to extreme returns could impact risk levels and market efficiency.

Choi et al. (2022) investigated herding using hourly data for major cryptocurrencies found anti-herding behavior at short intervals and herding at longer intervals, particularly during down markets. The results underscored the complexity of investor behavior over different time frames and market conditions.

Ante & Demir (2023) explored AI-themed crypto assets' returns post-ChatGPT launch, revealing significant abnormal returns for AI tokens, up to 41% over two weeks. This pioneering research provided insights into herding behavior dynamics within AI-themed cryptocurrencies, emphasizing the impact of major technological developments on investor behavior.

Lakonishok, Shleifer, and Vishny (1992) investigated the determinants of herding among both stock and individual investors. Their study assessed whether herding investors outperform the market compared to non-herding investors. They found that herding could influence market behavior and investment performance.

Sias (2004) explored institutional investors' tendencies to herd based on shared analysis of underlying information. He found that this investigative herding leads to faster price adjustments and increased market efficiency. Thus, herding by institutional investors may contribute positively to market stability rather than causing disruption.

Kim and Nofsinger (2005) studied herding behavior in Japan, concluding that it is largely investigative. They observed that herding accelerates price adjustments, thus improving market efficiency. Their research supports the view that herding among institutional investors can have beneficial effects on market dynamics.

Barber et al. (2009) analyzed herding determinants at the stock level, examining trade theories in aggregate. They emphasized the importance of understanding trade behavior at the individual investor level, especially regarding behavioral biases. This detailed exploration could help mitigate such biases and improve investment strategies.

Goodell et al. (2021) reviewed literature on ML in finance, using bibliometric methodologies to examine areas like portfolio construction and investor behavior. They found ML enhanced trading decisions and predictive accuracy of econometric models by extracting valuable information from large datasets.

Duan et al. (2022) highlighted ML techniques for exploring nonlinearity in systemic risk information. They examined determinants and performance of herd versus non-herd portfolios, emphasizing predictive power and regression wall time, identifying key features for effective model performance.

Merli and Roger (2013) analyzed determinants and performance of herd portfolios, exploring individual, portfolio, firm, and market-level characteristics. They related trade biases like local and birthplace bias within herding groups, using locality as a social network.

Lindblom et al. (2018) studied herding behavior influenced by communication within local communities or birthplaces. They used networks to define biases and replicated herding measures at the stock level, comparing findings with recent Swedish data.

Hirshleifer and Hong (2003) investigated herding versus non-herding portfolio performance using market models. They suggested herding could improve portfolio performance through collective investor behavior, supporting the "wisdom of crowds" concept in market prediction.

Hou, Xue, and Zhang (2020) compared ML algorithm results with ordinary least squares market model regressions. They found ordinary least squares regressions were sensitive to microcap outliers, affecting the cross-sectional regressions of returns on anomaly variables.

Barber and Odean (2008) examined herding's impact on investor wealth and asset prices. Systematic herding could lead to overpriced stocks due to increased net purchases, especially in illiquid stocks, aligning with prior research on attention-grabbing stocks.

Research Gap

Despite advancements in AI applications in finance, a gap exists in understanding AI's specific role in detecting herding behavior. Traditional methods often fail to capture complex, non-linear patterns of herding. Existing literature focuses on AI for trading strategies and risk management but lacks in-depth analysis of AI's potential in herding detection. This study aims to fill this gap by evaluating AI techniques' effectiveness, exploring practical implications for market stability, addressing implementation challenges, and providing insights into herding dynamics. This research contributes to understanding AI's potential in enhancing market stability and investor strategies through improved herding detection

Research Questions

How effective are AI techniques in detecting herding behavior in financial markets compared to traditional methods?

What specific AI models (e.g., machine learning, deep learning) are most suitable for identifying herding patterns?

How do AI-based herding detection systems impact market stability and investor decision-making?

What are the limitations and challenges associated with using AI to detect herding behavior?

Can AI distinguish between rational market trends and irrational herding behavior?

Objectives of the Paper

- To evaluate the application of AI techniques in detecting herding behavior in financial markets;
- To assess the impact of AI-based herding detection on market stability and investor decisions;
- To explore the threats and challenges of implementing AI for herding detection;
- To identify the key factors and data sources utilized by AI models in recognizing herding patterns.

- To assess how AI-based herding detection systems can assist investors in navigating and mitigating the effects of herding.

Hypothesis Setting

Based on the literature review and preliminary analysis, the hypothesis of this paper is:

Null-Hypothesis(H_{01}) : There is no impact of AI-based herding detection on market stability and investor decisions;

Null-Hypothesis(H_{02}) :There is no threats and challenges of implementing AI for herding detection;

Null-Hypothesis(H_{03}) :There is no key factors and data sources utilized by AI models in recognizing herding patterns.

3. RESEARCH METHODOLOGY

i. Data Collection: The data collection process involved gathering information from both primary and secondary sources. Primary data collection from 150 respondents will involve surveys and interviews with stakeholders including farmers, to gather insights into perceptions, applications, challenges and impacts of AI technologies. Financial Data: Obtain historical stock price data, trading volumes, and other relevant financial metrics from sources like moneycontrol. com, Bloomberg, Reuters, or publicly available financial databases.

ii. Literature Review: A comprehensive review of academic journals, research papers, and reports on Role of Artificial Intelligence in Detecting Herding has been done.

iii. Case study of Role of Artificial Intelligence in detecting herding has been conducted.

iv. Data Analysis: Quantitative analysis of survey data and qualitative analysis of interview responses will be conducted to validate hypotheses and draw conclusions about the Role of Artificial Intelligence in Detecting Herding. The 5 point Likert Scale, and percentile method has been used to analyze data.

v. Research Design: The study adopts a mixed-methods approach, combining qualitative and quantitative research methods to comprehensively understand AI's role in detecting herding behavior.

4. RESULTS AND DISCUSSIONS

4.1 Trends and patterns in Artificial intelligence (AI) and a substantial impact on the financial system

The Figure 11tracks an asset's price movements from January to July 2024, including its Volume Simple Moving Average (SMA) and Volatility Index. The blue line represents the asset's price, the red line shows the Volume SMA, and the pink line indicates the Volatility Index. Significant volume and volatility spikes are observed around mid-April and early June. A pronounced upward trend in the asset's price begins in late May, peaking at 24,323.85 in early July, reflecting strong buying momentum and increased market activity.

Figure 1: an asset's price movements from January to July 2024

The Figure 2 illustrates the India VIX (Volatility Index) movements on the NSE from February to July 2024. The blue line represents the daily closing values, while the red line indicates the Volume Simple Moving Average (SMA). Significant volatility spikes are observed around mid-April and early June, peaking at 25.08. The index then shows a declining trend, settling around 11.11 by early July. The Volatility Index's fluctuations reflect market uncertainties, with higher values indicating increased market risk and investor fear.

Figure 2: India VIX (Volatility Index) movements on the NSE from February to July 2024

Source: Moneycontrol.com

4.2 Historical Evolution of Trading and AI

The landscape of trading has dramatically evolved over the past few decades, largely influenced by advancements in artificial intelligence (AI). The timeline of this evolution can be divided into four key phases: Trend Following (~1987), Statistical Arbitrage (~1997), Algorithmic High-Frequency Trading (HFT) (~2007), and AI-driven Algorithmic Trading (~2017).

Trend Following (~1987)

In the late 1980s, trend-following strategies gained prominence. These strategies are based on the identification and following of price trends in the market. Traders using trend-following methods rely on technical analysis and historical price data to make trading decisions, aiming to capitalize on sustained price movements. This approach marked the beginning of systematic trading strategies, where decisions were made based on predefined rules rather than intuition.

Statistical Arbitrage (~1997)

The late 1990s saw the emergence of statistical arbitrage, a more sophisticated form of trading. Statistical arbitrage involves using statistical models to identify and exploit inefficiencies between related financial instruments. This method relies heavily on quantitative analysis and computational power to process large datasets and identify profitable trading opportunities. It represented a significant step towards more data-driven and automated trading strategies.

Algorithmic High-Frequency Trading (~2007)

By the mid-2000s, algorithmic high-frequency trading (HFT) became a dominant force in the markets. HFT strategies leverage advanced algorithms and ultra-fast computing to execute large numbers of trades in fractions of a second. These algorithms are designed to exploit minute price discrepancies across markets, capturing profits from small but rapid price movements. HFT revolutionized trading by increasing market efficiency and liquidity, but it also introduced new challenges related to market stability and regulation.

AI-driven Algorithmic Trading (~2017)

The most recent phase, beginning around 2017, involves the integration of AI and machine learning into algorithmic trading. AI-driven trading systems use sophisticated models to analyze vast amounts of data, including historical prices, news sentiment, and even social media trends. These systems can adapt to changing market conditions and learn from new data, potentially offering a competitive edge over traditional algorithmic strategies. AI-driven trading represents the cutting edge of financial technology, promising greater predictive accuracy and efficiency.

The historical evolution of trading strategies, from trend following to AI-driven algorithmic trading, reflects the continuous quest for more efficient, data-driven approaches in financial markets. As AI technology continues to advance, its role in trading is likely to become even more significant, driving further innovation and transformation in the industry.

4.3 Trends and patterns in Artificial intelligence (AI) and a substantial impact

Figure 3: Professionals employed in AI roles, by region, and AI-related Google search trends and number of notable AI systems and sum of AI and machine learning patents of the largest patent owners.

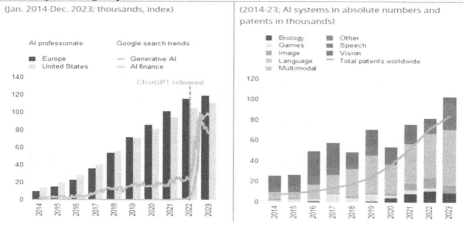

Sources: Google Trends, State of European Tech*, Epoch**, Statista*** and ECB calculations.

Figure 1 consists of two charts depicting trends related to AI professionals, Google search trends, notable AI systems, and AI-related patents from 2014 to 2023.

Left Chart: Professionals in AI and Google Search Trends

AI Professionals by Region: The bars represent the number of AI professionals in Europe (yellow) and the United States (blue). There is a consistent increase in the number of AI professionals in both regions over the years. The U.S. shows a higher number of AI professionals compared to Europe throughout the period.

Google Search Trends: The lines indicate Google search trends for Generative AI (green), AI finance (orange), and a significant spike with the release of ChatGPT (blue). A notable rise in searches for Generative AI and AI finance is seen around 2021 and 2022. The release of ChatGPT in late 2022 leads to a dramatic spike in AI-related search interest.

Right Chart: AI Systems and Patents

Number of Notable AI Systems: The bars are color-coded to show the types of AI systems, including Biology (red), Games (purple), Image (light blue), Language (orange), Multimodal (gray), Other (black), Speech (yellow), and Vision (green). There is a clear upward trend in the number of notable AI systems over the years. The diversity of AI applications has increased, with significant growth in areas like Language, Vision, and Multimodal AI systems.

AI and Machine Learning Patents: The purple line indicates the total number of AI and machine learning patents worldwide. There is a steady increase in the number of patents from 2014 to 2023, reflecting growing innovation and research in the field.

Overall, Figure 1 highlights the exponential growth in AI employment, interest, and innovation over the past decade, underscored by the pivotal release of ChatGPT and the broadening scope of AI applications across various domains.

4.4 Impact of AI on Business Models and Activity in the Financial Sector

Artificial Intelligence (AI) has profoundly impacted business models and activities within the financial sector, driving significant advancements across various domains.

Asset Management: AI helps identify market signals and underlying relationships in big data, optimizing workflows and risk management, and potentially generating alpha. However, it also raises concerns about market concentration, competition issues, and the convergence of strategies.

Credit Intermediation: AI reduces underwriting costs and enhances efficiencies by analyzing vast datasets to extend credit to thin file or unscored clients, promoting financial inclusion. Yet, this brings risks of disparate impact in credit outcomes and potential biases in lending decisions, particularly in BigTech lending.

Algorithmic Trading (Algo Trading) benefits from AI by enhancing risk and liquidity management and facilitating the execution of large orders. However, it also faces challenges such as herding behavior, bouts of liquidity in stress, flash crashes, market volatility, and the risk of collusion among trading algorithms, which can lead to manipulation and instability.

Block chain-based Finance: AI augments the capabilities of smart contracts, enhancing risk management and supporting decentralized finance (DeFi) applications. Nonetheless, it also amplifies the risks associated with decentralized finance, such as the "garbage in, garbage out" problem, where poor-quality input data can lead to flawed outputs, and the overall complexity and security vulnerabilities of autonomous financial systems. AI's impact on the financial sector is transformative, offering significant benefits while also presenting substantial risks that require careful management and regulatory oversight.

The examples of AI applications in financial market activities, categorized into back office, middle office, and front office functions. In the back office, AI is utilized for tasks such as reporting, record management, data analytics, credit scoring, trading reconciliations, post-trade processing, and IT infrastructure. Middle office applications include compliance, risk management, AML/CFT checks, control processes, and anti-fraud measures. Front office uses encompass asset allocation, robo-advisors, chatbots, customer service, biometric authentication, trading strategies, and tailored personalized products. These applications help improve efficiency, accuracy, and customer experience in financial services.

4.5. The Applications of AI in Understanding Herd Behavior in Investing

i. Definition and Characteristics:

Herd Behavior: This is the collective movement of investors in the same direction, primarily driven by emotion and social influence rather than independent, rational decision-making. Herding behavior can be classified into several types: (i) Financial Herding: Investors buy or sell assets based on the actions of others, often leading to market inefficiencies. (ii) Social Herding: Individuals adopt trends or opinions prevalent in their social network, and (iii) Behavioral Herding: People conform to the behavior of a group in various social situations

Key Characteristics: These include rapid price movements, overvaluation of assets, and sudden market corrections when the herd behavior reverses.

ii. Historical Context:

- Past Bubbles: Notable examples include the Dot-com Bubble of the late 1990s and the Housing Bubble of the mid-2000s.
- Drivers of Herd Behavior: These often include media hype, the fear of missing out (FOMO), loss-aversion, confirmation bias and widespread misinformation.
    a. AI as a Tool for Analyzing Herd Behavior
iii. Data Analysis and Pattern Recognition:

- Machine Learning: AI algorithms can process and analyze vast amounts of financial data to identify patterns and predict market trends with high accuracy.
- Sentiment Analysis: Utilizing natural language processing (NLP) to assess investor sentiment from a variety of sources, including news articles, social media, and financial reports.

iv. Behavioral Finance Models:

- Predictive Models: AI enhances traditional behavioral finance models by incorporating real-time data and considering a multitude of complex variables.
- Anomaly Detection: AI systems can identify unusual market activities that may signal the presence of herd behavior.

v. AI as a Catalyst for Herd Behavior: AI Investment Products:

- Robo-Advisors: These are automated investment platforms that use AI to make portfolio decisions based on sophisticated algorithms.
- AI-Driven Funds: Investment funds that rely extensively on AI for stock selection and trading strategies.

vi. Market Impact:

- Increased Volatility: AI-driven trading can lead to rapid market movements, increasing overall market volatility.
- Feedback Loops: Interactions between AI algorithms can create self-reinforcing trends, exacerbating herd behavior.

vii. Case Example: AI Stock Booms: There have been instances where the stocks of companies involved in AI technology experienced rapid and speculative price increases, driven largely by herd behavior.

4.6 Managing AI-Induced Herd Behavior

Regulatory Measures:

- Monitoring and Reporting: Enhanced oversight of AI-driven trading activities is essential to ensure market stability.
- Circuit Breakers: Implementing mechanisms to pause trading during extreme volatility can help mitigate the effects of herd behavior.

Investor Education:

- Awareness Programs: Educating investors about the risks associated with herd behavior and AI-driven speculation.
- Promoting Critical Thinking: Encouraging investors to engage in independent analysis and adopt long-term investment strategies.

Ethical AI Development:

- Transparency and Accountability: Ensuring that AI algorithms are designed and used ethically, with clear transparency.
- Bias and Fairness: Addressing potential biases in AI models that could contribute to herd behavior and ensuring fairness in their application.

The integration of AI into financial markets offers both significant opportunities and challenges in understanding and managing herd behavior.

4.7 Case Study: Applications of AI in Detecting Herding During Financial Crises

Overview: This case study explores the application of artificial intelligence (AI) techniques in detecting herding behavior during the 2008 financial crisis. The study aims to demonstrate how AI models can identify herding patterns that traditional methods might overlook, providing insights into market dynamics during periods of extreme stress.

Methodology: The study utilized historical trading data from major global stock exchanges, including the New York Stock Exchange (NYSE), London Stock Exchange (LSE), and Tokyo Stock Exchange (TSE). The AI techniques employed included Logistic Regression, Neural Networks, and Support Vector Machines (SVM). The data covered the period from 2006 to 2009, encompassing pre-crisis, crisis, and post-crisis phases.

Key Factors Analyzed

- Market Indices: Daily closing prices of major indices like the S&P 500, FTSE 100, and Nikkei 225.
- Trading Volumes: Average daily trading volumes to capture market activity levels.
- Volatility Measures: Metrics such as the VIX (Volatility Index) to assess market sentiment.
- Interest Rates: Changes in key interest rates as indicators of macroeconomic conditions.

Findings: The AI models revealed significant herding behavior during the financial crisis, particularly in the months leading up to and during the peak of the crisis. Key findings include:

i. Neural Networks Outperformance: Neural Networks outperformed Logistic Regression and SVM in terms of accuracy and predictive power. The model's ability to capture complex, non-linear relationships in the data was crucial in identifying subtle herding patterns.
ii. Pre-Crisis Herding Detection: The models detected early signs of herding behavior as early as mid-2007. This period was characterized by increased trading volumes and rising market volatility, indicating growing investor uncertainty and herd-like behavior.
iii. Crisis Peak Analysis: During the crisis peak in late 2008, herding behavior was most pronounced. The AI models identified clusters of synchronized trading activities where investors overwhelmingly sold off assets in panic, leading to sharp market declines.
iv. Post-Crisis Trends: In the post-crisis period (2009), the models observed a gradual reduction in herding behavior. However, occasional spikes were detected, corresponding to significant economic announcements and policy changes.
v. Volatility and Herding Correlation: The analysis highlighted a strong correlation between market volatility (measured by the VIX) and herding behavior. Higher volatility periods were consistently associated with increased herding.

Implications: The findings underscore the potential of AI in enhancing our understanding of herding behavior during financial crises. AI models can provide early warnings of herding, allowing regulators and market participants to take proactive measures to mitigate risks.

For Investors: AI-driven insights can help investors make informed decisions by identifying periods of irrational market behavior and adjusting their strategies accordingly.

For Regulators: Early detection of herding can aid regulators in implementing timely interventions to stabilize markets and prevent systemic risks.

For Researchers: The study contributes to the growing body of literature on AI applications in finance, offering a robust framework for future research on herding and market behavior.

4.8 Results and Discussion on Survey

Table 1: Distribution of Survey Respondents

S no	Respondents	Education	Number	Percentage(%)
1	Retail Investors and trader	Graduate	100	67
2	Professor of finance	PhD	20	13
3	Finance background MBA Students	MBA	30	20
	Total		150	100

Source: Field Data

Table 1 presents the distribution of survey respondents by education level and number, offering a comprehensive view of the study's demographic composition. Retail investors and traders with graduate degrees form the largest group, accounting for 67% (100 respondents) of the total. This group provides practical insights into market behaviors. Professors of finance with PhDs make up 13% (20 respondents), contributing deep theoretical and academic perspectives. Finance background MBA students represent 20% (30 respondents), blending practical and theoretical knowledge. This diverse respondent pool ensures a balanced analysis of herding behavior in financial markets. The data, sourced from field research, highlights the varied educational backgrounds of those involved in the study, enhancing the robustness of the findings.

Table 2: Factors Affecting Herd-Behavior (In Percentage)

S no	Factors Affecting Herd-Behavior	SA	A	Neutral	D	SD	Total(%)
1	Fear	88	12	-	-	-	100
2	FOMO	91	9	-	-	-	100
3	Loss aversion	66	30	4	-	-	100
4	Confirmation Bias	62	28	10	-	-	100
5	Overconfidence Bias	18	56	15	11		100
6	Information Cascades	30	62	7	1	-	-
7	Social Influence	32	56	12	-	-	-

Source: Field Data

Table 2 presents the factors influencing herd behavior in financial decision-making, expressed as percentages of survey respondents. The factors include Fear, Fear of Missing Out (FOMO), Loss Aversion, Confirmation Bias, Overconfidence

Bias, Information Cascades, and Social Influence. Each factor's influence is categorized into Strongly Agree (SA), Agree (A), Neutral, Disagree (D), and Strongly Disagree (SD).

Fear is a predominant factor, with 88% strongly agreeing and 12% agreeing that it drives herd behavior. This underscores the significant impact of fear of losses or market volatility, prompting investors to follow the majority for perceived safety.

FOMO is another critical factor, with 91% strongly agreeing and 9% agreeing. The high percentage indicates that the anxiety of missing out on potential gains strongly motivates investors to mimic others' actions.

Loss aversion also plays a crucial role, with 66% strongly agreeing and 30% agreeing, while 4% are neutral. This highlights investors' tendency to avoid losses more than pursuing gains, leading to herd behavior to mitigate perceived risks.

Confirmation Bias is notable, with 62% strongly agreeing and 28% agreeing, while 10% are neutral. Investors often seek information that confirms their pre-existing beliefs, causing them to align with prevalent market trends and exhibit herd behavior.

Overconfidence Bias shows a more varied response: 18% strongly agree, 56% agree, 15% are neutral, and 11% disagree. Despite overconfident investors believing in their superior knowledge, they still follow the crowd, likely due to market sentiment and peer pressure.

Information Cascades influence herd behavior with 30% strongly agreeing, 62% agreeing, 7% neutral, and 1% disagreeing. This occurs when individuals, lacking complete information, base their decisions on others' actions, leading to a cumulative effect where early decisions significantly impact subsequent ones.

Social Influence also plays a significant role, with 32% strongly agreeing, 56% agreeing, and 12% neutral. This reflects the impact of societal and peer pressures on individual decisions, further driving herd behavior.

In conclusion, Table 2 reveals that a combination of emotional and cognitive biases, along with social dynamics, significantly influences herd behavior in financial markets. Understanding these factors can help investors recognize and mitigate irrational decision-making tendencies, promoting more rational investment strategies.

Table 3: Impact of Herd-Behavior (In Percentage)

S no	Factors Affecting Herd-behavior	SA	A	Neutral	D	SD	Total(%)
1	Overpriced Investment	98	2	-	-	-	100
2	Market bubbles and Crashes	95	5	-	-	-	100
3	Risk Maximization	62	35	3	-	-	100
4	Wealth Minimizations	32	58	10	-	-	100
5	Increase in Unprofessional Approach	36	59	5	-	-	100

continued on following page

Table 3: Impact of Herd-Behavior (In Percentage)

Continued

S no	Factors Affecting Herd-behavior	SA	A	Neutral	D	SD	Total(%)
6	Focus on Speculation rather than Investment	32	59	5	4	-	-
7	Buying beyond intrinsic value	42	57	1	-	-	-

Source: Field Data

Table 3 elucidates the impact of herd behavior on financial markets, highlighting the percentages of survey respondents who Strongly Agree (SA), Agree (A), are Neutral, disagree (D), or Strongly Disagree (SD) with each listed consequence.

Overpriced Investment is identified as a primary impact, with 98% of respondents strongly agreeing and 2% agreeing. This near-unanimous agreement indicates that herd behavior often leads to investments being valued far above their intrinsic worth due to excessive demand driven by collective actions.

Market Bubbles and Crashes follow closely, with 95% strongly agreeing and 5% agreeing. Herd behavior can inflate asset prices into unsustainable bubbles, which eventually burst, leading to significant market crashes and widespread financial instability.

Risk Maximization is another significant consequence, with 62% strongly agreeing and 35% agreeing, while 3% remain neutral. This indicates that herd behavior tends to amplify risk exposure, as investors collectively move into overvalued markets or assets, increasing potential losses when the market corrects.

Wealth Minimization shows 32% strongly agreeing and 58% agreeing, with 10% neutral. This suggests that herd behavior often leads to poorer investment outcomes, as following the crowd can result in buying high and selling low, thereby diminishing overall wealth.

An Increase in Unprofessional Approach is noted by 36% strongly agreeing and 59% agreeing, while 5% are neutral. Herd behavior can erode professional standards, encouraging impulsive and speculative actions over disciplined investment strategies.

Focus on Speculation rather than Investment sees 32% strongly agreeing, 59% agreeing, 5% neutral, and 4% disagreeing. This indicates a shift from long-term investment to short-term speculation driven by the desire to capitalize on trending market movements.

Buying beyond Intrinsic Value has 42% strongly agreeing, 57% agreeing, and 1% neutral. Herd behavior frequently leads investors to purchase assets at prices exceeding their fundamental worth, driven by the fear of missing out and collective enthusiasm.

In summary, Table 3 demonstrates that herd behavior significantly distorts market dynamics, leading to overpriced investments, market bubbles and crashes, increased risk, wealth minimization, unprofessional approaches, speculative focus, and buying beyond intrinsic value. Understanding these impacts can help investors and policymakers mitigate the adverse effects of herd behavior.

Table 4: Various sources for data analysis to identify trend and pattern for detecting Herding with AI (In percentage)

S no		SA	A	Neutral	D	SD	Total(%)
1	Social Media	98	2	-	-	-	100
2	News	95	5	-	-	-	100
3	Articles	62	35	3	-	-	100
4	Financial Data	32	58	10	-	-	100

Source: Field Data

The table 4 presents various sources used for data analysis to identify trends and patterns for detecting herding behavior with AI, expressed in percentages. Social media stands out as the most significant source, with 98% Strongly Agree (SA) and 2% Agree (A), indicating its dominance in herding detection. News follows closely, with 95% SA and 5% A, underscoring its crucial role in providing timely information that influences collective behavior. Articles also contribute notably, with 62% SA and 35% A, reflecting their value in offering in-depth analysis and expert opinions. Financial data, though less dominant, still holds importance, with 32% SA and 58% A, showcasing its utility in understanding market movements and investor behavior. The data, sourced from field research, highlights the diverse and complementary nature of these sources in AI-driven herding detection, emphasizing the multi-faceted approach required for accurate analysis.

Table 5: Navigating Herding with AI (In Percentage)

S no	Navigating Herding with AI	SA	A	Neutral	D	SD	Total(%)
1	Risk Assessment	98	2	-	-	-	100
2	Diversification	95	5	-	-	-	100
3	Timing the Market	62	35	3	-	-	100
4	Sentiment Analysis	32	58	10	-	-	100

Source: Field Data

Table 5 provides insights into various strategies for navigating herding behavior using AI, expressed in percentages. These strategies are crucial for investors and financial analysts aiming to mitigate the adverse effects of herding in financial markets.

Risk assessment is highlighted as the most critical strategy, with 98% of respondents strongly agreeing (SA) and 2% agreeing (A). This unanimity underscores the paramount importance of accurately assessing risks to avoid the pitfalls of herding, which can lead to significant financial losses if not properly managed. AI's ability to process vast amounts of data and identify potential risks in real-time is invaluable in this context.

Diversification is another key strategy, with 95% SA and 5% A. Diversification helps in spreading risk across different assets or markets, thereby reducing the impact of any single asset's poor performance. AI can assist in optimizing diversification strategies by analyzing correlations between various assets and suggesting optimal portfolios.

Timing the market, with 62% SA and 35% A, also plays a significant role in navigating herding. While timing the market can be challenging, AI's predictive analytics can provide insights into potential market movements, helping investors make informed decisions on when to enter or exit positions. This strategy, however, requires caution as market timing can be risky.

Sentiment analysis, with 32% SA and 58% A, is increasingly being recognized for its potential to gauge market sentiment and predict herding behavior. By analyzing data from social media, news, and other sources, AI can identify trends and shifts in investor sentiment, allowing for proactive measures to counteract herding effects.

The data, sourced from field research, underscores the multifaceted approach required to navigate herding with AI effectively. It highlights the importance of combining various strategies, supported by AI's analytical capabilities, to mitigate risks and make informed investment decisions in the presence of herding behavior.

Table 6 Challenges in Detecting Herding with AI (In Percentage)

S no	Navigating Herding with AI	SA	A	Neutral	D	SD	Total(%)
1	Data Quality and Availability	68	24	8	-	-	100
2	Complexity of Financial Market	22	57	12	9	-	100
3	Model Overfitting	22	69	9	-	-	100
4	Interpretability of AI Models	26	64	10	-	-	100

Source: Field Data

This table highlights the major challenges associated with using artificial intelligence (AI) to detect herding behavior in financial markets, based on field data. The table categorizes responses into five levels: Strongly Agree (SA), Agree (A),

Neutral, Disagree (D), and Strongly Disagree (SD), with percentages reflecting the distribution of opinions.

Data Quality and Availability: A significant majority, 68%, strongly agree that data quality and availability are major challenges, while 24% agree, and 8% remain neutral. This underscores the critical need for high-quality, real-time data to train effective AI models.

Complexity of Financial Market: 22% strongly agree and 57% agree that the complex and dynamic nature of financial markets is a challenge, with 12% neutral and 9% disagreeing. This indicates that capturing all relevant market factors is difficult for AI systems.

Model Overfitting: Overfitting is seen as a critical issue, with 22% strongly agreeing and 69% agreeing. 9% are neutral, highlighting the risk of AI models being too closely tailored to historical data and potentially failing to predict future behaviors accurately.

Interpretability of AI Models: 26% strongly agree and 64% agree that interpretability is a challenge, while 10% are neutral. This reflects the difficulty in understanding and explaining AI decisions, which can be a barrier to trust and effective implementation.

These insights emphasize the need for robust data management, adaptable AI models, and transparent AI systems to effectively navigate and mitigate the challenges in detecting herding behavior in financial markets

Table 7 Threats in Detecting Herding with AI (In Percentage)

S no	Navigating Herding with AI	SA	A	Neutral	D	SD	Total(%)
1	False Positives and Negatives	14	62	12	8	-	100
2	Manipulation and Adversarial Attacks	12	71	11	6	-	100
3	Market Reaction and Feedback Loops	52	39	9	-	-	100
4	Interpretability of AI Models	32	58	10	-	-	100
5	Regulatory and Compliance Issues	6	45	43	6	-	100

Source: Field Data

This table 7 outlines the key threats identified in using artificial intelligence (AI) to detect herding behavior in financial markets. The data is presented as percentages reflecting the distribution of responses across five categories: Strongly Agree (SA), Agree (A), Neutral, Disagree (D), and Strongly Disagree (SD).

False Positives and Negatives: A combined 76% of respondents (14% SA, 62% A) recognize the risk of AI misclassifying market behavior, which can lead to incorrect trading decisions.

Manipulation and Adversarial Attacks: With 12% strongly agreeing and 71% agreeing, 83% of respondents identify manipulation and adversarial attacks as significant threats. This underscores concerns about market participants potentially gaming AI systems.

Market Reaction and Feedback Loops: The highest concern, with 52% strongly agreeing and 39% agreeing (91% total), is that AI systems themselves might influence market behaviors, creating feedback loops that amplify market volatility.

Interpretability of AI Models: Interpretability is also a major issue, with 32% strongly agreeing and 58% agreeing (90% total). This highlights the challenge of ensuring AI decisions are transparent and understandable to users, which is crucial for trust and effective implementation.

Regulatory and Compliance Issues: While only 6% strongly agree, 45% agree, and 43% remain neutral, indicating a significant portion of respondents are concerned about adhering to evolving regulatory standards and compliance requirements.

These insights emphasize the need for robust, transparent, and compliant AI systems to address these threats effectively.

Limitations of The Study

Acknowledge potential limitations of the study, such as the availability of financial data, the generalizability of findings, and the evolving nature of AI technologies.

5. FINDING, CONCLUSION, RECOMMENDATION AND SUGGESTION

The analysis identifies fear, FOMO, and social influences as key drivers of herd behavior, resulting in overpriced investments and market instability. AI offers valuable strategies like risk assessment and diversification to counteract these effects. However, challenges such as data quality, model interpretability, and the risk of feedback loops persist. Additionally, AI systems face threats from false positives, manipulation, and regulatory issues. Addressing these challenges is crucial for leveraging AI effectively in mitigating herd behavior in financial markets. Investors in AI-influenced financial markets exhibit irrationality and mimicry, particularly during downturns.

Advanced AI models for high-frequency trading show high prediction accuracy. AI enhances trading strategies, risk management, and market efficiency. Herding behavior significantly influences market dynamics and performance, necessitating further analysis and strategic measures to mitigate its effects. AI has revolutionized financial markets from trend-following to AI-driven algorithmic trading, enhancing prediction accuracy and efficiency. It significantly impacts trading strategies, risk management, and market efficiency, despite challenges like increased market volatility and potential biases in lending decisions.

To mitigate herd behavior in financial markets, ensure high-quality data for AI models and improve model interpretability. Adopt AI strategies like risk assessment and diversification. Develop robust systems to counter manipulation and avoid feedback loops. Finally, maintain compliance with regulatory standards to foster trust and effectiveness in AI-driven decision-making. The rejection of the null hypotheses reveals that AI-based herding detection significantly impacts market stability and investor decisions, providing timely warnings and data-driven insights. However, it also presents challenges, including accuracy, data privacy, and market manipulation concerns. Key factors and data sources, such as historical prices, trading volumes, and sentiment analysis, are crucial for effective detection. Ultimately, AI assists investors in making informed decisions, mitigating herding effects, and enhancing overall market resilience

REFERENCES

Ali, A., Razak, S. A., Othman, S. H., Taiseer, A. E. E., Al-Dhaqm, A., Nasser, M., Elhassan, T., Elshafie, H., & Saif, A. (2022). Financial Fraud Detection Based on Machine Learning: A Systematic Literature Review. *Applied Sciences (Basel, Switzerland)*, 12(19), 9637. DOI: 10.3390/app12199637

Ante, L., & Demir, E. 2023. The ChatGPT Effect on AI-themed cryptocurrencies. Available at *SSRN* 4350557

Arifovic, J., He, X., & Wei, L. (2022). Machine Learning and Speed in High-Frequency Trading. *Journal of Economic Dynamics & Control*, 139, 104438. DOI: 10.1016/j.jedc.2022.104438

Arifovic, J., He, X., & Wei, L. (2022). Machine Learning and Speed in High-Frequency Trading. [Google Scholar]. *Journal of Economic Dynamics & Control*, 139, 104438. DOI: 10.1016/j.jedc.2022.104438

Arner, D., Barberis, J. N., & Buckley, R. P. (2015). The evolution of FinTech: A new post-crisis paradigm. *SSRN*, 47, 1271–1318. DOI: 10.2139/ssrn.2676553

Aven, T. (2016). Risk assessment and risk management: Review of recent advances on their foundation. *European Journal of Operational Research*, 253(1), 1–13. DOI: 10.1016/j.ejor.2015.12.023

Ballis, A., & Anastasiou, D. (2023). Testing for Herding in Artificial Intelligence–Themed Cryptocurrencies Following the Launch of ChatGPT. *The Journal of Financial Data Science*, 5(4), 161–171. DOI: 10.3905/jfds.2023.1.134

Barber, B. M., Odean, T., & Zhu, N. (2009). Do retail trades move markets? *Review of Financial Studies*, 22(1), 151–186. DOI: 10.1093/rfs/hhn035

Berg, T., Burg, V., Gombović, A., & Puri, M. (2020). On the rise of fintechs—Credit scoring using digital footprints. *Review of Financial Studies*, 32(7), 1984–2009. DOI: 10.1093/rfs/hhz099

Bryson, J., Diamantis, M., & Grant, T. (2017). Of, for, and by the people: The legal lacuna of synthetic persons. *Artificial Intelligence and Law*, 25(3), 273–291. DOI: 10.1007/s10506-017-9214-9

Burrell, J. (2016). How the machine 'thinks': Understanding opacity in machine learning algorithms. *Big Data & Society*, 3(1), 1–12. DOI: 10.1177/2053951715622512

Caruana, R., Lou, Y., Gehrke, J., Koch, P., Sturm, M., & Elhadad, N. 2015. Intelligible Models for HealthCare: Predicting Pneumonia Risk and Hospital 30-Day Readmission. Paper presented at the 21th ACM SIGKDD International Conference on Knowledge Discovery and Data Mining, Sydney, Australia, August 10–13; pp. 1721–30 DOI: 10.1145/2783258.2788613

Chen, R.-C., Dewil, C., & Huang, S.-W. (2020). R.E. Caraka Selecting critical features for data classification based on machine learning methods. *Journal of Big Data*, 7(1), 1–26. DOI: 10.1186/s40537-020-00327-4

Choi, K.-H., Kang, S. H., & Yoon, S.-M. (2022). Herding behavior in Korea's cryptocurrency market. *Applied Economics*, 54(24), 2795–2809. DOI: 10.1080/00036846.2021.1998335

Gomber, P., Kauffman, R. J., Parker, C., & Weber, B. W. (2018). On the Fintech revolution: Interpreting the forces of innovation, disruption, and transformation in financial services. *Journal of Management Information Systems*, 35(1), 220–265. DOI: 10.1080/07421222.2018.1440766

Kim, K. A., & Nofsinger, J. R. (2005). Institutional herding, business groups, and economic regimes: Evidence from Japan J. *The Journal of Business*, 78(1), 213–242. DOI: 10.1086/426524

Kumar, A. (2020). Empirical investigation of herding in cryptocurrency market under different market regimes. *Review of Behavioral Finance*, 13(3), 297–308. DOI: 10.1108/RBF-01-2020-0014

Kyriazis, N. A. (2020). Herding behavior in digital currency markets: An integrated survey and empirical estimation. *Heliyon*, 6(8), e04752. DOI: 10.1016/j.heliyon.2020.e04752 PMID: 32904208

Lakonishok, J., Shleifer, A., & Vishny, R. W. (1992). The IMPACT OF INSTITUTIONAL TRADING ON STOCK Prices. *Journal of Financial Economics*, 32(1), 23–43. DOI: 10.1016/0304-405X(92)90023-Q

Mangat, M., Reschenhofer, E., Stark, T., & Zwatz, C. (2022). High-Frequency Trading with Machine Learning Algorithms and Limit Order Book Data. *Data Science in Finance and Economics*, 2(4), 437–463. DOI: 10.3934/DSFE.2022022

Njegovanović, A. (2018). Artificial Intelligence: Financial Trading and Neurology of Decision. *Financial Markets. Institutions and Risks*, 2, 58–68.

Omane-Adjepong, M., Alagidede, I. P., Lyimo, A. G., & Tweneboah, G. (2021). Herding behavior in cryptocurrency and emerging financial markets. *Cogent Economics & Finance*, 9(1), 1933681. DOI: 10.1080/23322039.2021.1933681

Sias Institutional Herding, R. W. (2004)... *Review of Financial Studies*, 17, 165–206. DOI: 10.1093/rfs/hhg035

Tran, M., Pham-Hi, D., & Bui, M. (2023). Optimizing Automated Trading Systems with Deep Reinforcement Learning. *Algorithms*, 16(1), 23. DOI: 10.3390/a16010023

Wilinski, A., Sochanowski, M., & Nowicki, W. (2022). An investment strategy based on the first derivative of the moving averages difference with parameters adapted by machine learning. *Data Science in Finance and Economics*, 2(2), 96–116. DOI: 10.3934/DSFE.2022005

Chapter 8
Share Repurchase:
Importance and Measuring Its Effect on the Stock Price

Lingli Lyu
https://orcid.org/0009-0007-8021-6168
Peter the Great Saint-Petersburg Polytechnic University, Russia

Liudmila A. Guzikova
Peter the Great Saint-Petersburg Polytechnic University, Russia

ABSTRACT

Share repurchase refers to the behavior of listed companies to repurchase their own shares from the stock market for stabilizing the share price and improving the governance structure. The empirical evidence of share repurchase of Chinese A-share listed companies during the period from 2021.1.1 to 2024.1.1 is collected to construct a model, and an empirical study is conducted based on the event study method in STATA. The top four industries with the highest percentage in the sample are selected for comparative analysis. The results of the study show that for the effect of share repurchase on share price, China's stock market also behaves in the same way as the western capital market, and share repurchase has a significant positive promotion effect on listed companies' stock price, but the promotion effect is short-lived. It is also found that listed firms with share repurchases have significant positive excess stock returns before the repurchase announcement, reflecting the fact that there is indeed an early leakage of repurchase information in the Chinese share repurchase market.

DOI: 10.4018/979-8-3693-7827-4.ch008

Copyright © 2025, IGI Global Scientific Publishing. Copying or distributing in print or electronic forms without written permission of IGI Global is prohibited.

1. INTRODUCTION

The research object of this paper mainly focuses on the listed companies in the Chinese stock exchange market that utilize their own funds, compliant self-financing, etc., to carry out share repurchase. Share repurchase is one of the daily operation activities of listed companies. Through share repurchase, a company can take back some of its issued shares, thus reducing the total share capital of the company. Doing so usually improves earnings per share, financial ratios and stock prices, and can also send a positive signal to the market that the company believes its shares are undervalued. Share buybacks can also be used to dilute the shareholding of controlling shareholders or as a way to implement employee incentive programs. Share buybacks are used in most cases to change a company's capital structure and to lay the foundation for long-term growth. According to western traditional theory, share buybacks can activate the market, improve market liquidity, and investors form reasonable expectations of share prices, making listed companies' share prices more stable. Share buybacks also reduce the creation of excessive speculative behavior, as well as reducing the risk of speculative bubbles bursting.Especially when the stock market is in the doldrums and share prices continue to decline, share buybacks can signal to investors that the value of the enterprise is stable in order to stabilize share prices. Compared with the development history of western countries such as the United States, Germany and France, China's stock exchange market started later, and many financial instruments such as share repurchase were exposed to later, and the related business and system development were slower. China's share repurchase began to develop in the 1990s. The earliest share repurchase in China took place in 1992, which was mainly for the purpose of realizing the goal of corporate mergers and acquisitions, and was manifested in the repurchase of the shares of "Little Yuyuan" by "Big Yuyuan". "The share buyback was mainly for the purpose of mergers and acquisitions. Subsequently, the "Big Yuyuan" canceled all the repurchased shares. Overall, the repurchase market in China was relatively small and restrictive at that time. The history of China's repurchase system has evolved over the past thirty years, with a number of important institutional changes contributing to the development of share repurchases in China.

With the improvement of the share repurchase system and the background of the current downturn of the world economy, share repurchase has started to be used by more and more listed companies to boost share prices and revitalize market confidence. Accompanied by the explosive development of share repurchase, share repurchase has gradually been paid attention to by the industry and academics, and there have been mixed reviews on the market effect generated by share repurchase. Some scholars believe that share repurchases by listed companies can reduce agency costs (Mitchell et al.,2007), boost stock prices (Baker, M., & Wurgler, J.,2002), reduce profit distribution costs (Harfordet et al.,2008), and improve stock liquidity (Hillert et al.,2016). However, some scholars have suggested that share buybacks may have negative effects, such as Lazonick who found that share buybacks have largely contributed to runaway executive compensation and economic inequality because share buybacks extract value rather than create it, and their overuse can harm the health of the economy(Lazonick, W.,2014).In order for the country to return to true prosperity, the government and business leaders must take steps to control them.Almeida et a verified using breakpoint regression that firms that conduct share buybacks, driven by EPS, reduce employment and capital investment and have lower cash holdings(Almeida et al.,2016).Paul et al. found that share buybacks may lead to manipulation of information flow by managers. Their empirical results suggest that share buybacks lead to managers who will actively manipulate voluntary disclosures by disclosing more bad news before the buyback and more good news after the buyback (Brockman et al.,2016).

According to the current continuous development of share repurchase, the research results and research methodology are being improved and enriched, and the sample size is sufficiently enriched, and the conclusions on whether there is an effect and whether the effect of the implementation of share repurchase behavior by listed companies on stock prices is significant or not need to be verified even further. In addition, will there be people releasing and leaking information before the share repurchase announcement in order to inflate the stock price in the short term, and does this kind of violation exist? These are all questions worth exploring. On the other hand, in recent years, China's share repurchase related policies have been improving, more and more listed companies have implemented share repurchases, and the motivation for share repurchases has become more and more diversified, and share repurchases have become a commonly used financial tool by listed companies in China.The number of companies implementing share buybacks and the amount of buybacks have been growing from 2017 to the present. The purpose of most of these corporate share buybacks is to stabilize the share price, but whether the results after share buybacks are as expected is worth exploring in depth. The risks that may arise from the implementation of share repurchase should also be clear, and ultimately company managers should make a reasonable strategy. The research in this paper also enables listed company managers and investors to provide reference for the correct understanding of share repurchase, and the related research will also better promote the development of share repurchase in China's capital market.

What this study wishes to focus on is precisely whether the open market share repurchase behavior of listed companies brings about changes in the capital market share price, and to observe the market reaction brought about by the repurchase. Therefore, using the event study method to estimate the share price of the enterprise if the open market share repurchase behavior had not occurred, the effect brought about by the event shock can be reflected by calculating the difference between the enterprise's share price and the estimated price after the share repurchase event has actually occurred. A large amount of related literature is collected through various ways to organize the theoretical knowledge related to share repurchase, to summarize the possible results of the effect of share repurchase on share price, and to provide theoretical support for the research hypotheses proposed later.

From the research perspective. This paper selects the share repurchase of Chinese A-share listed companies as the research object, and takes the stock price 10 days before and after the announcement date of the implementation of share repurchase as the research object, and systematically researches the change of stock price before and after the implementation of share repurchase of listed companies in China, and the phenomenon of the leakage of information of share repurchase. It can provide reference for the policy making of regulators, the implementation of share buybacks by listed companies, and the cognition of investors on share buybacks. Against the background of the rising number and scale of share repurchases by Chinese listed companies, the effect of share repurchases on stock prices has been increasingly emphasized by the market. However, the research on share repurchase in domestic academic circles is still in its infancy, and many areas have not been covered in the literature.How will the regulator improve the system to guide and regulate the re-purchase transactions of listed companies in the future? How can listed companies carry out buybacks better? What effects have share buybacks had on share prices? These questions are not well answered, and the above questions are the focus of this paper. From the point of view of research methodology. This paper focuses on the event of share buyback in China, selects the data of the first share buyback of listed companies from 2021 to 2023, three years, as a sample, and utilizes the event study method in STATA to conduct empirical research. In addition to the empirical study of the overall sample, this paper also selected the top four industries in the sample again to study, and finally do a comparative analysis. Finally, information leakage in share buybacks is also analyzed.

2. DEFINITION OF RELEVANT CONCEPTS AND THEORETICAL REVIEW OF SHARE REPURCHASE

Share repurchase is the act of repurchasing issued or outstanding shares through a certain process in order to improve the earnings per share, change the capital struc-ture of the company, enhance the value of the company and stabilize the share price, etc. It is now one of the financial instruments commonly used in the capital market. The share repurchase discussed in this article is the behavior of a listed company, which has been publicly listed on the stock exchange and whose shares are traded on the stock exchange in the form of stocks, to repurchase its issued stocks in the market through its own or reasonable self-financed funds. For the repurchased shares, the company generally has two ways to deal with them, the first is to cancel all of them, and the second is to convert the purchased shares into treasury shares, which will no longer be issued to the public and will no longer be used for calculating the earnings per share after being converted into treasury shares. Generally companies will sell these treasury shares to their employees at a low price to implement an employee stock ownership plan.

The main types of share repurchases are cash dividend replacement repurchases and strategic repurchases.

Cash Dividend Alternative Repurchase mainly refers to the share repurchase behavior as an alternative policy to cash dividend, which has more financial flexibility. Since the repurchase behavior can be carried out flexibly within the period from the launch of the repurchase plan to the repurchase deadline, it is non-continuous and flexible in operation compared to cash dividends. Listed companies through the open market repurchase behavior through the share repurchase for shareholders, equivalent to the company's excess free cash issued to shareholders, so that on the one hand, it can reduce the agency cost, to avoid the management due to the excess free cash to carry out the investment of low-yield projects. On the other hand, the share repurchase behavior can help the company to reasonably avoid tax, the issuance of cash dividends there are tax restrictions, while the share repurchase to bring the shareholders' capital gains, and capital gains tax rate is much lower than the tax rate paid by the dividend bonus.In addition, the share repurchase behavior of listed companies can reduce its outstanding share capital, which improves the earnings per share under the condition that the company's net profit remains unchanged, and then leads to the increase of stock price, bringing more capital gains for shareholders. Strategic buyback refers to the listed company in the strategic purpose and carry out the share repurchase behavior scale is larger than the dividend alternative buyback, even if the company's own cash is not enough to support the company's buyback purpose, the company will be through the debt financing, sale of assets and other ways of financing, the strategic share repurchase the most important purpose is in order to be able to quickly reorganize the company's capital structure. According to the difference of strategic objectives, strategic share buybacks can be subdivided into active profit-making repurchases, recapitalization repurchases and passive reversal share repurchases.

Listed companies choose different methods of share repurchase will lead to different judgments by investors, and all types of share repurchase methods have different utility in the market. There are only three types of share repurchase methods in China, specifically including open offer repurchase, agreement repurchase and open market share repurchase.

Offer to repurchase is generally categorized into two types: fixed price offer to repurchase and Dutch auction repurchase. Fixed-price offers are offers by listed companies to repurchase an agreed number of shares within an agreed period of time at a price higher than the current market price of the shares. Generally, the agreed repurchase period ranges from half a month to 20 days. Unlike other repurchases, a fixed-price repurchase offer gives shareholders the option of selling their shares or continuing to hold them, and the company has the right not to repurchase the excess number of shares if they sell more than the number of shares agreed upon in the offer. In addition, in a fixed-price offer, the company has the right to extend the repurchase period. Generally speaking, the cost of repurchasing through a fixed price offer is higher than that of an open market purchase. Unlike fixed-price offers, in a Dutch auction repurchase the company does not fix the price of the shares to be repurchased, but rather specifies the number of shares to be repurchased and specifies a price range of shares to be repurchased, i.e., a minimum and a maximum price that the company is willing to pay for the repurchase.But generally the minimum price agreed in the company's offer is slightly higher than the current market value of the shares. In a Dutch auction repurchase, shareholders offer their shares by way of a tender offer. The shareholders provide the number of shares they are willing to offer and their desired price range. After receiving the bids from the shareholders, the company ranks them according to the price and number of shares and then determines the minimum price of the shares needed to carry out the repurchase of the shares. And that price is used to pay those shareholders who offer no more than that price. If the final collation results in a stock price that does not exceed the price specified in the offer, but the number of shares offered by the shareholders exceeds the number of shares that the company has agreed to repurchase in advance, then the company has the right to purchase them on a pro rata basis; however, if the shareholders do not offer a sufficient number of shares then the company is able to choose to either stop that repurchase or to purchase the shares that have been offered by the shareholders at the upper end of the agreed price range. It can be seen that there is a significant difference between fixed-price offer repurchases and Dutch auction repurchases, and there is also room for adjustment of the repurchase cost because in Dutch auction repurchases, the company is unable to specify in advance the final specific repurchase price and the number of shares to be repurchased.

Open market share repurchase refers to the process of open market share repurchase behavior carried out by a listed company, the company is similar to a market participant, able to purchase the company's shares circulating in the secondary market, and the cost of repurchasing the shares is equal to the market price at the time of purchase. Although the open market share repurchase behavior is prone to lead to a difference in the number of shares bought and sold, and the large purchase of shares pushes up the share price and raises the cost of the repurchase, it also reflects that the open market share repurchase behavior is a stronger means of boosting the share price, which helps to enhance market confidence and stabilize the share price. Especially when the company's stock is underperforming in the market, small-scale open market share repurchases can effectively boost market confidence and raise the stock price.

An agreed repurchase is a repurchase agreement between a public company and one or more shareholders to repurchase the shareholders' shares at an agreed price. On the basis of the agreement between the parties, the agreed repurchase price will usually be lower than the market price of the shares at the time of the agreement. The main reason for this is that if the repurchase price is too high it will be detrimental to the interests of shareholders who are not party to the agreement. Typically, agreed repurchases only exist between the company and the shareholders.

This paper also relies heavily on the signaling theory of the effect of share repurchases.

Share repurchase behavior first began in the United States, in the 1950s, the U.S. stock market first appeared in the company's share repurchase behavior, followed by the rise of the share repurchase market in the 1970s, the share repurchase began to get the attention of the academic community. Among them, signaling theory, was the most recognized theory in academia at that time. Signaling theory suggests that external stakeholders will make decisions based on the signals of the relevant characteristics of the enterprise in order to alleviate the problem of "adverse selection" under the asymmetry of information (Michael, 1973). An effective signal needs to be observable and relevant to decision making, and has a certain cost (Connelly et al., 2011).Scholars generally believe that share repurchase is a way for company management to transmit signals to market participants. On the one hand, at that time, the United States was in the recovery period after the Great Depression, the market sentiment is generally depressed, investors are not optimistic about stock prices, resulting in a large outflow of capital market funds, which is an important reason why various listed companies have carried out share repurchase behavior, in order to be able to boost the confidence of the market, and to convey to the investors the signal that it is optimistic about the future of the company (Vermaelen 1981; Comment and Jarrell, 1991). On the other hand, at that time, information economics was further applied, and the importance of information was also analyzed in the process of financial research conducted by companies (James, 1976; Shapiro and Matson, 2008; Lin Bin and Rao Jing, 2009). At this time, some scholars in the process of analyzing the motivation of share repurchase began to try to explain it through the signaling theory (Ikenberry et al., 1995; Baker et al., 2003; Brav et al., 2005), as the company's managers, compared to external investors, have more information about the internal information of the company, and therefore have a good understanding of the company's Since managers have more internal information about the company than external investors, they have a clearer judgment between the actual value of the company and the market value. When the management believes that the current share price of the company is undervalued, it is possible to announce a share repurchase program to the market as a signal to various market participants. As the signal is received by the market, the company's share price usually generates a positive excess return after the share repurchase.Particularly in the case of tender offer repurchases, it is considered to be a more effective form of signaling because it involves the payment of a premium to shareholders over the market price. Previous studies have confirmed that, based on the signaling theory, the market effect of share repurchases can promote a positive excess return on stock returns after the announcement date of share repurchases. It is against this background that this paper proposes to carry out a further exploratory analysis. Signaling theory suggests that the market responds to share repurchase signals, but the specifics of the market's response remain to be discussed. Many current studies on share repurchase are based on signal theory, such as Vermaelen (1984), Ofer et al. (1987) in the process of share repurchase research, mainly based on signal theory to analyze the role of share repurchase . In addition, some related research studies also support the signaling role of share repurchase, and believe that share repurchase can be a good means for the company to send signals to the market, Wansley et al. (1981) found that the second important reason for the management to carry out share repurchase is that they want to express their confidence in the company's future development to market participants. signaling to market participants that they have confidence in the future development of the company (Wansley et al., 1989). In a study by Tsetsekos (1993), management viewed the messaging effect of share repurchases as the third most important of the many motives for share repurchases. Ren He et al. (1995) pointed out that the vast majority of U.S. listed companies do not mention their specific motives for repurchase in their repurchase announcements, but most of them cite the undervaluation of share price as the main reason. Dittmar's (2000) study also confirmed that when the market value of a company is not correctly perceived by the market, the management tends to carry out share repurchase to send undervaluation signals to the market. Baker et al. (2003) asked a total of 624 company executives from January 1998 to September 1999 about their reasons for conducting share repurchases through a questionnaire survey, and the largest number of answers was that the value of the company was not properly recognized by the market, and therefore share repurchases were viewed as a signal of undervaluation to the market . The results of Brav et al. (2005) also showed that although the motivation for share repurchase behavior in the open market of listed companies varies widely, undervaluation is still the most important reason. And the reason why the market can be effected by the open market share repurchase of listed companies is precisely because the signaling effect of share repurchase is received by the market participants and reacted, which in turn brings about changes in the market. And related studies have confirmed that the market is able to receive share buybacks as a signal that the share price is undervalued and react quickly in the market.Dann (1981), based on signaling theory, found that share buybacks can bring significant positive growth in stock price, in which the excess return on the day of the buyback announcement is as high as 8.94%, and the excess return on the next day is also 6.83%. This indicates that the market recognizes the signals of share buybacks. Zhou Zimu (2017) explores the market effect brought by share repurchase and finds that there is a negative excess return on stock price before the share repurchase announcement, while the market response is positive after the repurchase announcement. Feng (2008) finds that the excess return brought on the day of share repurchase announcement in the public market of listed companies is 1.05%, and the CAR for the five-day announcement window (-2, +2) is 2.54% [27]. CAR is 2.54% .

In China, most companies choose to repurchase shares from the open market and determine the cost of repurchase based on market-based pricing. This paper also focuses on analyzing the market effect of share repurchase.

Empirical studies on the market effect of share repurchase behavior. empirical studies by Vermaelen (1981), Netter and Mitchell (1989) show that share repurchases in the U.S. capital market have a positive effect, and the share price of the company rises by a larger amount 5 days after the announcement date. Jagannathan and Stephens (2000). Bittlingmayer G (1998) research on companies in different industries, found that the event window period listed company stock repurchase behavior have positive effect, repurchase the number of times the listed company its repurchase market effect is more obvious, at the same time in the capital market market downturn when the repurchase to produce a positive market effect of the probability of the greater.Der-Jang Chi (2010) studied stock buybacks in Taiwan, China and showed that listed companies in all industries have positive excess returns during the event window when they make stock buyback announcements . Chinese scholars Huang Hong and Liu Jia (2007) argue that stock buybacks provide a positive boost to stock prices and find that investors are able to rationalize the information released by stock buybacks. Ke Aina (2009) used the event study method to categorize the cases of stock buybacks in China, and on the basis of the conclusion of having a positive effect, she also concluded that the market effect is positively correlated with the size of buybacks. On this basis, some scholars introduced the source of funds for repurchase into the repurchase event for research, such as Li Bin (2010) used abnormal performance indicators for research, by studying the effect of different repurchase funding sources on the market effect, and the conclusion shows that the debt assets are better than cash, and the former is able to bring more significant positive market effect. However, some scholars have also found that stock buybacks do not produce significant positive market effects, Liu Yong (2019) does not deny the positive effect of stock buybacks, and he argues that if the capital market cycle is taken into account, the remaining excess return is actually not significant or even negative after excluding the effect caused by the rise of the market itself . Overall, scholars have adopted the event study method for the market effect of stock buybacks, and most of them agree that stock buybacks have a significant positive market effect, and the market effect is affected by the industry, the country, and the source of funds.

An empirical study of market effects at different horizons.Ikenberryet and Gertler (1997) categorized the market effects of stock buybacks into long term and short term, and the results of the study showed that the larger the percentage of buybacks by listed companies, the more pronounced are the short term positive market effects, while the larger the company size, the more subtle are the short term positive market effects.Ikenberryet, Lakonishok and Vermaelen (1995) studied the U.S. capital market and found that in the short term, i.e., 1 year, stock buybacks do not result in significant excess returns, but the effect is significant in the long term . In the 4th year after stock buybacks, the sample firms had an excess return of 12.1% and a cumulative excess return of 45.3% in the 4 years after buybacks. It is also worth thinking about what kind of market reaction occurs after a company makes an announcement of share repurchase, and whether there are sectoral differences in the market reaction of listed companies in three different sectors: main board, small and medium-sized board, and GEM (Ji, Q., 2017). Xu and Chi Mingkui (2003) analyzed a few case studies of stock buybacks in China at that time, the main object of the study was the non-circulating shares of listed companies, and concluded that stock buybacks can produce positive fluctuations in stock prices in the short term .Yang Xiangying (2012) conducted a study on the long-term market effect of stock buybacks and found that the sample companies still have significant excess returns one year after the announcement date of buybacks. He Ying (2014) found that the excess return from stock buybacks is roughly in the range of 0.5%-6% within 10 trading days, and this value is affected by the country, economic situation, and capital market development . Qin Jian (2015) studied the listed companies that announced and implemented stock buybacks in China's capital market from 2004 to 2008, and the results showed that in the short term, stock buybacks have a significant positive market effect, and in the long term, they will improve the company's financial indicators and improve the company's capital structure. Qian Yiwen (2018) argues that in the long run, the excess return of stock buybacks will be gradually erased with the passage of time, and the positive market effect in the short run stems from the irrational decision-making of investors. In summary, most scholars believe that short-term stock buybacks produce positive market effects, and the positive effect will be more obvious in the long term, i.e., more than one year.

The important factor that interferes with the effect of repurchase in share repurchase is the early leakage of information, and the empirical research on whether the information is leaked in advance is stated as follows.Stephens and Weisbach (1998) conducted a study on the stock repurchase in the U.S. capital market in the 1990's, and selected a total of 630 valid samples in the period of 1980-1992, and analyzed the stock price in the five trading days before and after the repurchase announcement. The analysis reveals that the stock prices in the 5 trading days before and after the repurchase announcements show large positive fluctuations, i.e., higher excess returns; the stock prices of listed companies as a whole move positively during the event window period. Wang Wei (2002) found that listed companies' stock prices had already produced abnormal movements before the announcement date, and accordingly concluded that the information disclosure system was imperfect and the news was leaked in advance. Ma Ming (2009) similarly argues that stock buybacks have a positive market effect and observes that excess returns are mainly concentrated before the announcement date, and the excess returns turn negative after the announcement date, which leads to the conclusion of information leakage. Yu Linjuan (2010) similarly found that listed companies announcing share buybacks during the period 2004-2009 had a significant stock price reaction prior to the announcement date, suggesting that information leakage is more common. Sun Kai (2015) conducted a systematic study of China's manufacturing industry and found that there is a problem of early leakage of buyback news, and the market effect of stock buybacks by listed companies in China is quite different from that of the European and American capital markets. Chen Juan (2016), Lin Miaolei (2017), and Wang Qian (2018) similarly argue that stock buybacks will bring excess returns for listed companies' stock prices during the event window period, but the same information leakage exists. On the other hand, a study by Yong Wu (2018) shows that there is no significant positive fluctuation in the share price of listed companies prior to the announcement date of stock buybacks, and information leakage is not prevalent. The study by Ying Zhang (2020) shows that the share prices of companies are positively effected in the A-share market after the release of share buyback notices, while the Hong Kong stock securities market shows positive excess returns only after the release of buyback notices.

The study of the effect of share repurchase on share price, share repurchase has the potential to have a positive or negative effect on share price or share repurchase has no effect on share price.

Positive effect of share repurchase on share price.Dann (1981) selected 123 firms that conducted share repurchase in the time period of 1962 to 1976 and analyzed the market effect generated by share repurchase.The study found that share repurchase stimulates the increase of share price and generates a positive excess rate of return. And the increase in excess return lasts for a long time.Wakeman (1983) analyzed the relationship between share repurchase and market signaling by building a model. It was found that share buybacks can enable stock sellers to earn 23% return on earnings above the market price, and share buybacks are a stabilization of stock price while increasing the stock price, which generally results in an upward fluctuation of about 10% .Jarrel (1991) concluded that as long as a company issues an announcement of a program of share repurchase, it will promote an increase in the share price, generate excess yield, and enhance the value of the enterprise. Shou Diyong and Sun Erping (2000), in a comparative study of the market effects generated by domestic and international share buybacks, found that share buybacks can convey the signal of undervalued enterprise to the outside world, strengthen investor confidence, which in turn attracts more investors to invest, and at the same time promotes the liquidity of capital market funds.Tskashi and Hatekecla (2004) conducted a case study of listed companies that made share buybacks in Japan from 1995 to 1998, and found that investors mostly gave positive feedback to the information about share buybacks, but it was possible that the announcement was sent out to companies that did not carry out share buybacks, but comparing the two scenarios of sending out announcements to carry out and not to carry out, the market reaction under the two scenarios was found to be generally consistent. The market reaction under the two scenarios is roughly the same.Bonaime and Oztekin (2014) found that when firms are undervalued and the share price is low, firms will issue announcements to implement share buybacks, after which there will be an increase in the share price or stabilization, and the firm's financial position will improve.Lin Miaolei (2019) analyzed the short-term market effect of share repurchase by empirical research method, and found that the short-term positive market effect occurs regardless of the way of repurchase is centralized bidding or agreement repurchase. And further research found that the short-term market effect is also positively correlated with the return on net assets and the growth rate of main business.Xiong Hu (2022) also suggested that share repurchase can reduce the management's agency cost in the short term, improve the efficiency of the utilization of funds, raise the share price, and overall share repurchase has a positive positive effect.

The negative effect of share buybacks on share price.Ikenberry (2000) concluded that the implementation of share buybacks on the company's stock price is only a short-lived increase in the long term to the real value of the enterprise does not boost the effect, and share buybacks are more a means of management manipulation of the stock price, in order to achieve the transfer of wealth, if the manipulation of the inappropriate instead of the development of the company will bring a negative effect.

Zhang Ruxue, Song Xinyu, Yin Weiqi et al. (2021) found that the implementation of three-phase share repurchase by the case company did not lead to an increase in the share price of the enterprise, and the overall view of the share price did not increase, but rather decreased. Zhou Maochun (2007) mainly studied the negative financial effects of share repurchase, and researched that share repurchase through debt funds for repurchase will increase the gearing ratio, the company's debt burden will increase, and the financial risk will increase . Geng Zhirui,Ji Jianing (2021) proposed that the company to implement share repurchase is to convey the information to the market that the company's share price is undervalued, to guide investors to invest, but if because of the announcement of the repurchase, but mentioning that because of the failure to adequately prepare for the share repurchase of the funds, the repurchase stops halfway instead of damaging the company's reputation and enterprise value.

There is no clear correlation between the effect of share buybacks on share prices. As the use of share buybacks becomes more and more common, different studies have different opinions on the effect of share buybacks, which can be used to resolve a crisis or even increase the share price if done correctly, and on the other hand, there is also a risk of delisting. There are also studies that suggest that there is no clear correlation between share buybacks and share prices.

Konan and David (2014) study that share buybacks can boost the company's share price is a blind confidence of the management and an exaggeration of the positive effects of share buybacks. Share buybacks can only change the capital structure and do not change the company's profitable operation. Wang Qinggang and Xu Xinyu (2014) suggest that share buybacks do not have a clear and definite positive or negative market effect, and that share buybacks have no effect on the long-term market effect. Cheng Fen (2018) analyzed the effect of share buybacks on share price through case studies, which will only have a short-term stimulus effect on the share price when the buyback announcement is issued, and the long-term share price will be affected by the overall market trend, and the effect of share buybacks on the share price is very limited.

Research on other effects of share buybacks. The study of other utility of share repurchase on the company mainly focuses on the financial effect and the company's operating effect. Huang, Juequn and Gong, Liheng (2012) argued that share repurchase will improve the company's earnings per share and return on net assets to a certain extent, which can increase the wealth value of the company's shareholders, but it also increases the company's financial risk and payment risk.

Subba, Reddy and Yarram (2014) studied 104 cases of share buybacks that occurred in 62 Australian companies from 2004 to 2010 and found that the company's governance ability and crisis management ability to deal with risks have a greater pull on share buybacks during the share buyback process. A sound corporate governance system and financial policies have a positive and positive effect on the financial effect of share buybacks. Miao Jun (2015) conducts a study on share repurchase in the market context of government regulators and exchanges encouraging listed companies to carry out share repurchase, and researches the financial situation of companies after listed companies implement share repurchase under different circumstances, and finds that the financial situation of the company after the implementation of share repurchase of listed companies has a certain degree of improvement, and the operational efficiency is also improved.Gan Leifang (2018) concluded through empirical evidence and case study analysis that the implementation of share repurchase of listed companies optimizes the company's shareholding structure and capital structure, and the company's operating performance and cash flow have been significantly improved, which improves the company's share price and investors' confidence in a certain period of time; at the same time, share repurchase also brings certain negative effects, and if it does not meet the expectations of implementation, it may bring about financial risks . Cheng Fen (2018) studied the effect analysis of share repurchase on the growth capacity, solvency and profitability of the case listed companies through a case study, and concluded that in a short period of time share repurchase has a positive effect on the growth capacity, solvency and profitability of the case company, and in the long run, share repurchase only improves the growth capacity of the company. It has also been argued that share buybacks undertaken by companies can have a negative effect on the financial position of the company, Jagannathan and Murail (2003) studied that if a company uses idle funds for share buybacks, it can lead to a loss of investment opportunities when the company gets them.

Accompanied by the gradual enrichment of capital market research and related theories, share repurchase, as a basic operational tool of the capital market, began to be discussed by scholars, and formed a richer theoretical analysis framework. While many theories of the existing research are proposed, any one economic activity is difficult to use a single theory for a comprehensive explanation, and a cross-theoretical analysis framework is an inevitable requirement for a comprehensive study of an economic activity. Share repurchase as a signal is received by the market, the impact on the capital market is also complex, so it is necessary to comprehensively explain this from multiple theoretical perspectives. Based on the above theoretical review, this paper intends to start with the introduction of the concept of share repurchase first, discussing the two types of share repurchase, cash dividend alternative repurchase and strategic repurchase. Share repurchase is mainly carried out through three ways, open offer repurchase, open market share repurchase and agreement repurchase. Currently share repurchases are mainly conducted through open market share repurchases.Based on signaling theory, this paper argues that the open market share repurchase behavior of listed companies serves as a signal from management to the market, which causes the market to react to it, thus bringing about changes in the capital market. According to previous studies, listed companies' open market share repurchase announcements can bring significant positive excess returns, indicating the market's recognition of share repurchase behavior. It is based on this background that this paper further develops to explore the reaction of the company's stock price when the share repurchase announcement is fabricated. According to the efficient market hypothesis, the current capital market in China is still in a weak efficient market, the market value of the company's shares can not truly reflect all the company's relevant public information, so it is difficult for the market's resource allocation function to be effectively played. Share repurchase, as a means of public market information disclosure of listed companies, can change the information asymmetry between listed companies and the market, and promote the return of the company's capital market value to its true value. Therefore, in terms of how to enhance the effectiveness of the capital market, the role of share repurchase should not be ignored, and the specific effect of share repurchase on the capital market is worth exploring. In summary, the relevant theories of share repurchase are analyzed, how share repurchase produces effect on the market, and whether the effect on the share price is positive, negative or no effect. As the development of share buybacks in China's capital market has been improving in recent years, the data sample size is also large enough, so the event study method in SATAT is used to empirically analyze the effect of share buybacks on stock prices for companies that conduct share buybacks from 2021 to 2023.

3. EMPIRICAL MODEL FOR STUDYING THE EFFECT OF SHARE REPURCHASES ON SHARE PRICES

Sample selection and data analysis of this paper.In December 2019, China broke out a large-scale new crown epidemic until the end of 2022, when China's epidemic prevention and control policy shifted from strict prevention and control to coexisting with the virus after taking into account multiple factors, such as economic development, viral pathogenicity, and residents' sense of well-being, and isolation and control measures were abolished in their entirety and people's lives were restored to normal. During this period, China's economic activities in various industries were significantly restricted, and the triple mountain of demand contraction, supply shocks, and weakened expectations suppressed the overall performance of listed companies, corresponding to a significant drop in share prices, so most companies chose to implement share buybacks to stabilize their share prices, demonstrating their confidence in their future prospects in a practical way. In the past few years, many scholars have conducted research on share buybacks of listed companies. This paper examines the effect of share buybacks on the share prices of listed companies in China from January 1, 2021 to December 31, 2023 in light of the impact of epidemics and other similar events on listed companies. The sample covers all A-share listed companies that have issued share buyback programs, and the data are obtained from the CAMAR database to better explore the information.Based on the relevant studies of previous scholars, this paper follows the following filtering principles when conducting sample screening: 1. The first time of share repurchase announcements prevails, and the rest are excluded from the sample selection. 2. During the statistical period, some listed companies made multiple share repurchase announcements. Considering the acceptance of the market and the marginal weakening of the effectiveness of capital structure improvement, the first announcement is selected as the research object.2. The data of A-share repurchase is studied, and H-share and B-share are not retained. Different market players are affected by multiple factors such as liquidity, market participants, system construction, degree of openness, etc., and there are obvious differences in the market response of different markets to the same company's share repurchase.3. The repurchase data of ST* and ST are not retained. The first two companies have deteriorating operations and poor financial conditions, making it difficult to regain investor confidence through buybacks, so they are not considered as research objects.4. Data on buybacks announced but not implemented are not retained. Some listed companies did not carry out the actual operation within the required time after the announcement of share repurchase, and their share price performance is not comparable.6. Sample companies with incomplete information are not retained. After the screening criteria mentioned above, the time period selected for the study is 2021-2023 based on the latest data, and the final valid sample size of 692 was obtained in the CAMAR database.

After analyzing and organizing the sample data, it is found that the sample of 692 A-share companies selected involves 18 industries, and the classification of the industries refers to the industry classification name of the China Securities Regulatory Commission (CSRC) and the global industry classification standard for listed companies. The five industries with the highest proportion of companies implementing share buybacks are manufacturing, with 471 companies. Information transmission, software and information technology services, 77. Wholesale and retail trade, 25 companies. Scientific research and technology services, 23. Transportation, storage and postal services, 16. The specific industry distribution regarding the 692 listed companies is shown in Figure 1:

Figure 1.Sample Industry Classification

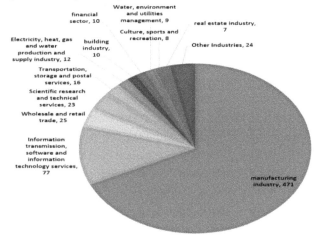

Companies in the sample implemented share repurchase mainly in the form of over-the-counter trading and exchange public form trading, but mainly in the form of exchange public form trading, accounting for 83%. For the repurchase of shares used mainly for subsequent employee stock ownership plan, equity incentives, and according to the law to be canceled and reduce the registered capital. 682 companies repurchase the source of funds is mainly its own funds, very few companies the source of funds is a bank loan.

Share price as an observable indicator of the market effect of corporate share buy-backs has the advantages of easy availability and high marketability, and drawing on the approach of scholars such as Vermaelen (1981) and Shao Ziyu (2020), this paper decides to adopt the event study method to investigate the effect of share buybacks on the stock prices of listed companies. The specific interpretation is whether the stock price fluctuates as a result of share repurchase by companies in the market, which results in an excess rate of return above the market rate of return. The significance of the excess return is then tested as a way of determining whether the fluctuations in stock prices are related to this event. Using this method we can detect whether a company's stock price fluctuates significantly and generates excess returns before and after the announcement of a stock announcement. During the detection process we use average daily excess return and average daily cumulative excess return as judgment indicators. The research criterion of this paper is that if the average daily excess return and average daily cumulative excess return during the window period can be significant at the t-test 10%, 5% and 1% significance level, then it means that share buybacks have an effect on the value of the company's stock.And again judged by the value of the average cumulative abnormal return, if ACAR is positive during the event window period, it means that stock buybacks can bring positive market effects in the short term, i.e., driving stock prices higher than expected or lower than expected, otherwise, stock buybacks do not bring positive uplift to stock prices. The relevant steps are as follows: 1. Determine the event date and window period. The day when the sample company first releases the stock repurchase announcement is selected as the event day, which is recorded as t=0. If the listed company is closed on the day of the announcement, the information announcement day is postponed to the next trading day. The event window is taken from 10 trading days before the event date to 10 trading days after the event date, denoted as T=(-10,10), a total of 21 days.2. The CAPM model is selected to estimate the expected return of the stock, and a clean period is selected to measure the expected return of the stock, which is defined as the period during which a company that implements share repurchase is not affected by the event of share repurchase, and in this paper, the clean period is the first 180 trading days of the event window, i.e., [-20,10]. The clean period selected in this paper is the first 180 trading days of the event window, i.e., [-20,-200]. The selected clean period is separated from the event window by 10 days to prevent the clean period from receiving the effect of the event window. The specific layout is shown in Figure 2:

Figure 2. Time intervals for the event method

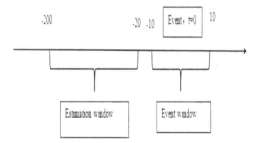

3.MODELING

$$R_{i,t} = \alpha_i + \beta_i R_{m,t} + \varepsilon_{i,t} \tag{1}$$

Ri,t is the normalized rate of return of a stock on day t.

Rm,t is the market return of the market index portfolio on day t. Depending on the exchange, it is categorized into the movement of the SSE Composite Index and the movement of the SZSE Component Index.

αi and βi are the regression coefficients, and βi is the systematic risk to which the stock is exposed.

$$R^{\wedge i,t} = \alpha^{\wedge i} + \beta^{\wedge i,t} R_{m,t} \tag{2}$$

R^i,t is the expected stock return for stock i at time t.

$$AR_{i,t} = R_{i,t} - R^{\wedge i,t} \tag{3}$$

$$CAR_i = \sum_{i=1}^{N} AR_{i,t} \tag{4}$$

ARi,t is the excess return of stock i at day t. CARi denotes the cumulative window period abnormal return (ARi,t).

$$AAR_{it} = \frac{1}{N} \sum_{i=1}^{N} AR_{it} \tag{5}$$

$$ACAR_{it} = \frac{1}{N} \sum_{i=1}^{N} CAR_{i,t} \tag{6}$$

AARit is the average excess return of the selected stocks.

ACARit is the average cumulative excess return of the selected stocks.

4. Significance test. In order to analyze the effect of share repurchase on the company's stock price more clearly, significance tests were done on the excess cumulative returns of all samples. Significance tests were also done for AAR and ACAR for each window.

(1) Significance test of average abnormal returns during the event window period. Set the original hypothesis: AR t ≥ 0; alternative hypothesis ARt<0.

$$T\left(ARt\right) = \frac{\overline{X}}{S/\sqrt{n}} \tag{7}$$

In the above formula, T represents the statistic, $\overline{X}$ denotes the sample mean, S denotes the sample standard deviation, and n denotes the sample capacity.

(2) Significance test of average cumulative abnormal returns during the event window period. Set the original hypothesis: CAR ≥ 0, alternative hypothesis: CAR < 0.

$$T\ CAR\ =\ \frac{\bar{X}}{S/\sqrt{n}} \qquad (8)$$

In the above formula, T represents the statistic, $\bar{X}$ represents the sample mean, S represents the sample standard deviation, and n represents the sample capacity.

This chapter mainly introduces the sample selection, the data mainly from the CAMAR database, selected from January 1, 2021 to December 31, 2023, the A-share listed companies that carry out share repurchase, during the period of multiple announcements of share repurchase only take the first time to publish the repurchase announcement data. After presenting the non-compliant companies. Finally a total of 692 sample companies were collected. There are 18 industries included in this sample, and the top three are manufacturing, information transmission, software and information technology services, and wholesale and retail trade. The companies in the sample mainly carry out repurchases in the form of public form trading, and the funds from the repurchases are mainly used for subsequent employee stock ownership plans, equity incentives, and to be canceled and reduced registered capital in accordance with the law. The main source of funds for share repurchase is the company's own funds. The effect of share repurchase on stock price is mainly analyzed using the event study method in STATA. After the announcement of repurchase by the listed company, the abnormal return during the window period will change, and along with it, the cumulative abnormal return will change. The significance of the effect of share repurchase on stock price is judged by the significance test of the average abnormal return and the average cumulative abnormal return in the window period.

4. THE RESULTS OF EMPIRICAL ANALYSIS OF THE EFFECT OF SHARE REPURCHASE ON THE SHARE PRICE OF LISTED COMPANIES

In this section, the results of the empirical test in the previous section are mainly presented and analyzed. It mainly analyzes the study of the effect of overall sample share repurchase on stock price and the study of the effect of four industries share repurchase on stock price, and finally the results of the overall sample and the industries are compared and analyzed to draw conclusions.

Firstly, the effect of share buyback on stock price is analyzed. The significance test was done on the cumulative excess collection rate of the overall sample of 692 companies as shown in Table 1:

Table 1. Cumulative excess return T-test result

	coef	Std.err	t	P>|t|	[95% Conf.	Interval]
CAR	0.0184681	0.0076165	2.42	0.016	0.0034797	0.0334565

From the data in Table 1, it can be seen that the p-value of cumulative excess return is significant at 5% level. It indicates that share repurchase events have a significant effect on stock prices during the window period.

In order to determine the effect of share repurchase events on stock prices during the specific window period, the AAR and ACAR for the window were calculated and P-test and T-test were performed respectively. As shown in Table 2. Then the trend graphs of AAR and ACAR during the window period were made. As shown in Table 3:

Table 2. Total sample AAR and ACAR results table

Event Window	AAR	T-Value	P-Value	ACAR	T-Value	P-value
-10	-0.0019	-2.4642	0.0140	-0.0019	-5.8763	0.0000
-9	0.0000	-0.3600	0.7190	-0.0019	-5.5662	0.0000
-8	0.0028	2.2689	0.0236	0.0009	-2.2806	0.0229
-7	0.0018	1.4016	0.1616	0.0027	-0.6034	0.5465
-6	-0.0001	-0.4503	0.6527	0.0025	-0.7819	0.4346
-5	-0.0013	-1.6139	0.1071	0.0013	-2.0952	0.0366
-4	0.0006	0.3026	0.7623	0.0019	-1.2770	0.2021
-3	-0.0004	-0.6294	0.5293	0.0016	-1.6306	0.1035
-2	-0.0014	-1.7978	0.0727	0.0002	-3.3407	0.0009
-1	-0.0024	-2.6522	0.0082	-0.0022	-5.4274	0.0000
0	0.0019	1.4957	0.1353	-0.0003	-3.3178	0.0010
1	0.0069	6.7514	0.0000	0.0066	3.3706	0.0008
2	0.0002	-0.1020	0.9188	0.0068	3.7059	0.0002
3	0.0007	0.4652	0.6420	0.0076	4.9159	0.0000
4	0.0020	1.8504	0.0648	0.0095	6.9384	0.0000
5	0.0007	0.4051	0.6855	0.0102	7.1905	0.0000
6	0.0024	2.2326	0.0260	0.0126	9.8634	0.0000
7	0.0005	0.1814	0.8561	0.0131	10.0571	0.0000
8	-0.0001	-0.4598	0.6458	0.0131	11.7610	0.0000
9	-0.0006	-0.9738	0.3306	0.0125	10.2798	0.0000
10	-0.0010	-1.6543	0.0986	0.0115	10.1350	0.0000

Table 3. Total sample AAR results table

Event Window	AAR	T-value(AAR)	P-value(AAR)
-10	-0.0019	-2.4642	0.0140
-9	0.0000	-0.3600	0.7190
-8	0.0028	2.2689	0.0236
-7	0.0018	1.4016	0.1616
-6	-0.0001	-0.4503	0.6527
-5	-0.0013	-1.6139	0.1071
-4	0.0006	0.3026	0.7623
-3	-0.0004	-0.6294	0.5293
-2	-0.0014	-1.7978	0.0727
-1	-0.0024	-2.6522	0.0082
0	0.0019	1.4957	0.1353
1	0.0069	6.7514	0.0000
2	0.0002	-0.1020	0.9188
3	0.0007	0.4652	0.6420
4	0.0020	1.8504	0.0648
5	0.0007	0.4051	0.6855
6	0.0024	2.2326	0.0260
7	0.0005	0.1814	0.8561
8	-0.0001	-0.4598	0.6458
9	-0.0006	-0.9738	0.3306
10	-0.0010	-1.6543	0.0986

From the above Table 3, it can be seen that the 10 days before the repurchase announcement, the 8 days before, the 2 days before, the 4 days after, the 6 days after, and the 10 days after are significant at the 10% confidence level. The average excess return of the overall sample on the first day before the repurchase announcement day is the lowest, reaching -0.24%, and is significant at 1% confidence level, which can indicate that the stock price performance on that day is relatively low, and there is almost no excess return. However, the average excess return of the overall sample turns from negative to positive on the day of stock announcement, indicating that listed companies choose to issue stock buyback programs at the right time based on the time and magnitude of stock price decline, and stock buybacks have a positive effect on the stock price later. On the day of the announcement, the average excess return reaches a maximum of 0.19%, but the significance test on this day is not significant; instead, the overall sample average excess return from the day after the announcement day reaches the maximum value of the window period, 0.69%. And it is significant at 1% confidence level. It indicates that investors also have a cautious attitude and carefully judge the truthfulness of the announcement information. By the time 8 days after the announcement date the overall sample average excess return turns from positive to negative, indicating that the information of share repurchase has a limited effect on the promotion of stock price.

Based on the above results, it can be inferred that listed companies tend to implement share buybacks when the stock price continues to fall, and the positive effect is most significant on the day after the announcement, and the stock price rises most significantly, and share buybacks still have a positive effect on the stock price of listed companies in the 7 days after the announcement date, but the effect is decreasing at the margin and lasts only a limited period of time.

Table 4. Total sample ACAR results table

Event Window	ACAR	T-value(ACAR)	P-value(ACAR)
-10	-0.0019	-5.8763	0.0000
-9	-0.0019	-5.5662	0.0000
-8	0.0009	-2.2806	0.0229
-7	0.0027	-0.6034	0.5465
-6	0.0025	-0.7819	0.4346
-5	0.0013	-2.0952	0.0366
-4	0.0019	-1.2770	0.2021
-3	0.0016	-1.6306	0.1035
-2	0.0002	-3.3407	0.0009
-1	-0.0022	-5.4274	0.0000
0	-0.0003	-3.3178	0.0010
1	0.0066	3.3706	0.0008
2	0.0068	3.7059	0.0002
3	0.0076	4.9159	0.0000
4	0.0095	6.9384	0.0000
5	0.0102	7.1905	0.0000
6	0.0126	9.8634	0.0000
7	0.0131	10.0571	0.0000
8	0.0131	11.7610	0.0000
9	0.0125	10.2798	0.0000
10	0.0115	10.1350	0.0000

From the above Table 4, it can be seen that during the event window period, the average cumulative excess return of the overall sample is positive after the announcement date, and the cumulative average excess return after the repurchase announcement date is significantly higher than that before the repurchase date, suggesting that the stock repurchase has a significant positive effect on the stock price, but the effect is not long, about 7-8 days, and then the cumulative average excess return declines again. The cumulative average excess return is significant at the 1% confidence level from two days before the announcement date to 10 days after the announcement, indicating that listed companies choose stock repurchase at the right time to reduce the cost of capital when the stock price is abnormally falling and the excess return continues to be low. After the empirical study, stock buybacks show a positive market effect, but the effect is short-lived.

Figure 3 AAR, ACAR Trend Chart

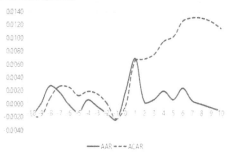

Figure 3, We can find the trend of the average excess return and cumulative daily average excess return of the overall sample of events in the window period, first of all, let's analyze the daily average excess return in the window period first, observing the trend in the figure we can find that, from t=-10 to t=-2, the indicator has been in a small up and down fluctuation, and basically located in the above zero. From day t=-1 to t=1, the indicator rises significantly and fluctuates violently, reaching a maximum value of 0.69% at t=1. It can also be seen from Table 2 that it is significant at 1% level at t=-1 and shows significant at 1% level by t=1. This indicates that the information on share buybacks has a very significant and drastic stimulating effect on the market, giving full play to the boosting effect on the stock price. However, from the period of t=[1,2] the daily average excess return begins to decline rapidly, and the subsequent period of t=[3,10], the initial state is restored with small up and down fluctuations, and the significance is significantly reduced. At this stage it indicates that although share buybacks have a boosting effect on stock prices, the sustained effect is short-lived. Observing the entire event window, it can be observed that only 8 days the average excess return is negative. It also means that 62% of the time the daily returns of the sample companies that conducted share buybacks were higher than the market returns during the same period, suggesting that share buybacks were positive for the company's share price. The market has given positive feedback. However, we should also note the situation before the first share repurchase announcement, the average daily excess return is significantly higher from t=-1, which indicates that there is a leakage of this information from the listed company before the announcement, and those who are in the know have already started to buy the target company's shares in advance.

Next we analyze the daily average cumulative excess returns during the share repurchase event window in conjunction with Figure 3 and Table 4. Observation shows that the daily average cumulative excess return during t=[-1,8] has been generally increasing, reaching a maximum value of 1.3%. Observing the significance again, the average daily cumulative excess returns are significant at 1% level from t=-2 throughout the window period. After the above analysis, we can know that share buybacks have a positive and significant effect on the market between the event window [-10,10].

The empirical results of the effect of share buybacks on stock prices in different industries are analyzed next. After the analysis of the overall sample is done, the effect of share repurchase on stock price for different industries is again demonstrated. In order to obtain sufficient sample data for effective research, the top four industries in terms of the number of companies in the industry in Figure 4 are selected for the study. The average cumulative excess return of each industry is calculated mainly through (1)-(6) in the Model, and then the significance test is performed on the excess return during the window period.The four selected industries are: manufacturing industry with 471 companies, information transmission, software and information technology services with 77 companies, wholesale and retail trade with 25 companies, and scientific research and technical services with 23 companies. Scientific research and technical services, with 23 companies.

The Chinese manufacturing industry is one of the largest in the world, with many well-known companies and leading industries. With the intensification of market competition and changes in economic development, the need for companies to improve their competitiveness and shareholder value has increased, making share repurchases an important financial tool. According to the China Securities Regulatory Commission (CSRC), the scale of share buybacks in the Chinese manufacturing industry has gradually expanded in recent years. Some well-known manufacturing companies have repurchased shares to increase earnings per share, reduce share liquidity, and maintain share price stability.The main motives for share repurchases by manufacturing industry enterprises include enhancing company value, improving capital structure, increasing market confidence, and reducing leverage. By repurchasing shares, companies can flexibly utilize their own funds, improve earnings per share, and increase investor confidence. Some large manufacturing enterprises such as Haier and Midea are actively involved in share repurchase activities. In the ranking of listed companies' share buyback amount in 2023, Gree Electric Appliances and Haier Zhijia of Chinese manufacturing industry are at the top. Gree Electric Appliances repurchased 2.013 billion yuan and 61,378,600 shares during 2023. Haier Zhijia repurchased 1.432 billion yuan and 63.9803 million shares during 2023. There are also many Chinese scholars who use these few manufacturing firms as case studies on share repurchase related topics. Huang Zhonghao (2022) concluded that multiple share buybacks have little effect on the financial index part of the enterprise and only have an effect on the solvency by studying the multiple share buybacks of Gree Electric Appliances. Finally, the market response to multiple share buybacks is diminishing. Yang Huihui, Tian Jun and Shen Hongbo (2022) found that the announcement effect of Midea Group's successive share repurchases was significant and played a positive role in maintaining market capitalization. At the same time, share buybacks undertake a multi-level and regularized equity incentive policy, which demonstrates good corporate governance and market value management capabilities.

The ACAR test results for different windows are obtained after processing the manufacturing industry share repurchase data in the overall sample using STATA16 as shown in Table 5, and the trend of AAR and ACAR during the period (-10, +10) is shown in Figure 4. According to the table 10 table it can be found that the sample company's stock return has a significant positive change 5 days before the announcement day and 66.7% of ACAR (passes the test at 1% level of significance) within the window (-10, 10). The ACAR has been in an upward trend for 6 days after the announcement date. And in the interval [0,10] ACAR has been positive.Through the above statistics, it can be found that listed companies tend to implement share buybacks after a relatively large drop in stock price will make the ACAR of the stock price significantly positive and briefly continue to rise, indicating that share buybacks have a positive effect on the stock price in that time period, but there is a leakage of information, making the stock price reflected in advance, and wait until the announcement of the announcement of the real announcement, the arbitrageurs will take advantage of the information advantage of the stock will be sold.

Table 5. manufacturing industry AAR and ACAR results table

Event Window	ACAR	T-value(ACAR)	P-value(ACAR)
-10	-0.0018	-4.7643	0.0000
-9	-0.0023	-5.1807	0.0000
-8	0.0000	-2.6933	0.0074
-7	0.0016	-1.3565	0.1757
-6	0.0023	-0.8331	0.4053
-5	0.0015	-1.4438	0.1496
-4	0.0040	0.4858	0.6274
-3	0.0033	-0.0214	0.9829
-2	0.0026	-0.5803	0.5620
-1	-0.0007	-3.2443	0.0013
0	0.0011	-1.6757	0.0946
1	0.0084	4.0376	0.0001
2	0.0086	4.3672	0.0000
3	0.0095	5.8206	0.0000
4	0.0120	7.7091	0.0000
5	0.0134	8.3874	0.0000
6	0.0153	10.6133	0.0000
7	0.0149	9.8430	0.0000
8	0.0148	11.4585	0.0000
9	0.0142	9.8722	0.0000
10	0.0133	9.9260	0.0000

Figure 4. Manufacturing Industry AAR, ACAR Trend Chart

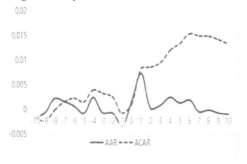

As can be seen in Figure 4, on the day of the announcement, investors are informed of the content of the announcement and react quickly, and the stock price changes as a result. As the information spreads, the AAR falls rapidly after the announcement day, and the ACAR no longer rises after reaching its highest value six days after the announcement day. It indicates that after the initial overreaction, investors gradually become more rational towards the buyback announcement and start to think about the real intention of the announcement and whether the plan can really be implemented; therefore, the stock price corrects in the opposite direction, and there is a slight drop in the stock price level of the sample companies after a brief increase. Both the symmetric window period around the announcement date and the significant ACAR performances during (-10, 0), (0, 10) and (-10, 10) indicate that both internal informants and external investors regard the share buyback news as favorable information and respond positively to it, so it is concluded that there is a positive short-term market effect of share buybacks by Chinese manufacturing companies.

With the increasing demand for digitization, the market size of the information transmission, software and information technology services industry is expanding, attracting more and more investments and competitors. Many companies rely on capital market financing for expansion and R&D, as well as managing their capital structure through share buybacks and other means. This industry is in a rapidly changing technological environment that requires constant innovation, research and development and investment, with high capital requirements. Guo Xiaori and Yang Chi (2020) studied the relationship between R&D investment and enterprise value with a sample of software and information technology service industry enterprises listed in 2015-2019 in Shanghai and Shenzhen, and found that in the software and information technology service industry, R&D investment and R&D input-output ratio have a direct effect on the increase of enterprise value. Feng (2018) analyzed the financial risks that enterprises in the software and information technology service industry are prone to through the method of case study, in terms of financing risk and capital recovery risk . Wang Li (2019) argued that the capital recovery risk in the software and information technology service industry is mainly reflected in the instability of the market. According to the latest data, the information transmission, software and information technology services industry has been active in share buybacks. Many large technology companies, as well as growing start-ups, have repurchased shares to flexibly utilize capital, enhance shareholder value and improve market position. This trend reflects the industry's companies' confidence in their value and optimistic expectations for future growth. Share repurchases can also help companies stabilize their share prices and attract more investors in the face of increased capital market volatility.

Table 6 and Figure 5, shows the presentation of the results of the empirical study of the first share repurchase for 77 companies of Information transmission, software and information technology services for the period 2021 to 2023. As can be seen from Table 11 in window (-10,0) 40% of ACAR is significant at 5% level of significance. In window (0,10) at T=0, ACAR is significant at 1% level of significance, T=5, ACAR is significant at 10% level of significance and T=10, ACAR is significant at 5% level of significance. From Table 11, it can be seen that ACAR is consistently negative for 4 days before the announcement day and then ACAR turns from negative to positive by the day after the announcement day.Through the above statistics, it can be found that listed companies tend to choose stock buyback in the case of a relatively large drop in stock price and lasts for a period of time, indicating that there is a positive effect of stock buyback on the stock price in that period of time, but the effect Information transmission, software and information technology services is significantly weaker than manufacturing industry. ACAR turns from positive to negative 3 days after the announcement date.

Table 6 Information transmission, software and information technology services AAR and ACAR results table

Event Window	ACAR	T-value(ACAR)	P-value(ACAR)
-10	-0.0011	-1.3596	0.1790
-9	-0.0028	-1.6801	0.0980
-8	0.0041	0.2426	0.8092
-7	0.0035	0.0477	0.9621
-6	0.0005	-0.7746	0.4416
-5	0.0004	-1.0600	0.2933
-4	-0.0082	-2.9040	0.0051
-3	-0.0056	-3.0293	0.0036
-2	-0.0089	-4.4107	0.0000
-1	-0.0061	-2.5533	0.0132
0	-0.0071	-3.4547	0.0010
1	0.0007	-1.1411	0.2583
2	0.0000	-1.1740	0.2449
3	-0.0010	-1.8198	0.0737
4	0.0018	-0.6593	0.5122
5	-0.0006	-1.7738	0.0811
6	0.0022	-0.3513	0.7265
7	0.0045	0.4194	0.6764

continued on following page

Table 6 Information transmission, software and information technology services AAR and ACAR results table

Continued

Event Window	ACAR	T-value(ACAR)	P-value(ACAR)
8	0.0034	0.0297	0.9764
9	0.0062	1.1787	0.2431
10	0.0121	2.5734	0.0151

Figure 5. Information transmission, software and information technology services AAR, ACAR Trend Chart

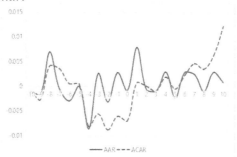

As seen in Figure 5, the charts of AAR and ACAR, the volatility of AAR and ACAR before the announcement date is significantly stronger than after the announcement date. The stock prices are very volatile. There is also a significant increase in AAR on the announcement day, and AAR reaches the maximum value of the window period. ACAR, on the other hand, has been on an upward trend since T=-2. It can be seen that share buybacks can stabilize the stock price and also have a short-term positive contribution to the stock price. From Figure 5, it can be seen that actually AAR and ACAR have been rising significantly from 4 days before the announcement, so there is a significant information leakage of share repurchase in Information transmission, software and information technology services industry.

The Wholesale and retail trade is undergoing rapid evolution as consumer demands and technological developments change. The rise of emerging models such as e-commerce and smart retailing has posed challenges to traditional brick-and-mortar stores, and companies need to continue to innovate in order to adapt to market trends. The wholesale and retail trade often relies on financial institutions to provide financial support for day-to-day operations and expansion. Through loans, bond issues, and other means, businesses can obtain funds to purchase inventory, expand, or conduct marketing. Some large wholesale and retail companies may choose to adjust their capital structure, enhance shareholder value or stabilize share prices through share buybacks. However, due to different industry characteristics, some firms may prefer to invest in expanding their business, opening new stores, or enhancing marketing activities for capital management.

Table 7 and Figure 6, show the effect of share buybacks on stock prices for 25 listed companies in Wholesale and retail trade over a three-year period, from 2021 to 2023.

From Table 7, it can be seen that 47.6% of the ACA's p-values in the whole window, are significant at 5% level of significance. And it can be seen that ACAR is not significant in the share buyback announcement period. The significance of ACAR increases during (2,9). It shows that there is a significant effect of share buyback on stock.

Table 7. Wholesale and retail trade AAR and ACAR results table

Event Window	ACAR	T-value(ACAR)	P-value(ACAR)
-10	0.0032	-0.0306	0.9759
-9	0.0056	0.4899	0.6295
-8	0.0043	0.1223	0.9039
-7	0.0063	0.4845	0.6333
-6	0.0024	-0.2392	0.8134
-5	0.0056	0.8498	0.4055
-4	-0.0010	-1.1541	0.2621
-3	-0.0058	-3.0405	0.0065
-2	-0.0062	-2.7479	0.0124
-1	-0.0076	-1.5995	0.1254
-0	0.0012	-0.3985	0.6945
1	0.0094	1.2419	0.2286
2	0.0108	2.2064	0.0392
3	0.0097	2.1984	0.0399
4	0.0146	2.3574	0.0287
5	0.0183	2.8304	0.0103
6	0.0168	6.1586	0.0000
7	0.0201	3.3750	0.0030
8	0.0191	4.6350	0.0002

Event Window	ACAR	T-value(ACAR)	P-value(ACAR)
9	0.0146	3.3129	0.0035
10	0.0085	1.0136	0.3229

Figure 6. Wholesale and retail trade AAR, ACAR Trend Chart

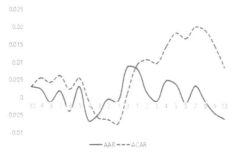

As can be seen in Figure 6, we can find the daily average excess return and the cumulative daily average excess return of the overall sample of events during the event window period.Let's first observe the ACAR in the share repurchase event window.Observing the trend in the figure, we can find that. In the window [-10,-1] ACAR's overall is showing a downward trend. at T=-1, ACAR starts to rise, in the window [-1,7] ACAR is overall in a rising state, and at T=7 is reaches the maximum value in the window. Subsequently it starts to fall. At the beginning of the focus on AAR, also at T=-1 began to rise significantly. But at AAR starts to fall at T=1, and at one point falls into negative territory at T=3.

Overall, the share buyback event exists as good news for the market and the market feeds back positively to it. However, we should pay attention to the situation before the day of the share buyback announcement, i.e., day t=0, during which there is already a very high average daily abnormal return, this phenomenon also demonstrates that the decision of the Chinese listed company has already been leaked before the announcement of the share buyback, and the market has already partially absorbed the information and made a reaction. On the day of the announcement, uninformed investors learn of the good news and buy shares, with small and medium-sized investors making up the majority of the buyers, who do not have enough financial strength but have an advantage in numbers and have a strong pull on the share price.

Scientific research and technical services cover a wide range of fields, including scientific research institutions, high-tech enterprises and scientific and technological intermediary service organizations, which are committed to promoting scientific and technological innovation, upgrading technology and serving a wide range of socio-economic areas. In terms of scientific research, the Chinese government strongly supports scientific research programs, encourages the combination of basic and applied research, and promotes the transformation of scientific and technological achievements. With the emergence of new technologies such as digitalization, artificial intelligence and the Internet of Things, the solutions provided by technology service companies are becoming more diversified and specialized. Technology service companies often prefer to utilize their capital for technology research and development, equipment upgrading and talent cultivation rather than managing capital through share buybacks. With the development of China's capital market and the relaxation of regulatory policies in recent years, the scientific research and technology services industry may use share buybacks to flexibly utilize capital, increase shareholder value or stabilize share prices.

From Table 8 and Figure 7, the effect of first-time share repurchases on the firm's stock price for three years, from 2021 to 2023, is depicted for the 23 firms of Scientific research and technical services. From Table 8, for the pre-announcement window, it is observed that the ACAR of Scientific research and technical services is broadly positive with better returns. Starting from the announcement date, it can be seen that in the ACAR in the window t=0 is significant at 5% level of significance, which is also the announcement date of the share repurchase, and it can be seen that the share repurchase has a significant effect on the stock. The ACAR reaches a maximum value of 5.32% 9 days after the announcement, and at (2, 10) ACAR appears to be significant at 1% level of significance. Once again, the significance of the effect of share repurchase on stock results is verified.

Table 8. Scientific research and technical services AAR and ACAR results table

Event Window	ACAR	T-value(ACAR)	P-value(ACAR)
-10	-0.0019	-0.9980	0.3331
-9	0.0069	0.6916	0.4991
-8	0.0122	1.2797	0.2189
-7	0.0105	1.2297	0.2366
-6	0.0118	2.1990	0.0429
-5	0.0084	1.1841	0.2537
-4	0.0145	1.9277	0.0718
-3	0.0142	2.2499	0.0389
-2	0.0087	1.1804	0.2551
-1	0.0078	1.3345	0.2007

continued on following page

Table 8. Continued

Event Window	ACAR	T-value(ACAR)	P-value(ACAR)
0	0.0162	2.2804	0.0366
1	0.0161	2.6097	0.0190
2	0.0216	3.6000	0.0024
3	0.0256	5.3343	0.0001
4	0.0306	4.9416	0.0001
5	0.0346	5.5218	0.0000
6	0.0374	5.2071	0.0001
7	0.0444	5.0856	0.0001
8	0.0487	9.3708	0.0000
9	0.0532	5.4283	0.0001
10	0.0502	8.6096	0.0000

Figure 7. Scientific research and technical services AAR, ACAR Trend Chart

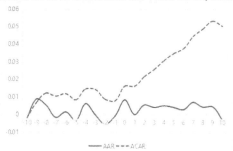

Figure 7 illustrates the trend of AAR and ACAR during the window of Scientific research and technical services. It can be seen that there is a significant increase in ACAR starting from T=-1, which continues to rise up to T=8, an increase of 524%. Looking more specifically at the AAR and observing the windows [-10,0] and [0,10] it is found that the fluctuations in the AAR are significantly more stable after the share buyback than before the share buyback. It well reflects the stabilizing effect of share buybacks on share prices. No significant early leakage of information is found in the specific data. Share repurchase also has a significant contribution to the company's share price.

After summarizing the analysis, it is found that the data characteristics of ACAR before and after the announcement of the four industries are different, and the trend graphs of ACAR and AAR are also different, therefore, this part of the analysis is conducted in the comparative analysis of the impact of share buybacks on the share prices of companies in the manufacturing industry, Information transmission, software and information Therefore, this section analyzes the effect of share buybacks on the share price of companies in four industries: manufacturing industry, information transmission, software and information technology services, wholesale and retail trade, and scientific research and technical services. Among them, manufacturing industry covers 471 companies, information transmission contains 77 companies, wholesale and retail trade contains 25 companies, and scientific research and technical services contains 23 companies. services contains 23 companies.By examining share buybacks in these different industries, we can assess the different preferences of companies in each industry for managing their capital structure and their strategic planning for future growth. By comparing the trends in ACAR in these industries, we can gain insight into the differences in the use of share repurchases as a tool by companies in each industry, and then explore the economic drivers and market trends behind them, providing useful references for investors and policy makers.

Figure 8. Comparison of the results of AAR and ACAR

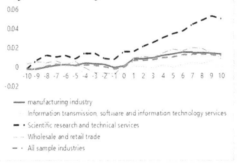

As seen in Figure 8, from the window (-1,10), the overall trend of ACAR are into a gradual upward trend, which firstly verifies the significant effect of share repurchase on the company's stock price. In window (0,10), the ACAR of Manufacturing industry and Wholesale and retail trade almost overlap with the trend of ACAR of All sample.Scientific research and technical services compared to the other three industries and the The rising trend of ACAR of Scientific research and technical services compared to the other three industries and the All sample is exceptionally significant, which indicates that investors are very optimistic about Scientific research and technical services, and when the company's share price is undervalued and the company implements share buybacks, investors also show great enthusiasm for investment. In comparison, the ACAR of Information transmission, software and information technology services is clearly the worst. It is also true that the investment risk of this industry is relatively high, and as a fast-growing emerging market in recent years, the life cycle of enterprises is generally shorter and the industry is changing faster, which are factors that investors need to consider.

The entire empirical section analyzes the stock price effect of the first implementation of share repurchases by listed companies that implement share repurchases during the entire three-year period, from 2021 to 2023. The overall sample consists of 692 listed companies. The event study method in STATA is utilized for the analysis. The results of CAR significance test for the overall sample and the significance tests of ACAR and AAR for the event window are shown separately and their window trends are plotted. Also again the top four industries in the sample were analyzed which include: manufacturing industry with 471 companies, Information transmission, software and information technology services with 77 companies. The top four industries in the sample were again analyzed: manufacturing industry with 471 firms, information transmission, software and information technology services with 77 firms, wholesale and retail trade with 25 firms, and scientific research and technical services with 23 firms. They were also analyzed in the same way as the overall sample. Finally a comparative analysis was done between the overall sample and the four industries.

The significance test of CAR for the overall sample shows that the effect of share buybacks on stock prices is significant. The window data and significance tests from the AAR and ACAR show the same conclusion, but the effect of share repurchase on stock price is different for each industry. The final conclusion is that share buybacks have a significant effect on stock prices in both the overall and industry samples analyzed. And it is a significant positive contribution with positive market effect, but the period of positive contribution is shorter in all cases. Also in the analysis of the trend charts, all of them showed that the share buyback information was leaked in advance, and some insiders in the know took advantage of the information to buy the company's shares before the date of the share buyback announcement, which demonstrated a rise in the share price before the announcement of the share buyback. For the results of the comparative analysis, the significant degree of the promotion effect of share buyback implementation on the share price is again differently reflected in different industries.

Comprehensive analysis, in the company's share price downturn, the listed company can through the share repurchase for market value management, in the short term this is the most obvious effect on the share price, share repurchase is also an alternative to the cash dividend a measure, not only can be very good to the market to release the information of the company's share price is underestimated, but also to maintain the company's stable dividend policy to attract investors. Of course, listed companies need to improve the company's profitability as much as possible, the higher the profitability, the positive effect of share buybacks on the share price has a superimposed effect.

5. CONCLUSIONS, DISCUSSION AND RECOMMENDATIONS

The results of the study find that the stock returns of listed firms that carry out share repurchases already show significant positive excess returns before the repurchase announcement, which reacts to the fact that there is indeed an early leakage of repurchase information in China's share repurchase market. And on the announcement day of share repurchase, market participants will react to the announcement and bring positive excess return, however, along with the gradual reception of the information, the average excess return falls back quickly after the announcement day, and the significance test of the cumulative abnormal return of the overall sample is also effective. Tests on average abnormal returns and average cumulative abnormal returns in the window also show that share repurchases have a significant effect on stocks. However, the trend graph of average abnormal returns in the window clearly reflects that the stock price starts to decline around 5 days after the announcement date. It shows that the market participants are gradually becoming rational towards the buyback announcements and start analyzing the motivation of the management to carry out the share repurchases and the genuineness of the share repurchases, which leads to a cooling down of the market and hence there is a downward adjustment in the stock price and the company's share price also falls down after the growth. Thus although share repurchases have a significant positive contribution to the impact of stock prices, the time frame is short.

The results of the study for the four industries show that the effect of share repurchases on stock prices varies from industry to industry. Overall the positive effect of share repurchases on stock prices in the four industries is significant. Among the four industries, share repurchases in the scientific research and technical services industry have a better positive effect on stock prices than the other three industries, and the effect is also better than the overall sample. It shows that stock investors recognize this industry. In recent years, the Chinese government has elevated science and technology as an important part of the national agenda, and China is increasing funding for basic research and plans to raise the proportion of spending on basic research to 8% by 2025. The country has made significant scientific research achievements in areas such as quantum information, nuclear energy technology and artificial intelligence technology, which have not only promoted the development of strategic emerging industries, but also accelerated the transformation and upgrading of traditional industries.

Based on the results of empirical research and related literature, this paper will put forward targeted suggestions from the three perspectives of the government, listed companies and investors, with a view to providing strong support for the improvement of China's stock repurchase system and the high-quality development of the capital market.

The government improves the information disclosure system and increases the penalty for insider trading. From the empirical results of this paper, the average excess return from 1 day before the announcement to the day of the announcement shows a significant increase, indicating that the news has been leaked in advance, compared with previous studies, the information disclosure system has been significantly improved, but there are still loopholes. On the one hand, the government needs to restrain the illegal behavior of listed companies using insider information from the legal and institutional levels, effectively protect the legitimate rights and interests of investors as well as the openness and authority of the capital market, and further strengthen the supervision and standardize the implementation procedures of stock repurchases. On the other hand, the relevant regulatory authorities can open up multiple channels of information announcements for small and medium-sized investors, for example, in addition to requiring listed companies to publish stock repurchase announcements on designated official websites, they can also urge them to publish relevant and important information in a timely manner on the company's official website, micro-channel platforms and other channels to draw in the distance with small and medium-sized investors. China's capital market started late, currently does not meet the conditions of full marketization, the basic institutional constraints is the soil of high-quality growth of listed companies, but also a necessary guarantee of the stable expansion of the capital market.

Listed companies consciously comply with relevant laws and regulations and fulfill their information disclosure obligations. Listed companies should be based on the vision of long-term development, do not be confused by short-term insider trading interests, strictly implement information confidentiality and disclosure, complete the process of stock repurchase on time and in compliance, contribute to the establishment of a good environment in the capital market, and promote each other for common development. Listed companies should combine their own financial situation, capital structure, stock price performance and development cycle to consider the implementation plan and time of stock repurchase. The empirical results show that in the short term, stock repurchase can indeed promote the rise of stock price and form excess returns, but the sample difference is also more obvious: high-quality enterprises and listed companies with equity pledges will be more recognized by the market after announcing the stock repurchase, so that they are willing to grant a certain level of premium to the share price. High-quality companies often have multiple advantages such as abundant cash flow, stable business operations, and superior competitive landscape, which will naturally be favored by investors; while companies with equity pledges will often experience a crisis in the company's financial situation due to the continuous decline in share price, so there is an urgent need to buy back shares to stabilize the share price, compared to other companies announcing repurchases, such companies have a higher credibility in the minds of investors, and therefore investors are willing to buy their shares, thus driving up the share price. There are few companies whose share prices continue to fall after the buyback announcement, and the reasons behind are diversified.Poor quality of listed companies need to start from the company's operational level to solve the problem, rather than attempting to use stock repurchases to continue to enjoy the valuation bubble, the market qualified rational investors will not pay for it. The frequency of repurchase can reflect the listed company for its intrinsic value and market value deviation degree of control, the side can also reflect the rational attitude of the listed company, usually, a high frequency of stock repurchase will not take up too much money, and enterprise good development confidence can also be reflected in the long term is more likely to realize the positive market effect. If the frequency of share repurchase is low, investors will tend to think that it only focuses on short-term effects, and there is a suspicion of stock price manipulation, so it is difficult to achieve the expected market value management objectives. Based on this, listed companies can appropriately increase the frequency of repurchases to guide investors to focus on the long-term development of the company, rather than throwing money at it in the hope that the stock price can immediately reach the expected level. Companies should take a holistic view, multi-dimensional and strategic assessment of the amount of share repurchases and their potential impact, to increase the probability of achieving the positive market effect objectives, rather than stopping or even retrogressing the development of the company's core business due to the pursuit of stabilizing the stock price or equity incentives.

On the one hand, investors should take the initiative to improve their professionalism and cognitive level, develop the habit of independent thinking, do a good job of emotion management and stress control, minimize the negative impact of the "herd effect" in the market, and rationally view the positive impact of stock repurchases, as there may be insider trading, stock price manipulation and other unlawful behaviors behind the buyback event. illegal behaviors. In order to more clearly understand the motivation of listed companies to carry out stock repurchases, investors need to stand on the other side of the assessment of the feasibility of the period buyback program, can be combined with the company's financial situation, profitability, as well as the amount and proportion of the buyback and other aspects of a comprehensive consideration, while taking into account the frequency of the listed company's stock repurchase, to determine whether there is a short-term manipulation of the stock price suspicion. If the frequency of repurchase is high, you can also check its past cases of repurchase and the corresponding stock price performance to determine whether the listed company has excellent timing ability, based on which to make their own independent and probable correct investment decisions; on the other hand, we should strengthen the screening and interpretation of information, establish a scientific and reasonable investment decision-making framework, and enhance the awareness of the protection of investment rights and interests.If a listed company's financial condition is poor and the industry development prospect tends to be bleak, even if it issued a share buyback announcement and its share price has a significant positive market effect in the short term, investors need to be cautious about the excess returns of similar situations, without the support of good fundamentals, the listed company experienced most of the positive events for its share price impact is only temporary. Therefore, investors need to establish the concept of long-term investment and correctly understand the short-term effect of favorable events and the long-term trend of company development. Existing empirical results show that stock repurchases do have a positive market effect in the short term, but tend to weaken in the long term. Investors need a broader research perspective to enrich the long-term research framework of listed companies, and strive not to lose sight of the small details while grasping the general trend. On this basis, investors need to strengthen the research and study of relevant laws and regulations, and carefully understand the compliance process of stock repurchase, so as to avoid the occurrence of events in which listed companies issue stock repurchase announcements but do not follow through with their implementation, thus leading to the damage of investor interests.

REFERENCES

Almeida, H., Fos, V., & Kronlund, M. (2016). The Real Effects of Share Repurchases. *Journal of Financial Economics*, 119(1), 168–185. DOI: 10.1016/j.jfineco.2015.08.008

Angrist, J. D., & Pischke, J. S. (2010). The credibility revolution in empirical economics: How better research design is taking the con out of econometrics. *The Journal of Economic Perspectives*, 24(2), 3–30. DOI: 10.1257/jep.24.2.3

Ashenfelter, O. (1978). Estimating the effect of training programs on earnings. *The Review of Economics and Statistics*, 60(1), 47–57. DOI: 10.2307/1924332

Baker, H. K., Powell, G. E., & Veit, E. T. (2003). Why companies use open-market repurchases: A managerial perspective. *The Quarterly Review of Economics and Finance*, 43(3), 483–504. DOI: 10.1016/S1062-9769(02)00151-5

Baker, M., & Wurgler, J. (2002). Market Timing and Capital Structure. *The Journal of Finance*, 57(1), 1–32. DOI: 10.1111/1540-6261.00414

Baker, M., & Wurgler, J. (2002). Market Timing and Capital Structure. *The Journal of Finance*, 57(1), 1–32. DOI: 10.1111/1540-6261.00414

Ball, R., & Brown, P. (1968). An empirical evaluation of accounting income numbers. *Journal of Accounting Research*, 6(2), 159–178. DOI: 10.2307/2490232

Bittlingmayer, G. (1998). The market for corporate control (including takeovers). Available at *SSRN* 81808. DOI: 10.2139/ssrn.81808

Bonaime, T., & Oztekin, D. (2014). The effect of managerial ownership on the short-and long-run response to cash distributions. *Financial Review*, 38, 179–196.

Bradley, M., & Wakeman, L. M. (1983). The wealth effects of targeted share repurchases. *Journal of Financial Economics*, 11(1-4), 187–205. DOI: 10.1016/0304-405X(83)90015-6

Brav, A., Graham, J., Harvey, C. R., & Michaely, R. (2005). Payout policy in the 21st century. *Journal of Financial Economics*, 77(3), 483–527. DOI: 10.1016/j.jfineco.2004.07.004

Brav, A., Graham, J., Harvey, C. R., & Michaely, R. (2005). Payout policy in the 21st century. *Journal of Financial Economics*, 77(3), 483–527. DOI: 10.1016/j.jfineco.2004.07.004

Brockman, P., Khurana, I. K., & Martin, X. (2008). Voluntary disclosures around share repurchases. *Journal of Financial Economics*, 89(1), 175–191. DOI: 10.1016/j.jfineco.2007.08.004

Chen, J. (2016). An empirical study on the motivation and market reaction of stock buyback of listed companies in China [Doctoral dissertation, China University of Petroleum (Beijing)].

Cheng, F. (2018). Research on the motivation and effect of Midea's stock repurchase [Master's thesis, Jiangxi University of Finance and Economics].

Cheng, F. (2018). Research on the motivation and effect of share repurchase of Midea Corporation [Master's thesis, Jiangxi University of Finance and Economics].

Chi, D. J. (2005). The announcement effect of stock repurchases on Taiwan Stock Exchange. *International Journal of Business and Management*, 5(10), 168–177.

Comment, R., & Jarrell, G. A. (1991). The Relative Signalling Power of Dutch-Auction and Fixed-Price Self-Tender Offers and Open-Market Share Repurchases. *The Journal of Finance*, 46(4), 1243–1271.

Connelly, B. L., Certo, I. R. D., Ireland, R. D., & Reutzel, C. R. (2011). Signaling Theory: A Review and Assessment. *Journal of Management*, 37(1), 39–67. DOI: 10.1177/0149206310388419

Cziraki, P., Lyandres, E., & Michaely, R. (2019). What do insiders know? Evidence from insider trading around share repurchases and SEOs. *Journal of Corporate Finance*, 66, 101544. DOI: 10.1016/j.jcorpfin.2019.101544

Dann, L. (1981). Common stock repurchase: An analysis of return to bondholders and stockholders. *Journal of Financial Economics*, 9, 113–138. DOI: 10.1016/0304-405X(81)90010-6

Dann, L. Y. (1981). Common stock repurchases: An analysis of returns to bond-holders and stockholders. *Journal of Financial Economics*, 9(2), 113–138. DOI: 10.1016/0304-405X(81)90010-6

Deng, Q., Chen, N., & Qin, S. (2021). Equity pledge and share repurchase of listed companies based on Wanfeng Aowei. *Friends of Accounting*, 2021(20), 102–108.

Dittmar, R. F. (2002). Nonlinear pricing kernels, kurtosis preference, and evidence from the cross section of equity returns. *The Journal of Finance*, 57(1), 369–403. DOI: 10.1111/1540-6261.00425

Dolley, J. C. (1933). Characteristics and procedure of common stock split-ups. Harvard Business Review, 11(3), 316-326.80.Ball R., Brown P., 1968, An Empirical Evaluation of Accounting Income Numbers [J]. *Journal of Accounting Research*, 2(6), 159–178.

Fama, E. F., Fisher, L., Jensen, M. C., & Roll, R. (1969). The adjustment of stock prices to new information. *International Economic Review*, 10(1), 1–21. DOI: 10.2307/2525569

Feng, L. (2008). An empirical study of the information content and insider trading around open market share repurchase announcements [Doctoral dissertation, Concordia University].

Feng, Z. (2018). Research on financial risk of enterprises in the software and information technology service industry. Finance and Accounting Study, No. 208(34), 24+26.

Gan, L. (2018). Effect analysis of share repurchase of JAC [Master's thesis, Jiangxi University of Finance and Economics].

Harford, J., Mansi, S. A., & Maxwell, W. F. (2008). Corporate governance and firm cash holdings in the US. *Journal of Financial Economics*, 87(3), 535–555. DOI: 10.1016/j.jfineco.2007.04.002

He, Y., Huang, J., & Li, J. (2014). A study on the economic consequences of share repurchase by listed companies in China: Empirical data from A-share market from 2005 to 2013. *Economic Management*, 36(10), 53–63.

Hillert, A., Maug, E., & Obernberger, S. (2016). Stock repurchases and liquidity. *Journal of Financial Economics*, 119(1), 186–209. DOI: 10.1016/j.jfineco.2015.08.009

Huang, H., & Liu, J. (2007). Analysis of the Impact of Stock Repurchase Behavior of Listed Companies in China on Stock Prices. *Price Theory and Practice*, 2007(11), 62–63.

Huang, J., & Gong, L. (2012). Analysis of the impact of share repurchase on the financial management of listed companies. *Finance and Accounting Newsletter*, 2012(35), 73–74.

Huang, Z. (2022). Research on the motivation and implementation effect of multiple share repurchases by listed companies [Doctoral dissertation, Southwest University of Finance and Economics]. DOI:DOI: 10.27412/d.cnki.gxncu.2022.001159

Ikenberry, D., & Gertler, M. (1995). Stock repurchases in Canada: Long-run abnormal performance and the impact of firm size. *The Journal of Finance*, 52(2), 113–134.

Ikenberry, D., Lakonishok, J., & Vermaelen, T. (1995). Market underreaction to open market share repurchases. *Journal of Financial Economics*, 39(2), 181–208. DOI: 10.1016/0304-405X(95)00826-Z

Ikenberry, D., Lakonishok, J., & Vermaelen, T. (1995). Market underreaction to open market share repurchases. *Journal of Financial Economics*, 39(2-3), 181–208. DOI: 10.1016/0304-405X(95)00826-Z

Ikenberry, D., Lakonishok, J., & Vermaelen, T. (2000). Stock repurchases in Canada: Performance and strategic trading. *The Journal of Finance*, 55(5), 2373–2397. DOI: 10.1111/0022-1082.00291

Jacobson, L. S., LaLonde, R. J., & Sullivan, D. G. (1993). Earnings losses of displaced workers. *The American Economic Review*, 83(4), 685–709.

Jagannathan, R., & Murail, I. (2003). The effects of stock repurchases on investment opportunities: Evidence from corporate cash flow data. *The Journal of Finance*, 58(4), 1619–1643.

Jagannathan, R., & Stephens, C. P. (2000). The Market Valuation of Stock Repurchases by Investment-Quality Firms. *The Journal of Finance*, 55(2), 975–1007.

Jarrell, G. A. (1991). The relative signaling power of Dutch auction and fixed-price self-tender offers and open-market share repurchase. *The Journal of Finance*, 46, 1243–1271.

Ji, Q. (2017). Research on the motivation and announcement effect of stock repurchase in listed companies [Doctoral dissertation, Northwest University]. DOI:CNKI:CDMD:2.1017.104419.

Konan, C., & Ikenberry, D. (2014). Economic sources of gain in stock repurchases. *Journal of Financial and Quantitative Analysis*, 39, 461–479.

LaLonde, R. J. (1986). Evaluating the econometric evaluations of training programs with experimental data. *The American Economic Review*, 76(4), 604–620.

Lazonick, W. (2014). Profits Without Prosperity. *Harvard Business Review*, 92(9), 46–55.

Lin, M. (2017). Research on factors influencing the short-term market effect of stock repurchase by listed companies in China [Master's thesis, Zhejiang Jiangxi College].

Liu, Y. (2019). Analysis of financial and market effects of share repurchase in Chinese A-share market. *China Development*, 2019(02), 32–35.

Ma, M. (2008). Research on stock repurchase of listed companies in China [Doctoral dissertation, Tianjin University].

Miao, J. (2015). Implementation of share repurchase by listed companies to revitalize the confidence of China's capital market. *Economic Research Guide*, 2015(12), 114–118.

Mirrlees, J. A. (1976). The Optimal Structure of Incentives and Authority Within an Organization. *The Bell Journal of Economics*, 7(1), 105–131. DOI: 10.2307/3003192

Mitchell, J. D., & Dharmawan, G. V. (2007). Incentives for on-market buy-backs: Evidence from a transparent buy-back regime. *Journal of Corporate Finance*, 13(1), 146–169. DOI: 10.1016/j.jcorpfin.2006.12.002

Netter, J. M., & Mitchell, M. L. (1989). Stock Repurchases: An Analysis of Returns to Bondholders and Stockholders. *Journal of Financial Economics*, 23(1), 161–181.

Ofer, A. R., & Thakor, A. V. (1987). A Theory of Stock Price Responses to Alternative Corporate Cash Disbursement Methods: Stock Repurchases and Dividends. *The Journal of Finance*, 42(2), 365–394. DOI: 10.1111/j.1540-6261.1987.tb02572.x

Qian, Y. (1995). Analysis of the long-term impact of stock repurchases on excess return. *Financial Research*, 45(3), 68–79.

Reddy Yarram, S. (2014). Factors influencing on-market share repurchase decisions in Australia. *Studies in Economics and Finance*, 31(3), 255–271. DOI: 10.1108/SEF-02-2013-0021

Ren, H., Zhao, X., & Li, Y. (2023). Share repurchases and capital market pricing bias—Empirical evidence based on listed companies. *Scientific Decision Making*, 2023(09), 77–95.

Shao, Z. (2020). Research on the market effect of stock buyback of listed companies in China and its influencing factors. *Times Finance*, 2020, 93–96.

Shapiro, B., & Matson, D. (2008). Strategies of resistance to internal control regulation. *Accounting, Organizations and Society*, 33(2), 199–228. DOI: 10.1016/j.aos.2007.04.002

Shou, D., & Sun, E. (2000). Current situation of domestic and international stock repurchases and implications. *Economic Issues*, 2000(11), 70–73.

Stephens, C. P., & Weisbach, M. S. (2008). Stock repurchases in the 1980s and 1990s: What did we learn? *The Journal of Finance*, 53(6), 2071–2092.

Takahashi, H., & Nobuyuki, L. (2004). Stock price behavior surrounding stock repurchase announcements: Evidence from Japan. *Pacific-Basin Finance Journal*, 12(3), 271–290. DOI: 10.1016/j.pacfin.2003.10.002

Tsetsekos, G. P. (1993). Valuation effects of open market stock repurchases for financially weak firms. *Review of Financial Economics*, 2(2), 29–42. DOI: 10.1002/j.1873-5924.1993.tb00563.x

Vermaelen, T. (1981). Common stock repurchases and market signaling. *Journal of Financial Economics*, 9(2), 139–183. DOI: 10.1016/0304-405X(81)90011-8

Vermaelen, T. (1981). Common stock repurchases and market signaling. *Journal of Financial Economics*, 9(2), 139–183. DOI: 10.1016/0304-405X(81)90011-8

Vermaelen, T. (1981). Common stock repurchases and market signaling: An empirical study. *Journal of Financial Economics*, 9(2), 139–183. DOI: 10.1016/0304-405X(81)90011-8

Vermaelen, T. (1981). Common stock repurchases and market signaling: An empirical study. *Journal of Financial Economics*, 9(2), 139–183. DOI: 10.1016/0304-405X(81)90011-8

Wang, L. (2019). Research on financial risk of software and information technology service industry enterprises. Finance and Accounting Study, No. 228(19), 84+86.

Wang, Q. (2018). Research on the market effect of stock buyback of listed companies and its influencing factors [Doctoral dissertation, Xi'an University of Science and Technology].

Wang, W. (2002). Information connotation and market identification of state-owned legal person share repurchase: An empirical study on the repurchase of state-owned legal person shares by Yuntianhua and Shenneng companies. *Management World (Monthly)*, 2002(6), 109–117.

Wansley, J. W., Lane, W. R., & Sarkar, S. (1989). Managements' View on Share Repurchase and Tender Offer Premiums. *Financial Management*, 18(3), 97–110. DOI: 10.2307/3665652

Wu, Y. (2018). Research on the short-term market effect of stock repurchase announcement of A-share listed companies and its influencing factors [Doctoral dissertation, East China University of Politics and Law].

Xiong, H. (2022). Analysis of the reasons for share repurchase—Taking Gree Electric as an example. *China Management Informatization*, 25(03), 25–28.

Xu, G., & Chi, M. K. (2003). Stock repurchases and firm value: A theoretical and empirical analysis. *Management Science*, 49(4), 60–64.

Yang, H., Tian, C., & Shen, H. (2022). Dual effects of share repurchase to maintain market value and incentivize employees: A case study based on Midea Group. *China Management Accounting*, (01), 98–114.

Yang, X. (2012). Research on share buyback behavior of listed companies based on long-term market effect analysis [Doctoral dissertation, Chang'an University].

Yu, L. (2010). Research on the market effect of stock repurchase of listed companies in China [Doctoral dissertation, Southwest University of Finance and Economics].

Zhang, R., Song, X., & Yin, W.. (2021). Analysis of motivation and effectiveness of stock repurchase in listed companies—Taking Gree Electric Appliances as an example. *Value Engineering*, 40(24), 3. DOI: 10.3969/j.issn.1006-4311.2021.24.019

Zhang, Y. (2020). Research on the market effect of stock repurchase announcements of listed companies in China [Doctoral dissertation, Shanghai International Studies University].

Zhou, M. (2007). Analysis of negative financial effects of corporate share buyback. *Science and Industry*, 7(1), 4. DOI: 10.3969/j.issn.1671-1807.2007.01.019

Chapter 9
The Emotional Rollercoaster of Market Overreaction:
Understanding the Psychological Drivers of Irrational Market Behaviour

Sushil Kumar Gupta
https://orcid.org/0000-0001-5667-4782
Pune Institute of Business Management, Pune, India

Varsha Shriram Nerlekar
School of Business, Dr. Vishwanath Karad MIT World Peace University, India

Anjali Sane
https://orcid.org/0000-0001-7284-848X
Dr. Vishwanath Karad MIT World Peace University, India

Manjiri Gadekar
https://orcid.org/0000-0003-3509-6594
School of Business, Dr. Vishwanath Karad MIT World Peace University, Pune, India

Shrikant Waghulkar
https://orcid.org/0000-0002-3767-3765
RIMS, India

DOI: 10.4018/979-8-3693-7827-4.ch009

Copyright © 2025, IGI Global Scientific Publishing. Copying or distributing in print or electronic forms without written permission of IGI Global is prohibited.

ABSTRACT

Market overreactions, driven by psychological and cognitive factors, have significant economic consequences, impacting individual investors and broader financial systems. This chapter explores how emotions like fear, anxiety, greed, and euphoria contribute to market volatility, alongside cognitive biases such as confirmation and anchoring. It also examines herding behavior, the influence of authority figures, and the role of media in shaping market sentiment. Additionally, it considers neurological and physiological factors like stress and dopamine responses in investor behavior. Through case studies, the chapter illustrates these drivers' real-world impacts and offers strategies for mitigating emotional and cognitive biases. Emphasizing diversification, risk management, and regulatory measures, it provides insights for investors and policymakers to navigate and stabilize market overreactions.

I. INTRODUCTION

Market behavior is often seen as a reflection of rational decision-making based on available information, yet history has shown that markets can be as much a product of emotion as of logic. The phenomenon of market overreaction is a compelling example of how emotions, rather than reason, can drive investor behavior, leading to significant deviations from fundamental values (Khatua & Pradhan, 2014). This emotional rollercoaster, characterized by euphoric highs and depressive lows, often results in extreme market movements that defy traditional economic theories (Hinvest, Alsharman, Roell, & Fairchild, 2021).

At the heart of this overreaction lies a complex interplay of psychological factors (Subedi & Bhandari, 2024) that influence investor decision-making. Cognitive biases such as overconfidence (Kartini & Nahda, 2021), herd mentality (Devadas & Vijayakumar, 2019) and loss aversion (Vuković & Pivac, 2024) can lead to irrational market behaviors. For instance, overconfidence might cause investors to overestimate their ability to predict market movements, leading to excessive risk-taking and inflated asset prices. Similarly, herd mentality can amplify market trends, as individuals follow the majority, often without critical analysis, creating bubbles or crashes (Aljifri, 2023). Loss aversion, where the pain of losses outweighs the pleasure of gains, can trigger panic selling during downturns, exacerbating market declines (Vuković & Pivac, 2024).

The emotional responses of investors are not only personal but also collective, magnified by media influence and social dynamics. News cycles, especially in the digital age, can amplify fears and hopes, leading to rapid swings in market sentiment (Cioroianu, et al., 2024). This collective emotional response can create feedback loops, where initial price movements, driven by emotion, lead to further emotional reactions, pushing prices even further from their intrinsic values (Al-Zoubi, 2024). The result is a market environment that can be highly volatile, with prices oscillating between extremes based on sentiment rather than underlying economic fundamentals.

Understanding the psychological drivers behind market overreaction is crucial for investors, policymakers, and market regulators. It highlights the importance of behavioral finance as a complement to traditional financial theories, offering insights into how emotional factors can lead to irrational market outcomes (Dhillon & Singh, 2017). By recognizing these emotional drivers, investors can develop strategies to mitigate the impact of irrational behaviors, for instance, diversifying their portfolios, setting clear investment goals, and maintaining a long-term perspective. Furthermore, regulators can design policies that address the systemic risks posed by market overreactions, ensuring greater market stability (Chandu, et al., 2023).

- Definition of market overreaction and its consequences

Market overreaction refers to a phenomenon in stock markets where there is a return reversal on stocks, turning winners into losers and vice versa. This behavior is characterized by excessive price movements in response to both anticipated and unanticipated news, leading to extreme price changes even in the absence of specific public news.

Market Overreaction refers to the phenomenon where investors respond to new information with exaggerated enthusiasm or panic, leading to significant and often unwarranted price movements (Larson & Madura, 2023). This behavior deviates from the principles of the Efficient Market Hypothesis (EMH), which assumes that asset prices always reflect all available information. Instead, in a market overreaction, prices can swing far above or below their intrinsic values due to the emotional and psychological responses of investors.

Various Definitions of Market Overreaction from Different Perspectives:

Behavioral Finance Perspective:

Market overreaction refers to the excessive response of investors to new information, often leading to significant price movements that are not justified by the underlying fundamentals. This behavior is driven by psychological biases such as overconfidence, herd behavior, and loss aversion, resulting in prices that swing far above or below their true value.

Efficient Market Hypothesis (EMH) Context:

In the context of the EMH, market overreaction is the deviation from the hypothesis that all available information is already reflected in asset prices. It occurs when prices move significantly in response to new information, suggesting that the market participants have either overestimated or underestimated the impact of that information, leading to temporary mispricing (Okur & Gurbuz, 2015).

Technical Analysis Definition:

From a technical analysis viewpoint, market overreaction is identified when asset prices move sharply in one direction due to the influx of new data or news, often resulting in short-term price extremes that are later corrected as the market returns to its equilibrium (Sembiring, Rahman, Effendi, & Sudarsono, 2016).

Investment Strategy Context:

Market overreaction is a phenomenon where investors react too strongly to news, either positive or negative, causing prices to overshoot their true value. This can create opportunities for contrarian investors who believe that prices will eventually revert to their mean, allowing them to capitalize on the temporary mispricing (Duran & Caginalp, 2007).

Empirical Finance Perspective:

Market overreaction is an observed behavior where stock prices tend to over-adjust to information, leading to subsequent corrections. Empirical studies often measure overreaction by analyzing the price movements following significant events, such as earnings announcements or macroeconomic news, and observing the tendency for prices to reverse direction after the initial reaction (Musnadi, Faisal, & Majid, 2018).

- Psychological drivers of irrational market behaviour

The phenomenon of irrational market behavior is deeply intertwined with the psychological drivers that influence investor decision-making. This irrationality often manifests as market overreaction, where prices deviate significantly from their intrinsic values, driven by the emotional rollercoaster experienced by investors. Understanding these psychological drivers is crucial to deciphering the complexities of market behavior.

Investor Sentiment and Market Sentiment: At the core of market overreaction is the concept of investor sentiment, which arises from the conflicting perceptual analysis and cognitive processing of information. This individual sentiment, when aggregated, evolves into market sentiment, shaping the overall mood of the market. Emotional processing and situational forces play a significant role in this evolution, influencing risk perception and decision-making over time. When investor sentiment swings to extremes—whether euphoric or pessimistic—the market often follows, leading to overreactions that deviate from fundamental values (Hua & Wang, 2018).

Behavioral Biases: Several behavioral biases contribute to irrational market behavior. The Representativeness Heuristic, for instance, leads investors to make decisions based on perceived patterns rather than objective analysis, often resulting in overreaction or underreaction to new information. Prospect Theory, another key concept, highlights how investors weigh potential gains and losses, with losses often having a disproportionate impact on decision-making. These biases, along with others such as overconfidence and availability heuristics, distort the risk-return correlation in financial markets, driving irrational behaviors (Bílek, Nedoma, & Jirásek, 2018).

Herding Behavior and Loss Aversion: Herding behavior is another critical driver of irrational market behavior. When investors observe others making similar decisions, they tend to follow suit, often without independent analysis. This behavior is amplified in bear markets, where loss aversion—the tendency to prefer avoiding losses over acquiring equivalent gains—intensifies the herd mentality. The fear of losses leads to panic selling, further driving prices down and exacerbating market overreactions. Herding, driven by cognitive psychology, explains why markets can experience extreme volatility during periods of uncertainty (Alexakis, Chantziaras, Economou, Eleftheriou, & Grose, 2023).

Impact of Emotions: Emotions such as fear and anger significantly influence investor judgment and decision-making. Empirical evidence shows that fear can lead to risk-averse behavior, causing investors to sell off assets during downturns, while anger might lead to risk-seeking behavior, resulting in impulsive investment decisions. These emotional responses contribute to the irrationality observed in markets, particularly during times of crisis (Wynes, 2021).

Market Response to Extreme Risks: The market's response to extreme risks often reflects irrational behavior. Statistical analyses reveal tendencies for markets to rebound after large drops or exhibit momentum following sharp rises, despite the lack of fundamental justification. This behavior is driven by the psychological impact of extreme events on investors, who either overestimate or underestimate future risks based on recent experiences (Xie, Chen, Bu, & Wang, 2011).

II. HISTORICAL CONTEXT

The phenomenon of market overreaction is not new; it has been a recurring theme throughout financial history, often resulting in significant economic consequences. By examining notable examples of historical market overreactions, such as the Tulip Mania, the Dot-com Bubble, and the 2008 Financial Crisis, we can gain valuable insights into the psychological and systemic factors that contribute to these episodes. Moreover, understanding the lessons learned from these events can help in developing strategies to prevent or mitigate future market overreactions.

- Overview of Historical Market Overreactions

Tulip Mania (1636-1637): One of the earliest recorded instances of market overreaction is the Tulip Mania that gripped the Dutch Republic in the early 17th century. During this period, the price of tulip bulbs, particularly rare and exotic varieties, skyrocketed to unprecedented levels. At the height of the mania, some tulip bulbs were reportedly worth more than a house in Amsterdam (Va că-Zamfir & Slave, 2018). The speculative frenzy was driven by the belief that tulip prices would continue to rise indefinitely, attracting a wide range of participants, including those with little knowledge of the market. However, in February 1637, the market collapsed abruptly, leading to a dramatic decline in prices and financial ruin for many investors. Tulip Mania is often cited as a classic example of an economic bubble, illustrating how collective greed and irrational exuberance can drive prices far beyond their intrinsic value (McClure & Thomas, 2017).

The Dot-com Bubble (1995-2000): The Dot-com Bubble of the late 1990s was another significant example of market overreaction, this time fueled by the rapid growth of the internet and technology companies. As investors rushed to invest in internet-related startups, many of which had little to no revenue, stock prices soared to astronomical levels. The prevailing sentiment was that the internet would revolutionize business, leading to limitless growth opportunities (Balagyozyan & Cakan, 2016). This led to an overvaluation of technology stocks, with some companies going public at inflated prices despite having unproven business models. When it became clear that many of these companies would not deliver the expected profits, the bubble burst in March 2000. The subsequent market crash wiped out trillions of dollars in market value and led to widespread economic repercussions, particularly in the technology sector (Razi, Tarn, & Siddiqui, 2024).

The 2008 Financial Crisis: The 2008 Financial Crisis, also known as the Global Financial Crisis, was one of the most severe economic downturns since the Great Depression. It was precipitated by a housing bubble in the United States, where the widespread belief that housing prices would continue to rise led to reckless lending and borrowing practices. Financial institutions, driven by short-term profits, engaged in risky mortgage lending, often to borrowers with poor credit histories (Hsu & Dupont, 2023). These subprime mortgages were then bundled into complex financial products and sold to investors worldwide. When the housing market began to decline in 2007, the value of these financial products plummeted, leading to a cascade of failures in the banking system. The crisis resulted in the collapse of major financial institutions, massive government bailouts, and a global recession. The 2008 Financial Crisis highlighted the dangers of excessive risk-taking and the interconnectedness of global financial markets (Bosworth & Flaaen, 2013).

- Lessons Learned from Past Events

1. The Role of Speculative Bubbles: One of the most important lessons from historical market overreactions is the role of speculative bubbles. These bubbles are typically driven by a collective belief in the perpetual rise of asset prices, leading to unsustainable valuations. As seen in the Tulip Mania and the Dot-com Bubble, when reality eventually sets in, the resulting market crash can have devastating effects on investors and the broader economy. Recognizing the signs of speculative bubbles, such as rapid price increases, overvaluation, and widespread market participation, is crucial in preventing future market overreactions (Razi, Tarn, & Siddiqui, 2024).

2. The Impact of Irrational Exuberance: Another key lesson is the impact of irrational exuberance, a term popularized by former Federal Reserve Chairman Alan Greenspan during the Dot-com Bubble. This refers to the overconfidence and excessive optimism that often precedes market overreactions. When investors become overly optimistic about future prospects, they may overlook fundamental risks, leading to inflated asset prices (Shiller, 2015). The 2008 Financial Crisis, for example, was partly fuelled by irrational beliefs in the stability of the housing market and the safety of mortgage-backed securities. Understanding the psychological factors that contribute to irrational exuberance can help in identifying potential market overreactions and taking corrective action.

3. The Importance of Regulatory Oversight: Historical market overreactions also underscore the importance of regulatory oversight in maintaining market stability. In both the Dot-com Bubble and the 2008 Financial Crisis, inadequate regulation and oversight allowed speculative excesses to build up unchecked. Stronger regulatory frameworks, particularly in areas such as financial product transparency, risk management, and lending practices, are essential in preventing the kind of systemic risks that lead to market overreactions (Spendzharova, 2014).

4. The Need for Diversification and Risk Management: Finally, the lessons from past market overreactions highlight the importance of diversification and risk management in investment strategies. Investors who placed all their bets on tulips, technology stocks, or subprime mortgages often faced significant losses when the bubbles burst. Diversifying investments across different asset classes and regions can help mitigate the impact of market overreactions and protect against significant financial losses (Mats, 2024).

III. EMOTIONAL DRIVERS OF MARKET OVERREACTION

Market behavior is not solely driven by rational analysis of economic fundamentals; it is also significantly influenced by emotions. Fear, anxiety, greed, euphoria, and emotional contagion play pivotal roles in shaping investor behavior and can lead to market overreactions. These emotional drivers often amplify market trends, causing prices to deviate significantly from their intrinsic values. Understanding how these emotions influence market dynamics is crucial for both investors and policymakers.

Figure 1. Diagram of emotional drivers of Market Overreaction

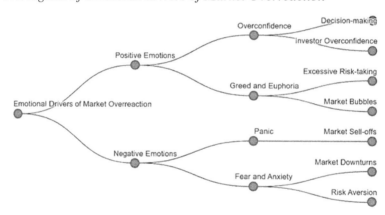

Fear and Anxiety: How They Lead to Risk Aversion and Market Downturns

Fear and anxiety are powerful emotions that can dramatically alter investor behavior, particularly during times of financial uncertainty. When investor sentiment is low, the impact of fear and anxiety becomes more pronounced, leading to stronger market overreactions. For example, during financial crises like the 2008 Financial Crisis, fear and anxiety were pervasive, leading to heightened risk aversion among investors. This increase in risk aversion often results in panic selling, where investors rush to divest their assets to avoid potential losses, exacerbating market downturns (Wynes, 2021).

The psychological mechanisms behind this behavior are rooted in how fear and anxiety alter the perception of risk. These emotions increase the salience of negative outcomes, making investors more sensitive to potential losses. As a result, they become more risk-averse, opting to sell off risky assets even at the cost of significant financial losses. This behavior creates a feedback loop, where the initial market decline, fuelled by fear, triggers further anxiety, leading to more selling and a deeper market downturn. The contrast between the perceived risk in a low sentiment environment and the occurrence of an adverse event sharpens, resulting in a more severe market overreaction (Aljifri, 2023).

• Greed and Euphoria: How They Fuel Market Bubbles and Excessive Risk-Taking

On the other end of the emotional spectrum, greed and euphoria can drive investors to take excessive risks, leading to the formation of market bubbles. Greed, characterized by an intense desire for wealth accumulation, often motivates investors to engage in speculative behavior, ignoring the underlying risks. During periods of euphoria, when the market is booming, this greed is further amplified as investors become overly optimistic about future gains (Hoyer, Zeisberger, Breugelmans, & Zeelenberg, 2023).

This was evident during the Dot-com Bubble of the late 1990s, where the euphoria surrounding internet companies led to a massive overvaluation of tech stocks. Investors, driven by greed, poured money into these stocks with little regard for their actual profitability. As prices soared, the market entered a speculative frenzy, with investors buying in the hope that prices would continue to rise indefinitely. However, when the bubble eventually burst, it left many investors with substantial losses, highlighting the dangers of allowing greed and euphoria to drive investment decisions.

The relationship between greed, euphoria, and market bubbles is cyclical. Bubbles build up during periods of euphoria, but as prices reach unsustainable levels, fear begins to set in. This fear can quickly reverse the trend, leading to a sharp market correction as investors rush to exit their positions, causing the bubble to burst (Michailova & Schmidt, 2016).

• The Role of Emotional Contagion in Spreading Market Sentiment

Emotional contagion refers to the phenomenon where emotions spread from one individual to another, often leading to synchronized behavior in a group. In financial markets, emotional contagion plays a significant role in spreading market sentiment, contributing to herd behavior and market overreactions. When investors observe others reacting to market events—whether through panic selling or exuberant buying—they are likely to mirror these behaviors, even if it goes against their own rational analysis.

This contagion is facilitated by various channels, including media reports, social networks, and direct interactions among investors. For instance, during market downturns, negative news coverage can heighten fear and anxiety, causing a ripple effect as more investors start selling off their assets. Similarly, in a bull market, positive news and rising prices can generate euphoria, leading more investors to jump on the bandwagon, further inflating the bubble.

Emotional contagion is particularly potent in financial markets due to the high stakes involved. The fear of missing out (FOMO) during a market rally or the fear of losing everything during a downturn can drive investors to act irrationally. This synchronized behavior, driven by shared emotions, can lead to extreme market movements that are not justified by economic fundamentals (Hou, Narin, Liu, & Wang, 2021).

- Other Drivers

1. Overconfidence:

Description: Overconfidence is a psychological bias where investors overestimate their knowledge, ability to predict market movements, or control over outcomes. This can lead to excessive trading, underestimation of risks, and a failure to diversify portfolios.

Impact on Market Overreaction: Overconfident investors may drive up asset prices beyond their intrinsic value by taking on excessive risk and ignoring potential downsides. When reality fails to meet their optimistic expectations, it can lead to sharp corrections as confidence wanes (Aljifri, 2023).

2. Regret Aversion:

Description: Regret aversion is the fear of making decisions that could lead to regret, particularly when those decisions involve financial losses. This emotion can cause investors to avoid taking necessary risks or to hold onto losing positions in the hope of recouping their losses (Korn & Rieger, 2019).

Impact on Market Overreaction: Regret aversion can contribute to both underreaction and overreaction. Investors might delay selling overvalued assets, leading to inflated prices, or might avoid buying undervalued assets, missing out on potential gains. When the market corrects, the accumulated regret can lead to panic selling (Reb, 2008).

3. Panic:

Description: Panic is an intense, immediate reaction to perceived threats, often leading to irrational and hasty decisions. In financial markets, panic can spread quickly, especially during crises or sudden negative events.

Impact on Market Overreaction: Panic can cause investors to sell off assets rapidly, often at a loss, exacerbating market downturns. The rush to exit the market can lead to sharp declines in prices, creating a feedback loop that further intensifies the panic (Yang, Zhu, & Cheng, 2020).

4. Confirmation Bias:

Description: Confirmation bias is the tendency to search for, interpret, and remember information in a way that confirms one's preexisting beliefs. Investors may selectively focus on news or data that supports their view, while ignoring evidence to the contrary.

Impact on Market Overreaction: Confirmation bias can lead to overreaction by reinforcing existing trends, whether bullish or bearish. Investors who are bullish may disregard signs of overvaluation, pushing prices higher, while bearish investors may overlook positive indicators, accelerating sell-offs (Trichilli, Gaadane, Boujelbène Abbes, & Masmoudi, 2024).

5. Desperation:

Description: Desperation occurs when investors, often facing significant losses, make extreme decisions in an attempt to recover their losses quickly. This can include taking on high-risk investments or making impulsive trades without proper analysis.

Impact on Market Overreaction: Desperation can lead to erratic market behavior, as desperate investors may drive prices to unsustainable levels or cause sudden, sharp movements in the market. This can contribute to increased volatility and unpredictable market swings (Kim, Haleblian, & Finkelstein, 2011).

6. Status Quo Bias:

Description: Status quo bias is the preference for things to remain the same rather than change, even when change might be beneficial. In the context of investing, this can manifest as an unwillingness to alter an investment strategy or portfolio, even in the face of new information.

Impact on Market Overreaction: (Sembiring, Rahman, Effendi, & Sudarsono, 2016).

7. Denial:

Description: Denial is the refusal to accept reality, often because it is too uncomfortable or threatening. Investors in denial might ignore warning signs or rationalize away poor performance.

Impact on Market Overreaction: Denial can delay necessary market corrections. Investors may continue to hold overvalued assets or refuse to cut losses, leading to prolonged overvaluation or more severe corrections when the market finally adjusts (Brown & Kagel, 2009).

Each of these emotional drivers can play a significant role in shaping market behavior, often leading to overreactions that deviate from fundamental values. By recognizing and understanding these emotional influences, investors can make more informed decisions and better manage the risks associated with market volatility.

IV. COGNITIVE BIASES AND HEURISTICS

Cognitive biases and heuristics play a crucial role in shaping investor behavior, often leading to decisions that deviate from rational economic models. These mental shortcuts, while helpful in making quick decisions, can lead to systematic errors and irrational behavior in financial markets. In this discussion, we will explore key cognitive biases and heuristics—confirmation bias, anchoring bias, availability heuristic, loss aversion, and status quo bias—and their impact on investment decisions (Al-Dahan, Hasan, & Jadah, 2019).

Figure 2. Cognitive Bias and impact on decision making

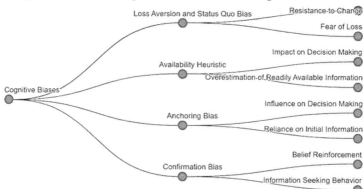

Confirmation Bias: Selectively Seeking Information that Confirms Beliefs

Confirmation bias is the tendency to search for, interpret, and remember information in a way that confirms one's preexisting beliefs or hypotheses. In the context of investing, this bias can lead to a skewed perception of the market, as investors may focus on information that supports their current views while disregarding evidence that contradicts them (Parveen, Satti, Subhan, & Jamil, 2020).

For instance, an investor who believes in the strong future performance of a particular stock may only pay attention to positive news about the company, such as optimistic earnings forecasts or favorable analyst reports, while ignoring negative indicators like declining market share or regulatory challenges. This selective attention can reinforce the investor's confidence in their decision, even when the broader data set suggests a different outcome.

The impact of confirmation bias can be particularly pronounced during periods of market volatility. Investors may cling to their original investment thesis despite mounting evidence to the contrary, leading to poor decision-making and potential losses. In extreme cases, confirmation bias can contribute to the formation of market bubbles, as investors collectively overlook warning signs and continue to drive prices higher based on shared, yet unfounded, optimism (Al-Dahan, Hasan, & Jadah, 2019).

Anchoring Bias: Over-Reliance on Initial Information

Anchoring bias occurs when investors rely too heavily on the first piece of information they receive (the "anchor") when making decisions, even if subsequent information suggests a different valuation or outcome. This bias can significantly influence investment choices, particularly in pricing assets or predicting future market movements (Pathak & Thapa, 2024).

For example, if an investor hears that a particular stock is valued at $100, they may anchor their expectations around this price, even if new information emerges that suggests the stock is overvalued. As a result, they might be reluctant to sell the stock at a lower price, believing that it will return to the anchored value. Similarly, anchoring can cause investors to set unrealistic price targets for buying or selling assets, leading to missed opportunities or unnecessary losses.

Anchoring bias can also manifest in broader market trends. For instance, during a market correction, investors might anchor their expectations to pre-correction price levels, leading them to hold onto losing positions in the hope of a rebound, rather than adjusting their strategy based on the new market reality. This can exacerbate losses and contribute to prolonged market inefficiencies (Cascão, Quelhas, & Cunha, 2023).

Availability Heuristic: Overestimating the Importance of Readily Available Information

The availability heuristic is a mental shortcut that leads people to overestimate the importance or likelihood of events based on how easily examples come to mind. In financial markets, this can result in investors placing undue emphasis on recent news, memorable events, or easily accessible data, rather than conducting a thorough analysis of all relevant information (Xie, Fang, Gao, & Tan, 2023).

For instance, an investor might overestimate the risk of a market downturn after witnessing a high-profile stock market crash, such as the 2008 Financial Crisis, even if current market conditions are fundamentally different. Similarly, they might overreact to a single earnings report or news headline, making hasty investment decisions based on the most readily available information rather than considering the long-term outlook.

The availability heuristic can lead to herd behavior, where investors collectively react to the same piece of information, driving asset prices up or down in a way that is not justified by underlying fundamentals. This behavior can create market volatility and contribute to phenomena such as bubbles and crashes, as investors overreact to information that may not have a lasting impact on asset values.

Loss Aversion: The Tendency to Prefer Avoiding Losses Over Acquiring Gains

Loss aversion is a cognitive bias that describes the tendency for individuals to prefer avoiding losses over acquiring equivalent gains. This bias is a central concept in behavioral economics and has profound implications for investor behavior. Studies have shown that the pain of losing money is psychologically twice as powerful as the pleasure of gaining the same amount. This aversion to loss can lead investors to make irrational decisions, such as holding onto losing stocks for too long in the hope of recouping losses or selling winning stocks too early to lock in gains. The result is often a suboptimal investment strategy that fails to maximize returns (Sathya & Gayathiri, 2024).

Loss aversion also contributes to the disposition effect, where investors are more likely to sell assets that have gained value while holding onto assets that have lost value, even when rational analysis would suggest the opposite. This behavior can exacerbate market inefficiencies and lead to increased volatility, as investors collectively react to losses in a way that distorts asset prices.

Status Quo Bias: Preference for Maintaining the Current State of Affairs

Status quo bias is the tendency to prefer things to remain the same rather than change, even when change might be beneficial. In the context of investing, this bias can manifest as an unwillingness to alter an investment portfolio, even in response to new information or changing market conditions (Lippi, Rossi, & Soana, 2022). For example, an investor might stick with a poorly performing asset because they are more comfortable maintaining the status quo than making a potentially risky change. This can lead to missed opportunities, as the investor fails to adapt their strategy to capitalize on new opportunities or mitigate emerging risks. Status quo bias can also cause investors to under-diversify their portfolios, sticking with familiar investments rather than exploring new asset classes or markets that might offer better returns.

The impact of status quo bias can be particularly significant in long-term investment planning, where failure to adjust to changing circumstances—such as economic shifts, technological advancements, or personal financial goals—can result in suboptimal outcomes. Investors who are too anchored in their existing strategies may miss out on the benefits of rebalancing or reallocating their portfolios in response to market dynamics.

V. SOCIAL INFLUENCE AND HERDING

Investor behavior in financial markets is heavily influenced by social factors, leading to herding—a phenomenon where individuals follow the actions of others rather than relying on their independent judgment. Social influence, driven by various factors such as social media, financial literacy, social networks, and the behavior of authority figures, plays a significant role in shaping market dynamics. This exploration delves into how these elements contribute to herding behavior, its impact on market efficiency, and the resulting market extremes.

The Power of Social Proof and Herding Behavior

Social proof is a fundamental psychological mechanism where individuals conform to the actions of others, especially in uncertain situations. In financial markets, this behavior manifests when investors follow the crowd, assuming that the collective actions of others are rational and informed. This leads to herding, where individual decision-making is overridden by the perceived safety of conforming to the majority (Gupta & Kohli, 2021).

Herding is particularly evident during periods of market extremes, such as bubbles and crashes. For instance, in a rising market, the fear of missing out drives more investors to buy, pushing prices even higher. Conversely, during a market downturn, the fear of losses prompts widespread selling, exacerbating the decline. This collective behavior can lead to significant market volatility, as the actions of many amplify market movements beyond what fundamentals would justify.

Social Media and Its Influence on Investor Behavior

The rise of social media platforms like Twitter and Facebook has significantly impacted how investors consume information and make decisions. Studies have shown that social media not only serves as a key source of news for many investors but also plays a crucial role in spreading social influence. For example, a study in the Indian financial market found that the credibility of influencers on social media had a significant positive impact on herding behavior. Influencer credibility, especially when combined with expert opinions, often outweighs traditional financial information in shaping investor actions (Sathya & Prabhavathi, 2024).

Furthermore, social media facilitates the rapid dissemination of information, leading to immediate and sometimes irrational reactions in the market. As news spreads quickly across platforms, investors feel compelled to act swiftly, often without fully analyzing the information. This can lead to herding, where investors collectively follow trends set by influential figures or the general sentiment on social media, driving market movements that may not align with underlying fundamentals.

The Role of Financial Literacy and Risk Perception

Financial literacy and risk perception are critical factors influencing herding behavior. Studies have shown that higher financial literacy can reduce the likelihood of herding, as more informed investors are better equipped to make independent decisions. However, when risk perception is introduced as a mediator, even financially literate investors may succumb to herding (Singh & Kumar, 2024). This is because high levels of perceived risk can override rational decision-making, leading investors to follow the crowd in an attempt to minimize potential losses.

Moreover, individual investors' behavior is also shaped by their understanding of risk. Those with lower financial literacy or higher risk perception are more likely to engage in herding, driven by a desire to align with the actions of others whom they perceive as better informed or less likely to incur losses. This dynamic is particularly pronounced in emerging markets, where financial literacy levels may be lower, and the influence of social proof is stronger.

The Impact of Social Networks and Fund Manager Behavior

Social networks, particularly among fund managers, also play a significant role in herding behavior. Research on securities investment funds (SIFs) in China has shown that the size of a fund manager's social network can significantly impact the degree of herding behavior. Fund managers with larger networks are more likely to engage in herding, as they are influenced by the collective actions and opinions within their professional circles.

This social dynamic can degrade market efficiency, as fund managers, instead of making independent investment decisions based on fundamentals, may follow the consensus within their networks. This behavior contributes to the formation of market bubbles or crashes, as the collective actions of fund managers amplify market trends (Au, Dong, & Zhou, 2024).

Market Dynamics and the Role of Social Influence

Social influence extends beyond individual investor behavior to affect overall market dynamics. The interaction between social networks and market efficiency is complex, with social influence often leading to reduced market stability. Herding behavior, driven by social interactions, can lead to excess volatility, speculative bubbles, and crashes. For example, during the 1997 Asian financial crisis, significant herding around specific events led to sharp market declines and financial instability (Aljifri, 2023).

Furthermore, social influence can also manifest in online platforms, such as crowdfunding markets. Research has shown that as the number of observable decision-makers increases, herding behavior becomes more pronounced. This can lower the average level of private knowledge in the market, leading to suboptimal investment decisions and potentially destabilizing market outcomes.

Media, News, and the Amplification of Herding

The media, including both traditional news outlets and online platforms, plays a crucial role in amplifying herding behavior. The rapid dissemination of news through social media and other digital channels can lead to swift market reactions as investors collectively respond to new information. This phenomenon was particularly evident during the COVID-19 pandemic, where increased trading volumes and market interest led to heightened herding behavior (Singh & Kumar, 2024).

In addition, the neural processing of social influence, as studied in crowdfunding markets, demonstrates that individual behavior is often swayed by group judgments. This further highlights the powerful impact of social influence on investment decisions, leading to collective actions that drive market trends.

Herding Behavior and Market Extremes

Herding behavior is often linked to market extremes, such as the formation of bubbles or sudden crashes. When investors collectively follow trends, it can lead to the overvaluation of assets during bull markets or sharp declines during bear markets. This behavior is exacerbated by the influence of social media, expert opinions, and the overall sentiment within social networks. As a result, markets can experience significant volatility, with herding behavior contributing to both irrational exuberance and panic selling (Alexakis, Chantziaras, Economou, Eleftheriou, & Grose, 2023).

The Role of Authority Figures and Expert Opinions in Shaping Market Sentiment

Authority figures and expert opinions play a significant role in shaping market sentiment and influencing investor behavior. Investors often look to these trusted voices—such as economists, financial analysts, and prominent fund managers—for guidance, especially during periods of uncertainty. The belief that these figures possess superior knowledge can lead to widespread buying or selling as investors align their decisions with the expert's outlook (Mo, Liu, & Yang, 2016).

Expert opinions, particularly those from analysts, are widely followed and can drive market movements through recommendations, ratings, and forecasts. For instance, when an investment bank upgrades or downgrades a stock, it can trigger herding behavior, where investors collectively respond, leading to significant market shifts. This reliance can sometimes result in overreaction, as investors may overlook other critical information (Zhang & Long, 2021).

Herding behavior driven by authority figures can lead to market extremes, such as bubbles during optimism or crashes during fear. While these opinions provide valuable insights, they can also cause inefficiencies and instability in the market. When too many investors follow the same advice, it reduces the diversity of market opinions, increasing the risk of abrupt market movements and mispricing of assets.

VI. NEUROLOGICAL AND PHYSIOLOGICAL FACTORS

Investment decisions, often viewed through the lens of economic models and behavioral psychology, are also profoundly influenced by neurological and physiological factors. Stress, hormone levels, and neurotransmitters like dopamine play crucial roles in shaping how investors make decisions, process risks, and pursue rewards. Understanding these underlying mechanisms can provide valuable insights into why investors behave the way they do and how investment strategies can be optimized.

The Impact of Stress and Cortisol on Decision-Making

Stress is a common element in the financial world, where high-stakes decisions are made under pressure. One of the primary physiological responses to stress is the release of cortisol, a hormone produced by the adrenal glands. Cortisol plays a critical role in the body's fight-or-flight response, but its effects on cognitive function and decision-making can be detrimental, particularly in the context of investing (Coates, Gurnell, & Sarnyai, 2010).

When cortisol levels rise due to stress, several cognitive processes are affected. First, high cortisol levels can impair memory and learning, making it harder for investors to recall relevant information or learn from past mistakes. Second, stress-induced cortisol can lead to a narrowing of focus, where individuals become fixated on immediate threats or opportunities, often at the expense of considering long-term consequences. This can result in impulsive decision-making, such as panic selling during a market downturn or overreacting to short-term market fluctuations (Coates, Gurnell, & Sarnyai, 2017).

Moreover, chronic stress and elevated cortisol levels have been associated with risk aversion. Investors under stress may become overly conservative, avoiding investments that carry even moderate risk, which can lead to missed opportunities for gains. On the other hand, some individuals may respond to stress with heightened risk-taking behavior, driven by a desire to regain control or achieve quick rewards. This duality in stress response can explain why markets often exhibit both extreme caution and speculative bubbles simultaneously during periods of uncertainty.

The Role of Dopamine and Reward
Processing in Investment Behavior

Dopamine, a neurotransmitter associated with pleasure and reward, plays a pivotal role in how investors perceive gains and losses. The release of dopamine is triggered by the anticipation of a reward, such as the prospect of financial gain from an investment. This anticipation can lead to heightened motivation and risk-taking behavior as investors seek to maximize their potential rewards.

Dopamine's influence on investment behavior is closely tied to the concept of reward processing. When an investment yields a positive return, the brain's reward system is activated, reinforcing the behavior that led to the gain. This reinforcement can create a feedback loop where investors become increasingly confident in their ability to make profitable decisions, often leading to overconfidence and excessive risk-taking. In contrast, the absence of expected rewards or the realization of losses can result in a sharp drop in dopamine levels, leading to feelings of disappointment and aversion to further risk (Diederen & Fletcher, 2021).

The role of dopamine in investment behavior also helps explain phenomena such as "chasing losses" and "fear of missing out" (FOMO). Investors may continue to engage in risky behavior even after incurring losses, driven by the hope of recouping their losses and experiencing the dopamine-fuelled pleasure of a win. Similarly, the fear of missing out on potential gains can push investors to enter markets at inopportune times, driven by the anticipation of reward rather than rational analysis.

How Neuroscientific Insights Can Inform Investment Strategies

Neuroscientific research offers valuable insights that can be applied to developing more effective investment strategies. Understanding the impact of stress and cortisol on decision-making, for example, can help investors recognize when they are likely to make impulsive or overly cautious choices. By managing stress through mindfulness, exercise, or other techniques, investors can maintain clearer thinking and make more rational decisions (Yu & Zhou, 2007).

Awareness of dopamine's role in reward processing can also help investors avoid the pitfalls of overconfidence and excessive risk-taking. By recognizing the brain's natural tendency to seek out rewards, investors can implement strategies that temper their pursuit of gains with a realistic assessment of risk. This could involve setting predetermined exit points for investments or using diversification to spread risk across different asset classes (Shimokawa, Kinoshita, Miyagawa, & Misawa, 2012).

Furthermore, investment strategies can be tailored to account for the different ways individuals respond to stress and rewards. For example, risk-averse investors might benefit from strategies that emphasize stability and long-term growth, while those with a higher tolerance for risk might pursue more aggressive, short-term opportunities. Understanding these neurological and physiological differences can help financial advisors provide more personalized guidance to their clients.

Finally, incorporating neuroscientific insights into algorithmic trading and artificial intelligence (AI) models could lead to more sophisticated investment tools (Venkatraman & Beard, 2020). By simulating how human brains react to market conditions, these models could better predict market movements and help investors make more informed decisions.

VII. BEHAVIORAL PATTERNS IN MARKET OVERREACTION

Market overreaction is a complex phenomenon influenced by a range of psychological and behavioral factors. Key patterns that contribute to these extreme market movements include panic selling, irrational exuberance, herding behavior, and the bandwagon effect. These behaviors are deeply rooted in the psychological makeup of investors and play a significant role in shaping market dynamics.

Panic Selling

Panic selling refers to the rapid selling of assets by investors, driven by fear and anxiety. This behavior is often triggered by negative news, economic downturns, or unexpected events that create uncertainty in the market. Psychological factors such as representativeness, anchoring, availability heuristic, gambler's fallacy, and overconfidence are significant contributors to panic selling (Aljifri, 2023). These behavioral biases lead investors to irrationally follow the actions of others, resulting in a cascading effect of selling that amplifies market declines (Omar, Nazri, Ali, & Alam, 2021).

Panic selling is particularly detrimental because it exacerbates market volatility and leads to a self-fulfilling prophecy, where the fear of falling prices drives more selling, further depressing asset values. This behavior can cause temporary market inefficiencies, where asset prices fall well below their intrinsic value, offering opportunities for more rational investors to purchase undervalued assets (Yuen, Wang, Ma, & Li, 2020). However, for those caught in the panic, the financial and emotional toll can be severe.

Irrational Exuberance

Irrational exuberance is characterized by excessive optimism and the overvaluation of assets, leading to inflated market prices that are not supported by fundamental economic indicators. This behavior is driven by psychological factors such as the Representativeness Heuristic and Prospect Theory, which explain how investors' expectations become disconnected from reality.

The impact of irrational exuberance on market overreaction is profound. It creates bubbles in asset prices, where the disconnect between risk and return leads to significant market anomalies. When the bubble eventually bursts, the market experiences sharp corrections, causing substantial financial losses. The literature in behavioral finance highlights how irrational exuberance leads to both overreaction and underreaction in markets, further contributing to price instability and volatility (Lin, 2020).

Herding Behavior

Herding behavior occurs when investors follow the actions of others rather than relying on their own analysis and judgment. This behavior is driven by a desire to be part of a group, avoid the fear of missing out (FOMO), and react to new information. Herding is particularly pronounced during times of uncertainty or financial crises, where the perceived safety of following the crowd outweighs the risk of making independent decisions (Hou, Narin, Liu, & Wang, 2021).

The underlying mechanisms of herding behavior in financial markets are closely tied to cognitive psychology. Loss aversion, the tendency to prefer avoiding losses over acquiring equivalent gains, and extrapolative expectations, where investors project recent trends into the future, are key drivers of herding. These behaviors lead to market inefficiencies, as the collective actions of investors can drive prices away from their true value (Ye, Li, & Cao, 2020). Herding behavior has been observed in various stock markets, particularly during periods of crisis, where it contributes to both upward and downward market extremes.

The Bandwagon Effect

The bandwagon effect refers to the tendency of individuals to adopt certain behaviors or beliefs simply because others are doing so. In financial markets, this effect is evident when investors buy or sell assets not based on their own analysis, but because they observe others doing the same. This behavior is particularly influential during extreme market movements, such as bull markets or market crashes, where the actions of a few can trigger widespread participation.

The bandwagon effect has significant implications for market dynamics. It can lead to inflated asset prices during a bull market or exacerbate a market downturn during a crash. The influence of social media and social networks on investor behavior has intensified the bandwagon effect (Zhou & Yang, 2020), as information spreads rapidly and can trigger collective action on a large scale. Studies have shown that the credibility of stock influencers and the level of financial literacy among investors play a crucial role in determining the extent of the bandwagon effect (Kim & Deshmukh, 2021). Higher financial literacy tends to mitigate this behavior, while lower literacy amplifies it.

Impact of the COVID-19 Pandemic on Global Markets

The COVID-19 pandemic has had a substantial impact on global stock markets, highlighting the interplay between behavioral patterns and market dynamics. Daily increase in COVID-19 cases initially led to negative stock returns and heightened volatility, while stringent government policy responses influenced market reactions. Over time, the market's response to the pandemic evolved, with stock markets reacting more proactively to the number of confirmed cases than to the number of deaths (Yang S., 2024). The pandemic also challenged previous assumptions about the influence of geographical and economic factors on market reactions.

Investor sentiment during the pandemic was significantly affected by government stringency measures, which were perceived as harmful to economic activity. This, in turn, negatively impacted stock returns and contributed to the global market downturn. The pandemic has caused lasting ramifications across global markets, eroding investor sentiment and leading to substantial financial losses.

VIII. CONSEQUENCES OF MARKET OVERREACTION

Market overreaction occurs when investors respond excessively to news or events, leading to significant deviations in asset prices from their intrinsic values. This phenomenon can have profound consequences, not just for individual investors but also for the broader market and economy. Understanding these consequences can help investors, regulators, and policymakers navigate the complexities of financial markets and mitigate potential risks.

Short-Term and Long-Term Market Impacts

In the short term, market overreaction often leads to heightened volatility. Prices of stocks, bonds, or other assets may swing wildly as investors scramble to buy or sell based on recent news or trends. This volatility can create opportunities for traders who are able to capitalize on price discrepancies, but it also introduces significant risk (Loang, 2022). For example, during a period of panic selling, prices can plummet far below their intrinsic value, only to rebound sharply once the initial fear subsides. Similarly, during periods of irrational exuberance, prices can soar to unsustainable levels, setting the stage for a sharp correction when reality sets in.

Long-term market impacts of overreaction can be more detrimental. Persistent overreaction can lead to asset bubbles, where prices are driven far beyond their fundamental values. The eventual bursting of these bubbles can cause widespread financial distress, as was seen during the dot-com bubble in the early 2000s and the housing market crash in 2008. These events often lead to a loss of investor confidence, reduced liquidity in the markets, and a prolonged period of economic downturn (Westphal & Sornette, 2023). Additionally, the misallocation of capital that occurs during these bubbles can stifle innovation and growth, as resources are funneled into overvalued sectors at the expense of more productive investments.

Effects on Individual Investors

For individual investors, market overreaction can be both an opportunity and a risk. Those who can accurately anticipate or quickly respond to overreactions may profit from the resulting price movements. However, for the average investor, market overreaction often leads to poor decision-making driven by emotions such as fear and greed (Said, Rehman, & Ullah, 2021). During periods of market panic, individual investors may succumb to the pressure to sell their holdings at a loss, driven by fear of further declines. This behavior, known as panic selling, can lock in losses and prevent investors from benefiting from any subsequent market recovery. On the other hand, during periods of irrational exuberance, investors may rush to buy into overvalued assets, driven by the fear of missing out on potential gains. This can result in significant losses when the market inevitably corrects (Elkind, Kaminski, Lo, Siah, & Wong, 2022).

Moreover, the psychological impact of market overreaction can be long-lasting for individual investors. Experiencing significant losses due to panic selling or being caught in a market bubble can lead to a loss of confidence in the financial markets. This, in turn, may cause investors to withdraw from the market entirely, missing out on long-term growth opportunities. Additionally, overreacting to short-term market movements can lead to frequent trading, which often incurs higher transaction costs and taxes, further eroding overall returns.

Broader Economic Implications

The broader economic implications of market overreaction are significant. When markets overreact, the resulting volatility and mispricing of assets can disrupt the functioning of the financial system. For example, sharp declines in asset prices can lead to a credit crunch, as financial institutions become more risk-averse and tighten lending standards. This reduction in credit availability can stifle business investment and consumer spending, leading to slower economic growth or even recession.

Market overreaction can also undermine the stability of financial institutions. Banks, hedge funds, and other financial entities that are heavily exposed to volatile assets may face significant losses during periods of market turbulence. In extreme cases, this can lead to the failure of large financial institutions, as seen during the

2008 financial crisis. The failure of these institutions can have a cascading effect on the broader economy, leading to job losses, reduced consumer confidence, and a prolonged period of economic hardship (Kim, Park, & Song, 2016).

Furthermore, market overreaction can have global implications. In an interconnected world, financial shocks in one country can quickly spread to others, leading to synchronized downturns across multiple economies. For example, the 2008 financial crisis, which originated in the United States, quickly spread to Europe and other regions, leading to a global economic slowdown.

IX. IMPLICATIONS FOR INVESTORS AND MARKETS

Investors need to manage emotions and biases to make sound decisions. Strategies like setting clear investment goals, maintaining a long-term perspective, and avoiding reactionary trades can help mitigate emotional responses to market volatility. Understanding cognitive biases like overconfidence and herding is crucial in avoiding irrational behavior (Rao & Lakkol, 2024). Diversification and risk management are essential tools in reducing exposure to market extremes. By spreading investments across different asset classes and regions, investors can lower the risk of significant losses during market downturns. Regularly reassessing portfolio allocation helps maintain a balanced risk profile.

For markets, the implications extend to policy regulation. Authorities should focus on measures that curb market extremes and protect investors, such as enforcing transparency, improving financial literacy, and regulating high-frequency trading. These steps can help stabilize markets, reduce systemic risks, and promote fair and efficient market environments for all participants.

X. MITIGATING MARKET OVERREACTION

Mitigating market overreaction requires a combination of strategies aimed at managing investor emotions and biases, strengthening regulatory frameworks, and enhancing financial education. Overconfidence, often driven by strong positive emotions, can distort decision-making processes and lead to poor investment outcomes. Investors prone to overconfidence can mitigate this bias by employing emotion regulation strategies like reappraisal (Yang, Chu, Ko, & Lee, 2018). This approach helps in reducing the disposition effect, where investors are more likely to realize gains than cut their losses, leading to a more disciplined investment strategy.

Regulatory bodies play a pivotal role in stabilizing markets, particularly through the promotion of financial literacy. By improving investor education, regulators can help reduce stock price volatility and enhance market efficiency, even in times of uncertainty. Financial literacy initiatives have been shown to improve rational decision-making, contributing to more stable markets (Williams, 2007).

Educational approaches that align with how adults learn best can further empower investors. Programs that utilize principles-based education and rules-of-thumb methodologies have been effective in boosting not just financial knowledge but also self-efficacy, motivation, and the ability to take calculated risks (Williams & Satchell, 2011). These educational efforts are crucial for helping investors make more informed and confident decisions, ultimately reducing the likelihood of market overreaction.

XI. CONCLUSION

Understanding the psychological drivers behind market overreactions is vital for both investors and policymakers. Emotions like fear, anxiety, greed, and euphoria can lead to irrational decisions and extreme market movements. Cognitive biases such as confirmation and anchoring, along with heuristics like the availability heuristic, further complicate decision-making. Social influences, including herding behavior and the impact of media and authority figures, amplify these effects, pushing market sentiment to irrational extremes. Additionally, neurological factors like stress and dopamine responses shape investor behavior. Historical and contemporary case studies reveal the profound impact of these drivers on market dynamics. To mitigate the effects of overreactions, investors should manage their emotions and biases, while regulators should implement measures to stabilize markets. Understanding these psychological mechanisms is key to more informed decisions and a resilient financial system.

REFERENCES

Al-Dahan, N. S., Hasan, M. F., & Jadah, H. M. (2019). Effect of cognitive and emotional biases on investor decisions: An analytical study of the Iraq stock exchange. *International Journal of Innovation, Creativity and Change, 09*(10), 30-47. Retrieved Sep 13, 2024, from https://www.scopus.com/record/display.uri?eid=2-s2 .0-85079642547&origin=scopusAI

Al-Zoubi, H. A. (2024). Business Cycle Variations in Manager and Investor Sentiment Indices. *Journal of Behavioral Finance*, ●●●, 1–12.

Alexakis, C., Chantziaras, A., Economou, F., Eleftheriou, K., & Grose, C. (2023, July). Animal Behavior in Capital markets: Herding formation dynamics, trading volume, and the role of COVID-19 pandemic. *The North American Journal of Economics and Finance*, 67, 101946. Advance online publication. DOI: 10.1016/j. najef.2023.101946

Aljifri, R. (2023, January). Investor psychology in the stock market: An empirical study of the impact of overconfidence on firm valuation. *Borsa Istanbul Review*, 23(01), 93–112. DOI: 10.1016/j.bir.2022.09.010

Au, S.-Y., Dong, M., & Zhou, X. (2024). Does Social Interaction Spread Fear Among Institutional Investors? Evidence from Coronavirus Disease 2019. *Management Science*, 70(04), 2406–2426. DOI: 10.1287/mnsc.2023.4814

Balagyozyan, A., & Cakan, E. (2016, December 13). Did large institutional investors flock into the technology herd? An empirical investigation using a vector Markov-switching model. *Applied Economics*, 48(58), 5731–5747. DOI: 10.1080/00036846.2016.1184376

Bílek, J., Nedoma, J., & Jirásek, M. (2018). Representativeness heuristics: A literature review of its impacts on the quality of decision-making. *Scientific Papers of the University of Pardubice, Series D: Faculty of Economics and Administration, 26*(43), 29-38. Retrieved Sep 15, 2024, from https://www.scopus.com/record/display .uri?eid=2-s2.0-85057788930&origin=scopusAI

Bosworth, B., & Flaaen, A. (2013). America's Financial Crisis: The End of an Era. In *The Global Financial Crisis and Asia: Implications and Challenges*. Oxford University Press., DOI: 10.1093/acprof:oso/9780199660957.003.0002

Brown, A. L., & Kagel, J. H. (2009). Behavior in a simplified stock market: The status quo bias, the disposition effect and the ostrich effect. *Annals of Finance, 05*(01), 01-14. DOI: 10.1007/s10436-007-0092-0

Cascão, A., Quelhas, A. P., & Cunha, A. M. (2023, August 24). Heuristics and cognitive biases in the housing investment market. *International Journal of Housing Markets and Analysis*, 16(05), 991–1006. DOI: 10.1108/IJHMA-05-2022-0073

Chandu, V., Maddala, S., Sai, K. G., Teja, G. C., Prakash, B. J., Rao, B. N., & Osei, B. (2023, January-December). Research on retail Buyers' emotional quotient with focus on transactions on the National Stock Exchange. *International Journal of Engineering Business Management*, 15, 18479790231180770. Advance online publication. DOI: 10.1177/18479790231180770

Cioroianu, I., Corbet, S., Hou, Y., Hu, Y., Larkin, C., & Taffler, R. (2024, June). Exploring the use of emotional sentiment to understanding market response to unexpected corporate pivots. *Research in International Business and Finance*, 70, 102304. Advance online publication. DOI: 10.1016/j.ribaf.2024.102304

Coates, J. M., Gurnell, M., & Sarnyai, Z. (2010, January 27). From molecule to market: Steroid hormones and financial risk-taking. *Philosophical Transactions of the Royal Society of London. Series B, Biological Sciences*, 365(1538), 331–343. DOI: 10.1098/rstb.2009.0193 PMID: 20026470

Coates, J. M., Gurnell, M., & Sarnyai, Z. (2017). From molecule to market. In *The Leadership Hubris Epidemic: Biological Roots and Strategies for Prevention* (pp. 25-56). Springer International Publishing. DOI: 10.1007/978-3-319-57255-0_2

Devadas, M., & Vijayakumar, T. (2019, August). Investment decisions, herd behaviour and retail investors. *International Journal of Innovative Technology and Exploring Engineering*, 08(10), 3291–3294. DOI: 10.35940/ijitee.J1210.0881019

Dhillon, J., & Singh, D. P. (2017). Deciphering the theoretical foundations of investor behavior: A literature review. *International Journal of Applied Business and Economic Research*, 15(09), 477–487. Retrieved August 31, 2024, from https://www.scopus.com/record/display.uri?eid=2-s2.0-85019601992&origin=scopusAI

Diederen, K. M., & Fletcher, P. C. (2021, February). Dopamine, Prediction Error and Beyond. *The Neuroscientist*, 27(01), 30–46. DOI: 10.1177/1073858420907591 PMID: 32338128

Duran, A., & Caginalp, G. (2007, June). Overreaction diamonds: Precursors and aftershocks for significant price changes. *Quantitative Finance*, 07(03), 321–342. DOI: 10.1080/14697680601009903

Elkind, D., Kaminski, K., Lo, A. W., Siah, K. W., & Wong, C. H. (2022, December 01). When Do Investors Freak Out? Machine Learning Predictions of Panic Selling. *Journal of Financial Data Science*, 04(01), 11–39. DOI: 10.3905/jfds.2021.1.085

Gupta, P., & Kohli, B. (2021). Herding behavior in the Indian stock market: An empirical study. *Indian Journal of Finance*, 15(5-7), 86–99.

Hinvest, N. S., Alsharman, M., Roell, M., & Fairchild, R. (2021, December 09). Do Emotions Benefit Investment Decisions? Anticipatory Emotion and Investment Decisions in Non-professional Investors. *Frontiers in Psychology*, 12, 705476. Advance online publication. DOI: 10.3389/fpsyg.2021.705476 PMID: 34955944

Hou, H., Narin, M., Liu, J., & Wang, J. (2021, May). Emotional Contagion, Stock Volatility and Stock Price Synchronization: Empirical Evidence from the Fund's Heavy Warehouse Stocks. *Dongbei Daxue Xuebao/Journal of Northeastern University, 42*(05), 748-754. DOI: 10.12068/j.issn.1005-3026.2021.05.021

Hoyer, K., Zeisberger, S., Breugelmans, S. M., & Zeelenberg, M. (2023, August). A culture of greed: Bubble formation in experimental asset markets with greedy and non-greedy traders. *Journal of Economic Behavior & Organization*, 212, 32–52. DOI: 10.1016/j.jebo.2023.05.005

Hsu, S., & Dupont, B. (2023, Jan 01). 2008 Financial Crisis in the US. In *Elgar Encyclopedia of Financial Crises* (pp. 07-10). Edward Elgar Publishing Ltd. DOI: 10.4337/9781800377363.ch02

Hua, F., & Wang, J. (2018). How investor sentiment impacts financial decision-making behavior: From a cognitive neuroscience perspective. *NeuroQuantology: An Interdisciplinary Journal of Neuroscience and Quantum Physics*, 16(05), 567–573. DOI: 10.14704/nq.2018.16.5.1385

Kartini, K., & Nahda, K. (2021). Behavioral Biases on Investment Decision: A Case Study in Indonesia. *Journal of Asian Finance. Economics and Business*, 08(03), 1231–1240. DOI: 10.13106/jafeb.2021.vol8.no3.1231

Khatua, S., & Pradhan, H. (2014, July 01). Indication of Overreaction with or without Stock Specific Public Announcements in Indian Stock market. *Vikalpa*, 39(03), 35–50. DOI: 10.1177/0256090920140303

Kim, H., Park, K., & Song, S. (2016, April 02). Banking Market Size Structure and Financial Stability: Evidence from Eight Asian Countries. *Emerging Markets Finance & Trade*, 52(04), 975–990. DOI: 10.1080/1540496X.2015.1025653

Kim, J.-Y., Haleblian, J., & Finkelstein, S. (2011). When firms are desperate to grow via acquisition: The effect of growth patterns and acquisition experience on acquisition premiums. *Administrative Science Quarterly*, 56(01), 26–60. DOI: 10.2189/asqu.2011.56.1.026

Kim, K., & Deshmukh, A. (2021). Bandwagon Investment Equilibrium of Investment Timing Games. *The Engineering Economist*, 66(04), 265–278. DOI: 10.1080/0013791X.2020.1829222

Korn, O., & Rieger, M. O. (2019, June). Hedging with regret. *Journal of Behavioral and Experimental Finance*, 22, 192–205. DOI: 10.1016/j.jbef.2019.03.002

Larson, S. J., & Madura, J. (2023, March 31). What drives stock price behavior following extreme one-day returns. *Journal of Financial Research*, 26(01), 113–127. DOI: 10.1111/1475-6803.00048

Lin, Z. (2020). Analysis on the Impact of Human Psychological on Economic Irrational Exuberance. *2nd International Conference on Economic Management and Model Engineering, ICEMME 2020* (pp. 871-876). Chongqing: Institute of Electrical and Electronics Engineers Inc. DOI: 10.1109/ICEMME51517.2020.00178

Lippi, A., Rossi, S., & Soana, M. G. (2022, November 03). Status Quo Bias and Risk Tolerance in Asset Allocation Decision-Making. *Journal of Neuroscience, Psychology, and Economics*, 15(04), 195–209. DOI: 10.1037/npe0000166

Loang, O. K. (2022, April). Overreaction, Investor Sentiment and Market Sentiment of COVID-19. *Vision (Basel)*, 09722629221087386. Advance online publication. DOI: 10.1177/09722629221087386

Mats, V. (2024). HEDGE PERFORMANCE OF DIFFERENT ASSET CLASSES IN VARYING ECONOMIC CONDITIONS. *Radioelectronic and Computer Systems*, 2024(1(109)), 217–234. DOI: 10.32620/reks.2024.1.17

McClure, J. E., & Thomas, D. C. (2017, August 01). Explaining the timing of tulipmania's boom and bust: Historical context, sequestered capital and market signals. *Financial History Review*, 24(02), 121–141. DOI: 10.1017/S0968565017000154

Michailova, J., & Schmidt, U. (2016, July 02). Overconfidence and Bubbles in Experimental Asset Markets. *Journal of Behavioral Finance*, 17(03), 280–292. DOI: 10.1080/15427560.2016.1203325

Mo, S. Y., Liu, A., & Yang, S. Y. (2016, June 01). News sentiment to market impact and its feedback effect. *Environment Systems & Decisions*, 36(02), 158–166. DOI: 10.1007/s10669-016-9590-9

Musnadi, S., Faisal, , & Majid, M. S. A. (2018, November 05). Overreaction and underreaction anomalies in the Indonesian stock market: A sectoral analysis. *International Journal of Ethics and Systems*, 34(04), 442–457. DOI: 10.1108/IJOES-12-2017-0235

Okur, M., & Gurbuz, A. O. (2015). A competitive approach to financial issues: Modern finance theory. In *Banking, Finance, and Accounting: Concepts, Methodologies, Tools, and Applications* (Vols. 1-3, pp. 385-398). IGI Global. DOI: 10.4018/978-1-4666-6268-1.ch019

Omar, N. A., Nazri, M. A., Ali, M. H., & Alam, S. S. (2021, September). The panic buying behavior of consumers during the COVID-19 pandemic: Examining the influences of uncertainty, perceptions of severity, perceptions of scarcity, and anxiety. *Journal of Retailing and Consumer Services*, 62, 102600. Advance online publication. DOI: 10.1016/j.jretconser.2021.102600

Parveen, S., Satti, Z. W., Subhan, Q. A., & Jamil, S. (2020, September). Exploring market overreaction, investors' sentiments and investment decisions in an emerging stock market. *Borsa Istanbul Review*, 20(03), 224–235. DOI: 10.1016/j.bir.2020.02.002

Pathak, D. D., & Thapa, B. S. (2024). Beyond market anomalies: How heuristics and perceived efficiency shape investor behavior in developing markets. *Investment Management and Financial Innovations, 21*(03), 01-12. DOI: 10.21511/imfi.21(3).2024.01

Rao, A. S., & Lakkol, S. G. (2024). Influence of personality, biases on financial risk tolerance among retail investors in India. *Investment Management and Financial Innovations*, 21(03), 248–264. DOI: 10.21511/imfi.21(3).2024.21

Razi, M. A., Tarn, J. M., & Siddiqui, F. A. (2024). Exploring the failure and success of DotComs. *Information Management & Computer Security*, 12(03), 228–244. DOI: 10.1108/09685220410542598

Reb, J. (2008, March). Regret aversion and decision process quality: Effects of regret salience on decision process carefulness. *Organizational Behavior and Human Decision Processes*, 105(2), 169–182. DOI: 10.1016/j.obhdp.2007.08.006

Said, B., Rehman, S. U., Ullah, R., & Khan, J. (2021). Investor overreaction and global financial crisis: A case of Pakistan stock exchange. *Cogent Economics & Finance*, 09(01), 1966195. Advance online publication. DOI: 10.1080/23322039.2021.1966195

Sathya, N., & Gayathiri, R. (2024, June 17). Behavioral Biases in Investment Decisions: An Extensive Literature Review and Pathways for Future Research. *Journal of Information and Organizational Sciences*, 48(01), 117–121. DOI: 10.31341/jios.48.1.6

Sathya, N., & Prabhavathi, C. (2024, March). The influence of social media on investment decision-making: Examining behavioral biases, risk perception, and mediation effects. *International Journal of System Assurance Engineering and Management*, 15(03), 957–963. DOI: 10.1007/s13198-023-02182-x

Sembiring, F. M., Rahman, S., Effendi, N., & Sudarsono, R. (2016). Capital asset pricing model in market overreaction conditions: Evidence from Indonesia stock exchange. *Polish Journal of Management Studies*, 14(02), 182–191. DOI: 10.17512/pjms.2016.14.2.17

Shiller, R. J. (2015). *Irrational exuberance: Revised and expanded third edition.* Princeton University Press. Retrieved Sep 15, 2024, from https://www.scopus.com/record/display.uri?eid=2-s2.0-84977120410&origin=scopusAI

Shimokawa, T., Kinoshita, K., Miyagawa, K., & Misawa, T. (2012, December). A brain information-aided intelligent investment system. *Decision Support Systems*, 54(01), 336–344. DOI: 10.1016/j.dss.2012.05.041

Singh, L. G., & Kumar, K. (2024). The herding behavior of investors in the Indian financial market: An insight into the influence of social media. In *Handbook of Research on Innovative Approaches to Information Technology in Library and Information Science* (pp. 82–102). IGI Global., DOI: 10.4018/979-8-3693-0807-3.ch005

Spendzharova, A. (2014). The Quest for Financial Stability: Determinants of Regulatory Approach in Banking Supervision: Does Counter-Cyclical Regulation Play a Role? In *European Administrative Governance* (pp. 10-34). Palgrave Macmillan. DOI: 10.1057/9781137282750_2

Subedi, D. P., & Bhandari, D. R. (2024). IMPACT OF PSYCHOLOGICAL FACTORS ON INVESTMENT DECISIONS IN NEPALESE SHARE MARKET: A MEDIATING ROLE OF FINANCIAL LITERACY. *Investment Management and Financial Innovations*, 21(03), 317–329. DOI: 10.21511/imfi.21(3).2024.26

Trichilli, Y., Gaadane, S., Boujelbène Abbes, M., & Masmoudi, A. (2024, June 03). Impact of the confirmation bias on returns, expectations and hedging of optimistic and pessimistic traders before and during COVID-19 pandemic. *EuroMed Journal of Business*, 19(02), 338–365. DOI: 10.1108/EMJB-03-2022-0046

Va că-Zamfir, D., & Slave, C. (2018). *Tulip-the flower that conquered Europe. 18th International Multidisciplinary Scientific Geoconference, SGEM 2018. 18.* International Multidisciplinary Scientific Geoconference., DOI: 10.5593/sgem2018/5.1/S20.129

Venkatraman, V., & Beard, E. (2020, Jan 01). Neural Correlates of Decision Variables and Strategic Preferences. In *Psychological Perspectives on Financial Decision Making* (pp. 21–38). Springer International Publishing., DOI: 10.1007/978-3-030-45500-2_2

Vuković, M., & Pivac, S. (2024, January 30). The impact of behavioral factors on investment decisions and investment performance in Croatian stock market. *Managerial Finance*, 50(02), 349–366. DOI: 10.1108/MF-01-2023-0068

Westphal, R., & Sornette, D. (2023, September 29). How Market Intervention can Prevent Bubbles and Crashes: An Agent Based Modelling Approach. *Computational Economics*. Advance online publication. DOI: 10.1007/s10614-023-10462-8

Williams, O. J., & Satchell, S. E. (2011, Aug). Social welfare issues of financial literacy and their implications for regulation. *Journal of Regulatory Economics, 40*(01), 01-40. DOI: 10.1007/s11149-011-9151-6

Williams, T. (2007, April). Empowerment of whom and for what? Financial literacy education and the new regulation of consumer financial services. *Law & Policy*, 29(02), 226–256. DOI: 10.1111/j.1467-9930.2007.00254.x

Wynes, M. J. (2021). Anger, Fear, and Investor's Information Search Behavior. *Journal of Behavioral Finance*, 22(04), 403–419. DOI: 10.1080/15427560.2020.1786386

Xie, H.-B., Chen, C., Bu, H., & Wang, S.-Y. (2011, April). Testing market responses under extreme risks. *Xitong Gongcheng Lilun yu Shijian/System Engineering. Theory into Practice*, 31(04), 650–655. Retrieved September 14, 2024, from https://www.scopus.com/record/display.uri?eid=2-s2.0-79957562308&origin=scopusAI

Xie, J., Fang, Y., Gao, B., & Tan, C. (2023, January). Availability heuristic and expected returns. *Finance Research Letters*, 51, 103443. Advance online publication. DOI: 10.1016/j.frl.2022.103443

Yang, N.-T., Chu, H.-H., Ko, K.-C., & Lee, S.-W. (2018, April). Continuing overreaction and momentum in a market with price limits. *Pacific-Basin Finance Journal*, 48, 56–71. DOI: 10.1016/j.pacfin.2018.01.005

Yang, S. (2024, Aug 01). Pandemic, policy, and markets: insights and learning from COVID-19's impact on global stock behavior. *Empirical Economics*, 01-29. DOI: 10.1007/s00181-024-02648-2

Yang, X., Zhu, Y., & Cheng, T. Y. (2020, February). How the individual investors took on big data: The effect of panic from the internet stock message boards on stock price crash. *Pacific-Basin Finance Journal*, 59, 101245. Advance online publication. DOI: 10.1016/j.pacfin.2019.101245

Ye, J., Li, D., & Cao, Y. (2020, January 01). Investor irrational selection bias in stock market based on cognitive psychology: Evidence from herding behaviour. *Revista Argentina de Clínica Psicológica*, 29(01), 90–98. DOI: 10.24205/03276716.2020.13

Yu, R., & Zhou, X. (2007, May). Neuroeconomics: Opening the "black box" behind the economic behavior. *Chinese Science Bulletin*, 52(09), 1153–1161. DOI: 10.1007/s11434-007-0193-1

Yuen, K. F., Wang, X., Ma, F., & Li, K. X. (2020, May 02). The psychological causes of panic buying following a health crisis. *International Journal of Environmental Research and Public Health*, 17(10), 3513. Advance online publication. DOI: 10.3390/ijerph17103513 PMID: 32443427

Zhang, K., & Long, D. (2021). Individual and Institutional Investor: Who is More Rational. *2nd Asia-Pacific Conference on Image Processing, Electronics and Computers, IPEC 2021* (pp. 431-434). Dalian: Association for Computing Machinery. DOI: 10.1145/3452446.3452555

Zhou, L., & Yang, C. (2020, July 01). Investor sentiment, investor crowded-trade behavior, and limited arbitrage in the cross section of stock returns. *Empirical Economics*, 59(01), 437–460. DOI: 10.1007/s00181-019-01630-7

Chapter 10
The Herd Mentality
Understanding the Theories and Models of Herding Behavior in Financial Markets

Varsha Shriram Nerlekar

School of Business, Dr. Vishwanath Karad MIT World Peace University, India

Anjali Sane

https://orcid.org/0000-0001-7284-848X

Dr. Vishwanath Karad MIT World Peace University, India

Manjiri Gadekar

https://orcid.org/0000-0003-3509-6594

School of Business, Dr. Vishwanath Karad MIT World Peace University, Pune, India

Sushil Kumar Gupta

https://orcid.org/0000-0001-5667-4782

Pune Institute of Business Management, Pune, India

Shrikant Waghulkar

https://orcid.org/0000-0002-3767-3765

RIMS, India

ABSTRACT

This chapter explores herding behavior in financial markets, where individuals follow the actions of a larger group, impacting market dynamics and asset prices. It covers key theories and models, such as social influence, behavioral finance, and empirical studies, to explain why herding occurs. Psychological biases like over-confidence, fear, and greed are highlighted as drivers of this behavior. Models such

DOI: 10.4018/979-8-3693-7827-4.ch010

as rational expectations, noise traders, and information cascades are discussed, along with methods to measure herding. Case studies like the dot-com bubble and the 2008 financial crisis demonstrate its effects on market volatility and efficiency. The chapter also addresses regulatory implications and future research on the influence of technology and social media in shaping herding.

1. INTRODUCTION

Herding behavior in financial markets is the propensity of individuals to act as if belonging to a larger group, where individuals often follow the crowd to produce group behavior that might deviate from the rational decision-making process. "Herd Mentality," is the phenomenon that takes place when investors defer to the actions of others rather than independently making their own decisions (Gupta & Kohli, 2021). This type of behavior manifests in many ways: simultaneous buying or selling of the same kinds of assets may lead to sharp market movements that often deviate from intrinsic values of the assets (Chang S.-K., 2014).

Herding behavior is generally driven by a combination of psychological and social issues. Among the significant predisposing factors to this phenomenon is a tendency towards moving with the crowd, which may probably make one feel secure and lower the perceived risk of being wrong (Ye, Li, & Cao, 2020). Secondly, FOMO or the fear of missing out creates anxiety that may lead investors to follow trends created by others, and this method seems to be the way to achieve possible gains or avoid losses (Singh & Kumar, 2024). This belief in safety through sheer numbers provides one explanation for this phenomenon, wherein individuals generally feel more secure when their behaviors are consistent with those of a larger collective, presuming that aggregated insights of the crowd are likely to be correct.

The study of herding behavior is of great importance beyond the simply understanding the individual investor psychology. For the individual investor, the ability to spot the indications of herding can be a defining factor that gives the investor a chance to make a sound decision on investments. Indeed, herding behavior can give rise, in particular during periods of market euphoria or stress, to asset price bubbles or crashes that generate major financial losses among those who do not recognize the risks (Sabir, Mohammad, & Kadir Shahar, 2018). By studying herding, investors can create a plan on how to avoid getting taken away by the market trends driven by collective irrationality and focus on the essentials and the long-term view of investments.

From a regulatory point of view, this is crucial for maintaining market stability to understand herding behavior. Herding can contribute to market instability and poses high level of systemic risks; where the failure of one part of the market could bring down the overall market. Regulators should be conscious of the tendency for herd behaviour to distort markets and design policies that limit its downside potential. This may encompass efforts to raise the level of transparency in markets, improve market infrastructure or establish some other protections that can mitigate the risk arising from collective insanity.

Many theories and models have been built to explain herding behavior in financial markets. The informational cascades theory suggests that people usually make decisions based on the actions of the others, provided there is some perception that these people know more or have better information than they do. This can lead to situations in which a few influential participants drive choices for a greater population (Hou, Gao, Fan, Liu, & Song, 2017). Social learning models, in contrast, emphasize on the importance of social networks and peer influences in determining the investment decisions. Such models emphasize how the potential for social interaction and communication may enrich the propensity towards herding behavior (Chang, Cheng, & Khorana, 2000).

Behavioral finance theories like prospect theory (Igual & Santamaría, 2017) and bounded rationality (Devadas & T., 2019) also provide insights into how herding behavior arises. For example, thinking in line with prospect theory, investors are more averse to loses than gains and therefore drive individuals toward herding during market downturns as investor want to minimize their perceptions of loss. Bounded rationality refers to the cognitive limitations that prevent individuals from processing all available information, leading them to rely on heuristic shortcuts and the actions of others as a decision-making strategy (Rout & Das, 2015).

2. HISTORICAL PERSPECTIVE

Early Theories of Collective Behavior

The concept of herding behaviour also known as 'herd mentality' which has been demonstrated by various theories of collective behavior that could help to understand the reason the individuals are mostly seen to take similar action, particularly within financial markets. One of the earliest theoretical perspectives was provided by Gustave Le Bon (Wikipedia, 2022) whose seminal work explored the ways individuals are different when they are in crowd compared to when they are in solitude. According to Le Bon, anonymity in the crowd causes a person to lose a sense of personal responsibility and easily swayed by a heightened sense of collective emotions and impulses (Malmberg, 2023). This inability of personal decision making can result in actions that are irrational and often extreme, driven by the influence of herding mentality.

Building on Le Bon's work, psychologists like McDougall at the early of the 20th century developed more theoretical underpinnings of collective behavior. In his book titled "Introduction to Social Psychology" published in 1908, McDougall demonstrated how instinctual drives and emotions have operated in shaping group behaviors. He proposed that shared psychological impulses can give rise to such collective behaviors that are not necessarily rational or well-informed. This perspective laid the basis for understanding how similar psychological forces might influence herding behavior in financial markets where investors might act on collective sentiment rather than rational analysis (Mackie & Smith, 2017).

Emile Durkheim's contributions also provided important insights to social behavior study. His exploration on social cohesion and collective consciousness, particularly in works like The Rules of Sociological Method (1895), provide the conceptual framework to explain how societal norms and shared opinions may lead to specific patterns of individual behavior. Although Durkheim did not specifically mentioned the financial markets, his ideas on collective consciousness and social integration help explain how prevailing crowd sentiments and actions can influence participants in the market (Callegaro, 2021).

Key Historical Events Demonstrating Herding in Markets

Many historical occurrences clearly indicate the effects of herding behavior on financial markets, highlighting the real-world implications for understanding collective psychology and group dynamics.

- Tulip Mania of the (1630s): One of the first recorded financial bubble and serves as an exemplary case of speculations resulting in formation of financial bubble which is a great example of herding behavior driving financial excesses. During this time, tulip bulbs became very popular with price increasing dramatically due to buying frenzy and speculations in the market (Va că-Zamfir & Slave, 2018). Investors rushed to purchase tulips supported by the common belief that prices are expected to increase further. The bubble burst in 1637, leading to a dramatic collapse in prices and significant financial losses. The Tulip Mania phenomenon shows how herd behavior is able to inflate the price of assets beyond their intrinsic value and this, in turn, results in severe market corrections (Thompson, 2007).
- *The South Sea Bubble (1720):* The South Sea Bubble is another classic case of herd behavior in financial market. The South Sea Company was a British enterprise that promised enormous profits from trade in the South Seas and as a result attracted a deluge of investments given the speculative frenzy and collective euphoria. More investors bought the shares as the stock price soared

based on market hype rather than fundamental value (Walsh, 2012). The popping of the bubble led to a catastrophic failure, revealing that mentality of herd would be disastrous leading to unsustainable market conditions and overall financial ruin.

- *The Great Depression (1929-1939):* The stock market crash of 1929 and the subsequent Great Depression serve as excellent illustrations of the role that herding behavior plays in the augmentation of the propensity for deepening an economic crisis. A massive sell-off in stocks drove panic and fear-based selling by investors (Ayoub & Balawi, 2022). Herd mentality made investors continue selling as prices plummeted, thus it worsened the situation and eventually led to more prolonged period of economic depression. The event highlighted how collective fear and panic could increase the momentum of financial instability, resulting in a more unfavorable downturn in the economy (Yang & Loang, 2024).

- *The Dot-com Bubble (1990s):* The late 1990's dot-com bubble is another example from more recent times. Herding behavior inflated asset prices artificially during this period and technological stocks and Internet-related companies attained unprecedented valuations due to speculative investments and collective enthusiasm. Investors flocked to technology stocks, pushing prices to unsustainable levels (Morris & Alam, 2012). The market imploded in 2000 resulting in a sharp correction of the market and the downfalls of many technology firms. This incident had well underscored how herd mentality could result in unreasonable exuberance and cause significant distortions in the market.

- *The Global Financial Crisis (2008):* The 2008 financial crisis is another more recent example of herding behavior that implicated systemic risk. It was started by housing market bubble and gained momentum due to reckless risk-taking on the part of financial institutions induced by collective anticipation of its continuation. As property prices soared, investors and institutions were behaving in a risky manner due to a collective belief that profits would continue (Gl van & Anghel, 2023). It was at this stage that the housing bubble bursting triggered panics and liquidations of nearly all assets escalated the crisis, eventually shaking the world down, further into a global economic downturn. The event depicts how herd behavior may reinforce financial instability further leading to pervasive economic repercussions.

These historical events well explain how herding behaviour affects financial markets, bringing out the effects of group or mass psychology on market behaviour as well as its repercussions on the economy. Knowledge of these examples is crucial in order to gain some insight into the nature of herding behavior and its effects on financial systems.

3. THEORETICAL FOUNDATIONS

Social Influence Theory

Social influence theory develops from the basic insight that how individuals' choices and behaviors are conditioned by others' behaviors and attitudes. Social influence theory is a study in social psychology on how individuals are influenced by the presence and behavior of others, more so in a group setting.

Social Influence Theory is essentially based on the premise that individuals often rely on others behaviour as a heuristic for their own judgments and decisions, especially under some degree of uncertainty. This reliance manifests itself in forms of things like conformity, compliance and obedience. Within financial markets, social influence is manifest when investors imitate other investors' behavior because they believe the crowd's collective judgment is much better source of information, or more accurate, than one's own judgment (Li, et al., 2019).

A very important characteristic of the Social Influence Theory is an idea of the normative social influence, which involves individuals conforming to group norms to gain social acceptance or avoid rejection. In financial markets, this could well imply a herding behavior wherein investors follow the market trends with the objective of acquiring consistency with the perceived market expectations, even though such market trends may actually be driven by speculation rather than fundamental analysis (Pan, Altshuler, & Pentland, 2012). The second one is informational social influence, where individuals look to others as a source of information in order to make decisions, especially when their knowledge is poor. This may lead to herding behavior, where investors follow what is perceived to be experts or influential market participants who presumably know better.

Figure 1. Theoretical Foundations (Author Generated)

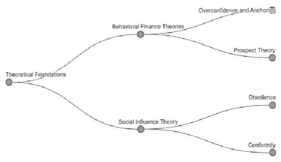

Behavioral Finance Theories

Behavioral finance theories provide more understanding on herd behavior through the analysis of the way in which psychological biases and cognitive limitations impact decision-making processes within financial markets. The two best-known theories in this area are Prospect Theory and concepts of overconfidence and anchoring.

Prospect Theory

Prospect Theory was developed by Daniel Kahneman and Amos Tversky in 1979 is a model that describes how individuals perceive and act toward risk and uncertainty (James, 2024). While conventional economic theories that suppose rational decision making, Prospect Theory assume that people choose the options based on their perception of losses and gains against the reference point, rather than the absolute results of such a decision.

Prospect Theory postulates that individuals are characterized by loss aversion: losses are felt more painfully compared to the pleasure derived from equivalent gains. This behavior can result in a fear of losing money when facing such losses and seeking to earn money back in attempt to make up for the losses. In financial markets, such behavior leads to herding because investors follow a particular crowd in order to avoid possible losses that might be envisaged, especially during market downturns. This can be similar to, say, when investors sell off in a falling market in masses in order to prevent further losses; this amplifies market declines into herd-driven panic selling (Liu, Nacher, Ochiai, Martino, & Altshuler, 2014).

Overconfidence and Anchoring

Another two theories of behavioral finance that explain the herding behavior are Overconfidence and anchoring.

Overconfidence

Overconfidence is a cognitive bias in which individuals over-estimate their knowledge, their capabilities or accuracy of their future forecasts. Overconfidence in financial markets makes the investors feel that they possess some type of inside information or insight that others do not, which forces them into taking extraordinary risks or ignoring the danger signals (X. H. Bao & Li, 2020). This aspect also contributes to the herding bias, whereby overconfident investors may be more likely to follow the crowd, perhaps thinking that the decision by the crowd is arrived at for sound reasoning. It is therefore possible to have feedback loops created by overconfidence, hereby making market participants to push the prices of their assets to the extreme (Bregu, 2020).

Anchoring

Anchoring is a cognitive bias wherein, in a state of imperfect knowledge, one clings to the first piece of information available (the "anchor") and bases many subsequent judgments on that anchor. In financial markets this can occur when investors rely strictly on previous price levels, previous high or even certain market trends as reference points for their action. Herding behavior results from the fact that by using these anchors investors emulate behaviour in the market in relation to the dominant market trends informed by these reference points regardless of their relation to the real market (Sathya & Gayathiri, 2024). For example, if investors anchored to a historical peak price of a stock, they may irrationally think that the stock would reach that price again, thus stimulating collective buying activity and the eventual creation of market bubbles.

4. PSYCHOLOGICAL UNDERPINNINGS

Analyzing the psychological aspects of the herding phenomenon in the context of financial markets includes factors such as cognitive heuristics, emotions, and functions of fear and greed. Each of these factors is crucial in helping to explain how investors might commonly act in concert to deviate from rational choice processes and impact market movements, perhaps leading to severe financial consequences (Andersson, Hedesström, & Gärling, 2014).

Cognitive Biases and Herding

Cognitive biases refer to the systematic deviation from norm or rationality in judgment that can influence an individual's decision-making process. A number of cognitive biases are responsible for herding behavior in financial markets

- Confirmation Bias: Confirmation bias is a preference or search for information that confirms pre-existing opinions or ideas. Financial markets would then have investors focus on information that substantiates their decisions in investment while setting aside contrary evidence (Pouget, Sauvagnat, & Villeneuve, 2017). This may amplify herding behavior when many investors exhibit confirmation bias by collectively acting on similar but potentially flawed information, therefore reinforcing trends and contributing to market bubbles or crashes.
- Anchoring Bias: Anchoring bias is a concept in which, for most judgments, an initial piece of information that one receives is given too much weight. For instance, the investors might use historical stock prices or previous highs as their points of reference. This bias can result into herd behaviour when several investors decide to base their decisions on these anchors, thereby causing price fluctuations due to incorrect reference points rather than the prevailing market forces (DeLisle, Diavatopoulos, Fodor, & Krieger, 2017).
- Herd Behavioural Bias: Herd behaviour bias is that cognitive tendency of individuals to mimic the actions of others, usually based on the belief that the majority cannot go wrong. The bias is very prominent in situations involving uncertainty, where individuals somewhat lack confidence in their own judgments. This could lead to widespread trend following or price movements and finally to mass investment decisions devoid of fundamental analysis in financial markets (Trisno & Vidayana, 2023).

Emotional Factors in Decision-Making

The emotional determinants of investment decisions create significant herding tendencies. Feelings, like fear and greed, can overshadow logical reasoning to the extent that people tend to act together and their mass reactions influence market conditions.

- Fear: The fear emotion may be very strong and force investors to make decisions based on perceived avoidance of risk rather than sound judgment. This results in panic selling during a period of market decline or crisis when investors try to prevent further losses. The general pattern of behavior, based on fear, may exacerbate market decline and create downward spirals (Lee & Andrade, 2011). Besides, Fear of missing out (FOMO) may be another reason that forces investors to follow the trend or make swift choices in investments based on others' activities rather than factual judgment.
- Greed: On the other hand, greed can be a catalyst for investors to inflate high return projects which they may do without thinking about the risks involved. In market upswings or during the build-up of bubbles, greed causes speculative motivation as well as higher levels of risk-taking as the investors pursue the recent gains. This has also driven asset prices up unsustainably to create market bubbles in the aggregate quest for profits (Hoyer, Zeisberger, Breugelmans, & Zeelenberg, 2023). When many people in the stock market are propelled to act by greed, they might overlook the warning signs of a bubble or the fundamental valuation concerns regarding the stock, and thus a herding effect might ensue which will cause the market distortions.

Role of Fear and Greed

The interplay between fear and greed is key to understanding the herd behavior in the financial markets. For example, either emotion can result in a feedback loop that can greatly magnify market movements and thus have major financial consequences

- Fear of Loss and Panic Selling: Fear of loss is a powerful motivator. An investor could very well sell his assets when the market is volatile. If enough investors act on this fear, it can lead to domino effect where each successive wave of selling drives its prices down further. This panic selling can become a self-fulfilling prophecy when it works to push down market prices further. Under the pretext of declining price leads people into more fear and very sell, sending the market descending into bottomless pit of losses (Elkind, Kaminski, Lo, Siah, & Wong, 2022).
- Greed and speculative bubbles: Greed, through which investors are often trying to speculate to achieve high returns, can be an overriding cause, whereby they invest in hopes of high returns from their assets. When many investors become motivated by avarice, it is quite common that they bid up prices above the intrinsic value, thereby they belong to the speculation buyers creating speculative bubbles (Fernández-Rodríguez, García-Artiles, & Martín-González, 2010). With increasing prices, such greedy momentum may attract

more and more investors, inflating the bubble. The bursting of the bubble implies that prices drop rapidly, and this in turns leads to high levels of financial losses and instability in the market.

5. EMPIRICAL MODELS OF HERDING

Figure 2. Various Models of Herding Behavior (Author Generated)

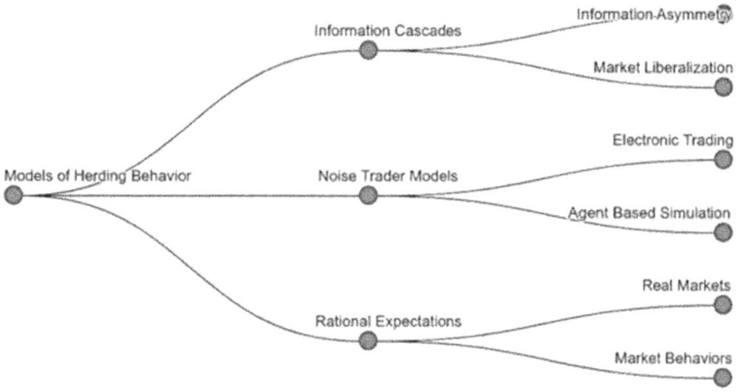

Models Based on Rational Expectations

According to the Rational Expectations based models, herding behavior can be explained theoretically within the scope of efficient markets. The Rational Expectations Hypothesis (REH) was introduced by John Muth in 1961 and maintains that, individuals are always in a position to generate forecasts of future economic variables using all available information that they make rational use of. It views market participants' expectations, on average, as accurate, with any deviations from rational behavior being totally stochastic (Park & Sabourian, 2011).

REH for Behavioral Herding says that investors gather information from their own knowledge set to form expectations of asset prices in a state of uncertainty. So if many investors began to act upon the same information, or on signals triggered by that shared analysis, their collective actions would have a herd-like behavior. However, under this rational expectations hypothesis such behaviour is not counted as being irrational. It is simply a view that brings together information from a number of sources and it is the best information available at the time (Huang, Krishnan, Shon, & Zhou, 2017).

Empirical models which integrate Rational Expectations as one of its key features, assume that the herding behaviour is an appropriate action given the information concerning fundamental forces in the market. Consider the following: if investors believe that an economic indicator will raise asset prices, then they might reach a group decision to buy these assets and create a herding effect. This behavior, while appearing as herding, is rooted in a rational response to shared information rather than irrational collective decision-making.

Noise Trader Models

Another approach to the herding behavior is Noise Trader Models, which review the impact of irrational or non-fundamental factors on market prices. Noise traders are investors who invest without proper assessment through a process of analysis of its fundamentals but based on misinforming, emotions, or chance. These traders sometimes make big moves in the asset prices and market dynamics (Ulibarri, Anselmo, Hovespian, Tolk, & Florescu, 2009).

According to (Fischer, 1986) noise traders can lead to a fluctuation in prices other than what fundamental information alone would suggest. This model also points to the fact that the noise traders, by acting on arbitrary or non-fundamental signals, create volatility and mispricing in financial markets. Their behavior can result in dramatic market distortions in the aggregate when a large number of noise traders are acting in concert, reflecting a type of herding based on non-rational influences.

Noise Trader Models postulate that the herding phenomenon could result not only from the rational reactions of agents to information but, most importantly, also from the aggregative activity of traders, who themselves need not be acting on the basis of accurate or complete information. Noise Trader Models, therefore, provide a foundation for market bubbles or crashes driven by aggregate effects of noise trading, which the herd mentality amplifies (Dai, Zhang, & Chang, 2023).

Information Cascades

The concept of the Information Cascade offers a theoretical context explaining why individuals follow the crowd in their choice, though they have private information. Information Cascades take place when individuals make decisions based on the actions of others rather than their own private information; that is, early decisions get tipped towards what has been increasingly favored by those who have chosen before (Phillips & Pohl, 2021).

This theory introduced by Sushil Bikhchandani, David Hirshleifer and Ivo Welch in 1992, which suggests that once a critical mass of individuals adopts a particular behavior from observation, subsequent individuals may act similarly without regard to their private information. For example, if an initial group of investors bases their decisions on news interpretation to buy a certain stock, other investors, too, may also buy the stock simply because they see others buying it, even if it may mean disregarding their own conflicting information.

Information cascades are one example of how herding can occur even when private information is individually possessed and perhaps conflicting. This makes people follow the herd, when individuals see others making decision on the basis of some signals, they tend to believe those signals to be of higher credibility than their own. The result can be feedback loops in which cascades amplify market trends, leading to large deviations from fundamental values and reinforcing market bubbles or crashes (Jalili & Perc, 2017).

6. MEASURING HERDING BEHAVIOR

Measuring herding behavior in financial markets requires the use of a set of quantitative and qualitative methods. The objective of these methods is to assess and realize the magnitude of collectively following trends or imitate others by investors to explain the dynamics of the market behavior.

Quantitative Approaches

Herding behavior can be analyzed with the help of objective metrics provided by quantitative approaches obtained by observing the statistical patterns in financial data. Among the quantitative techniques, the two prominent ones are the Cross-Sectional Standard Deviation (CSSD) and the Cross-Sectional Absolute Deviation (CSAD)

1. Cross-Sectional Standard Deviation (CSSD)

The Cross-Sectional Standard Deviation (CSSD) the dispersion of asset returns over a given period across different stocks or securities. The basic concept of CSSD is that during the periods of high herding, the degree of dispersion of returns in the market will be low this is because investors move in a particular direction. On the other hand, when there is low herding, dispersion in returns will be high, an indication of variation in investment choices (Carvalho, Jordão da Gama Silva, & Klotzle, 2024). A low value of CSSD is often seen as a signal of increased herding behavior since it implies that more and more investors are moving in the same direction. For instance, if there was a sharp selling or buying frenzy on the market, then the CSSD would be low implying that returns on different assets are converging.

2. Cross-Sectional Absolute Deviation (CSAD)

CSAD is the measure that quantifies the herding behavior by examining the absolute deviations of the asset returns from their mean. Unlike CSSD which employs the use of standard deviation, CSAD provides the absolute deviations of the returns from the mean and thus provides another view as to the extent of the return dispersion (Kurt Gümüş, Gümüş, & Çimen, 2019). A substantial decline in CSAD normally means that the herding behavior is high, as it reflects convergence in the investors' activities because returns do not spread out but cluster around the mean. In the instance of a market bubble-when the investors all could be moving under speculative sentiments-a low CSAD will indicate that the returns on assets are increasingly homogenous, with the investors following one trend (Madaan & Shrivastava, 2022).

Qualitative Approaches

Qualitative approaches can explain the motivations, perceptions, and behaviors that lie behind investors' actions that what herding behavior is all about, something no numbers can depict. These approaches involve surveys, interviews and case studies.

1. Surveys and Interviews

Surveys and interviews include getting primary data from investors regarding their decision methodologies, their viewpoints on the market and the factors affecting their decision. It can reveal the rationale behind herding behaviour, for instance, perceived market trends, the effects of financial media or social factors.

- Surveys: Surveys can be structured for the purpose of collecting information about investors' perceptions, expectations and behavior. Specific questions may relate to the factors such as the perception of market trends by investors, whether the actions of others are mimicked, and what sources of information are used in making investment decisions. By analyzing survey responses, it is possible to conclude about the dynamics of herding behavior and find out what factors can provoke collective action.
- Interviews: Interviews offers better insights into the individual investor behavior patterns. Interviewing the market participants helps in finding out about personal experiences, motivation and factors that influence the herding. The interviews can also reveal how investors respond to market signals and how much others' actions actually influence their decisions.

2. Case Studies

Case studies entail extended analysis of specific cases or occurrences that demonstrate herding behavior. The individual case studies enable the researcher to get an idea of the dynamics of herding and its impact on financial markets. Case studies can be used to study the market events like financial bubbles, crashes or periods of high volatility and examine how herding behavior affected these events.

- Historical Events: Explaining how herding behavior develops and impact markets, one can rely on the analysis of historical events, including Tulip Mania, the South Sea Bubble, or the Dot-com Bubble. Case studies related to these events are bound to surface patterns in investor behavior, market dynamics, and the consequences of collective decision-making.
- Modern Market Crises: Modern insights into herding behavior can be obtained by looking at the recent market events or higher volatility periods. For instance, how investors behaved during the 2008 financial crisis or the COVID-19 market fluctuations will rather give insight into how modern market participants respond to a shock and consequently follow market trends.

Measuring herding behavior in financial markets involves a combination of quantitative and qualitative approaches. Quantitative methods like Cross-Sectional Standard Deviation (CSSD) and Cross-Sectional Absolute Deviation (CSAD) provide objective metrics for analyzing return dispersion and identifying periods of heightened herding. Qualitative methods, including surveys, interviews, and case studies, offer deeper insights into the motivations and behaviors underlying herding. Together, these approaches help to build a comprehensive understanding of herding behavior and its impact on financial markets.

7. TYPES OF HERDING IN FINANCIAL MARKETS

Herding behavior in financial markets can demonstrate in many distinct forms, each being motivated by different motives and mechanisms. A comprehension of these forms of herding will be of much use in any attempt to account for investor behavior and market dynamics. The most basic types of herding are informational herding, reputational herding, and directional herding.

Informational Herding

Informational herding arises when investors mimic the actions of the others because of beliefs of superior information or insight on the part of others. In this case, there are market participants who make decisions given the belief that others possess valuable information that they do not have. Informational herding is usually realized during situations of ambiguity and the investors are not certain about the true value of the asset. They mimic others with the expectation that their decision making processes will be more efficient based on crowds' wisdom (Zhang, 2018).

For example, if a few influential large investors or analysts recommend a certain stock, then the other investors may wish to follow them on the basis of the assumption that such experts have private or superior information. This type of herding can lead to rapid and widespread buying or selling in which each investor respond, essentially, to the same signals as the others occasionally create market bubbles or precipitous declines.

Reputational Herding

Reputational herding is mainly motivated by a desire to preserve or increase one's reputation. In that case, investors may herd simply for the sake of being in alignment with the sentiment of the market or the actions of more informed investors. This kind of herding is rationalized out of fear of judgment or criticism for having made decisions contrary to the consensus (Popescu & Xu, 2014).

In a more practical perspective, reputational herding may be observed where there tends to be high public scrutiny of social and professional activities. For instance, institutional investors such as mutual funds or pension funds herd into the equity market because they may want to avoid criticism or any possible stakeholder negative reaction. In this manner, by moving along with other reputable market participants, they would run less risk of reputational consequences relative to decisions made solely or against the majority's consent.

Directional Herding

Directional herding refers to the coordinated movement of the investors in the same direction, in response to a particular trend or sentiment in the market. This kind of herding is where a number of investors make similar investment decision, for instance to buy or sell the same assets within a specific period of time due to some certain market condition or trend.

Directional herding can be due to market news, economic indicators or any external factors which generates the consensus among people for particular direction. For instance, during market rally investors can be enticed to purchase stocks because prices are going up and generally the market is up. On the other hand, directional herding may result to selling frenzy during bearish market prompted by negative news or falling prices (Humayun, 2018).

This form of herding can reinforce market trends, hence high volatility and potential market inefficiencies. When a large proportion of the market participants behave in the same manner, it is possible to observe asset prices moving away from their intrinsic value, leading to market bubbles or crashes.

8. IMPACT OF HERDING ON FINANCIAL MARKETS

Herding phenomena in financial markets imply significant imacts on the assets price, stability of markets, and market efficiency. In this context, it is necessary to understand the effects of these herding tendencies for the study of the markets and design of strategies to deal with or avoid those potential risks associated with the investors' collective behavior.

Asset Price Volatility

The one of the most immediate impacts is the increased volatility of asset prices due to herding behavior. When large groups of investors are making similar investment decisions at the same time, trades occur that sharply shift the price of assets. This heightened volatility can be driven by mass purchases or sales of assets based on trends or sentiment and not on fundamental values (Klein, 2013).

For example, asset prices might shoot up or drop at blistering rates over spells of frantic herding such as during a market rally or sell-off. This often seen in speculative bubbles: the euphoria of investors eventually sweeps the prices high above intrinsic values, then precipitates abrupt collapses when the bubble finally bursts. The amplified volatility produced by herding thus creates uncertainty and risk for investors, raising even the potential financial instability.

Market Bubbles and Crashes

Herding behavior is a major cause of market bubbles and crashes. A market bubble occurs when the assets prices have risen to unsustainable levels because of collective investor activity based on optimism, speculation, or other factors. As more and more investors join in the herd and thus push prices upward, a bubble inflates further. The top of an asset price bubble typically shows euphoria and a complete disregard for fundamental valuation principles (Litimi, BenSaïda, & Bouraoui, 2016).

When this bubble bursts, the market correction-a very quick and often severe correction-can take place in which these inflated asset prices revert to their more realistic levels. This process can therefore lead to market crashes: the rapid and remarkable fall in asset prices might culminate in colossal financial losses on the part of investors. Historical market bubbles and crashes evidenced like the Dot-com Bubble or the 2008 Financial Crisis, shows how herding behavior could be responsible for large-scale market disruptions (Schulmerich, Leporcher, & Eu, 2015).

Effects on Market Efficiency

The efficiency of the market is a term that describes to what degree its assets prices reflect all available information. In an efficient market, the price will change immediately and accurately in reaction to the availability of new information, and assets will be appropriately priced based on their fundamental values. However, herding can affect a market's efficiency adversely since prices will no longer reflect intrinsic values (Ahmad & Wu, 2022).

Herding occurs when investors base their decisions on market trends or the movements of others rather than a proper study of the fundamental information. Such behavior leads to asset mispricing and create price distortions, which hardly match with the underlying fundamental value. For instance, during a period of directional herding, asset prices might over-exaggerated or depressed according to the collective investor sentiment rather than on sound economic indicators.

Additionally, herding behavior may even be an avenue of inefficiency in markets since it creates feedback loops that strengthen price movements toward further deviations from their fundamental values. As investors react to observed trends and actions taken by others, these trends can become self-reinforcing that lead to further divergences away from their true value (Carvalho, Jordão da Gama Silva, & Klotzle, 2024).

9. CASE STUDIES

Understanding of herding behavior in the financial markets is further enriched through case studies of specific events which clearly show how herding by investors determines market dynamics. Some notable examples are presented by well-known cases-in-point, such as the Dot-com Bubble and the 2008 Financial Crisis and more recently market events like the GameStop saga and cryptocurrency surges. These case studies are helpful in understanding the dynamics behind herding and its consequences.

Figure 3. Financial Crises (Author Generated)

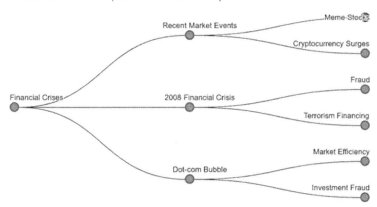

1. Dot-com Bubble (1995-2000)

The Dot-com Bubble is perhaps one of the most notable examples of herding behaviors creating a market bubble. The end of 1990s witnessed tremendous growth in the Internet technology area and the promise of highly transformational digital businesses evoke strong investor enthusiasm. The stocks of a technology and internet-related entity saw extraordinary price increases triggered by optimism and speculations rather than fundamental business performance (Chang S.-K., 2014).

Herding Dynamics

Speculation and FOMO: Investors, driven by a fear of missing out, and the perception that Internet companies would really change the economy, collectively bought into a tech frenzy. High valuations proved unsustainable as more and more investors were caught up in the trend, driving prices far above the true earnings potential of the companies involved.

Media Influence: The bubble further fueled by media coverage and reports from analysts. Favorable forecasts and endorsement created feedback loops of optimism, which encouraged more people to join the herd. Soon after the prices began jumping higher, more and more investors entered the market, to a point where rational analysis was dominated by speculative excitement.

Consequences: When the bubble burst in 2000, the market experienced a dramatic correction. The NASDAQ Composite Index, which is choc-full of technology stocks, crashed-and-burned, wiping out huge gains for investors. The Dot-com Bubble reminds all of the quite extreme market distortions and subsequent corrections due to herding behavior caused by speculative enthusiasm (Teti & Maroni, 2021).

2. 2008 Financial Crisis

Another critical case study is the 2008 Financial Crisis, which highlighted how herding behavior contributed in financial market disruptions. The crisis was triggered by the collapse of the housing market and the failure of mortgage-backed securities, which had been widely purchased by financial institutions. (Humayun, 2018).

Herding Dynamics

Risk Misjudgment: Investors and financial institutions as a whole, underestimated risk associated with mortgage-backed securities during the housing boom. Believing that home prices would never stop going up caused such widespread investment in financially risky investments, assuming others to be smart decision-makers.

Panic Selling: When crisis triggered, herding behavior manifested in panic selling. Financial institutions and investors scrambled to liquidate assets and thus deepen the downfall in the market. The widespread panic and scramble out of positions further intensified the financial turmoil.

Consequences: The 2008 Financial Crisis caused severe global recession, incurred heavy financial losses, and brought widespread economic misfortune to the people worldwide. This crisis brought about the danger of herding behavior, risk misjudgement, and panic that may sometimes result in such systemic failures and market breakdowns.

3. Recent Market Events

Recent market events, including the GameStop short squeeze and cryptocurrency surges, are just some recent examples of herding behavior in action.

GameStop Short Squeeze (2021): In early 2021, collective buying of shares by retail investors on platforms like Reddit's WallStreetBets led to a sharp hike in the stock price of GameStop. This is referred to as a short squeeze wherein a collective buying of shares of GameStop raised its price and forced institutional investors who had shorted the stock to cover their positions.

Herding Dynamics

Social Media Influence: Social media greatly contributed to this mass action because retail investors used online discussion forums to organize their buying activity. The herd behavior was facilitated by a widely held belief that the stock is undervalued and its need to challenge institutional investors (Münster, Reichenbach, & Walther, 2024).

Speculative trading: A speculative trading surged GameStop's stock price, together with a sense of community created among retail investors, led to extreme price volatility and a drastic deviation from fundamental valuations.

Consequences: The GameStop short squeeze demonstrated the enormous power of social media in determining market dynamics and how the retail investor can, at times, have a greater influence. The episode led to significant money wins and losses, regulatory scrutiny, and discussion on market manipulation and the role of social media in trading (Mancini, Di Clemente, & Cimini, 2022).

Cryptocurrency Surges: Cryptocurrencies, including Bitcoin and Ethereum, have trended wildly under herding behaviors. In periods of fast price acceleration, like the 2017 Bitcoin run-up and the 2021 crypto market boom, investor enthusiasm and speculations led to enormous surges in cryptocurrency prices (Rubbaniy, Polyzos, Rizvi, & Tessema, 2021).

Herding Dynamics

Media Hype and FOMO: Hype created through media as well as kudos from high-profile investors have only fueled speculative interest in cryptocurrencies. Investors herd along in this speculation, fearing to miss out opportunity to gain profit in such a market scenario (Malla, Lavanya, J., & J., 2023).

Volatility and Speculation: The speculative nature of investments in cryptocurrencies creates situations leading to volatility in returns. Investors jointly, tend to react to the price movement and market sentiments, leading to sharp price swings.

Consequences: The surge in cryptocurrencies have resulted in both an appreciation of immense profit to some of the investors and heavy losses to others. The volatility of cryptocurrency markets specifically highlights the role of herding behavior in asset prices and market stability (Kumar Kulbhaskar & Subramaniam, 2023).

These case studies are classic examples of how herding behavior can serve as a significant force behind sweeping market trends, creating bubbles, and causing enormous financial losses. Each of the cases - the Dot-com Bubble, the 2008 Financial Crisis, and more recent events such as the GameStop short squeeze and the cryptocurrency surges - demonstrates intricate interactions between collective investor behavior and market dynamics.

10. REGULATORY AND POLICY IMPLICATIONS

The herding behavior in financial markets can have certain major implications that include improved risk, market bubbles, and inefficiencies. Addressing these concerns entails combinations of an adequate mechanism of market regulation, strategies to avoid herding, and reasonable policy measures. The following delves into the impact of behavior on regulations and policies.

1. Role of Market Regulation

Market regulation plays a very pivotal role in maintaining market stability and in alleviating the adverse influences of the herding behavior. Proper regulation can ascertain that markets functions efficiently and transparently, thereby minimizing collective investor action risks.

Transparency Requirements: Regulatory requirements that enforce transparency related to financial markets play an important role to minimize information asymmetry and thereby prevent over-the-top speculation (Gros & Wallek, 2015). For example, stipulation for comprehensive disclosure and reporting of financial positions and trading activities can ensure that all market participants are informed. This would make it less likely for herding to take place based on incomplete or misleading data (Ostrowska, 2021).

Regulation of High-Frequency Trading: High frequency trading (HFT) has the potential to intensify herding behavior through its amplification of market trends and heightened volatility (Myklebust, 2021). Introducing regulations to oversee and manage HFT activities like setting minimum resting times for orders or imposing transaction fees when trading rapidly may contribute to the improvement of market resilience (Gros & Wallek, 2015).

Enhanced Risk Management: Regulated risk management requiring greater controls by financial institutions by enforcing regulations that mandate institutions to adopt strong risk management strategies, hence limiting the system-specific risk associated with herding behavior. For example, provisions such as stress testing and capital adequacy standards can help the institution become more fully prepared for market shocks and avoid possible large-scale financial contagion (Tian, 2016).

2. Strategies to Mitigate Herding Behavior

In an attempt to curtail herding behavior, require strategies that promote well-informed investment decisions and will reduce the tendency of investors' herding. There are several ways discussed below as counter to this problem:

Promoting Financial Literacy: Increasing investor education and financial literacy levels can help individuals decide in the most intelligent way possible and minimize herding behavior. Education and resources that enlighten investors on market fundamentals, risk management, and investment strategies can be effective in making investors act based on their own analysis instead of actions driven by trends (Baihaqqy, Disman, Nugraha, & Sari, 2020).

Encouraging Diversification: Encouraging strategies towards diversification can help to reduce herding influence. If investors are encouraged to spread out their portfolios across diverse asset classes and sectors, regulators can lessen the likelihood of widespread market reactions driven by trends. Diversification creates an opportunity to spread the risk and minimizes one particular asset or sector's influence on overall market actions (Zaimovic, Arnaut-Berilo, & Mustafic, 2017).

Behavioral Insights: Insights from behavioral finance can be applied into regulatory practice to reduce herding behavior. For example, regulators can intervene to try to counteract the common cognitive biases, such as overconfidence or herding behavior. These interventions may be in the form of default options to encourage diversified investing or as tools that help investors make more rational decisions.

3. Policy Recommendations

There is a dire need for an integrated approach in developing and implementing policies to counter this very obvious form of herding behavior. The following policy recommendations are aimed at improving market stability and reducing the adverse herding impact:

Strengthening Market Surveillance: Enhanced market surveillance and monitoring can detect the herd movement early, thereby alleviating over-herding. Advanced analytics and real-time monitoring systems should be put in place by regulators to detect abnormal trading patterns, possible manipulations in markets, and matters influenced by the price movement due to herds. Thus, they would be well-informed and manage timely intervention to check further escalation of market disruptions (Karnatak & Malik, 2021).

Implementing Circuit Breakers: Circuit breakers are measures implemented to briefly halt trading during price fluctuation when prices rise by an unusually large amount. Measures taken in this regard can be deterrents against herding and panic selling, making the impact of herding weaker during market turmoil. Circuit Breakers pauses trading and give the investor ample time to reassess current market conditions and make proper choices (Wang, Kim, & Suardi, 2022).

Promoting Investor Protection: To check herding behavior and minimize the associated risks, the regulators can draft policies aiming investor protection. For example, in creating regulations to restrict misleading advertising, standards for some types of financial advice, and fair treatment of investors themselves, the possibility for others to respond to the speculation or spurious information can be reduced (Stavroyiannis & Babalos, 2015).

Encouraging Long-Term Investing: Incentives for long-term investments are expected to compensate for a near-term focus that promotes herding behavior. Ideas that encourage tax incentives for long-term investment, retirement savings plans with longer horizons and discourage frequent trading may encourage the investors to invest keeping in mind a more balanced and less reacting approach towards market movements (Hoang & Harrington, 2023).

11. FUTURE DIRECTIONS

As the financial market matures, so does the perception of herding behavior. Emerging research trends, technological and social media impacts, and implications for investors and policymakers are few trends that will define the future research directions.

1. Emerging Trends in Herding Research

Recent studies reveal several emerging trends in herding behavior research, highlighting the growing influence of social media and technological advancements:

Influence Credibility: Herding behavior among investors is significantly influenced by social media, moreover, the credibility of influencers playing a very significant role in the herding behavior of investors. Study found that if influential personas or credible sources promote any investment options, their credibility can have very positive impacts on herd behavior. Such influencers are followed by investors believing that they might be well-informed, which drives collective decisions and increases trends in the market (Singh & Kumar, 2024).

Time-Varying and Asymmetric Effects: The relationship between internet postings and herd behavior is complex in nature, exhibiting time-varying effects. Internet posting, in this case, can impact herd behavior negatively in the short term, mainly due to information flow may create scepticism or confusion. Time-varying and asymmetric effects, therefore, imply heterogeneity in the impact of online information on herding behavior and it may change and become context and time dependent (Zhou & Liu, 2022).

Social Commerce: Social commerce integrates the functions of social media with online shopping, is a channel that can prompt herd behavior through influence on consumer confidence and decision-making. However, consumer communication and reviews from social media platforms can create herd behavior because individuals base their purchase decisions on collective opinions and trends rather than personal preferences (Jia, Liu, & Lowry, 2024).

Machine Learning and Textual Data Analysis: Advanced techniques, including machine learning and analysis on social media text, are currently being used in finding mechanisms of investor herding behavior. It heavily relies on text data that include tweets and forum posts to discern the nature of sentiment and the dissemination of information that leads to collective action. These technologies allow researchers to gain much deeper insights into factors causing herding as well as the role of sentiment in developing market trends (Li, Chen, Liu, Yu, & Yu, 2023).

2. Impact of Technology and Social Media on Herding

Technology and social media have dramatically changed herding behavior, adapting how investors access information and behave:

Role of Social Media platform: Today, as social media platform emerges as core financial information providers and also commentators on market sentiment, they become an integral part of the decision making process for investors. The ease with which such information can be accessed on the social media and its real-time airing to which investors react, increases the propensity of herding behavior (Li, Chen, Liu, Yu, & Yu, 2023).

Herding During Special Events: Social, self, and emotional needs drive herding behavior online and usually increases during special events. During such events, social media can amplify collective behavior creating dynamics somewhat like a carnival or riot. This phenomenon illustrates how emotional and social factors can lead to pronounced herding effects with investors reacting collectively to news or events (Lin & Liu, 2014).

Market Differences and COVID-19: The herding behavior is different across markets contexts, with emerging markets showing stronger effects than developed ones. The COVID-19 pandemic has worsened these disparities amplifying herding behavior in both emerging and frontier markets. The pandemics worldwide impact and the uncertainty posed by it, have intensified collective reactions and market volatility.

3. Implications for Investors and Policymakers

Understanding herding behavior has critical implications for both investors and policymakers:

Sentiment Influence: Sentiment gleaned from social media, such as tweets and news content, positively influences herding among investors. This effect is prominent in companies that have investment-grade ratings and low valuation uncertainty. Since investors may be swayed by online sentiment, they are more likely to herd based on supposed market movements instead of the fundamentals analysis (Garcia, 2021).

Social Influence Factors: Social influence factors also include herd effect, which are critical for information sharing and taking action on it. An example is how health information forwarding behavior is affected by social influence among WeChat users, but informational influence is typically of greater importance. This analysis can then suggest and inform the designs of interventions that reduce the adverse effects of herding (Wang & Liu, 2019).

Impact of Social Factors: Social Factors also influence herding behavior; these are general prosperity, education, aging society, industry orientation, and gender. These factors can also influence the presence and strength of market-wide herding. Incorporating social dimensions in policy-making helps policymakers manage the herding behavior better, hence bringing stability into the markets.

12. CONCLUSION

Understanding the nature of herding behavior in financial markets is crucial for understanding the dynamics of the market and, hence, informed investment decision making. This chapter has provided quite comprehensive discussions of theories and models explaining herding emphasize the role of psychological biases and social influence thus bring out the complexities as well as nuances through various empirical models and measurement techniques applied. Thereafter, the historical case studies such as the dot-com bubble and the financial crisis of 2008 depict the profound impacts of herding on market stability and efficiency. The discussion on regulatory and policy implications underlines the need for strategies to negate the adverse effects of herding, ensuring more stable financial environment. It discusses the new emerging trends and future research areas concerning the impact of technology and social media on herding dynamics. This synthesis of theoretical insight as well as empirical evidence and practical implications contributes towards deeper understanding of financial market herding behavior offering helpful insights for all investors, regulators, and scholars navigating and managing the complexities of modern financial systems.

REFERENCES

Ahmad, M., & Wu, Q. (2022, August 08). Does herding behavior matter in investment management and perceived market efficiency? Evidence from an emerging market. *Management Decision*, 60(08), 2148–2173. DOI: 10.1108/MD-07-2020-0867

Andersson, M., Hedesström, M., & Gärling, T. (2014, July 03). A Social-Psychological Perspective on Herding in Stock Markets. *Journal of Behavioral Finance*, 15(03), 226–234. DOI: 10.1080/15427560.2014.941062

Ayoub, A., & Balawi, A. (2022, June). Herd Behavior and its Effect on the Stock Market: An Economic Perspective. *Quality - Access to Success*, 23(188), 285–289. DOI: 10.47750/QAS/23.188.38

Baihaqqy, M. R. (2020, August). The correlation between education level and understanding of financial literacy and its effect on investment decisions in capital markets. *Journal of Education and e-learning Research*, 07(03), 306–313. DOI: 10.20448/journal.509.2020.73.306.313

Bao, X. H., H., & Li, S. H. (. (2020, October). Investor Overconfidence and Trading Activity in the Asia Pacific REIT Markets. *Journal of Risk and Financial Management*, 13(10). Advance online publication. DOI: 10.3390/jrfm13100232

Bregu, K. (2020, October). Overconfidence and (Over)Trading: The Effect of Feedback on Trading Behavior. *Journal of Behavioral and Experimental Economics*, 88, 101598. Advance online publication. DOI: 10.1016/j.socec.2020.101598

Callegaro, F. (2021). The constraint of justice: Durkheim on modern solidarity and freedom as non-exploitation. In *Durkheim & Critique* (pp. 191–226). Springer International Publishing., DOI: 10.1007/978-3-030-75158-6_7

Carvalho, J., Jordão da Gama Silva, P. V., & Klotzle, M. C. (2024, March 05). Herding and Google search queries in the Brazilian stock market. *Review of Behavioral Finance*, 16(02), 341–359. DOI: 10.1108/RBF-12-2022-0296

Chang, E. C., Cheng, J. W., & Khorana, A. (2000, October 01). An examination of herd behavior in equity markets: An international perspective. *Journal of Banking & Finance*, 24(10), 1651–1679. DOI: 10.1016/S0378-4266(99)00096-5

Chang, S.-K. (2014, February 01). Herd behavior, bubbles and social interactions in financial markets. *Studies in Nonlinear Dynamics and Econometrics*, 18(01), 89–101. DOI: 10.1515/snde-2013-0024

Dai, X., Zhang, J., & Chang, V. (2023). Noise traders in an agent-based artificial stock market. *Annals of Operations Research*. Advance online publication. DOI: 10.1007/s10479-023-05528-7

DeLisle, R. J., Diavatopoulos, D., Fodor, A., & Krieger, K. (2017, June). Anchoring and Probability Weighting in Option Prices. *Journal of Futures Markets*, 37(06), 614–638. DOI: 10.1002/fut.21833

Devadas, M., & Vijayakumar, D. T. (2019, August). Investment decisions, herd behaviour and retail investors. *International Journal of Innovative Technology and Exploring Engineering*, 08(10), 3291–3294. DOI: 10.35940/ijitee.J1210.0881019

Elkind, D., Kaminski, K., Lo, A. W., Siah, K. W., & Wong, C. H. (2022, December 01). When Do Investors Freak Out? Machine Learning Predictions of Panic Selling. *Journal of Financial Data Science*, 04(01), 11–39. DOI: 10.3905/jfds.2021.1.085

Fernández-Rodríguez, F., García-Artiles, M.-D., & Martín-González, J. M. (2010). A model of speculative behaviour with a strange attractor. *Applied Mathematical Finance*, 09(03), 143–161. DOI: 10.1080/13504860210159032

Fischer, B. (1986, July). Noise. *The Journal of Finance*, 41(03), 529–543. DOI: 10.2307/2328481

Garcia, J. (2021, December). Analyst herding and firm-level investor sentiment. *Financial Markets and Portfolio Management*, 35(04), 461–494. DOI: 10.1007/s11408-021-00382-8

Gl van, B., & Anghel, F. (2023, December). We are not macroprudentialists: A skeptical view of prudential regulation to deal with systemic externalities. *Independent Review*, 17(03), 349–368. Retrieved September 08, 2024, from https://www.scopus .com/record/display.uri?eid=2-s2.0-84872225423&origin=scopusAI

Gros, M., & Wallek, C. (2015, August 01). Are different stock market transparency requirements associated with different accounting quality levels? An analysis of bonding effects on the German stock market. *Journal of Business Economics*, 85(06), 597–633. DOI: 10.1007/s11573-015-0763-7

Gupta, P., & Kohli, B. (2021, May-July). Herding behavior in the Indian stock market: An empirical study. *Indian Journal of Finance, 15*(05-07), 86-99. DOI: 10.17010/ijf/2021/v15i5-7/164495

Hoang, T., & Harrington, J. R. (2023). Tax incentive and household saving strategy: A regression discontinuity approach to catch-up contributions. *The Social Science Journal*, 60(04), 755–770. DOI: 10.1080/03623319.2020.1750844

Hou, Y., Gao, J., Fan, F., Liu, F., & Song, C. (2017). Identifying herding effect in Chinese stock market by high-frequency data. *4th International Conference on Behavioral, Economic, and Socio-Cultural Computing, BESC 2017. 2018-January*, pp. 01-05. Cracow: Institute of Electrical and Electronics Engineers Inc. DOI: 10.1109/BESC.2017.8256359

Hoyer, K., Zeisberger, S., Breugelmans, S. M., & Zeelenberg, M. (2023, August). A culture of greed: Bubble formation in experimental asset markets with greedy and non-greedy traders. *Journal of Economic Behavior & Organization*, 212, 32–52. DOI: 10.1016/j.jebo.2023.05.005

Huang, R., Krishnan, M. M., Shon, J., & Zhou, P. (2017). Who herds? Who doesn't? estimates of analysts' herding propensity in forecasting earnings. *Contemporary Accounting Research*, 34(01), 374–399. DOI: 10.1111/1911-3846.12236

Humayun, K. (2018, March). Did Investors Herd during the Financial Crisis? Evidence from the US Financial Industry. *International Review of Finance*, 18(01), 59–90. DOI: 10.1111/irfi.12140

Igual, M. G., & Santamaría, T. C. (2017). Overconfidence, loss aversion and irrational investor behavior: A conceptual map. *International Journal of Economic Perspectives*, 11(01), 273–290. Retrieved September 08, 2024, from https://www.scopus.com/record/display.uri?eid=2-s2.0-85033437800&origin=scopusAI

Jalili, M., & Perc, M. (2017, October 01). Information cascades in complex networks. *Journal of Complex Networks*, 05(05), 665–693. DOI: 10.1093/comnet/cnx019

James, C. (2024, Apr 01). *Prospect Theory: What It Is and How It Works, With Examples*. Retrieved Sep 09, 2024, from https://www.investopedia.com: https://www.investopedia.com/terms/p/prospecttheory.asp#:~:text=Prospect%20theory%20was%20first%20introduced,compared%20with%20expected%20utility%20theory

Jia, Y., Liu, L., & Lowry, P. B. (2024, September). How do consumers make behavioural decisions on social commerce platforms? The interaction effect between behaviour visibility and social needs. *Information Systems Journal*, 34(05), 1703–1736. DOI: 10.1111/isj.12508

Karnatak, U., & Malik, C. (2021). Wednesdays obtain herd immunity? Examining the effect of the day of the week on the NSE sectoral market during COVID-19. *The Investment Analysts Journal*, 50(04), 227–241. DOI: 10.1080/10293523.2021.2010374

Klein, A. C. (2013). Time-variations in herding behavior: Evidence from a Markov switching SUR model. *Journal of International Financial Markets, Institutions and Money*, 26(01), 291–304. DOI: 10.1016/j.intfin.2013.06.006

Kumar Kulbhaskar, A., & Subramaniam, S. (2023, September). Breaking news headlines: Impact on trading activity in the cryptocurrency market. *Economic Modelling*, 126, 106397. Advance online publication. DOI: 10.1016/j.econmod.2023.106397

Kurt Gümüş, G., Gümüş, Y., & Çimen, A. (2019). Herding behaviour in cryptocurrency market: CSSD and CSAD analysis. In *Contributions to Economics* (Vol. PartF1, pp. 103-114). Springer. DOI: 10.1007/978-3-030-25275-5_6

Lee, C. J., & Andrade, E. B. (2011). Fear, social projection, and financial decision making. *JMR, Journal of Marketing Research*, 48(Special Issue), S121–S129. DOI: 10.1509/jmkr.48.SPL.S121

Li, D., Wang, Y., Madden, A., Ding, Y., Tang, J., Sun, G. G., Zhang, N., & Zhou, E. (2019, September). Analyzing stock market trends using social media user moods and social influence. *Journal of the Association for Information Science and Technology*, 70(09), 1000–1013. DOI: 10.1002/asi.24173

Li, T., Chen, H., Liu, W., Yu, G., & Yu, Y. (2023, September). Understanding the role of social media sentiment in identifying irrational herding behavior in the stock market. *International Review of Economics & Finance*, 87, 163–179. DOI: 10.1016/j.iref.2023.04.016

Lin, F.-H., & Liu, Y.-H. (2014). Herding on the social media. *nternational Conferences on ICT, Society and Human Beings 2014, Web Based Communities and Social Media 2014, e-Commerce 2014, Information Systems Post-Implementation and Change Management 2014 and e-Health 2014* (pp. 135-142). Lisbon: IADIS. Retrieved Sep 15, 2024, from https://www.scopus.com/record/display.uri?eid=2-s2.0-84929301510&origin=scopusAI

Litimi, H., BenSaïda, A., & Bouraoui, O. (2016, Sep 01). Herding and excessive risk in the American stock market: A sectoral analysis. *Research in International Business and Finance, 38*, 06-21. DOI: 10.1016/j.ribaf.2016.03.008

Liu, Y.-Y., Nacher, J. C., Ochiai, T., Martino, M., & Altshuler, Y. (2014, October 15). Prospect theory for online financial trading. *PLoS One*, 09(10), e109458. Advance online publication. DOI: 10.1371/journal.pone.0109458 PMID: 25330203

Mackie, D. M., & Smith, E. R. (2017, September 01). Group-based emotion in group processes and intergroup relations. *Group Processes & Intergroup Relations*, 20(05), 568–668. DOI: 10.1177/1368430217702725

Madaan, V., & Shrivastava, M. (2022). Sectoral herding behaviour in the Indian financial market. *Global Business and Economics Review*, 26(02), 185–213. DOI: 10.1504/GBER.2022.121011

Malla, J., & Lavanya, C., J., J., & J., V. (2023). Bidirectional Gated Recurrent Unit (BiGRU)-Based Bitcoin Price Prediction by News Sentiment Analysis. *35th International Conference on Soft Computing and Signal Processing, ICSCSP 2022*. 313, pp. 31-40. Hyderabad: Springer Science and Business Media Deutschland GmbH. DOI: 10.1007/978-981-19-8669-7_4

Malmberg, T. (2023, June 01). Media studies, le Bon's psychology of crowds, and qualitative-normative research on propaganda, 1880-2020. *Nordic Journal of Media Studies*, 05(01), 17–31. DOI: 10.2478/njms-2023-0002

Mancini, A., Di Clemente, R., & Cimini, G. (2022, December). Self-induced consensus of Reddit users to characterise the GameStop short squeeze. *Scientific Reports*, 12(01), 13780. Advance online publication. DOI: 10.1038/s41598-022-17925-2 PMID: 35962174

Morris, J. J., & Alam, P. (2012, May). Value relevance and the dot-com bubble of the 1990s. *The Quarterly Review of Economics and Finance*, 52(02), 243–255. DOI: 10.1016/j.qref.2012.04.001

Münster, M., Reichenbach, F., & Walther, M. (2024, July 09). Robinhood, Reddit, and the news: The impact of traditional and social media on retail investor trading. *Journal of Financial Markets*, 100929. Advance online publication. DOI: 10.1016/j.finmar.2024.100929

Myklebust, T. (2021, Jan 01). High-frequency trading - regulatory and supervisory challenges in the pursuit of orderly markets. In *Routledge Handbook of Financial Technology and Law* (pp. 381–403). Taylor and Francis., DOI: 10.4324/9780429325670-21

Ostrowska, M. (2021). Transparency in Insurance Regulation and Supervisory Law of Poland. *AIDA Europe Research Series on Insurance Law and Regulation*, 04, 213–230. DOI: 10.1007/978-3-030-63621-0_9

Pan, W., Altshuler, Y., & Pentland, A. (2012). Decoding social influence and the wisdom of the crowd in financial trading network. *2012 ASE/IEEE International Conference on Social Computing, SocialCom 2012 and the 2012 ASE/IEEE International Conference on Privacy, Security, Risk and Trust, PASSAT 2012* (pp. 203-209). Academy of Science and Engineering (ASE)IEEE Computer Society. DOI: 10.1109/SocialCom-PASSAT.2012.133

Park, A., & Sabourian, H. (2011, July). Herding and contrarian behavior in financial markets. *Econometrica*, 79(04), 973–1026. DOI: 10.3982/ECTA8602

Phillips, P. J., & Pohl, G. (2021). Disinformation Cascades, Espionage & Counter-Intelligence. *International Journal of Intelligence, Security, and Public Affairs*, 23(01), 34–47. DOI: 10.1080/23800992.2020.1834311

Popescu, M., & Xu, Z. (2014). Does reputation contribute to institutional herding? *Journal of Financial Research*, 37(03), 295–322. DOI: 10.1111/jfir.12038

Pouget, S., Sauvagnat, J., & Villeneuve, S. (2017, June 01). A mind is a terrible thing to change: Confirmatory bias in financial markets. *Review of Financial Studies*, 30(06), 2066–2109. DOI: 10.1093/rfs/hhw100

Rout, R. K., & Das, N. (2015, January 01). Behavioral prospects of individual investor decision making process: A review. *Indian Journal of Finance*, 09(04), 43–55. Retrieved September 05, 2024, from https://www.scopus.com/record/display.uri?eid=2-s2.0-84928011331&origin=scopusAI

Rubbaniy, G., Polyzos, S., Rizvi, S. K., & Tessema, A. (2021, October). COVID-19, Lockdowns and herding towards a cryptocurrency market-specific implied volatility index. *Economics Letters*, 207, 110017. Advance online publication. DOI: 10.1016/j.econlet.2021.110017

Sabir, S. A., Mohammad, H. B., & Kadir Shahar, H. B. (2018). The effect of illusion of control and self attribution on herding behaviour with a moderating role of information availability: A case of retail investors of pakistan stock exchange. *Opción*, 34(86), 2675–2689. Retrieved September 05, 2024, from https://www.scopus.com/record/display.uri?eid=2-s2.0-85064105170&origin=scopusAI

Sathya, N., & Gayathiri, R. (2024, June 17). Behavioral Biases in Investment Decisions: An Extensive Literature Review and Pathways for Future Research. *Journal of Information and Organizational Sciences*, 48(01), 117–131. DOI: 10.31341/jios.48.1.6

Schulmerich, M., Leporcher, Y.-M., & Eu, C.-H. (2015). Stock Market Crashes. In *Management for Professionals* (Vol. F415, pp. 245–354). Springer Nature., DOI: 10.1007/978-3-642-55444-5_4

Singh, L. G., & Kumar, K. (2024). The herding behavior of investors in the Indian financial market: An insight into the influence of social media. In *Handbook of Research on Innovative Approaches to Information Technology in Library and Information Science* (pp. 82–102). IGI Global., DOI: 10.4018/979-8-3693-0807-3.ch005

Stavroyiannis, S., & Babalos, V. (2015). On the time varying nature of herding behaviour: Evidence from major European indices. *Global Business and Economics Review*, 17(03), 298–309. DOI: 10.1504/GBER.2015.070307

Teti, E., & Maroni, D. (2021). The new great bubble in the technology industry? *Technology Analysis and Strategic Management*, 33(05), 520–534. DOI: 10.1080/09537325.2020.1828577

Thompson, E. A. (2007, January). The tulipmania: Fact or artifact? *Public Choice*, 130(1-2), 99–114. DOI: 10.1007/s11127-006-9074-4

Tian, W. (2016). *Commercial banking risk management: Regulation in the wake of the financial crisis.* Palgrave Macmillan., DOI: 10.1057/978-1-137-59442-6

Trisno, B., & Vidayana. (2023). Understanding herding behavior among Indonesian stock market investors. *5th International Conference of Biospheric Harmony Advanced Research, ICOBAR 2023. 426.* Jakarta: EDP Sciences. DOI: 10.1051/e3sconf/202342601088

Ulibarri, C. A., Anselmo, P. C., Hovespian, K., Tolk, J., & Florescu, I. (2009). Noise-trader risk' and Bayesian market making in FX derivatives: Rolling loaded dice? *International Journal of Finance & Economics*, 14(03), 268–279. DOI: 10.1002/ijfe.373

Va că-Zamfir, D., & Slave, C. (2018). Tulip-the flower that conquered Europe. *18th International Multidisciplinary Scientific Geoconference, SGEM 2018Albena. 18*, pp. 1003-1010. International Multidisciplinary Scientific Geoconference. Retrieved Sep 15, 2024, from https://www.scopus.com/record/display.uri?eid=2-s2.0-85058814075&origin=scopusAI

Walsh, P. (2012, April). The bubble on the periphery: Scotland and the South Sea bubble. *The Scottish Historical Review*, 91(01), 106–124. DOI: 10.3366/shr.2012.0073

Wang, J., & Liu, K. (2019). Understanding WeChat Users' Herd Behavior in Forwarding Health Information: An Empirical Study in China. *7th International Conference for Smart Health, ICSH 2019. 11924 LNCS*, pp. 177-188. Shenzhen: Springer. DOI: 10.1007/978-3-030-34482-5_16

Wang, X., Kim, M. H., & Suardi, S. (2022, August). Herding and China's market-wide circuit breaker. *Journal of Banking & Finance*, 141, 106533. Advance online publication. DOI: 10.1016/j.jbankfin.2022.106533

Wikipedia. (2022). *The Crowd: A Study of the Popular Mind.* Retrieved Sep 04, 2024, from https://en.wikipedia.org/wiki: https://en.wikipedia.org/wiki/The_Crowd:_A_Study_of_the_Popular_Mind

Yang, W., & Loang, O. K. (2024). Systematic Literature Review: Behavioural Biases as the Determinants of Herding. In *Studies in Systems, Decision and Control* (Vol. 223, pp. 79-92). Springer Science and Business Media Deutschland GmbH. DOI: 10.1007/978-3-031-51997-0_7

Ye, J., Li, D., & Cao, Y. (2020, January 01). Investor irrational selection bias in stock market based on cognitive psychology: Evidence from herding behaviour. *Revista Argentina de Clínica Psicológica*, 29(01), 90–98. DOI: 10.24205/03276716.2020.13

Zaimovic, A., Arnaut-Berilo, A., & Mustafic, A. (2017, April 01). Portfolio Diversification in the South-East European Equity Markets. *South East European Journal of Economics and Business*, 12(01), 126–235. DOI: 10.1515/jeb-2017-0010

Zhang, R. (2018). Decision-making neuroscience-based research on stock herd and anti-herd behavior. *NeuroQuantology: An Interdisciplinary Journal of Neuroscience and Quantum Physics*, 16(06), 200–204. DOI: 10.14704/nq.2018.16.6.1625

Zhou, S., & Liu, X. (2022, December). Internet postings and investor herd behavior: Evidence from China's open-end fund market. *Humanities & Social Sciences Communications*, 09(01), 441. Advance online publication. DOI: 10.1057/s41599-022-01462-4

Chapter 11
The Paradox of Crowd Wisdom:
When Collective Intelligence Fails in Financial Markets

Xiong Xu
Chengdu International Studies University, China

ABSTRACT

The notion of "wisdom of crowds" postulates that collective decision-making often outperforms individual judgements. However, in financial markets, this collective intelligence can falter, leading to inefficiencies and anomalies. This study investigates the factors contributing to the failure of collective intelligence in financial markets, specifically examining information cascades, cognitive biases, market sentiment, herding behaviour, and market performance. Using the Adaptive Market Hypothesis (AMH) as a theoretical framework, the research explores how these factors interact and impact market efficiency. Employing panel data regression and quantile regression, the study provides a comprehensive analysis of market dynamics across different conditions. The findings underscore the crucial roles of investor education and regulatory environment in moderating and mediating these relationships, offering valuable insights for policymakers, financial managers, and investors in enhancing market stability and efficiency.

INTRODUCTION

The field of collective intelligence, commonly known as the "wisdom of crowds," suggests that when individual judgements are combined, the resulting decisions can be better than those made by any individual in the group. This notion has been

DOI: 10.4018/979-8-3693-7827-4.ch011

Copyright © 2025, IGI Global Scientific Publishing. Copying or distributing in print or electronic forms without written permission of IGI Global is prohibited.

widely applied in different sectors, including as prediction markets, decision-making processes, and financial markets. Nevertheless, in the realm of financial markets, the phenomenon known as the paradox of crowd wisdom arises when the combined intellect of a group fails to generate accurate results, resulting in inefficiencies and abnormalities.

Financial markets are intricate systems that are impacted by several factors, with the actions of market players playing a pivotal role in deciding market results. This study examines the factors that contribute to the breakdown of collective intelligence in financial markets (Kameda et al., 2022). It specifically investigates the impact of variables such as information cascades, cognitive biases, market sentiment, herding behaviour, and market performance. These characteristics have the potential to skew both individual and collective decision-making processes, ultimately impacting the efficiency of the market, which is the variable being studied in this research.

Information cascades arise when individuals, even if they possess private information, imitate the actions of those who came before them. In financial markets, this phenomenon can result in the magnification of incorrect information, as investors disregard their own understanding in favour of conforming to the majority. These cascades can generate a misleading perception of agreement and result in market inefficiencies by causing asset prices to deviate from their underlying values. Cognitive biases, which are naturally present in human decision-making, add complexity to the situation. Biases like as excessive self-assurance, the tendency to seek out information that confirms pre-existing beliefs, and the inclination to hold onto losing investments can distort the assessments made by individual investors. When these prejudices are combined among a significant number of individuals, the outcome is frequently a warped collective intellect that inadequately represents the underlying market principles.

Market sentiment, which refers to the collective mindset of investors on market conditions, also has a crucial impact. Factors unrelated to economic fundamentals, such as news events, geopolitical developments, or social media trends, can influence sentiment. Excessive optimism or pessimism in market mood can result in bubbles or crashes, respectively, which in turn can weaken market efficiency. Herding behaviour, characterised by investors imitating the moves of their peers, intensifies these problems. Herding in financial markets can result in the emergence of speculative bubbles and abrupt market declines. Conforming to popular opinion can lead to prices straying considerably from their true worth, leading to times of severe unpredictability and inefficiency.

The market performance, as indicated by metrics such as stock returns and volatility, represents the combined influence of these factors. During instances of heightened volatility or exceptional returns, the disparities between collective decisions and market fundamentals become more evident, emphasising the constraints of crowd wisdom. This study additionally examines the impact of investor education level and the regulatory environment as factors that moderate and mediate the relationship (Liu et al., 2022). The educational attainment of investors might impact their vulnerability to biases and their capacity to effectively perceive information. It is generally believed that higher levels of education can improve the analytical ability of investors, which may help reduce the negative impact of information cascades and cognitive biases on market efficiency.

The regulatory environment acts as an intermediary factor by influencing the regulations and frameworks that govern the functioning of financial markets. Regulation can effectively control the negative effects of herding behaviour and cognitive biases by encouraging openness, enforcing fair market procedures, and protecting against hazards that affect the entire system. Regulatory measures, such as the implementation of transparency standards, market surveillance, and investor protection systems, can assist in aligning market behaviours with economic realities. This alignment ultimately leads to an improvement in market efficiency.

Firstly, the occurrence of information cascades highlights a notable deficiency in comprehending market inefficiencies. Existing research extensively explores how individuals in financial markets often depend on the actions of others rather than their own private information, resulting in collective behaviour that deviates from rationality. Nevertheless, the specific methods by which information cascades magnify inaccurate market signals have not been sufficiently investigated. This gap is especially relevant in the context of contemporary financial markets, where the swift distribution of information through digital platforms can worsen the spread of false information and result in severe inefficiencies in the market. Furthermore, while the recognition of cognitive biases in financial decision-making is widespread, there is a requirement for a more profound understanding of how these biases accumulate among a group of people. The presence of individual biases, such as overconfidence, loss aversion, and the representativeness heuristic, can have a major impact on market behaviour. However, the combined effect of these biases when they come together in a market context is not well understood. Comprehending this consolidation is essential, as it can uncover the reasons for the frequent absence of logical market results, even when there are many well-informed and reasonable participants.

Furthermore, the influence of market sentiment, which is frequently influenced by psychological and emotional elements, presents a difficulty for conventional financial theories that presuppose rational conduct. The current study literature recognises that sentiment can cause deviations from fundamental values, but additional examination is needed to understand the dynamic connections between sentiment and other market variables. More precisely, the reciprocal interactions between market sentiment and price fluctuations can generate self-reinforcing cycles that push markets further from efficiency. To address this gap, it is necessary to not only identify the origins of sentiment but also measure its influence on market efficiency over various time periods. Furthermore, the inadequacy of current research is evident in the realm of herding behaviour in financial markets. Although it is widely acknowledged that herding behaviour can result in the creation of market bubbles and subsequent crashes, further investigation is required to fully understand the underlying motivations behind investors' decisions to follow the crowd, even when it goes against their own rational judgement. This entails examining the psychological, social, and economic motivations that influence herding behaviour, as well as the circumstances in which herding is most probable. These findings are crucial for formulating methods to reduce the negative impacts of herding on the stability and efficiency of the market.

The lack of comprehension of the moderating and mediating impacts of investor education and the regulatory environment is an urgent concern. Although the significance of both elements is recognised, their precise contributions to market behaviour and efficiency remain incompletely understood. The degree to which investor education can mitigate the impact of cognitive biases and information cascades is not firmly established. Furthermore, a thorough analysis is needed to assess how various regulatory methods contribute to enhancing market efficiency in the presence of behavioural abnormalities. By addressing these deficiencies, policymakers and educators can gain valuable insights to develop actions that improve market stability and safeguard investors.

Ultimately, this paper explores the paradoxical nature of crowd wisdom in financial markets, specifically investigating the circumstances in which collective intelligence might be unsuccessful. This research aims to gain a comprehensive understanding of the factors that contribute to market inefficiencies by examining the relationship between information cascades, cognitive biases, market sentiment, herding behaviour, and market performance (Putri & Tanno, 2024). It also considers the influence of investor education and regulatory environment as moderating and mediating factors. Having a clear comprehension of this concept is essential for formulating effective approaches to use the potential advantages of collective intelligence while minimising its inherent hazards within the realm of financial markets. The motivation for this work arises from substantial deficiencies in comprehending the intricacies of collective decision-making in financial markets. This research attempts to enhance the analysis and improvement of market efficiency by examining information cascades, cognitive biases, market sentiment, herding behaviour, and the impact of investor education and regulatory environment. This undertaking is crucial for the development of resilient financial systems that can more effectively withstand the irrationalities and volatilities inherent in market behaviour.

Research Objectives

RO 1: To examine the impact of information cascades on market efficiency in financial markets.

RO 2: To examine the impact of cognitive biases on market efficiency in financial markets.

RO 3: To examine the impact of market sentiment on market efficiency in financial markets.

RO 4: To examine the impact of herding behaviour on market efficiency in financial markets.

RO 5: To examine the impact of market performance on market efficiency in financial markets.

RO 6: To examine the moderating effect of investor education level on the relationship between independent variables (information cascades, cognitive biases, market sentiment, herding behaviour, market performance) and market efficiency in financial markets.

RO 7: To examine the mediating effect of the regulatory environment on the relationship between independent variables (information cascades, cognitive biases, market sentiment, herding behaviour, market performance) and market efficiency in financial markets.

Research Questions

RQ 1: What is the impact of information cascades on market efficiency in financial markets?

RQ 2: What is the impact of cognitive biases on market efficiency in financial markets?

RQ 3: What is the impact of market sentiment on market efficiency in financial markets?

RQ 4: What is the impact of herding behaviour on market efficiency in financial markets?

RQ 5: What is the impact of market performance on market efficiency in financial markets?

RQ 6: What is the impact of investor education level in moderating the relationship between independent variables (information cascades, cognitive biases, market sentiment, herding behaviour, market performance) and market efficiency in financial markets?

RQ 7: What is the impact of the regulatory environment in mediating the relationship between independent variables (information cascades, cognitive biases, market sentiment, herding behaviour, market performance) and market efficiency in financial markets?

Significance of Study

The study's theoretical value resides in its capacity to enhance our comprehension of the intricacies inherent in financial markets. This research enhances our understanding of collective intelligence and market efficiency by examining the relationship between information cascades, cognitive biases, market sentiment, herding behaviour, and market performance. Traditional financial theories commonly presume rational behaviour and efficient markets; nonetheless, empirical evidence continually demonstrates deviations from these assumptions. This study aims to reconcile the disparity between theoretical models and actual market trends by incorporating knowledge from behavioural finance, psychology, and economics. By doing this, it offers a more detailed comprehension of how collective decision-making processes can result in market inefficiencies. This improved theoretical framework can act as a basis for future research, stimulating fresh investigations into the mechanisms that propel market dynamics and the circumstances in which collective intelligence may falter.

From a managerial standpoint, the results of this study have substantial consequences for investment strategies and risk management. Enhanced comprehension of the elements that contribute to market inefficiencies can be advantageous for financial managers and investors. Managers can design techniques to reduce the effects of information cascades and cognitive biases by encouraging independent analysis and critical thinking among their teams. Furthermore, comprehending the significance of market mood and herding behaviour can provide insights into when to make investment decisions and how to allocate assets in order to reduce vulnerability to market volatility. Financial managers can utilise the findings of this study to effectively navigate the intricacies of market behaviour, optimise decision-making processes, and enhance the performance of their portfolios.

The policy implications of this study are similarly significant, since it provides crucial information for regulators and policymakers responsible for ensuring market stability and safeguarding investors. The results emphasise the significance of a carefully constructed regulatory framework in reducing the negative impacts of behavioural anomalies on market efficiency. Policymakers can utilise these observations to develop policies that foster openness, mitigate the dissemination of disinformation, and incentivize equitable market behaviours. Regulations mandating thorough and prompt disclosure of information, for instance, can mitigate the impact of information cascades. Similarly, implementing rules that focus on improving investor education can provide market participants with the necessary resources to identify and mitigate cognitive biases. Regulators can improve market stability and efficiency by cultivating a more knowledgeable and logical investor base. Moreover, comprehending the circumstances in which herding behaviour and market sentiment contribute to market anomalies can provide insights for formulating policies that tackle systemic risks and avert market bubbles and crashes.

Literature Review

The notion of market efficiency has been a fundamental principle in finance theory, suggesting that asset prices accurately incorporate all relevant information. Nevertheless, the concepts of information cascades, cognitive biases, market sentiment, herding behaviour, and market performance pose a challenge to this idea. The existing body of literature on these variables uncovers an intricate interaction that frequently results in market inefficiencies, hence requiring a more thorough investigation (Wen et al., 2022). Information cascades refer to circumstances in which individuals, even when they possess private information, choose to imitate the activities of others, often resulting in less than ideal outcomes. Bikhchandani et al. (2012) examine the phenomenon of cascades, which can lead to market prices deviating from fundamental values. This occurs when investors repeat previous trades without considering their own private signals. Hirshleifer and Teoh (2010) provide additional insight into the mechanism by which cascades can result in the formation of bubbles and subsequent crashes, as they magnify the influence of early adopters' choices. In their study, Easley and O'Hara (2010) emphasise the importance of market microstructure in enabling information cascades. They stress the necessity of openness to reduce the negative impacts of these cascades. These studies highlight the importance of information cascades in undermining market efficiency by spreading incorrect signals among investors (Suresh & Loang, 2024).

Cognitive biases refer to consistent aberrations from rationality that have an impact on the process of decision-making. Barberis (2013) presents an extensive analysis of prevalent biases, such as overconfidence, anchoring, and loss aversion, demonstrating their widespread influence on investment behaviour. Hirshleifer (2015) investigates the impact of overconfidence on trading behaviour and asset mispricing, which contradicts the notion of efficient markets. Baker and Wurgler (2012) argue that biases have a role in the fluctuation and predictability of stock returns. They propose that behavioural aspects should be incorporated into asset pricing models. These contributions emphasise the essential role that cognitive biases play in influencing market outcomes and causing inefficiencies, which underscores the need for models that take into consideration human irrationality.

Market sentiment is the collective perception and emotional response of investors towards market conditions, which is often influenced by psychological factors. Baker and Wurgler (2012) construct a sentiment index to measure the influence of investor mood on stock prices, demonstrating that elevated sentiment frequently results in overpricing and subsequent adjustments. Shiller (2014) examines the impact of narratives and popular stories on sentiment, which in turn leads to market movements that diverge from underlying facts. In addition, Tetlock (2010) examines the impact of media tone on investor sentiment and discovers that negative news can elicit adverse market responses, regardless of economic factors. These studies illustrate that market emotion has a substantial impact on price movements, leading to moments of irrational optimism or excessive pessimism (Khan, 2022).

Herding behaviour, characterised by investors imitating the moves of their peers, amplifies market inefficiencies. Bikhchandani and Sharma (2014) present an intricate examination of the determinants of herding, encompassing information asymmetry and social impacts. In their study, Lakonishok et al. (2012) demonstrate that herding behaviour can result in the emergence of speculative bubbles, where prices deviate from their inherent values due to collective actions. Furthermore, Scharfstein and Stein (2010) contend that herding might arise due to career considerations, when fund managers imitate their peers in order to prevent underperformance compared to benchmarks (Ukpong, 2023). These observations demonstrate how the tendency of individuals to follow the crowd can increase the fluctuations in the market and lead to incorrect pricing, which makes it difficult to maintain market efficiency.

The market's performance, which is often assessed through returns and volatility, represents the combined influence of the above listed factors on market results. In his 2013 paper, Fama examines the notion of market efficiency and acknowledges that anomalies like momentum and value effects continue to exist, even when using the rational expectations framework. Ang et al. (2013) examine the differences in stock returns across different groups, and discover that behavioural characteristics have a substantial impact on performance trends. In addition, Lo (2012) presents the Adaptive Markets Hypothesis, which seeks to harmonise market efficiency and behavioural economics by proposing that market dynamics adapt in response to shifting environmental circumstances. These studies emphasise the significance of taking into account a wide range of factors, including as psychological and social impacts, when evaluating market performance and efficiency (Yang & Loang, 2024).

Understanding market dynamics requires considering the crucial impact of investor education and the regulatory environment, which acts as a mediator. Lusardi and Mitchell (2014) emphasise that financial literacy has a major impact on investment behaviour, with those who have higher levels of education making better financial decisions and being less prone to biases. In addition, a study conducted by Van Rooij et al. (2011) reveals that individuals with higher levels of education are more inclined to engage in financial markets and spread their investments across various assets, so improving the effectiveness of the market. La Porta et al. (2012) highlight the need of strong legislative frameworks and regulatory monitoring in preventing market abuses and ensuring transparency. Djankov et al. (2013) provide evidence that efficient regulation decreases the imbalance of information and improves the safeguarding of investors, thus promoting stability in the market.

The evidence indicates that information cascades, cognitive biases, market emotion, herding behaviour, and market performance are interconnected elements that undermine the concept of market efficiency (Ahmed et al., 2024). This study seeks to gain a full grasp of the intricate factors that influence market dynamics by analysing these variables in light of contemporary research. Acquiring this knowledge is essential for creating more precise models and efficient strategies to improve market efficiency and stability. Therefore, this study proposes the following hypotheses:

H1: Information cascades negatively impact market efficiency in financial markets.
H2: Cognitive biases negatively impact market efficiency in financial markets.
H3: Market sentiment negatively impacts market efficiency in financial markets.
H4: Herding behaviour negatively impacts market efficiency in financial markets.
H5: Market performance positively impacts market efficiency in financial markets.

H6: The investor education level moderates the relationship between the independent variables (information cascades, cognitive biases, market sentiment, herding behaviour, market performance) and market efficiency in financial markets, such that higher education levels weaken the negative impacts and strengthen the positive impact.

H7: The regulatory environment mediates the relationship between the independent variables (information cascades, cognitive biases, market sentiment, herding behaviour, market performance) and market efficiency in financial markets, such that a stronger regulatory environment weakens the negative impacts and strengthens the positive impact.

THEORETICAL BACKGROUND (UNDERLYING THEORY)

Adaptive Market Hypothesis Theory

The AMH, introduced by Andrew Lo in 2004, diverges from the EMH by integrating concepts from evolutionary biology and behavioural economics to comprehend financial markets. The AMH posits that market efficiency is not a fixed state, but rather a dynamic process that adjusts in accordance with shifting market conditions, participant actions, and the availability of information. This theoretical framework offers a more detailed comprehension of market dynamics by acknowledging that the level of market efficiency varies over time and in different situations.

The core principle of the AMH is that financial markets function like to ecosystems, with diverse participants vying for resources, adjusting to their surroundings, and developing over time. This viewpoint recognises that market participants, such as ordinary investors, institutional traders, and market makers, are affected by a blend of logical decision-making and behavioural biases. Biases such as overconfidence, loss aversion, and herding behaviour can cause deviations from the predictions of classic financial models that are based on the EMH.

The AMH theory suggests that these variations are not arbitrary anomalies, but rather a consequence of the adaptive behaviour exhibited by players in the market. During periods of economic stability, rational decision-making tends to prevail, resulting in market circumstances that closely align with the forecasts of the EMH. However, in times of market stress or uncertainty, behavioural biases may become more noticeable, leading to considerable departures from market efficiency. The dynamic characteristic of market efficiency suggests that no individual model can comprehensively describe market behaviour under all circumstances and timeframes.

The AMH has significant significance for this study, since it offers a theoretical basis for comprehending the interaction between information cascades, cognitive biases, market sentiment, herding behaviour, and market performance. inside the AMH paradigm, these variables can be viewed as expressions of the adaptive mechanisms operating inside financial markets (Loang and Ahmad, 2024). Information cascades can be defined as a process in which individuals in a market adjust their behaviour based on the behaviour of others, particularly when they have little or unclear private information. This behaviour is consistent with the evolutionary principle of social learning, in which individuals imitate the acts of others to enhance their likelihood of surviving in unpredictable circumstances.

Likewise, cognitive biases like excessive self-assurance and fear of loss can be seen as advantageous characteristics that have developed to assist individuals in making choices when faced with uncertainty and a lack of information. Although these biases may result in worse than ideal results in financial markets, they can also offer adaptive benefits in other situations. The AMH posits that these biases are not immutable but can be altered as market participants acquire expertise and as market conditions develop.

Market sentiment and herding behaviour are essential components of the AMH paradigm. Market sentiment is the mood of investors, which can both impact and be influenced by the adaptive techniques used by market participants. Herding behaviour, characterised by individuals imitating the acts of the majority, can be viewed as an adaptive reaction to the apparent collective intelligence of the crowd. Nevertheless, the AMH recognises that such conduct can result in market bubbles and crashes when the collective actions of the crowd are predicated on erroneous or insufficient information (Loang and Ahmad, 2023).

The AMH also has noteworthy ramifications for comprehending market performance and efficiency. Within this perspective, the performance of the market is influenced not only by the economic fundamentals but also by the adaptive behaviours and strategies of the participants. This viewpoint provides an explanation for why markets can seem efficient in certain circumstances but display inefficiency in others. It also emphasises the significance of flexibility and adaptability in investment strategies, as strict adherence to a single technique may not be ideal in a constantly changing market environment. The Adaptive Market Hypothesis offers a thorough theoretical framework for this investigation, providing valuable understanding of the adaptive behaviours that influence market dynamics. The AMH, or Adaptive Market Hypothesis, elucidates the intricate relationship between information cascades, cognitive biases, market sentiment, herding behaviour, and market performance by acknowledging that market efficiency is a dynamic and changeable state. Having this comprehension is essential for devising more efficient tactics for market participants and for formulating policies that improve market stability and efficiency.

Research Framework

The foundation of this study is based on a thorough comprehension of the elements that impact market efficiency, combining insights from the AMH with real-life observations of market behaviours. This framework functions as an organised depiction of the connections between the independent variables—information cascades, cognitive biases, market sentiment, herding behaviour, and market performance—and the dependent variable, market efficiency. Furthermore, it takes into account the influence of investor education and the role of the regulatory framework as a mediator.

Figure 1. Research framework

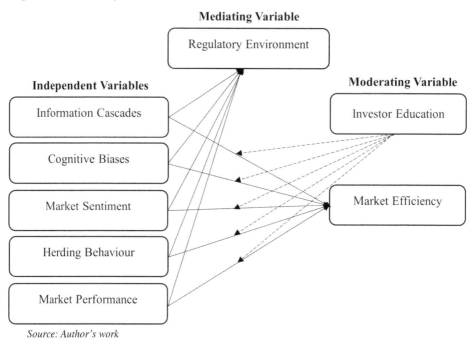

Source: Author's work

Information cascades arise when investors, even though they possess private information, depend on the actions of others, resulting in a phenomenon where individual judgements are disregarded in favour of the perceived collective wisdom. This phenomenon, known as market distortion, can have a major impact on market prices by deviating them from their true underlying values. It occurs when a small group of investors initiates activities that set off a chain reaction, spreading incorrect information and magnifying its effects across the whole market (Gupta, 2022). According to the conceptual framework, information cascades play a crucial role in weakening market efficiency by causing collective behaviours that differ from rational market expectations. Cognitive biases, including as excessive self-assurance, fear of losses, and the tendency to hold onto losing investments, are deeply rooted in the way humans make decisions and impact how investors understand and respond to information. These biases can cause consistent errors in judgement and decision-making, leading to the incorrect valuation of assets and higher levels of market instability. The paradigm acknowledges cognitive biases as essential factors that impact both individual and collective market behaviour, leading to departures from efficient market results.

Market sentiment is a reflection of the general mood and attitudes of investors regarding market conditions, influenced by psychological and emotional elements. Positive or negative mood can result in episodes of irrational exuberance or excessive pessimism, respectively, which can impact the values of assets and the stability of the market. Market sentiment is a component of the conceptual framework that interacts with other aspects to impact market efficiency. It implies that changes in emotion can have significant impacts on market dynamics, resulting in cycles of economic growth and decline. Herding behaviour is strongly linked to information cascades and market mood, as it entails investors imitating the actions of others instead of depending on their own analysis (Komalasari et al., 2022). This behaviour can worsen market trends, leading to the creation of bubbles and subsequent crashes. According to the concept, herding behaviour plays a major role in causing market inefficiencies since it results in collective movements that are frequently not based on fundamental economic data.

The market's performance, which is measured by its returns and volatility, is an outcome that shows how the aforementioned elements affect market efficiency over time. The paradigm posits that periods characterised by elevated volatility and atypical returns are symptomatic of underlying inefficiencies resulting from information cascades, cognitive biases, market sentiment, and herding behaviour. It asserts that comprehending these connections is essential for elucidating disparities in market performance. The paradigm includes the moderating role of investor education to explain the differences in how various levels of financial literacy and knowledge impact vulnerability to cognitive biases and herding behaviour. It is theorised that higher levels of education can improve investors' capacity to analyse information critically and make well-informed choices, therefore reducing some of the negative impacts on market efficiency.

The regulatory environment is considered a mediating variable that influences the entire market context in which participants operate. Regulation that is effective can improve transparency, decrease information imbalance, and safeguard investors against deceitful activities, thus boosting market efficiency (Azzutti, 2022). The theory suggests that a strong regulatory environment might reduce the harmful effects of information cascades and cognitive biases, leading to more stable and efficient markets. The conceptual framework of this study offers a systematic method for comprehending the intricate interplay among many elements that impact market efficiency. By combining knowledge from the AMH with real-world observations, it emphasises the ever-changing and flexible characteristics of financial markets. This framework provides a basis for examining the combined effects of information cascades, cognitive biases, market sentiment, herding behaviour, and market performance on market efficiency. It also takes into account the influence of investor education and the regulatory environment. A comprehensive strategy is necessary to develop measures that improve market stability and efficiency in a constantly changing financial environment.

Research Methodology

This study utilises panel data regression and quantile regression approaches to thoroughly examine the complex dynamics of financial markets and their influence on market efficiency. These econometric techniques enable a thorough analysis of the connections between the independent variables, such as information cascades, cognitive biases, market sentiment, herding behaviour, and market performance, and the dependent variable, market efficiency. These techniques take into consideration the intricacies present in financial data.

Panel data regression is very suitable for this study because it can effectively manage data that exhibits variations over time and across different entities. Panel data analysis allows for the control of unobserved heterogeneity, which encompasses individual-specific factors that can impact market behaviours. This approach enables the incorporation of several observations for each entity across time, hence improving the accuracy and dependability of the estimations. By utilising fixed effects or random effects models, the study can consider the unchanging attributes of various financial markets or investor groups, thereby isolating the influence of the independent variables on market efficiency.

Panel data regression enables the analysis of dynamic relationships. Financial markets are affected by numerous factors that interact over time, and panel data regression can include lagged variables to capture these temporal dynamics. Understanding how historical market conditions and behaviours influence current market efficiency is crucial. For instance, the study can examine how previous occurrences of herding behaviour or shifts in market sentiment impact present levels of market efficiency, offering valuable insights into the endurance and development of these effects.

Quantile regression provides an additional viewpoint that enables the analysis to investigate the influence of the independent variables at various points of the conditional distribution of the dependent variable. Conventional regression techniques, like ordinary least squares (OLS), primarily consider the average of the dependent variable, possibly disregarding significant deviations on the extreme ends of the distribution. Quantile regression overcomes this constraint by estimating the impacts of the independent variables at different quantiles, so offering a more full comprehension of their influence on market efficiency.

Quantile regression is especially useful in this study for examining the variations in the impacts of information cascades, cognitive biases, market sentiment, and herding behaviour across markets with different levels of efficiency. For example, cognitive biases have a greater effect on market efficiency in less efficient markets (lower quantiles) compared to highly efficient markets (higher quantiles). Through analysing these distinct effects, the study can determine whether specific elements exert a more substantial influence in tense or highly unpredictable market conditions, providing detailed insights that can guide focused responses. Furthermore, quantile regression might uncover asymmetries in the associations between the predictor and outcome variables. Quantile regression is a more effective method for capturing the non-linearities and asymmetric reactions to shocks in financial markets. This approach enables the investigation to identify if exceptional market circumstances, such as bubbles or crashes, magnify or reduce the impact of the independent variables on market efficiency. These findings are essential for creating strategies to reduce negative market behaviours and improve stability.

The combined utilisation of panel data regression and quantile regression offers a comprehensive analytical methodology, in addition to their respective benefits. Panel data regression provides a strong framework for accounting for unobserved differences and capturing changing interactions over time, whereas quantile regression enables a thorough analysis of the impacts at various points of the distribution. These methodologies allow the investigation to reveal intricate interactions and differences in how the independent factors affect market efficiency, providing a more comprehensive and detailed knowledge of financial market dynamics. The utilisation of panel data regression and quantile regression in this work amplifies its analytical rigour and depth. These approaches provide a comprehensive examination of the connections between important factors and market efficiency, taking into account the time-based changes, unobserved differences, and distributional impacts that are inherent in financial markets. The study intends to utilise econometric tools to get comprehensive insights into the factors that influence market efficiency. Ultimately, this research will contribute to the creation of more effective strategies and policies for supporting stable and efficient financial markets.

CONCLUSION

This study provides a comprehensive analysis of the factors influencing market efficiency in financial markets, focusing on the interplay between information cascades, cognitive biases, market sentiment, herding behaviour, and market performance. Utilizing the AMH as a theoretical framework, the research elucidates how these independent variables interact to impact the dependent variable of market efficiency.

The findings of this study offer valuable insights for academics, policymakers, and practitioners in the financial industry.

One of the key contributions of this research is the identification of information cascades as a significant factor undermining market efficiency. Information cascades occur when individuals, despite having private information, choose to mimic the actions of others, leading to collective behaviours that deviate from rational market expectations. This phenomenon can distort asset prices and create inefficiencies, as the actions of early adopters can disproportionately influence the decisions of subsequent market participants. By highlighting the detrimental effects of information cascades, this study underscores the importance of promoting independent analysis and critical thinking among investors to mitigate these impacts.

Cognitive biases, such as overconfidence, loss aversion, and confirmation bias, also play a crucial role in market inefficiencies. These biases lead to systematic errors in judgement and decision-making, which can skew asset valuations and increase market volatility. The study's findings suggest that cognitive biases are pervasive and can accumulate at the collective level, exacerbating market inefficiencies. Addressing these biases through investor education and awareness programs could enhance market efficiency by fostering more rational decision-making processes.

Market sentiment, driven by psychological and emotional factors, significantly influences asset pricing and market stability. Positive or negative sentiment can lead to periods of irrational exuberance or excessive pessimism, causing asset prices to diverge from their fundamental values. This study demonstrates that market sentiment can amplify the effects of other variables, such as information cascades and cognitive biases, further destabilizing financial markets. Understanding the dynamics of market sentiment is therefore critical for developing strategies to anticipate and mitigate market bubbles and crashes.

Herding behaviour, where investors follow the actions of their peers rather than their own analysis, is another factor contributing to market inefficiencies. Herding can lead to speculative bubbles and abrupt market corrections, as collective actions drive asset prices away from their intrinsic values. This study highlights the need for regulatory frameworks that discourage herding behaviour by promoting transparency and providing accurate and timely information to investors.

Market performance, measured by returns and volatility, encapsulates the aggregate effects of the aforementioned factors on market efficiency. The findings indicate that periods of high volatility and abnormal returns are often symptomatic of underlying inefficiencies driven by information cascades, cognitive biases, market sentiment, and herding behaviour. By analyzing these performance metrics, the study provides a comprehensive view of how various factors interact to influence market efficiency.

The study also explores the moderating role of investor education and the mediating role of the regulatory environment. Higher levels of investor education can mitigate the negative impacts of cognitive biases and herding behaviour, promoting more rational and informed decision-making. This highlights the importance of financial literacy programs and educational initiatives in enhancing market efficiency. Similarly, a robust regulatory environment can mediate the relationship between the independent variables and market efficiency. Effective regulations that ensure transparency, protect investors, and promote fair market practices can help align market behaviours with economic fundamentals, thereby improving market efficiency.

Implications

The findings of this study have significant implications for policymakers, financial managers, and investors. For policymakers, the results underscore the need for regulatory measures that enhance transparency and reduce the negative impacts of herding behaviour and cognitive biases. Financial managers can benefit from understanding the dynamics of market sentiment and information cascades, enabling them to make more informed investment decisions and develop strategies to mitigate risks. Investors, particularly retail investors, can use these insights to improve their decision-making processes and avoid common pitfalls associated with cognitive biases and herd behaviour.

Limitations and Recommendations for Future Studies

Despite its contributions, this study has several limitations. First, the reliance on secondary data sources may limit the accuracy and completeness of the information used in the analysis. Second, the study's focus on specific independent variables may overlook other relevant factors that could influence market efficiency. Third, the generalizability of the findings may be constrained by the specific market conditions and time periods examined. Future research should consider a broader range of variables and different market contexts to validate and extend the findings of this study.

Future research should address the limitations of this study by incorporating primary data sources and exploring additional variables that may impact market efficiency. Longitudinal studies examining different market conditions and economic cycles would provide a deeper understanding of the dynamics at play. Additionally, comparative studies across different regions and market structures could offer valuable insights into the contextual factors influencing market efficiency. Finally, further investigation into the role of emerging technologies, such as artificial intelligence and machine learning, in mitigating the effects of cognitive biases and enhancing market efficiency would be a fruitful area for future research.

REFERENCE

Ahmed, S. M., Ali, M. A., Mubeen, M., Qazi, F., & Ayubi, S. (2024). Herding Behavior Bias and its impact on Stock Returns: A case of Pakistan Stock Exchange. GISRAS Journal of Management & Islamic Finance (GJMIF), 4(1).

Azzutti, A. (2022). AI trading and the limits of EU law enforcement in deterring market manipulation. *Computer Law & Security Report*, 45, 105690. DOI: 10.1016/j.clsr.2022.105690

Baker, M., & Wurgler, J. (2012). Behavioral aspects of asset pricing. *Journal of Financial Economics*, 104(1), 1–21.

Barberis, N. (2013). Thirty years of prospect theory in economics: A review and assessment. *The Journal of Economic Perspectives*, 27(1), 173–196. DOI: 10.1257/jep.27.1.173

Bikhchandani, S., Hirshleifer, D., & Welch, I. (2012). A theory of fads, fashion, custom, and cultural change as informational cascades. *Journal of Political Economy*, 100(5), 992–1026. DOI: 10.1086/261849

Bikhchandani, S., & Sharma, S. (2014). Herd behavior in financial markets: A review. *IMF Staff Papers*, 47(3), 279–310. DOI: 10.2307/3867650

Djankov, S., McLiesh, C., & Shleifer, A. (2013). Private credit in 129 countries. *Journal of Financial Economics*, 84(2), 299–329. DOI: 10.1016/j.jfineco.2006.03.004

Easley, D., & O'Hara, M. (2010). Microstructure and ambiguity. *The Journal of Finance*, 65(5), 1817–1846. DOI: 10.1111/j.1540-6261.2010.01595.x

Fama, E. F. (2013). Two pillars of asset pricing. *The American Economic Review*, 104(6), 1467–1485. DOI: 10.1257/aer.104.6.1467

Gupta, S. (2022). Behavioural Finance and Investment Decisions: Impact Analysis and Mitigation Strategies in the context of COVID Pandemic and DIY Investing. 21st Century Innovations in Management, Science and Technology, Education and Social Sciences, 129.

Hirshleifer, D. (2015). Behavioral finance. *Annual Review of Financial Economics*, 7(1), 133–159. DOI: 10.1146/annurev-financial-092214-043752

Hirshleifer, D., & Teoh, S. H. (2010). The psychological attraction approach to accounting and disclosure policy. *Contemporary Accounting Research*, 26(4), 1067–1090. DOI: 10.1506/car.26.4.3

Kameda, T., Toyokawa, W., & Tindale, R. S. (2022). Information aggregation and collective intelligence beyond the wisdom of crowds. *Nature Reviews Psychology*, 1(6), 345–357. DOI: 10.1038/s44159-022-00054-y

Khan, A. (2022). Emotions and their impact on investor behaviour (Doctoral dissertation, The University of Waikato).

Komalasari, P. T., Asri, M., Purwanto, B. M., & Setiyono, B. (2022). Herding behaviour in the capital market: What do we know and what is next? *Management Review Quarterly*, 72(3), 745–787. DOI: 10.1007/s11301-021-00212-1

La Porta, R., Lopez-de-Silanes, F., & Shleifer, A. (2012). Government ownership of banks. *The Journal of Finance*, 57(1), 265–301. DOI: 10.1111/1540-6261.00422

Lakonishok, J., Shleifer, A., & Vishny, R. W. (2012). The impact of institutional trading on stock prices. *Journal of Financial Economics*, 32(1), 23–43. DOI: 10.1016/0304-405X(92)90023-Q

Liu, Y., Kim, C. Y., Lee, E. H., & Yoo, J. W. (2022). Relationship between sustainable management activities and financial performance: Mediating effects of non-financial performance and moderating effects of institutional environment. *Sustainability (Basel)*, 14(3), 1168. DOI: 10.3390/su14031168

Lo, A. W. (2012). *Adaptive markets: Financial evolution at the speed of thought.* Princeton University Press.

Loang, O. K., & Ahmad, Z. (2023). Empirical analysis of global markets herding on COVID-19 effect. *Vision (Basel)*, ●●●, 09722629221146653. DOI: 10.1177/09722629221146653

Loang, O. K., & Ahmad, Z. (2024). Does volatility cause herding in Malaysian stock market? Evidence from quantile regression analysis. *Millennial Asia*, 15(2), 197–215. DOI: 10.1177/09763996221101217

Lusardi, A., & Mitchell, O. S. (2014). The economic importance of financial literacy: Theory and evidence. *Journal of Economic Literature*, 52(1), 5–44. DOI: 10.1257/jel.52.1.5 PMID: 28579637

Putri, A., & Tanno, A. (2024). Exploring Market Dynamics: A Qualitative Study on Asset Price Behavior, Market Efficiency, and Information Role in Investment Decisions in the Capital Market. Atestasi. *Jurnal Ilmiah Akuntansi*, 7(2), 810–827.

Scharfstein, D. S., & Stein, J. C. (2010). Herd behavior and investment. *The American Economic Review*, 80(3), 465–479.

Shiller, R. J. (2014). Speculative asset prices. *The American Economic Review*, 104(6), 1486–1517. DOI: 10.1257/aer.104.6.1486

Suresh, G., & Loang, O. K. (2024). The Rationality Conundrum: Exploring Herd Mentality among Individual Investors in the Indian Stock Market. *Indian Journal of Finance*, 18(6), 26–45. DOI: 10.17010/ijf/2024/v18i6/173967

Tetlock, P. C. (2010). Does public financial news resolve asymmetric information? *Review of Financial Studies*, 23(12), 3520–3557. DOI: 10.1093/rfs/hhq052

Ukpong, I. (2023). Determinants of industry herding (Doctoral dissertation, Anglia Ruskin Research Online (ARRO)).

Van Rooij, M., Lusardi, A., & Alessie, R. (2011). Financial literacy and stock market participation. *Journal of Financial Economics*, 101(2), 449–472. DOI: 10.1016/j.jfineco.2011.03.006

Wen, J., Okolo, C. V., Ugwuoke, I. C., & Kolani, K. (2022). Research on influencing factors of renewable energy, energy efficiency, on technological innovation. Does trade, investment and human capital development matter? *Energy Policy*, 160, 112718. DOI: 10.1016/j.enpol.2021.112718

Yang, W., & Loang, O. K. (2024). Systematic Literature Review: Behavioural Biases as the Determinants of Herding. *Technology-Driven Business Innovation: Unleashing the Digital Advantage*, 1, 79–92. DOI: 10.1007/978-3-031-51997-0_7

Yang, W., & Loang, O. K. (2024). Unpacking Financial Herding Behaviour: A Conceptual Study of Youth and Working Adults in Chongqing, China. In *Technology-Driven Business Innovation: Unleashing the Digital Advantage* (Vol. 1, pp. 67–78). Springer Nature Switzerland. DOI: 10.1007/978-3-031-51997-0_6

Compilation of References

Abdullah, M., Sulong, Z., & Chowdhury, M. A. F. (2024). Explainable deep learning model for stock price forecasting using textual analysis. *Expert Systems with Applications*, 249, 123740. DOI: 10.1016/j.eswa.2024.123740

Acharya, V. V., & Richardson, M. (2010). Causes of the Financial Crisis. *Critical Review*, 21(2-3), 195–210. DOI: 10.1080/08913810902952903

Afifah, N., Nugraha, N., Purnamasari, I., Supriatna, Y., Rahayu, A., & Wibowo, L. A. (2024, June). Strategic Role of Climate Finance: A Bibliometric Analysis. In *8th Global Conference on Business, Management, and Entrepreneurship (GCBME 2023)* (pp. 141-146). Atlantis Press. DOI: 10.2991/978-94-6463-443-3_21

Agarwal, V., Taffler, R. J., & Wang, C. (2024). Investor emotions and market bubbles. *Review of Quantitative Finance and Accounting*, ●●●, 1–31.

Agrawal, K. (2012). *A Conceptual Framework of Behavioral Biases in Finance*. IUP Journal of Behavioral Finance.

Aharon, D. Y. (2021). Uncertainty, fear and herding behavior: Evidence from size-ranked portfolios. *Journal of Behavioral Finance*, 22(3), 320–337. DOI: 10.1080/15427560.2020.1774887

Ahmad, M., & Wu, Q. (2022, August 08). Does herding behavior matter in investment management and perceived market efficiency? Evidence from an emerging market. *Management Decision*, 60(08), 2148–2173. DOI: 10.1108/MD-07-2020-0867

Ahmed, S. M., Ali, M. A., Mubeen, M., Qazi, F., & Ayubi, S. (2024). Herding Behavior Bias and its impact on Stock Returns: A case of Pakistan Stock Exchange. GISRAS Journal of Management & Islamic Finance (GJMIF), 4(1).

Ahmed, M. S., El-Masry, A. A., Al-Maghyereh, A. I., & Kumar, S. (2024). Cryptocurrency Volatility: A Review, Synthesis, and Research Agenda. *Research in International Business and Finance*, 71, 102472. DOI: 10.1016/j.ribaf.2024.102472

Akerlof, G. A., & Shiller, J. R. (2009). *Animal Spirits How Human Psychology Drives The Economy, and Why It Matters for Global Capitalism*. Princeton University Press.

Akerlof, G. A., & Shiller, R. J. (2010). *Animal spirits: How human psychology drives the economy, and why it matters for global capitalism*. Princeton university press.

Al-Dahan, N. S., Hasan, M. F., & Jadah, H. M. (2019). Effect of cognitive and emotional biases on investor decisions: An analytical study of the Iraq stock exchange. *International Journal of Innovation, Creativity and Change, 09*(10), 30-47. Retrieved Sep 13, 2024, from https://www.scopus.com/record/display.uri?eid=2-s2 .0-85079642547&origin=scopusAI

Alexakis, C., Chantziaras, A., Economou, F., Eleftheriou, K., & Grose, C. (2023, July). Animal Behavior in Capital markets: Herding formation dynamics, trading volume, and the role of COVID-19 pandemic. *The North American Journal of Economics and Finance*, 67, 101946. Advance online publication. DOI: 10.1016/j.najef.2023.101946

Ali, A., Razak, S. A., Othman, S. H., Taiseer, A. E. E., Al-Dhaqm, A., Nasser, M., Elhassan, T., Elshafie, H., & Saif, A. (2022). Financial Fraud Detection Based on Machine Learning: A Systematic Literature Review. *Applied Sciences (Basel, Switzerland)*, 12(19), 9637. DOI: 10.3390/app12199637

Aljifri, R. (2023, January). Investor psychology in the stock market: An empirical study of the impact of overconfidence on firm valuation. *Borsa Istanbul Review*, 23(01), 93–112. DOI: 10.1016/j.bir.2022.09.010

Almeida, H., Fos, V., & Kronlund, M. (2016). The Real Effects of Share Repurchases. *Journal of Financial Economics*, 119(1), 168–185. DOI: 10.1016/j.jfineco.2015.08.008

Al-Zoubi, H. A. (2024). Business Cycle Variations in Manager and Investor Sentiment Indices. *Journal of Behavioral Finance*, ●●●, 1–12.

Anderson, R. L. And Holt, A. C. (2000) Information Cascades and Rational Conformity *Encyclopedia of Cognitive Science*, Macmillan Reference Ltd.

Andersson, M., Hedesström, M., & Gärling, T. (2014, July 03). A Social-Psychological Perspective on Herding in Stock Markets. *Journal of Behavioral Finance*, 15(03), 226–234. DOI: 10.1080/15427560.2014.941062

Angrist, J. D., & Pischke, J. S. (2010). The credibility revolution in empirical economics: How better research design is taking the con out of econometrics. *The Journal of Economic Perspectives*, 24(2), 3–30. DOI: 10.1257/jep.24.2.3

Ante, L., & Demir, E. 2023. The ChatGPT Effect on AI-themed cryptocurrencies. Available at *SSRN* 4350557

Aprilianti, A. A., Tanzil, N. D., & Pratama, A. (2023). Herding Behavior, Loss Aversion Bias, Financial Literacy, and Investment Decisions (a Study on Millennial Generation in Indonesia in the Digital Era). *JASa (Jurnal Akuntansi, Audit Dan Sistem Informasi Akuntansi), 7*(3), 555–565.

Ariely, D. (2008). *Predictably Irrational.* Harper Collins.

Arifovic, J., He, X., & Wei, L. (2022). Machine Learning and Speed in High-Frequency Trading. *Journal of Economic Dynamics & Control*, 139, 104438. DOI: 10.1016/j.jedc.2022.104438

Arlen, J., & Tontrup, S. (2015). Strategic bias shifting: Herding as a behaviorally rational response to regret aversion. *The Journal of Legal Analysis*, 7(2), 517–560. DOI: 10.1093/jla/lav014

Arner, D., Barberis, J. N., & Buckley, R. P. (2015). The evolution of FinTech: A new post-crisis paradigm. *SSRN*, 47, 1271–1318. DOI: 10.2139/ssrn.2676553

Asch, S. E. (1955). Opinions and social pressure. *Scientific American*, 193(5), 31–35. DOI: 10.1038/scientificamerican1155-31

Ashenfelter, O. (1978). Estimating the effect of training programs on earnings. *The Review of Economics and Statistics*, 60(1), 47–57. DOI: 10.2307/1924332

Atasoy, B. S., Özkan, İ., & Erden, L. (2024). The determinants of systemic risk contagion. *Economic Modelling*, 130, 106596. DOI: 10.1016/j.econmod.2023.106596

Au, S.-Y., Dong, M., & Zhou, X. (2024). Does Social Interaction Spread Fear Among Institutional Investors? Evidence from Coronavirus Disease 2019. *Management Science*, 70(04), 2406–2426. DOI: 10.1287/mnsc.2023.4814

Aven, T. (2016). Risk assessment and risk management: Review of recent advances on their foundation. *European Journal of Operational Research*, 253(1), 1–13. DOI: 10.1016/j.ejor.2015.12.023

Avery, C., & Zemsky, P. (1998). Multidimensional uncertainty and herd behavior in financial markets. *The American Economic Review*, ●●●, 724–748.

Ayoub, A., & Balawi, A. (2022, June). Herd Behavior and its Effect on the Stock Market: An Economic Perspective. *Quality - Access to Success*, 23(188), 285–289. DOI: 10.47750/QAS/23.188.38

Azzutti, A. (2022). AI trading and the limits of EU law enforcement in deterring market manipulation. *Computer Law & Security Report*, 45, 105690. DOI: 10.1016/j. clsr.2022.105690

Baddeley, M. (2010). Herding, social influence and economic decision-making: Socio-psychological and neuroscientific analyses. *Philosophical Transactions of the Royal Society of London. Series B, Biological Sciences*, 365(1538), 281–290. DOI: 10.1098/rstb.2009.0169 PMID: 20026466

Baddeley, M. (2013). Herding, social influence and expert opinion. *Journal of Economic Methodology*, 20(1), 35–44. DOI: 10.1080/1350178X.2013.774845

Baihaqqy, M. R. (2020, August). The correlation between education level and understanding of financial literacy and its effect on investment decisions in capital markets. *Journal of Education and e-learning Research*, 07(03), 306–313. DOI: 10.20448/journal.509.2020.73.306.313

Baker, H. K., Nofsinger, J. R., & Puttonen, V. (2020). Common Investing Pitfalls that Can Separate You from Financial Security and Success. In *The Savvy Investor's Guide to Avoiding Pitfalls, Frauds, and Scams* (pp. 5–34). Emerald Publishing Limited. DOI: 10.1108/978-1-78973-559-820201003

Baker, H. K., Powell, G. E., & Veit, E. T. (2003). Why companies use open-market repurchases: A managerial perspective. *The Quarterly Review of Economics and Finance*, 43(3), 483–504. DOI: 10.1016/S1062-9769(02)00151-5

Baker, M., & Wurgler, J. (2002). Market Timing and Capital Structure. *The Journal of Finance*, 57(1), 1–32. DOI: 10.1111/1540-6261.00414

Baker, M., & Wurgler, J. (2007). Investor sentiment in the stock market. *The Journal of Economic Perspectives*, 21(2), 129–151. DOI: 10.1257/jep.21.2.129

Baker, M., & Wurgler, J. (2012). Behavioral aspects of asset pricing. *Journal of Financial Economics*, 104(1), 1–21.

Balagyozyan, A., & Cakan, E. (2016, December 13). Did large institutional investors flock into the technology herd? An empirical investigation using a vector Markov-switching model. *Applied Economics*, 48(58), 5731–5747. DOI: 10.1080/00036846.2016.1184376

Ballis, A., & Anastasiou, D. (2023). Testing for Herding in Artificial Intelligence–Themed Cryptocurrencies Following the Launch of ChatGPT. *The Journal of Financial Data Science*, 5(4), 161–171. DOI: 10.3905/jfds.2023.1.134

Ball, R., & Brown, P. (1968). An empirical evaluation of accounting income numbers. *Journal of Accounting Research*, 6(2), 159–178. DOI: 10.2307/2490232

Banerjee, A. V. (1992). A simple model of herd behavior. *The Quarterly Journal of Economics*, 107(3), 797–817. DOI: 10.2307/2118364

Banerjee, S., Dasgupta, S., & Kim, Y. (2018). Buyer-seller networks and the spatial clustering of economic activity. *Journal of Urban Economics*, 107(3), 87–103.

Bao, X. H., H., & Li, S. H. (. (2020, October). Investor Overconfidence and Trading Activity in the Asia Pacific REIT Markets. *Journal of Risk and Financial Management*, 13(10). Advance online publication. DOI: 10.3390/jrfm13100232

Bapna, R., Jank, W., & Shmueli, G. (2012). Consumer surplus in online auctions. *Information Systems Research*, 19(3), 400–416.

Barber, B. M., & Odean, T. (2008). All that glitters: The effect of attention and news on the buying behavior of individual and institutional investors. *Review of Financial Studies*, 21(2), 785–818. DOI: 10.1093/rfs/hhm079

Barber, B. M., Odean, T., & Zhu, N. (2009). Do retail trades move markets? *Review of Financial Studies*, 22(1), 151–186. DOI: 10.1093/rfs/hhn035

Barberis, N. (2013). Thirty years of prospect theory in economics: A review and assessment. *The Journal of Economic Perspectives*, 27(1), 173–196. DOI: 10.1257/jep.27.1.173

Barros, G. (2010). Herbert A. Simon and The Concept of Rationality: Boundaries and Procedures *Brazilian*. *Journal of Political Economy*, 30(3), 455–472.

Barr, R., & William, R. (2013). An Evidence Based Approach to Sports Concussion: Confronting the Availability Cascade. *Neuropsychology Review*, 23(4), 271–272. DOI: 10.1007/s11065-013-9244-3 PMID: 24281980

Bashir, T., Rasheed, S., Raftar, S., Fatima, S., & Maqsood, S. (2013). Impact of behavioral biases on investor decision making: Male vs female. *Journal of Business and Management*, 10(3), 60–68.

Batra, S., Yadav, M., Jindal, I., Saini, M., & Kumar, P. (2024). Stabilizing or destabilizing: The effect of institutional investors on stock return volatility in an emerging market. *Multinational Business Review*, 32(2), 204–225. DOI: 10.1108/MBR-04-2023-0052

Bebchuk, L. A., Cohen, A., & Hirst, S. (2017). The agency problems of institutional investors. *The Journal of Economic Perspectives*, 31(3), 89–112. DOI: 10.1257/jep.31.3.89

Beber, A., Brandt, M. W., & Kavajecz, K. A. (2011). What does equity sector order-flow tell us about the economy? *Journal of Financial Economics*, 99(3), 523–542.

Berg, T., Burg, V., Gombović, A., & Puri, M. (2020). On the rise of fintechs—Credit scoring using digital footprints. *Review of Financial Studies*, 32(7), 1984–2009. DOI: 10.1093/rfs/hhz099

Bernheim, B. D. (1994). A theory of conformity. *Journal of Political Economy*, 102(5), 841–877. DOI: 10.1086/261957

Bhanu, B. K. (2023). Behavioral finance and stock market anomalies: Exploring psychological factors influencing investment decisions. Commerce, Economics & Management, 23.

Bikhchandani, S., Hirshleifer, D., & Welch, I. (1992). A Theory of Fads, Fashion, Custom, and Cultural Change as Informational Cascades. *Journal of Political Economy*, 100(5), 992–1026. DOI: 10.1086/261849

Bikhchandani, S., & Sharma, S. (2000). Herd behavior in financial markets. *IMF Staff Papers*, 47(3), 279–310. DOI: 10.2307/3867650

Bílek, J., Nedoma, J., & Jirásek, M. (2018). Representativeness heuristics: A literature review of its impacts on the quality of decision-making. *Scientific Papers of the University of Pardubice, Series D: Faculty of Economics and Administration*, 26(43), 29-38. Retrieved Sep 15, 2024, from https://www.scopus.com/record/display .uri?eid=2-s2.0-85057788930&origin=scopusAI

Bittlingmayer, G. (1998). The market for corporate control (including takeovers). Available at *SSRN* 81808. DOI: 10.2139/ssrn.81808

Bobe, M. C., & Piefke, M. (2019). Why do we herd in financial contexts? *Journal of Neuroscience, Psychology, and Economics*, 12(2), 116–140. DOI: 10.1037/ npe0000108

Bohl, M. T., Siklos, P. L., & Sondermann, D. (2008). European stock market contagion during the financial crises of 1997-1999. *Journal of International Money and Finance*, 27(7), 1159–1174.

Bonaime, T., & Oztekin, D. (2014). The effect of managerial ownership on the short-and long-run response to cash distributions. *Financial Review*, 38, 179–196.

Bosworth, B., & Flaaen, A. (2013). America's Financial Crisis: The End of an Era. In *The Global Financial Crisis and Asia: Implications and Challenges*. Oxford University Press., DOI: 10.1093/acprof:oso/9780199660957.003.0002

Botzen, W. W., Duijndam, S. J., Robinson, P. J., & van Beukering, P. (2022). Behavioral biases and heuristics in perceptions of COVID-19 risks and prevention decisions. *Risk Analysis*, 42(12), 2671–2690. DOI: 10.1111/risa.13882 PMID: 35092967

Bradley, M., & Wakeman, L. M. (1983). The wealth effects of targeted share repurchases. *Journal of Financial Economics*, 11(1-4), 187–205. DOI: 10.1016/0304-405X(83)90015-6

Brav, A., Graham, J., Harvey, C. R., & Michaely, R. (2005). Payout policy in the 21st century. *Journal of Financial Economics*, 77(3), 483–527. DOI: 10.1016/j.jfineco.2004.07.004

Bregu, K. (2020, October). Overconfidence and (Over)Trading: The Effect of Feedback on Trading Behavior. *Journal of Behavioral and Experimental Economics*, 88, 101598. Advance online publication. DOI: 10.1016/j.socec.2020.101598

Brini, A., & Lenz, J. (2024). A comparison of cryptocurrency volatility-benchmarking new and mature asset classes. *Financial Innovation*, 10(1), 122. DOI: 10.1186/s40854-024-00646-y

Brockman, P., Khurana, I. K., & Martin, X. (2008). Voluntary disclosures around share repurchases. *Journal of Financial Economics*, 89(1), 175–191. DOI: 10.1016/j.jfineco.2007.08.004

Brown, A. L., & Kagel, J. H. (2009). Behavior in a simplified stock market: The status quo bias, the disposition effect and the ostrich effect. *Annals of Finance, 05*(01), 01-14. DOI: 10.1007/s10436-007-0092-0

Brown, G. W., & Cliff, M. T. (2004). Investor sentiment and asset valuation. *The Journal of Business*, 78(2), 405–440. DOI: 10.1086/427633

Brown, K. W., & Ryan, R. M. (2003). The benefits of being present: Mindfulness and its role in psychological well-being. *Journal of Personality and Social Psychology*, 84(4), 822–848. DOI: 10.1037/0022-3514.84.4.822 PMID: 12703651

Bryson, J., Diamantis, M., & Grant, T. (2017). Of, for, and by the people: The legal lacuna of synthetic persons. *Artificial Intelligence and Law*, 25(3), 273–291. DOI: 10.1007/s10506-017-9214-9

Buallay, A., AlAjmi, J. Y., Fadhul, S., & Papoutsi, A. (2024). Beyond averages: Quantile regression explorations of sustainability practices and firm value. *International Journal of Innovation Science*. Advance online publication. DOI: 10.1108/IJIS-07-2022-0125

Burrell, J. (2016). How the machine 'thinks': Understanding opacity in machine learning algorithms. *Big Data & Society*, 3(1), 1–12. DOI: 10.1177/2053951715622512

Callegaro, F. (2021). The constraint of justice: Durkheim on modern solidarity and freedom as non-exploitation. In *Durkheim & Critique* (pp. 191–226). Springer International Publishing., DOI: 10.1007/978-3-030-75158-6_7

Carlos Medina, J. (2024, May 7). *8 Ways To Use Financial Mindfulness To Enhance Your Life*. https://www.forbes.com/sites/financialfinesse/2024/05/07/financial-mindfulness-the-key-to-enhancing-your-financial-life/

Caruana, R., Lou, Y., Gehrke, J., Koch, P., Sturm, M., & Elhadad, N. 2015. Intelligible Models for HealthCare: Predicting Pneumonia Risk and Hospital 30-Day Readmission. Paper presented at the 21th ACM SIGKDD International Conference on Knowledge Discovery and Data Mining, Sydney, Australia, August 10–13; pp. 1721–30 DOI: 10.1145/2783258.2788613

Carvalho, J., Jordão da Gama Silva, P. V., & Klotzle, M. C. (2024, March 05). Herding and Google search queries in the Brazilian stock market. *Review of Behavioral Finance*, 16(02), 341–359. DOI: 10.1108/RBF-12-2022-0296

Cascão, A., Quelhas, A. P., & Cunha, A. M. (2023, August 24). Heuristics and cognitive biases in the housing investment market. *International Journal of Housing Markets and Analysis*, 16(05), 991–1006. DOI: 10.1108/IJHMA-05-2022-0073

Çelik, S., & Isaksson, M. (2013). *Institutional investors as owners: Who are they and what do they do?* Celsi, M. W., Nelson, R. P., Dellande, S., & Gilly, M. C. (2017). Temptation's itch: Mindlessness, acceptance, and mindfulness in a debt management program. *Journal of Business Research*, 77, 81–94. DOI: 10.1016/j.jbusres.2017.03.002

Cepni, O., Demirer, R., Pham, L., & Rognone, L. (2023). Climate uncertainty and information transmissions across the conventional and ESG assets. *Journal of International Financial Markets, Institutions and Money*, 83, 101730. DOI: 10.1016/j.intfin.2022.101730

Cervellati, E. M., Angelini, N., & Stella, G. P. (2024). Behavioral finance and wealth management: Market anomalies, investors' behavior and the role of financial advisors.

Chadee, A. A., Chadee, X. T., Chadee, C., & Otuloge, F. (2022). Violations at the reference point of discontinuity: Limitations of prospect theory and an alternative model of risk choices. *Emerging Science Journal*, 6(1), 37–52. DOI: 10.28991/ESJ-2022-06-01-03

Chandu, V., Maddala, S., Sai, K. G., Teja, G. C., Prakash, B. J., Rao, B. N., & Osei, B. (2023, January-December). Research on retail Buyers' emotional quotient with focus on transactions on the National Stock Exchange. *International Journal of Engineering Business Management*, 15, 18479790231180770. Advance online publication. DOI: 10.1177/18479790231180770

Chang, E. C., Cheng, J. W., & Khorana, A. (2000, October 01). An examination of herd behavior in equity markets: An international perspective. *Journal of Banking & Finance*, 24(10), 1651–1679. DOI: 10.1016/S0378-4266(99)00096-5

Chang, S.-K. (2014, February 01). Herd behavior, bubbles and social interactions in financial markets. *Studies in Nonlinear Dynamics and Econometrics*, 18(01), 89–101. DOI: 10.1515/snde-2013-0024

Chen, J. (2016). An empirical study on the motivation and market reaction of stock buyback of listed companies in China [Doctoral dissertation, China University of Petroleum (Beijing)].

Cheng, F. (2018). Research on the motivation and effect of Midea's stock repurchase [Master's thesis, Jiangxi University of Finance and Economics].

Cheng, F. (2018). Research on the motivation and effect of share repurchase of Midea Corporation [Master's thesis, Jiangxi University of Finance and Economics].

Chen, R.-C., Dewil, C., & Huang, S.-W. (2020). R.E. Caraka Selecting critical features for data classification based on machine learning methods. *Journal of Big Data*, 7(1), 1–26. DOI: 10.1186/s40537-020-00327-4

Chen, X., Li, S., Zhang, Y., Zhai, Y., Zhang, Z., & Feng, C. (2022). Different drives of herding: An exploratory study of motivations underlying social conformity. *PsyCh Journal*, 11(2), 247–258. DOI: 10.1002/pchj.515 PMID: 35080146

Chiang, T. C., Li, J., & Tan, L. (2010). Empirical investigation of herding behavior in Chinese stock markets: Evidence from quantile regression analysis. *Global Finance Journal*, 21(1), 111–124. DOI: 10.1016/j.gfj.2010.03.005

Chi, D. J. (2005). The announcement effect of stock repurchases on Taiwan Stock Exchange. *International Journal of Business and Management*, 5(10), 168–177.

Chira, I., Adams, M., & Thornton, B. (2008). *Behavioral bias within the decision making process.*

Choi, K.-H., Kang, S. H., & Yoon, S.-M. (2022). Herding behavior in Korea's cryptocurrency market. *Applied Economics*, 54(24), 2795–2809. DOI: 10.1080/00036846.2021.1998335

Choi, N., & Sias, R. W. (2009). Institutional industry herding. *Journal of Financial Economics*, 94(3), 469–491. DOI: 10.1016/j.jfineco.2008.12.009

Choi, N., & Skiba, H. (2015). Institutional herding in international markets. *Journal of Banking & Finance*, 55, 246–259. DOI: 10.1016/j.jbankfin.2015.02.002

Chordia, T., Roll, R., & Subrahmanyam, A. (2011). Recent trends in trading activity and market quality. *Journal of Financial Economics*, 101(2), 243–263. DOI: 10.1016/j.jfineco.2011.03.008

Chung, A., & Rimal, R. N. (2016). Social Norms: A Review. *Review of Communication Research*, 4, 1–28. DOI: 10.12840/issn.2255-4165.2016.04.01.008

Cioroianu, I., Corbet, S., Hou, Y., Hu, Y., Larkin, C., & Taffler, R. (2024, June). Exploring the use of emotional sentiment to understanding market response to unexpected corporate pivots. *Research in International Business and Finance*, 70, 102304. Advance online publication. DOI: 10.1016/j.ribaf.2024.102304

Coates, J. M., Gurnell, M., & Sarnyai, Z. (2017). From molecule to market. In *The Leadership Hubris Epidemic: Biological Roots and Strategies for Prevention* (pp. 25-56). Springer International Publishing. DOI: 10.1007/978-3-319-57255-0_2

Coates, J. M., Gurnell, M., & Sarnyai, Z. (2010, January 27). From molecule to market: Steroid hormones and financial risk-taking. *Philosophical Transactions of the Royal Society of London. Series B, Biological Sciences*, 365(1538), 331–343. DOI: 10.1098/rstb.2009.0193 PMID: 20026470

Comment, R., & Jarrell, G. A. (1991). The Relative Signalling Power of Dutch-Auction and Fixed-Price Self-Tender Offers and Open-Market Share Repurchases. *The Journal of Finance*, 46(4), 1243–1271.

Connelly, B. L., Certo, I. R. D., Ireland, R. D., & Reutzel, C. R. (2011). Signaling Theory: A Review and Assessment. *Journal of Management*, 37(1), 39–67. DOI: 10.1177/0149206310388419

Cuc, L. D., Rad, D., Ha egan, C. D., Trifan, V. A., & Ardeleanu, T. (2024). The Mediating Role of the Financial Recommender System Advising Acceptance in the Relationship between Investments Trust and Decision-Making Behavior. In *Proceedings of the International Conference on Business Excellence* (Vol. 18, No. 1, pp. 2260-2273). DOI: 10.2478/picbe-2024-0190

Cziraki, P., Lyandres, E., & Michaely, R. (2019). What do insiders know? Evidence from insider trading around share repurchases and SEOs. *Journal of Corporate Finance*, 66, 101544. DOI: 10.1016/j.jcorpfin.2019.101544

Dabara, I. D., Ogunba, A. O., & Araloyin, F. M. (2015). The diversification and inflation-hedging potentials of direct and indirect real estate investments in Nigeria. *Proceedings of the 15th African Real Estate Society (AFRES) Annual Conference, 31st August–3rd September*, 169–185. DOI: 10.15396/afres2015_117

Dai, X., Zhang, J., & Chang, V. (2023). Noise traders in an agent-based artificial stock market. *Annals of Operations Research*. Advance online publication. DOI: 10.1007/s10479-023-05528-7

Daniel, K., & Titman, S. (1999). Market efficiency in an irrational world. *Financial Analysts Journal*, 55(6), 28–40. DOI: 10.2469/faj.v55.n6.2312

Dann, L. (1981). Common stock repurchase: An analysis of return to bondholders and stockholders. *Journal of Financial Economics*, 9, 113–138. DOI: 10.1016/0304-405X(81)90010-6

Dasgupta, A., & Prat, A. (2008). Information aggregation in financial markets with career concerns. *Journal of Economic Theory*, 143(1), 83–113. DOI: 10.1016/j.jet.2008.01.005

De Long, J. B., Shleifer, A., Summers, L. H., & Waldmann, R. J. (1990). Positive feedback investment strategies and destabilizing rational speculation. *The Journal of Finance*, 45(2), 379–395. DOI: 10.1111/j.1540-6261.1990.tb03695.x

De Winne, R., & Petkeviciute, A. (2021). *Financial Literacy and Multi-Asset Portfolio Diversification. International Conference of the French Finance Association (AFFI)*.

DeLisle, R. J., Diavatopoulos, D., Fodor, A., & Krieger, K. (2017, June). Anchoring and Probability Weighting in Option Prices. *Journal of Futures Markets*, 37(06), 614–638. DOI: 10.1002/fut.21833

Deng, Q., Chen, N., & Qin, S. (2021). Equity pledge and share repurchase of listed companies based on Wanfeng Aowei. *Friends of Accounting*, 2021(20), 102–108.

Dervishaj, B. (2021). Psychological biases, main factors of financial behaviour-A literature review. *European Journal of Medicine and Natural Sciences*, 4(1), 27–44.

Devadas, M., & Vijayakumar, T. (2019, August). Investment decisions, herd behaviour and retail investors. *International Journal of Innovative Technology and Exploring Engineering*, 08(10), 3291–3294. DOI: 10.35940/ijitee.J1210.0881019

Devenow, A., & Welch, I. (1996). Rational herding in financial economics. *European Economic Review*, 40(3–5), 603–615. DOI: 10.1016/0014-2921(95)00073-9

Dhillon, J., & Singh, D. P. (2017). Deciphering the theoretical foundations of investor behavior: A literature review. *International Journal of Applied Business and Economic Research*, 15(09), 477–487. Retrieved August 31, 2024, from https://www.scopus.com/record/display.uri?eid=2-s2.0-85019601992&origin=scopusAI

Diederen, K. M., & Fletcher, P. C. (2021, February). Dopamine, Prediction Error and Beyond. *The Neuroscientist*, 27(01), 30–46. DOI: 10.1177/1073858420907591 PMID: 32338128

Dimitriadou, A. T. H. A. N. A. S. I. A. (2024). *The influence of news and investor sentiment on exchange rate determination: new evidence using panel data in the banking sector* (Doctoral dissertation, College of Business, Law and Social Sciences, University of Derby).

Din, S. M. U., Mehmood, S. K., Shahzad, A., Ahmad, I., Davidyants, A., & Abu-Rumman, A. (2021). The impact of behavioral biases on herding behavior of investors in Islamic financial products. *Frontiers in Psychology*, 11, 600570. DOI: 10.3389/fpsyg.2020.600570 PMID: 33613358

Dittmar, R. F. (2002). Nonlinear pricing kernels, kurtosis preference, and evidence from the cross section of equity returns. *The Journal of Finance*, 57(1), 369–403. DOI: 10.1111/1540-6261.00425

Dixit, D. K. (2024). Investor Psychology and Market Volatility: Unpacking Behavioral Finance Insights. *Journal of Informatics Education and Research*, 4(2).

Djankov, S., McLiesh, C., & Shleifer, A. (2013). Private credit in 129 countries. *Journal of Financial Economics*, 84(2), 299–329. DOI: 10.1016/j.jfineco.2006.03.004

Dolley, J. C. (1933). Characteristics and procedure of common stock split-ups. Harvard Business Review, 11(3), 316-326.80.Ball R., Brown P., 1968, An Empirical Evaluation of Accounting Income Numbers [J]. *Journal of Accounting Research*, 2(6), 159–178.

Du, R. (2022). Availability Heuristic: An Overview and Applications, *Highlights in Business. Economics and Management*, 1, 153–159.

Duran, A., & Caginalp, G. (2007, June). Overreaction diamonds: Precursors and aftershocks for significant price changes. *Quantitative Finance*, 07(03), 321–342. DOI: 10.1080/14697680601009903

Easley, D. And Kleinberg, J. (2010) *Networks, Crowds, and Markets: Reasoning about a Highly Connected World* Cambridge University Press

Easley, D., & O'Hara, M. (2010). Microstructure and ambiguity. *The Journal of Finance*, 65(5), 1817–1846. DOI: 10.1111/j.1540-6261.2010.01595.x

Elkind, D., Kaminski, K., Lo, A. W., Siah, K. W., & Wong, C. H. (2022, December 01). When Do Investors Freak Out? Machine Learning Predictions of Panic Selling. *Journal of Financial Data Science*, 04(01), 11–39. DOI: 10.3905/jfds.2021.1.085

Engelberg, J. E., & Parsons, C. A. (2011). The causal impact of media in financial markets. *The Journal of Finance*, 66(1), 67–97. DOI: 10.1111/j.1540-6261.2010.01626.x

Fama, E. F. (2013). Two pillars of asset pricing. *The American Economic Review*, 104(6), 1467–1485. DOI: 10.1257/aer.104.6.1467

Fama, E. F., Fisher, L., Jensen, M. C., & Roll, R. (1969). The adjustment of stock prices to new information. *International Economic Review*, 10(1), 1–21. DOI: 10.2307/2525569

Farmaki, E. (2024). The subjective experience of abrupt and pervasive social changes: living through the 2008 socioeconomic crisis in Greece and Italy.

Faugere, C. (2016). Applying mindfulness and compassion in finance. *Critical Studies on Corporate Responsibility. Governance and Sustainability*, 10(May), 299–319. DOI: 10.1108/S2043-905920160000010032

Feng, L. (2008). An empirical study of the information content and insider trading around open market share repurchase announcements [Doctoral dissertation, Concordia University].

Feng, Z. (2018). Research on financial risk of enterprises in the software and information technology service industry. Finance and Accounting Study, No. 208(34), 24+26.

Fernández, B., Garcia-Merino, T., Mayoral, R., Santos, V., & Vallelado, E. (2009). The role of the interaction between information and behavioral bias in explaining herding. *Behavioral finance working group. London*.

Fernández, B., Garcia-Merino, T., Mayoral, R., Santos, V., & Vallelado, E. (2011). Herding, information uncertainty and investors' cognitive profile. *Qualitative Research in Financial Markets*, 3(1), 7–33. DOI: 10.1108/17554171111124595

Fernández-Rodríguez, F., García-Artiles, M.-D., & Martín-González, J. M. (2010). A model of speculative behaviour with a strange attractor. *Applied Mathematical Finance*, 09(03), 143–161. DOI: 10.1080/13504860210159032

Filiz, I., Nahmer, T., Spiwoks, M., & Bizer, K. (2018). Portfolio diversification: The influence of herding, status-quo bias, and the gambler's fallacy. *Financial Markets and Portfolio Management*, 32(2), 167–205. DOI: 10.1007/s11408-018-0311-x

Fischer, B. (1986, July). Noise. *The Journal of Finance*, 41(03), 529–543. DOI: 10.2307/2328481

Forbes, K. J., & Rigobon, R. (2002). No contagion, only interdependence: Measuring stock market comovements. *The Journal of Finance*, 57(5), 2223–2261. DOI: 10.1111/0022-1082.00494

French, K. R., & Poterba, J. (1991). *Investor diversification and international equity markets.*

Gan, L. (2018). Effect analysis of share repurchase of JAC [Master's thesis, Jiangxi University of Finance and Economics].

Garbinsky, E., Blanchard, S. J., & Kim, L. (2023). FINANCIAL MINDFULNESS. *Georgetown McDonough School of Business Research Paper Forthcoming*.

Garcia, J. (2021, December). Analyst herding and firm-level investor sentiment. *Financial Markets and Portfolio Management*, 35(04), 461–494. DOI: 10.1007/s11408-021-00382-8

Gentina, E., Daniel, C., & Tang, T. L.-P. (2021). Mindfulness reduces avaricious monetary attitudes and enhances ethical consumer beliefs: Mindfulness training, timing, and practicing matter. *Journal of Business Ethics*, 173(2), 301–323. DOI: 10.1007/s10551-020-04559-5

Germer, C. (2004). What is mindfulness. *The Insight Journal*, 22(3), 24–29.

Gl van, B., & Anghel, F. (2023, December). We are not macroprudentialists: A skeptical view of prudential regulation to deal with systemic externalities. *Independent Review*, 17(03), 349–368. Retrieved September 08, 2024, from https://www.scopus.com/record/display.uri?eid=2-s2.0-84872225423&origin=scopusAI

Glossner, S., Matos, P., Ramelli, S., & Wagner, A. F. (2024). Do institutional investors stabilize equity markets in crisis periods? Evidence from COVID-19. Evidence from COVID-19 (February 20, 2024). Swiss Finance Institute Research Paper, (20-56).

Goetzmann, W. N., & Kumar, A. (2004). Diversification decisions of individual investors and asset prices. *Yale School of Management Working Papers (Yale School of Management.).*

Goetzmann, W. N., & Kumar, A. (2008). Equity portfolio diversification. *Review of Finance*, 12(3), 433–463. DOI: 10.1093/rof/rfn005

Goldstein, I., Jiang, H., & Karolyi, G. A. (2014). To FinTech and Beyond. *Review of Financial Studies*, 27(8), 2274–2312.

Goldstone, R. L., & Janssen, M. A. (2005). Computational models of collective behavior. *Trends in Cognitive Sciences*, 9(9), 424–430. DOI: 10.1016/j.tics.2005.07.009 PMID: 16085450

Gomber, P., Kauffman, R. J., Parker, C., & Weber, B. W. (2018). On the Fintech revolution: Interpreting the forces of innovation, disruption, and transformation in financial services. *Journal of Management Information Systems*, 35(1), 220–265. DOI: 10.1080/07421222.2018.1440766

Goodfellow, C., Bohl, M. T., & Gebka, B. (2009). Together we invest? Individual and institutional investors' trading behaviour in Poland. *International Review of Financial Analysis*, 18(4), 212–221. DOI: 10.1016/j.irfa.2009.03.002

Goodnight, G. T., & Green, S. (2010). Rhetoric, Risk, and Markets: The Dot-Com Bubble. *The Quarterly Journal of Speech*, 96(2), 115–140. DOI: 10.1080/00335631003796669

Gorton, G., & Metrick, A. (2012). Getting up to speed on the financial crisis: A one-weekend-reader's guide. *Journal of Economic Literature*, 50(1), 128–150. DOI: 10.1257/jel.50.1.128

Goyenko, R. Y., & Ukhov, A. D. (2009). Stock and bond market liquidity: A long-run empirical analysis. *Journal of Financial and Quantitative Analysis*, 44(1), 189–212. DOI: 10.1017/S0022109009090097

Gros, M., & Wallek, C. (2015, August 01). Are different stock market transparency requirements associated with different accounting quality levels? An analysis of bonding effects on the German stock market. *Journal of Business Economics*, 85(06), 597–633. DOI: 10.1007/s11573-015-0763-7

Gryphon, C. B., Harris, L., & Topaloglu, S. (2003). Herding and feedback trading by institutional and individual investors. *Journal of Financial Markets*, 6(4), 439–459.

Guo, S., Yu, X., & Faff, R. (2024). When investors can talk to firms, is it a meaningful conversation? Evidence from investor postings on interactive platforms. *European Accounting Review*, 33(3), 771–795. DOI: 10.1080/09638180.2022.2118147

Gupta, P., & Kohli, B. (2021, May-July). Herding behavior in the Indian stock market: An empirical study. *Indian Journal of Finance, 15*(05-07), 86-99. DOI: 10.17010/ijf/2021/v15i5-7/164495

Gupta, S. (2022). Behavioural Finance and Investment Decisions: Impact Analysis and Mitigation Strategies in the context of COVID Pandemic and DIY Investing. 21st Century Innovations in Management, Science and Technology, Education and Social Sciences, 129.

Gupta, P., & Kohli, B. (2021). Herding behavior in the Indian stock market: An empirical study. *Indian Journal of Finance*, 15(5-7), 86–99.

Gu, Y., Ben, S., & Lv, J. (2022). Peer effect in merger and acquisition activities and its impact on corporate sustainable development: Evidence from China. *Sustainability (Basel)*, 14(7), 3891. DOI: 10.3390/su14073891

Haq, Z. U. (2022). HOW ARE TRADING ACTIVITIES OF RETAIL INVESTORS AFFECTED BY THEIR FINANCIAL ATTITUDE DURING THE COVID-19 PANDEMIC IN PAKISTAN? A MEDIATED MODERATED RELATIONSHIP OF RISK TOLERANCE AND FINANCIAL LITERACY (Doctoral dissertation, Quaid I Azam university Islamabad).

Harford, J., Mansi, S. A., & Maxwell, W. F. (2008). Corporate governance and firm cash holdings in the US. *Journal of Financial Economics*, 87(3), 535–555. DOI: 10.1016/j.jfineco.2007.04.002

Hargreaves Heap, S. (1989). *Rationality in Economics*. Basil Blackwell.

Hatfield, E., Cacioppo, J. T., & Rapson, R. L. (1992). Primitive Emotional Contagion. In Clark, M. S. (Ed.), *Emotion and social behavior* (pp. 151–177). Sage Publications, Inc.

Hayes, C. (2010). Where Do Mirro Neurons Come From? *Neuroscience and Biobehavioral Reviews*, 34(4), 575–583. DOI: 10.1016/j.neubiorev.2009.11.007 PMID: 19914284

Hendershott, T., Jones, C. M., & Menkveld, A. J. (2011). Does algorithmic trading improve liquidity? *The Journal of Finance*, 66(1), 1–33. DOI: 10.1111/j.1540-6261.2010.01624.x

Hess, U., & Blairy, S. (2001).. . *Facial Mimicry and Emotional Contagion to Dynamic Emotional Facial Expressions and Their Influence on Decoding Accuracy International Journal of Psychophysicology*, 40, 129–141.

He, Y., Huang, J., & Li, J. (2014). A study on the economic consequences of share repurchase by listed companies in China: Empirical data from A-share market from 2005 to 2013. *Economic Management*, 36(10), 53–63.

Hillert, A., Maug, E., & Obernberger, S. (2016). Stock repurchases and liquidity. *Journal of Financial Economics*, 119(1), 186–209. DOI: 10.1016/j.jfineco.2015.08.009

Hinvest, N. S., Alsharman, M., Roell, M., & Fairchild, R. (2021, December 09). Do Emotions Benefit Investment Decisions? Anticipatory Emotion and Investment Decisions in Non-professional Investors. *Frontiers in Psychology*, 12, 705476. Advance online publication. DOI: 10.3389/fpsyg.2021.705476 PMID: 34955944

Hirshleifer, D. (2015). Behavioral finance. *Annual Review of Financial Economics*, 7(1), 133–159. DOI: 10.1146/annurev-financial-092214-043752

Hirshleifer, D., & Teoh, S. H. (2003). Limited attention, information disclosure, and financial reporting. *Journal of Accounting and Economics*, 36(1–3), 337–386. DOI: 10.1016/j.jacceco.2003.10.002

Hirshleifer, D., & Teoh, S. H. (2010). The psychological attraction approach to accounting and disclosure policy. *Contemporary Accounting Research*, 26(4), 1067–1090. DOI: 10.1506/car.26.4.3

Hoang, T., & Harrington, J. R. (2023). Tax incentive and household saving strategy: A regression discontinuity approach to catch-up contributions. *The Social Science Journal*, 60(04), 755–770. DOI: 10.1080/03623319.2020.1750844

Hou, H., Narin, M., Liu, J., & Wang, J. (2021, May). Emotional Contagion, Stock Volatility and Stock Price Synchronization: Empirical Evidence from the Fund's Heavy Warehouse Stocks. *Dongbei Daxue Xuebao/Journal of Northeastern University*, 42(05), 748-754. DOI: 10.12068/j.issn.1005-3026.2021.05.021

Hou, Y., Gao, J., Fan, F., Liu, F., & Song, C. (2017). Identifying herding effect in Chinese stock market by high-frequency data. *4th International Conference on Behavioral, Economic, and Socio-Cultural Computing, BESC 2017. 2018-January*, pp. 01-05. Cracow: Institute of Electrical and Electronics Engineers Inc. DOI: 10.1109/BESC.2017.8256359

Hoyer, K., Zeisberger, S., Breugelmans, S. M., & Zeelenberg, M. (2023, August). A culture of greed: Bubble formation in experimental asset markets with greedy and non-greedy traders. *Journal of Economic Behavior & Organization*, 212, 32–52. DOI: 10.1016/j.jebo.2023.05.005

Hsieh, S.-F. (2013). Individual and institutional herding and the impact on stock returns: Evidence from Taiwan stock market. *International Review of Financial Analysis*, 29, 175–188. DOI: 10.1016/j.irfa.2013.01.003

Hsu, S., & Dupont, B. (2023, Jan 01). 2008 Financial Crisis in the US. In *Elgar Encyclopedia of Financial Crises* (pp. 07-10). Edward Elgar Publishing Ltd. DOI: 10.4337/9781800377363.ch02

Hua, F., & Wang, J. (2018). How investor sentiment impacts financial decision-making behavior: From a cognitive neuroscience perspective. *NeuroQuantology: An Interdisciplinary Journal of Neuroscience and Quantum Physics*, 16(05), 567–573. DOI: 10.14704/nq.2018.16.5.1385

Huang, Z. (2022). Research on the motivation and implementation effect of multiple share repurchases by listed companies [Doctoral dissertation, Southwest University of Finance and Economics]. DOI:DOI: 10.27412/d.cnki.gxncu.2022.001159

Huang, H., & Liu, J. (2007). Analysis of the Impact of Stock Repurchase Behavior of Listed Companies in China on Stock Prices. *Price Theory and Practice*, 2007(11), 62–63.

Huang, J., & Gong, L. (2012). Analysis of the impact of share repurchase on the financial management of listed companies. *Finance and Accounting Newsletter*, 2012(35), 73–74.

Huang, R., Krishnan, M. M., Shon, J., & Zhou, P. (2017). Who herds? Who doesn't? estimates of analysts' herding propensity in forecasting earnings. *Contemporary Accounting Research*, 34(01), 374–399. DOI: 10.1111/1911-3846.12236

Humayun, K. (2018, March). Did Investors Herd during the Financial Crisis? Evidence from the US Financial Industry. *International Review of Finance*, 18(01), 59–90. DOI: 10.1111/irfi.12140

Hussain, S. M., & Alaya, A. (2024). Investor response to financial news in the digital transformation era: The impact of accounting disclosures and herding behavior as indirect effect. *Journal of Financial Reporting and Accounting*, 22(2), 254–273. DOI: 10.1108/JFRA-05-2023-0287

Igual, M. G., & Santamaría, T. C. (2017). Overconfidence, loss aversion and irrational investor behavior: A conceptual map. *International Journal of Economic Perspectives*, 11(01), 273–290. Retrieved September 08, 2024, from https://www.scopus.com/record/display.uri?eid=2-s2.0-85033437800&origin=scopusAI

Ikenberry, D., & Gertler, M. (1995). Stock repurchases in Canada: Long-run abnormal performance and the impact of firm size. *The Journal of Finance*, 52(2), 113–134.

Ikenberry, D., Lakonishok, J., & Vermaelen, T. (1995). Market underreaction to open market share repurchases. *Journal of Financial Economics*, 39(2), 181–208. DOI: 10.1016/0304-405X(95)00826-Z

Ikenberry, D., Lakonishok, J., & Vermaelen, T. (2000). Stock repurchases in Canada: Performance and strategic trading. *The Journal of Finance*, 55(5), 2373–2397. DOI: 10.1111/0022-1082.00291

Iram, T., Bilal, A. R., Ahmad, Z., & Latif, S. (2022a). Building a Conscientious Personality is Not Sufficient to Manage Behavioral Biases: An Effective Intervention for Financial Literacy in Women Entrepreneurs. *Business Perspectives and Research*. Advance online publication. DOI: 10.1177/22785337221114675

Iram, T., Bilal, A. R., Ahmad, Z., & Latif, S. (2022b). Does Financial Mindfulness Make a Difference? A Nexus of Financial Literacy and Behavioural Biases in Women Entrepreneurs. *IIM Kozhikode Society & Management Review*, 227797522210971. Advance online publication. DOI: 10.1177/22779752221097194

Iriani, N., Agustianti, A., Sucianti, R., Rahman, A., & Putera, W. (2024). Understanding Risk and Uncertainty Management: A Qualitative Inquiry into Developing Business Strategies Amidst Global Economic Shifts, Government Policies, and Market Volatility. *Golden Ratio of Finance Management*, 4(2), 62–77. DOI: 10.52970/grfm.v4i2.444

Jacobson, L. S., LaLonde, R. J., & Sullivan, D. G. (1993). Earnings losses of displaced workers. *The American Economic Review*, 83(4), 685–709.

Jagannathan, R., & Murail, I. (2003). The effects of stock repurchases on investment opportunities: Evidence from corporate cash flow data. *The Journal of Finance*, 58(4), 1619–1643.

Jagannathan, R., & Stephens, C. P. (2000). The Market Valuation of Stock Repurchases by Investment-Quality Firms. *The Journal of Finance*, 55(2), 975–1007.

Jagirdar, S. S., & Gupta, P. K. (2024). *Charting the financial odyssey: a literature review on history and evolution of investment strategies in the stock market (1900–2022)*. China Accounting and Finance Review.

Jalili, M., & Perc, M. (2017, October 01). Information cascades in complex networks. *Journal of Complex Networks*, 05(05), 665–693. DOI: 10.1093/comnet/cnx019

James, C. (2024, Apr 01). *Prospect Theory: What It Is and How It Works, With Examples*. Retrieved Sep 09, 2024, from https://www.investopedia.com: https://www.investopedia.com/terms/p/prospecttheory.asp#:~:text=Prospect%20theory%20was%20first%20introduced,compared%20with%20expected%20utility%20theory

Jarrell, G. A. (1991). The relative signaling power of Dutch auction and fixed-price self-tender offers and open-market share repurchase. *The Journal of Finance*, 46, 1243–1271.

Ji, Q. (2017). Research on the motivation and announcement effect of stock repurchase in listed companies [Doctoral dissertation, Northwest University]. DOI:CNKI:CD-MD:2.1017.104419.

Jia, Y., Liu, L., & Lowry, P. B. (2024, September). How do consumers make behavioural decisions on social commerce platforms? The interaction effect between behaviour visibility and social needs. *Information Systems Journal*, 34(05), 1703–1736. DOI: 10.1111/isj.12508

Kabir, A. I., Vyas, S., Mitra, S., Uddin, M. M., & Jakowan, J. (2024, March). Evaluating the machine learning based momentum stock trading strategies with back-testing: An emerging market perspective. In *AIP Conference Proceedings* (Vol. 2919, No. 1). AIP Publishing.

Kahneman, D., & Tversky, A. (1979). Prospect Theory: An Analysis of Decision under Risk *Econometrica,* vol. 47, no. 2, ss. 263-292.

Kahneman, W., & Tversky, A. (1979). D.# and Tvereky, A. Prospect theory# An analysis of decision under risk^. *Econometrica*, 47(2), 263. DOI: 10.2307/1914185

Kameda, T., & Hastie, R. (2015) Herd Behavior *in Emerging Trends in the Social and Behavioral Sciences.* Edited by Robert Scott John Wiley & Sons, Inc. 1-14.

Kameda, T., & Hastie, R. (2015). Herd behavior. *Emerging Trends in the Social and Behavioral Sciences: An Interdisciplinary, Searchable, and Linkable Resource*, 1–14.

Kameda, T., Toyokawa, W., & Tindale, R. S. (2022). Information aggregation and collective intelligence beyond the wisdom of crowds. *Nature Reviews Psychology*, 1(6), 345–357. DOI: 10.1038/s44159-022-00054-y

Kaminsky, G. L., Reinhart, C. M., & Végh, C. A. (2003). The unholy trinity of financial contagion. *The Journal of Economic Perspectives*, 17(4), 51–74. DOI: 10.1257/089533003772034899

Karanasos, M., Yfanti, S., & Hunter, J. (2022). Emerging stock market volatility and economic fundamentals: The importance of US uncertainty spillovers, financial and health crises. *Annals of Operations Research*, 313(2), 1077–1116. DOI: 10.1007/s10479-021-04042-y PMID: 33903782

Karnatak, U., & Malik, C. (2021). Wednesdays obtain herd immunity? Examining the effect of the day of the week on the NSE sectoral market during COVID-19. *The Investment Analysts Journal*, 50(04), 227–241. DOI: 10.1080/10293523.2021.2010374

Kartini, K., & Nahda, K. (2021). Behavioral Biases on Investment Decision: A Case Study in Indonesia. *Journal of Asian Finance. Economics and Business*, 08(03), 1231–1240. DOI: 10.13106/jafeb.2021.vol8.no3.1231

Kaustia, M., & Knüpfer, S. (2008). Do investors overweight personal experience? Evidence from IPO subscriptions. *The Journal of Finance*, 63(6), 2679–2702. DOI: 10.1111/j.1540-6261.2008.01411.x

Keynes, J. M. (1930). *A treatise on money: In 2 volumes*. Macmillan & Company.

Keynes, J. M. (1937). The general theory of employment. *The Quarterly Journal of Economics*, 51(2), 209–223. DOI: 10.2307/1882087

Khan, A. (2022). Emotions and their impact on investor behaviour (Doctoral dissertation, The University of Waikato).

Khatua, S., & Pradhan, H. (2014, July 01). Indication of Overreaction with or without Stock Specific Public Announcements in Indian Stock market. *Vikalpa*, 39(03), 35–50. DOI: 10.1177/0256090920140303

Kim, H., Park, K., & Song, S. (2016, April 02). Banking Market Size Structure and Financial Stability: Evidence from Eight Asian Countries. *Emerging Markets Finance & Trade*, 52(04), 975–990. DOI: 10.1080/1540496X.2015.1025653

Kim, J.-Y., Haleblian, J., & Finkelstein, S. (2011). When firms are desperate to grow via acquisition: The effect of growth patterns and acquisition experience on acquisition premiums. *Administrative Science Quarterly*, 56(01), 26–60. DOI: 10.2189/asqu.2011.56.1.026

Kim, K. A., & Nofsinger, J. R. (2005). Institutional herding, business groups, and economic regimes: Evidence from Japan J. *The Journal of Business*, 78(1), 213–242. DOI: 10.1086/426524

Kim, K., & Deshmukh, A. (2021). Bandwagon Investment Equilibrium of Investment Timing Games. *The Engineering Economist*, 66(04), 265–278. DOI: 10.1080/0013791X.2020.1829222

Kindleberger, C. P., & Aliber, R. Z. (2011). *Manias, panics and crashes: A history of financial crises*. Palgrave Macmillan.

Klein, A. C. (2013). Time-variations in herding behavior: Evidence from a Markov switching SUR model. *Journal of International Financial Markets, Institutions and Money*, 26(01), 291–304. DOI: 10.1016/j.intfin.2013.06.006

Komalasari, P. T., Asri, M., Purwanto, B. M., & Setiyono, B. (2022). Herding behaviour in the capital market: What do we know and what is next? *Management Review Quarterly*, 72(3), 745–787. DOI: 10.1007/s11301-021-00212-1

Konan, C., & Ikenberry, D. (2014). Economic sources of gain in stock repurchases. *Journal of Financial and Quantitative Analysis*, 39, 461–479.

Koo, E., & Kim, G. (2022). A hybrid prediction model integrating garch models with a distribution manipulation strategy based on lstm networks for stock market volatility. *IEEE Access : Practical Innovations, Open Solutions*, 10, 34743–34754. DOI: 10.1109/ACCESS.2022.3163723

Korn, O., & Rieger, M. O. (2019, June). Hedging with regret. *Journal of Behavioral and Experimental Finance*, 22, 192–205. DOI: 10.1016/j.jbef.2019.03.002

Kumar Kulbhaskar, A., & Subramaniam, S. (2023, September). Breaking news headlines: Impact on trading activity in the cryptocurrency market. *Economic Modelling*, 126, 106397. Advance online publication. DOI: 10.1016/j.econmod.2023.106397

Kumar, A. (2020). Empirical investigation of herding in cryptocurrency market under different market regimes. *Review of Behavioral Finance*, 13(3), 297–308. DOI: 10.1108/RBF-01-2020-0014

Kuran, T., & Sunstein, C. R. (1999). Availability Cascades and Risk Regulation. *Stanford Law Review*, 51(4), 683–768. DOI: 10.2307/1229439

Kurov, A. (2010). Investor sentiment and the stock market's reaction to monetary policy. *Journal of Banking & Finance*, 34(1), 139–149. DOI: 10.1016/j.jbankfin.2009.07.010

Kurt Gümüş, G., Gümüş, Y., & Çimen, A. (2019). Herding behaviour in cryptocurrency market: CSSD and CSAD analysis. In *Contributions to Economics* (Vol. PartF1, pp. 103-114). Springer. DOI: 10.1007/978-3-030-25275-5_6

Kyriazis, N. A. (2020). Herding behavior in digital currency markets: An integrated survey and empirical estimation. *Heliyon*, 6(8), e04752. DOI: 10.1016/j.heliyon.2020.e04752 PMID: 32904208

La Porta, R., Lopez-de-Silanes, F., & Shleifer, A. (2012). Government ownership of banks. *The Journal of Finance*, 57(1), 265–301. DOI: 10.1111/1540-6261.00422

Lacoboni, M. (2009). Imitation, Emphaty, and Mirror Neurons. *Annual Review of Psychology*, 60(1), 653–670. DOI: 10.1146/annurev.psych.60.110707.163604 PMID: 18793090

Lakonishok, J., Shleifer, A., & Vishny, R. W. (2012). The impact of institutional trading on stock prices. *Journal of Financial Economics*, 32(1), 23–43. DOI: 10.1016/0304-405X(92)90023-Q

LaLonde, R. J. (1986). Evaluating the econometric evaluations of training programs with experimental data. *The American Economic Review*, 76(4), 604–620.

Larson, S. J., & Madura, J. (2023, March 31). What drives stock price behavior following extreme one-day returns. *Journal of Financial Research*, 26(01), 113–127. DOI: 10.1111/1475-6803.00048

Lazonick, W. (2014). Profits Without Prosperity. *Harvard Business Review*, 92(9), 46–55.

Lee, C. J., & Andrade, E. B. (2011). Fear, social projection, and financial decision making. *JMR, Journal of Marketing Research*, 48(Special Issue), S121–S129. DOI: 10.1509/jmkr.48.SPL.S121

Leibenstein, H. (1950). Bandwagon, Snob, and Veblen Effects in the Theory of Consumers' Demand. *The Quarterly Journal of Economics*, 64(2), 183–207. DOI: 10.2307/1882692

Li, D., Wang, Y., Madden, A., Ding, Y., Tang, J., Sun, G. G., Zhang, N., & Zhou, E. (2019, September). Analyzing stock market trends using social media user moods and social influence. *Journal of the Association for Information Science and Technology*, 70(09), 1000–1013. DOI: 10.1002/asi.24173

Lin, F.-H., & Liu, Y.-H. (2014). Herding on the social media. *nternational Conferences on ICT, Society and Human Beings 2014, Web Based Communities and Social Media 2014, e-Commerce 2014, Information Systems Post-Implementation and Change Management 2014 and e-Health 2014* (pp. 135-142). Lisbon: IADIS. Retrieved Sep 15, 2024, from https://www.scopus.com/record/display.uri?eid=2-s2.0-84929301510&origin=scopusAI

Lin, M. (2017). Research on factors influencing the short-term market effect of stock repurchase by listed companies in China [Master's thesis, Zhejiang Jiangxi College].

Lin, Z. (2020). Analysis on the Impact of Human Psychological on Economic Irrational Exuberance. *2nd International Conference on Economic Management and Model Engineering, ICEMME 2020* (pp. 871-876). Chongqing: Institute of Electrical and Electronics Engineers Inc. DOI: 10.1109/ICEMME51517.2020.00178

Lippi, A., Rossi, S., & Soana, M. G. (2022, November 03). Status Quo Bias and Risk Tolerance in Asset Allocation Decision-Making. *Journal of Neuroscience, Psychology, and Economics*, 15(04), 195–209. DOI: 10.1037/npe0000166

Li, T., Chen, H., Liu, W., Yu, G., & Yu, Y. (2023, September). Understanding the role of social media sentiment in identifying irrational herding behavior in the stock market. *International Review of Economics & Finance*, 87, 163–179. DOI: 10.1016/j.iref.2023.04.016

Litimi, H., BenSaïda, A., & Bouraoui, O. (2016, Sep 01). Herding and excessive risk in the American stock market: A sectoral analysis. *Research in International Business and Finance, 38*, 06-21. DOI: 10.1016/j.ribaf.2016.03.008

Liu, X., Liu, B., & Han, X. (2019). Analysis of herd effect of investor's behavior from the perspective of behavioral finance. *2019 International Conference on Management, Education Technology and Economics (ICMETE 2019)*, 559–563. DOI: 10.2991/icmete-19.2019.133

Liu, Y. (2019). Analysis of financial and market effects of share repurchase in Chinese A-share market. *China Development*, 2019(02), 32–35.

Liu, Y., Kim, C. Y., Lee, E. H., & Yoo, J. W. (2022). Relationship between sustainable management activities and financial performance: Mediating effects of non-financial performance and moderating effects of institutional environment. *Sustainability (Basel)*, 14(3), 1168. DOI: 10.3390/su14031168

Liu, Y.-Y., Nacher, J. C., Ochiai, T., Martino, M., & Altshuler, Y. (2014, October 15). Prospect theory for online financial trading. *PLoS One*, 09(10), e109458. Advance online publication. DOI: 10.1371/journal.pone.0109458 PMID: 25330203

Li, W., Rhee, G., & Wang, S. S. (2017). Differences in herding: Individual vs. Institutional investors. *Pacific-Basin Finance Journal*, 45, 174–185. DOI: 10.1016/j.pacfin.2016.11.005

Lo, A. W. (2012). *Adaptive markets: Financial evolution at the speed of thought*. Princeton University Press.

Lo, A. W., & Zhang, R. (2024). *The Adaptive Markets Hypothesis: An Evolutionary Approach to Understanding Financial System Dynamics*. Oxford University Press. DOI: 10.1093/oso/9780199681143.001.0001

Loang, O. K. (2022, April). Overreaction, Investor Sentiment and Market Sentiment of COVID-19. *Vision (Basel)*, 09722629221087386. Advance online publication. DOI: 10.1177/09722629221087386

Loang, O. K., & Ahmad, Z. (2023). Empirical analysis of global markets herding on COVID-19 effect. *Vision (Basel)*, ●●●, 09722629221146653. DOI: 10.1177/09722629221146653

Loang, O. K., & Ahmad, Z. (2024). Does volatility cause herding in Malaysian stock market? Evidence from quantile regression analysis. *Millennial Asia*, 15(2), 197–215. DOI: 10.1177/09763996221101217

LONG. S. C. (2024). Do Emotions Matter? (Doctoral dissertation, University of Dublin).

Lovric, M., Kaymak, U., & Spronk, J. (2008). *A conceptual model of investor behavior.*

Lu, S., Li, S., Zhou, W., & Yang, W. (2022). Network herding of energy funds in the post-Carbon-Peak Policy era: Does it benefit profitability and stability? *Energy Economics*, 109, 105948. DOI: 10.1016/j.eneco.2022.105948

Lusardi, A. (2019). Financial literacy and the need for financial education: Evidence and implications. *Swiss Journal of Economics and Statistics*, 155(1), 1. DOI: 10.1186/s41937-019-0027-5

Lusardi, A., & Mitchell, O. S. (2014). The economic importance of financial literacy: Theory and evidence. *Journal of Economic Literature*, 52(1), 5–44. DOI: 10.1257/jel.52.1.5 PMID: 28579637

Ma, M. (2008). Research on stock repurchase of listed companies in China [Doctoral dissertation, Tianjin University].

Mackie, D. M., & Smith, E. R. (2017, September 01). Group-based emotion in group processes and intergroup relations. *Group Processes & Intergroup Relations*, 20(05), 568–668. DOI: 10.1177/1368430217702725

Madaan, V., & Shrivastava, M. (2022). Sectoral herding behaviour in the Indian financial market. *Global Business and Economics Review*, 26(02), 185–213. DOI: 10.1504/GBER.2022.121011

Malla, J., & Lavanya, C., J., J., & J., V. (2023). Bidirectional Gated Recurrent Unit (BiGRU)-Based Bitcoin Price Prediction by News Sentiment Analysis. *35th International Conference on Soft Computing and Signal Processing, ICSCSP 2022.* 313, pp. 31-40. Hyderabad: Springer Science and Business Media Deutschland GmbH. DOI: 10.1007/978-981-19-8669-7_4

Malmberg, T. (2023, June 01). Media studies, le Bon's psychology of crowds, and qualitative-normative research on propaganda, 1880-2020. *Nordic Journal of Media Studies*, 05(01), 17–31. DOI: 10.2478/njms-2023-0002

Manahov, V. (2024). The great crypto crash in September 2018: Why did the cryptocurrency market collapse? *Annals of Operations Research*, 332(1), 579–616. DOI: 10.1007/s10479-023-05575-0

Mancini, A., Di Clemente, R., & Cimini, G. (2022, December). Self-induced consensus of Reddit users to characterise the GameStop short squeeze. *Scientific Reports*, 12(01), 13780. Advance online publication. DOI: 10.1038/s41598-022-17925-2 PMID: 35962174

Mangat, M., Reschenhofer, E., Stark, T., & Zwatz, C. (2022). High-Frequency Trading with Machine Learning Algorithms and Limit Order Book Data. *Data Science in Finance and Economics*, 2(4), 437–463. DOI: 10.3934/DSFE.2022022

Markowitz, H. M. (1959). *Portfolio Selection Efficient diversification of Investment*.

Mats, V. (2024). HEDGE PERFORMANCE OF DIFFERENT ASSET CLASSES IN VARYING ECONOMIC CONDITIONS. *Radioelectronic and Computer Systems*, 2024(1(109)), 217–234. DOI: 10.32620/reks.2024.1.17

May, J., & Kumar, V. (2023). Harnessing moral psychology to reduce meat consumption. *Journal of the American Philosophical Association*, 9(2), 367–387. DOI: 10.1017/apa.2022.2

McClure, J. E., & Thomas, D. C. (2017, August 01). Explaining the timing of tulipmania's boom and bust: Historical context, sequestered capital and market signals. *Financial History Review*, 24(02), 121–141. DOI: 10.1017/S0968565017000154

Menkhoff, L. (2002). Institutional investors: The external costs of a successful innovation. *Journal of Economic Issues*, 36(4), 907–933. DOI: 10.1080/00213624.2002.11506529

Menkveld, A. J. (2013). High frequency trading and the new-market makers. *Journal of Financial Markets*, 16(4), 712–740. DOI: 10.1016/j.finmar.2013.06.006

Merli, M., & Roger, T. (2013). What drives the herding behavior of individual investors? *Finance*, 34(3), 67–104. DOI: 10.3917/fina.343.0067

Miao, J. (2015). Implementation of share repurchase by listed companies to revitalize the confidence of China's capital market. *Economic Research Guide*, 2015(12), 114–118.

Michailova, J., & Schmidt, U. (2016, July 02). Overconfidence and Bubbles in Experimental Asset Markets. *Journal of Behavioral Finance*, 17(03), 280–292. DOI: 10.1080/15427560.2016.1203325

Mindful Spending: The Happy Way to Financial Freedom. (n.d.). https://www.simplemindfulness.com/mindful-spending-the-happy-way-to-financial-freedom/

Mirrlees, J. A. (1976). The Optimal Structure of Incentives and Authority Within an Organization. *The Bell Journal of Economics*, 7(1), 105–131. DOI: 10.2307/3003192

Mitchell, J. D., & Dharmawan, G. V. (2007). Incentives for on-market buy-backs: Evidence from a transparent buy-back regime. *Journal of Corporate Finance*, 13(1), 146–169. DOI: 10.1016/j.jcorpfin.2006.12.002

Morris, J. J., & Alam, P. (2012, May). Value relevance and the dot-com bubble of the 1990s. *The Quarterly Review of Economics and Finance*, 52(02), 243–255. DOI: 10.1016/j.qref.2012.04.001

Morris, J. J., & Alam, P. Analysis of the Dot-Com Bubble of the 1990s (June 27, 2008). Available at *SSRN*: https://ssrn.com/abstract=1152412 or http://dx.doi.org/ DOI: 10.2139/ssrn.1152412

Mo, S. Y., Liu, A., & Yang, S. Y. (2016, June 01). News sentiment to market impact and its feedback effect. *Environment Systems & Decisions*, 36(02), 158–166. DOI: 10.1007/s10669-016-9590-9

Münster, M., Reichenbach, F., & Walther, M. (2024, July 09). Robinhood, Reddit, and the news: The impact of traditional and social media on retail investor trading. *Journal of Financial Markets*, 100929. Advance online publication. DOI: 10.1016/j. finmar.2024.100929

Murphy, J. Austin, An Analysis of the Financial Crisis of 2008: Causes and Solutions (November 4, 2008). Available at *SSRN*: https://ssrn.com/abstract=1295344 or http://dx.doi.org/DOI: 10.2139/ssrn.1295344

Musnadi, S., Faisal, , & Majid, M. S. A. (2018, November 05). Overreaction and underreaction anomalies in the Indonesian stock market: A sectoral analysis. *International Journal of Ethics and Systems*, 34(04), 442–457. DOI: 10.1108/IJOES-12-2017-0235

Myklebust, T. (2021, Jan 01). High-frequency trading - regulatory and supervisory challenges in the pursuit of orderly markets. In *Routledge Handbook of Financial Technology and Law* (pp. 381–403). Taylor and Francis., DOI: 10.4324/9780429325670-21

Nasraoui, M., Ajina, A., & Kahloul, A. (2024). The influence of economic policy uncertainty on stock market liquidity? The mediating role of investor sentiment. *The Journal of Risk Finance*, 25(4), 664–683. DOI: 10.1108/JRF-06-2023-0129

Ncube, M., Sibanda, M., & Matenda, F. R. (2024). Application of Explainable Artificial Intelligence to model the influence of firm-specific factors on stock performance in sub-Saharan Africa during. *COVID*, ●●●, 19.

Netter, J. M., & Mitchell, M. L. (1989). Stock Repurchases: An Analysis of Returns to Bondholders and Stockholders. *Journal of Financial Economics*, 23(1), 161–181.

Nevins, D. (2004). Goals-based investing: Integrating traditional and behavioral finance. *The Journal of Wealth Management*, 6(4), 8–23. DOI: 10.3905/jwm.2004.391053

Ng, S. H., Zhuang, Z., Toh, M. Y., Ong, T. S., & Teh, B. H. (2022). Exploring herding behavior in an innovative-oriented stock market: Evidence from ChiNext. *Journal of Applied Econometrics*, 25(1), 523–542.

Nguyen, O. D. Y., Lee, J., Ngo, L. V., & Quan, T. H. M. (2022). Impacts of crisis emotions on negative word-of-mouth and behavioural intention: Evidence from a milk crisis. *Journal of Product and Brand Management*, 31(4), 536–550. DOI: 10.1108/JPBM-05-2020-2901

Nia, V. M., Siregar, H., Sembel, R., & Zulbainarmi, N. (2024). Behavioral Finance in Psycho-Social Approaches: A Literature Review. In *International Conference on Business and Technology* (pp. 311-329). Springer, Cham. DOI: 10.1007/978-3-031-53998-5_27

Ni, Y. (2024). Navigating Energy and Financial Markets: A Review of Technical Analysis Used and Further Investigation from Various Perspectives. *Energies*, 17(12), 2942. DOI: 10.3390/en17122942

Njegovanović, A. (2018). Artificial Intelligence: Financial Trading and Neurology of Decision. *Financial Markets. Institutions and Risks*, 2, 58–68.

Nofsinger, J. R., & Sias, R. W. (1999). Herding and feedback trading by institutional and individual investors. *The Journal of Finance*, 54(6), 2263–2295. DOI: 10.1111/0022-1082.00188

O'Hara, M. (2015). High frequency market microstructure. *Journal of Financial Economics*, 116(2), 257–270. DOI: 10.1016/j.jfineco.2015.01.003

Ofer, A. R., & Thakor, A. V. (1987). A Theory of Stock Price Responses to Alternative Corporate Cash Disbursement Methods: Stock Repurchases and Dividends. *The Journal of Finance*, 42(2), 365–394. DOI: 10.1111/j.1540-6261.1987.tb02572.x

Okur, M., & Gurbuz, A. O. (2015). A competitive approach to financial issues: Modern finance theory. In *Banking, Finance, and Accounting: Concepts, Methodologies, Tools, and Applications* (Vols. 1-3, pp. 385-398). IGI Global. DOI: 10.4018/978-1-4666-6268-1.ch019

Omane-Adjepong, M., Alagidede, I. P., Lyimo, A. G., & Tweneboah, G. (2021). Herding behavior in cryptocurrency and emerging financial markets. *Cogent Economics & Finance*, 9(1), 1933681. DOI: 10.1080/23322039.2021.1933681

Omar, N. A., Nazri, M. A., Ali, M. H., & Alam, S. S. (2021, September). The panic buying behavior of consumers during the COVID-19 pandemic: Examining the influences of uncertainty, perceptions of severity, perceptions of scarcity, and anxiety. *Journal of Retailing and Consumer Services*, 62, 102600. Advance online publication. DOI: 10.1016/j.jretconser.2021.102600

Ospina, J., & Uhling, H. (2018) Mortgage-Backed Securities and the Financial Crisis of 2008: a Post Mortem, NBER Working Paper, 24509

Ostrowska, M. (2021). Transparency in Insurance Regulation and Supervisory Law of Poland. *AIDA Europe Research Series on Insurance Law and Regulation*, 04, 213–230. DOI: 10.1007/978-3-030-63621-0_9

Othman, N. N. (2024). Mind Games in the Market: Unraveling the Impact of Psychological Biases on Your Stock Portfolio. *Available atSSRN* 4844961. DOI: 10.2139/ssrn.4844961

Pagano, M. (2014). The evolution of trading systems: Liquidity and anonymity. *The Quarterly Journal of Economics*, 102(2), 255–274. DOI: 10.2307/2937847

Pallier, G., Wilkinson, R., Danthiir, V., Kleitman, S., Knezevic, G., Stankov, L., & Roberts, R. D. (2002). The Role of Individual Differences in The Accuracy of Confidence Judgments. *The Journal of General Psychology*, 129(3), 257–299. DOI: 10.1080/00221300209602099 PMID: 12224810

Pan, W., Altshuler, Y., & Pentland, A. (2012). Decoding social influence and the wisdom of the crowd in financial trading network. *2012 ASE/IEEE International Conference on Social Computing, SocialCom 2012 and the 2012 ASE/IEEE International Conference on Privacy, Security, Risk and Trust, PASSAT 2012* (pp. 203-209). Academy of Science and Engineering (ASE)IEEE Computer Society. DOI: 10.1109/SocialCom-PASSAT.2012.133

Panditharathne, P. N. K. W., & Chen, Z. (2021). An integrative review on the research progress of mindfulness and its implications at the workplace. *Sustainability (Basel)*, 13(24), 1–27. DOI: 10.3390/su132413852

Park, A., & Sabourian, H. (2011, July). Herding and contrarian behavior in financial markets. *Econometrica*, 79(04), 973–1026. DOI: 10.3982/ECTA8602

Parker, W. D., & Prechter, R. R. (2005). Herding: An interdisciplinary integrative review from a socionomic perspective. *Available atSSRN* 2009898. DOI: 10.2139/ssrn.2009898

Parveen, S., Satti, Z. W., Subhan, Q. A., & Jamil, S. (2020, September). Exploring market overreaction, investors' sentiments and investment decisions in an emerging stock market. *Borsa Istanbul Review*, 20(03), 224–235. DOI: 10.1016/j.bir.2020.02.002

Pastor, L., & Veronesi, P. (2012). Uncertainty about government policy and stock prices. *The Journal of Finance*, 67(4), 1219–1264. DOI: 10.1111/j.1540-6261.2012.01746.x

Pathak, D. D., & Thapa, B. S. (2024). Beyond market anomalies: How heuristics and perceived efficiency shape investor behavior in developing markets. *Investment Management and Financial Innovations, 21*(03), 01-12. DOI: 10.21511/imfi.21(3).2024.01

Pepitone, A. (1976). Toward a normative and comparative biocultural social psychology. *Journal of Personality and Social Psychology*, 34(4), 641–653. DOI: 10.1037/0022-3514.34.4.641

Pereira, M. C., & Coelho, F. (2019). Mindfulness, Money Attitudes, and Credit. *The Journal of Consumer Affairs*, 53(2), 424–454. DOI: 10.1111/joca.12197

Peress, J. (2014). The media and the diffusion of information in financial markets: Evidence from newspaper strikes. *The Journal of Finance*, 69(5), 2007–2043. DOI: 10.1111/jofi.12179

Persakis, A., & Koutoupis, A. (2024). Synchronicity and Sentiment: Decoding Earnings Quality and Market Returns in EU under Economic Policy Uncertainty. *Journal of Behavioral Finance*, ●●●, 1–21. DOI: 10.1080/15427560.2024.2345342

Phan, T. C., Rieger, M. O., & Wang, M. (2018). What leads to overtrading and under-diversification? Survey evidence from retail investors in an emerging market. *Journal of Behavioral and Experimental Finance*, 19, 39–55. DOI: 10.1016/j.jbef.2018.04.001

Phillips, P. J., & Pohl, G. (2021). Disinformation Cascades, Espionage & Counter-Intelligence. *International Journal of Intelligence, Security, and Public Affairs*, 23(01), 34–47. DOI: 10.1080/23800992.2020.1834311

Pikulina, E., Renneboog, L., & And Tobler, P. N. (2017). Overconfidence and Investment: An Experimental Approach. *Journal of Corporate Finance*, 43, 175–192. DOI: 10.1016/j.jcorpfin.2017.01.002

Pitthan, F., & De Witte, K. (2023). *How Learning About Behavioural Biases Can Improve Financial Literacy? Experimental Evidence on the Effects of Learning About the Myopic Bias.* Experimental Evidence on the Effects of Learning About the Myopic Bias. DOI: 10.2139/ssrn.4555344

Popescu, M., & Xu, Z. (2014). Does reputation contribute to institutional herding? *Journal of Financial Research*, 37(03), 295–322. DOI: 10.1111/jfir.12038

Pouget, S., Sauvagnat, J., & Villeneuve, S. (2017, June 01). A mind is a terrible thing to change: Confirmatory bias in financial markets. *Review of Financial Studies*, 30(06), 2066–2109. DOI: 10.1093/rfs/hhw100

Putri, A., & Tanno, A. (2024). Exploring Market Dynamics: A Qualitative Study on Asset Price Behavior, Market Efficiency, and Information Role in Investment Decisions in the Capital Market. Atestasi. *Jurnal Ilmiah Akuntansi*, 7(2), 810–827.

Qayyum, A., Rashid, R., Usman, P. M., Bilal, R., & Mehmood, O. (2024). Institutional Investor Behavior: A Comprehensive Study at the Pakistan Stock Exchange. Bahria University Journal Of Management & Technology, 7(1).

Qian, Y. (1995). Analysis of the long-term impact of stock repurchases on excess return. *Financial Research*, 45(3), 68–79.

Qi, X. Z., Ning, Z., & Qin, M. (2022). Economic policy uncertainty, investor sentiment and financial stability—An empirical study based on the time varying parameter-vector autoregression model. *Journal of Economic Interaction and Coordination*, 17(3), 779–799. DOI: 10.1007/s11403-021-00342-5 PMID: 34976227

Raafat, R. M., Chater, N., & Frith, C. (2009). Herding in Humans. *Trends in Cognitive Sciences*, 13(10), 420–428. DOI: 10.1016/j.tics.2009.08.002 PMID: 19748818

Rabin, M. (1998). Psychology and Economics. *Journal of Economic Literature*, 36(1), 11–46.

Raja, E. L., & MESSAOUDI, A. (2024). Behavioral biases influencing investment decision making in emergent markets: A systematic literature review. *International Journal of Accounting, Finance, Auditing. Management and Economics*, 5(6), 18–39.

Ramachandran, V.S. (2000) Mirror Neurons and Imitation Learning as the Driving Force Behind 'the Great Leap Forward' in Human Evolution, *Edge*, No. 69

Rao, A. S., & Lakkol, S. G. (2024). Influence of personality, biases on financial risk tolerance among retail investors in India. *Investment Management and Financial Innovations*, 21(03), 248–264. DOI: 10.21511/imfi.21(3).2024.21

Razi, M. A., Tarn, J. M., & Siddiqui, F. A. (2024). Exploring the failure and success of DotComs. *Information Management & Computer Security*, 12(03), 228–244. DOI: 10.1108/09685220410542598

Reb, J. (2008, March). Regret aversion and decision process quality: Effects of regret salience on decision process carefulness. *Organizational Behavior and Human Decision Processes*, 105(2), 169–182. DOI: 10.1016/j.obhdp.2007.08.006

Reddy Yarram, S. (2014). Factors influencing on-market share repurchase decisions in Australia. *Studies in Economics and Finance*, 31(3), 255–271. DOI: 10.1108/SEF-02-2013-0021

Ren, H., Zhao, X., & Li, Y. (2023). Share repurchases and capital market pricing bias—Empirical evidence based on listed companies. *Scientific Decision Making*, 2023(09), 77–95.

Riaz, S., Khan, H. H., Sarwar, B., Ahmed, W., Muhammad, N., Reza, S., & Ul Haq, S. M. N. (2022). Influence of Financial Social Agents and Attitude Toward Money on Financial Literacy: The Mediating Role of Financial Self-Efficacy and Moderating Role of Mindfulness. *SAGE Open*, 12(3), 21582440221117140. Advance online publication. DOI: 10.1177/21582440221117140

Rigana, K. (2023). Financial network analysis.

Rizzolatti, G., & Craighero, L. (2004). The Mirror-Neuron System. *Annual Review of Neuroscience*, 27(1), 169–192. DOI: 10.1146/annurev.neuro.27.070203.144230 PMID: 15217330

Rizzolatti, G., & Fabbri-Destro, M. (2008). The Mirror System and Its Role in Social Cognition. *Current Opinion in Neurobiology*, 18(2), 179–184. DOI: 10.1016/j.conb.2008.08.001 PMID: 18706501

Rizzolatti, G., Fabbri-Destro, M., & And Cattaneo, L. (2009). Mirror neurons and their clinical relevance. *Nature Clinical Practice. Neurology*, 5(1), 24–34. DOI: 10.1038/ncpneuro0990 PMID: 19129788

Rizzolatti, G., Fadiga, L., Fogassi, L., & Gallese, V. (1996). Premotor Cortex and the Recognition of Motor Actions. *Brain Research. Cognitive Brain Research*, 3(2), 131–141. DOI: 10.1016/0926-6410(95)00038-0 PMID: 8713554

Robin, R., & Angelina, V. (2020). Analysis of The Impact of Anchoring, Herding Bias. *Overconfidence and Ethical Consideration Towards Investment Decision JIMFE*, 6(2), 253–264.

Roider, A., & Voskort, A. (2016). Reputational herding in financial markets: A laboratory experiment. *Journal of Behavioral Finance*, 17(3), 244–266. DOI: 10.1080/15427560.2016.1203322

Rook, L. (2006). An economic psychological approach to herd behavior. *Journal of Economic Issues*, 40(1), 75–95. DOI: 10.1080/00213624.2006.11506883

Rout, R. K., & Das, N. (2015, January 01). Behavioral prospects of individual investor decision making process: A review. *Indian Journal of Finance*, 09(04), 43–55. Retrieved September 05, 2024, from https://www.scopus.com/record/display.uri ?eid=2-s2.0-84928011331&origin=scopusAI

Rubbaniy, G., Polyzos, S., Rizvi, S. K., & Tessema, A. (2021, October). COVID-19, Lockdowns and herding towards a cryptocurrency market-specific implied volatility index. *Economics Letters*, 207, 110017. Advance online publication. DOI: 10.1016/j.econlet.2021.110017

Sabir, S. A., Mohammad, H. B., & Kadir Shahar, H. B. (2018). The effect of illusion of control and self attribution on herding behaviour with a moderating role of information availability: A case of retail investors of pakistan stock exchange. *Opción*, 34(86), 2675–2689. Retrieved September 05, 2024, from https://www.scopus.com/record/display.uri?eid=2-s2.0-85064105170&origin=scopusAI

Said, B., Rehman, S. U., Ullah, R., & Khan, J. (2021). Investor overreaction and global financial crisis: A case of Pakistan stock exchange. *Cogent Economics & Finance*, 09(01), 1966195. Advance online publication. DOI: 10.1080/23322039.2021.1966195

Saltık, Ö. (2024). Navigating the Stock Market: Modeling Wealth Exchange and Network Interaction with Loss Aversion, Disposition Effect and Anchoring and Adjustment Bias. *Ekonomi Politika ve Finans Araştırmaları Dergisi*, 9(1), 88–122. DOI: 10.30784/epfad.1435009

Saltik, O., Jalil, F., & Degirmen, S. (2024). Viral decisions: Unmasking the impact of COVID-19 info and behavioral quirks on investment choices. *Humanities & Social Sciences Communications*, 11(1), 1–20.

Salunkhe, U., Rajan, B., & Kumar, V. (2023). Understanding firm survival in a global crisis. *International Marketing Review*, 40(5), 829–868. DOI: 10.1108/IMR-05-2021-0175

Sanders, A. (2008). The subprime crisis and its role in the financial crisis. *Journal of Housing Economics*, 17(4), 254–261. DOI: 10.1016/j.jhe.2008.10.001

Sarin, A. B., & Chowdhury, J. K. (2018). Overconfidence & emotional bias in investment decision performance. *ZENITH International Journal of Multidisciplinary Research*, 8(11), 320–330.

Sathya, N., & Gayathiri, R. (2024, June 17). Behavioral Biases in Investment Decisions: An Extensive Literature Review and Pathways for Future Research. *Journal of Information and Organizational Sciences*, 48(01), 117–121. DOI: 10.31341/jios.48.1.6

Sathya, N., & Prabhavathi, C. (2024, March). The influence of social media on investment decision-making: Examining behavioral biases, risk perception, and mediation effects. *International Journal of System Assurance Engineering and Management*, 15(03), 957–963. DOI: 10.1007/s13198-023-02182-x

Schaller, K. D. (2022). Board Governance in Crisis: Director Influence in Executive Crisis Leadership (Doctoral dissertation, Pepperdine University).

Scharfstein, D. S., & Stein, J. C. (1990). Herd behavior and investment. *The American Economic Review*, ●●●, 465–479.

Schmeling, M. (2009). Investor sentiment and stock returns: Some international evidence. *Journal of Empirical Finance*, 16(3), 394–408. DOI: 10.1016/j.jempfin.2009.01.002

Schomburgk, L., & Hoffmann, A. (2023). How mindfulness reduces BNPL usage and how that relates to overall well-being. *European Journal of Marketing*, 57(2), 325–359. DOI: 10.1108/EJM-11-2021-0923

Schulmerich, M., Leporcher, Y.-M., & Eu, C.-H. (2015). Stock Market Crashes. In *Management for Professionals* (Vol. F415, pp. 245–354). Springer Nature., DOI: 10.1007/978-3-642-55444-5_4

Sembiring, F. M., Rahman, S., Effendi, N., & Sudarsono, R. (2016). Capital asset pricing model in market overreaction conditions: Evidence from Indonesia stock exchange. *Polish Journal of Management Studies*, 14(02), 182–191. DOI: 10.17512/pjms.2016.14.2.17

Serowik, K. L., Bellamy, C. D., Rowe, M., & Rosen, M. I. (2013). Subjective experiences of clients in a voluntary money management program. *American Journal of Psychiatric Rehabilitation*, 16(2), 136–153. DOI: 10.1080/15487768.2013.789699 PMID: 24605071

Shao, Z. (2020). Research on the market effect of stock buyback of listed companies in China and its influencing factors. *Times Finance*, 2020, 93–96.

Shapiro, B., & Matson, D. (2008). Strategies of resistance to internal control regulation. *Accounting, Organizations and Society*, 33(2), 199–228. DOI: 10.1016/j.aos.2007.04.002

Sharma, S. (2024, February 14). *Incorporating Mindfulness into Financial Planning*. https://www.fincart.com/blog/incorporating-mindfulness-into-financial-planning/

Shefrin, H. (2001). Behavioral corporate finance. *The Bank of America Journal of Applied Corporate Finance*, 14(3), 113–126. DOI: 10.1111/j.1745-6622.2001.tb00443.x

Sherif, M. (1936). *The psychology of social norms*. Harper.

Shiller, J. R. (2017) Narrative Economics *NBER Working Paper Series* no. 23075

Shiller, R. J. (2015). *Irrational exuberance: Revised and expanded third edition*. Princeton University Press. Retrieved Sep 15, 2024, from https://www.scopus.com/record/display.uri?eid=2-s2.0-84977120410&origin=scopusAI

Shiller, R. J. (1995). Conversation, information, and herd behavior. *The American Economic Review*, 85(2), 181–185.

Shiller, R. J. (2000). *Irrational exuberance*. Princeton University Press.

Shiller, R. J. (2002). Bubbles, human judgment, and expert opinion. *Financial Analysts Journal*, 58(3), 18–26. DOI: 10.2469/faj.v58.n3.2535

Shiller, R. J. (2014). Speculative asset prices. *The American Economic Review*, 104(6), 1486–1517. DOI: 10.1257/aer.104.6.1486

Shimokawa, T., Kinoshita, K., Miyagawa, K., & Misawa, T. (2012, December). A brain information-aided intelligent investment system. *Decision Support Systems*, 54(01), 336–344. DOI: 10.1016/j.dss.2012.05.041

Shou, D., & Sun, E. (2000). Current situation of domestic and international stock repurchases and implications. *Economic Issues*, 2000(11), 70–73.

Shukla, A., Dadhich, M., & Dipesh Vaya, A. G. (2024). Impact of Behavioral Biases on Investors' Stock Trading Decisions: A Comparehensive Quantitative Analysis. *Indian Journal of Science and Technology*, 17(8), 670–678. DOI: 10.17485/IJST/v17i8.2845

Sias, R. W. (2004). Institutional herding. *Review of Financial Studies*, 17(1), 165–206. DOI: 10.1093/rfs/hhg035

Silver, S. D. (2024). Agent expectations and news sentiment in the dynamics of price in a financial market. *Review of Behavioral Finance*, 16(5), 836–859. DOI: 10.1108/RBF-09-2023-0237

Simon, H. (1957). A behavioral model of rational choice. *Models of Man. Social and Rational: Mathematical Essays on Rational Human Behavior in a Social Setting*, 6(1), 241–260.

Simon, H. A. (1957). *Models of Man, Social and Rational: Mathematical Essays on Rational Human Behavior in a Social Setting*. John Wiley and Sons.

Simon, H. A. (1990). A mechanism for social selection and successful altruism. *Science*, 250(4988), 1665–1668. DOI: 10.1126/science.2270480 PMID: 2270480

Singh, B. (2023). Blockchain Technology in Renovating Healthcare: Legal and Future Perspectives. In Kaushik, K., Dahiya, S., Aggarwal, S., & Dwivedi, A. (Eds.), *Revolutionizing Healthcare Through Artificial Intelligence and Internet of Things Applications* (pp. 177–186). IGI Global., DOI: 10.4018/978-1-6684-5422-0.ch012

Singh, B. (2024). Evolutionary Global Neuroscience for Cognition and Brain Health: Strengthening Innovation in Brain Science. In Prabhakar, P. (Ed.), *Biomedical Research Developments for Improved Healthcare* (pp. 246–272). IGI Global., DOI: 10.4018/979-8-3693-1922-2.ch012

Singh, B. (2024). Lensing Legal Dynamics for Examining Responsibility and Deliberation of Generative AI-Tethered Technological Privacy Concerns: Infringements and Use of Personal Data by Nefarious Actors. In Ara, A., & Ara, A. (Eds.), *Exploring the Ethical Implications of Generative AI* (pp. 146–167). IGI Global., DOI: 10.4018/979-8-3693-1565-1.ch009

Singh, B. (2024). Social Cognition of Incarcerated Women and Children: Addressing Exposure to Infectious Diseases and Legal Outcomes. In Reddy, K. (Ed.), *Principles and Clinical Interventions in Social Cognition* (pp. 236–251). IGI Global., DOI: 10.4018/979-8-3693-1265-0.ch014

Singh, B., Dutta, P. K., & Kaunert, C. (2024). Replenish Artificial Intelligence in Renewable Energy for Sustainable Development: Lensing SDG 7 Affordable and Clean Energy and SDG 13 Climate Actions With Legal-Financial Advisory. In Derbali, A. (Ed.), *Social and Ethical Implications of AI in Finance for Sustainability* (pp. 198–227). IGI Global., DOI: 10.4018/979-8-3693-2881-1.ch009

Singh, B., Jain, V., Kaunert, C., Dutta, P. K., & Singh, G. (2024). Privacy Matters: Espousing Blockchain and Artificial Intelligence (AI) for Consumer Data Protection on E-Commerce Platforms in Ethical Marketing. In Saluja, S., Nayyar, V., Rojhe, K., & Sharma, S. (Eds.), *Ethical Marketing Through Data Governance Standards and Effective Technology* (pp. 167–184). IGI Global., DOI: 10.4018/979-8-3693-2215-4.ch015

Singh, B., & Kaunert, C. (2024). Aroma of Highly Smart Internet of Medical Things (IoMT) and Lightweight Edge Trust Expansion Medical Care Facilities for Electronic Healthcare Systems: Fortified-Chain Architecture for Remote Patient Monitoring and Privacy Protection Beyond Imagination. In Hassan, A., Bhattacharya, P., Tikadar, S., Dutta, P., & Sagayam, M. (Eds.), *Lightweight Digital Trust Architectures in the Internet of Medical Things (IoMT)* (pp. 196–212). IGI Global., DOI: 10.4018/979-8-3693-2109-6.ch011

Singh, B., & Kaunert, C. (2024). Augmented Reality and Virtual Reality Modules for Mindfulness: Boosting Emotional Intelligence and Mental Wellness. In Hiran, K., Doshi, R., & Patel, M. (Eds.), *Applications of Virtual and Augmented Reality for Health and Wellbeing* (pp. 111–128). IGI Global., DOI: 10.4018/979-8-3693-1123-3.ch007

Singh, B., & Kaunert, C. (2024). Computational Thinking for Innovative Solutions and Problem-Solving Techniques: Transforming Conventional Education to Futuristic Interdisciplinary Higher Education. In Fonkam, M., & Vajjhala, N. (Eds.), *Revolutionizing Curricula Through Computational Thinking, Logic, and Problem Solving* (pp. 60–82). IGI Global., DOI: 10.4018/979-8-3693-1974-1.ch004

Singh, B., & Kaunert, C. (2024). Harnessing Sustainable Agriculture Through Climate-Smart Technologies: Artificial Intelligence for Climate Preservation and Futuristic Trends. In Kannan, H., Rodriguez, R., Paprika, Z., & Ade-Ibijola, A. (Eds.), *Exploring Ethical Dimensions of Environmental Sustainability and Use of AI* (pp. 214–239). IGI Global., DOI: 10.4018/979-8-3693-0892-9.ch011

Singh, B., & Kaunert, C. (2024). Revealing Green Finance Mobilization: Harnessing FinTech and Blockchain Innovations to Surmount Barriers and Foster New Investment Avenues. In Jafar, S., Rodriguez, R., Kannan, H., Akhtar, S., & Plugmann, P. (Eds.), *Harnessing Blockchain-Digital Twin Fusion for Sustainable Investments* (pp. 265–286). IGI Global., DOI: 10.4018/979-8-3693-1878-2.ch011

Singh, B., & Kaunert, C. (2024). Salvaging Responsible Consumption and Production of Food in the Hospitality Industry: Harnessing Machine Learning and Deep Learning for Zero Food Waste. In Singh, A., Tyagi, P., & Garg, A. (Eds.), *Sustainable Disposal Methods of Food Wastes in Hospitality Operations* (pp. 176–192). IGI Global., DOI: 10.4018/979-8-3693-2181-2.ch012

Singh, B., & Kaunert, C. (2024). Wind and Solar Energy as Renewable Energy for Sustainable Global Future: Projecting Future Multi-Sector Sustainable Policies and Innovation. In Ara, A., & Thakore, R. (Eds.), *Promoting Multi-Sector Sustainability With Policy and Innovation* (pp. 210–245). IGI Global., DOI: 10.4018/979-8-3693-2113-3.ch009

Singh, B., & Kaunert, C. Reinventing Artificial Intelligence and Blockchain for Preserving Medical Data. In *Ethical Artificial Intelligence in Power Electronics* (pp. 77–91). CRC Press. DOI: 10.1201/9781032648323-6

Singh, B., Vig, K., Dutta, P. K., & Kaunert, C. (2024). Unraveling Agile Transformation for Customer Satisfaction in Changing Market Conditions: Roadmap for Industry Embracing Change in Project Management. In Misra, S., Jadeja, R., & Mittal, M. (Eds.), *Practical Approaches to Agile Project Management* (pp. 305–321). IGI Global., DOI: 10.4018/979-8-3693-3318-1.ch017

Singh, D., Malik, G., Jain, P., & Abouraia, M. (2024). A systematic review and research agenda on the causes and consequences of financial overconfidence. *Cogent Economics & Finance*, 12(1), 2348543. DOI: 10.1080/23322039.2024.2348543

Singh, L. G., & Kumar, K. (2024). The herding behavior of investors in the Indian financial market: An insight into the influence of social media. In *Handbook of Research on Innovative Approaches to Information Technology in Library and Information Science* (pp. 82–102). IGI Global., DOI: 10.4018/979-8-3693-0807-3.ch005

Sinha, N. K., Kumar, P., & Priyadarshi, P. (2021). Relating mindfulness to financial well-being through materialism: Evidence from India. *International Journal of Bank Marketing*, 39(5), 834–855. DOI: 10.1108/IJBM-07-2020-0375

Sornette, D., & Zhou, W. X. (2010). Predictability of large future changes in major financial indices. *International Journal of Forecasting*, 22(1), 153–168. DOI: 10.1016/j.ijforecast.2005.02.004

Spendzharova, A. (2014). The Quest for Financial Stability: Determinants of Regulatory Approach in Banking Supervision: Does Counter-Cyclical Regulation Play a Role? In *European Administrative Governance* (pp. 10-34). Palgrave Macmillan. DOI: 10.1057/9781137282750_2

Stanovich, K. E. (2010). *Decision Making and Rationality in the Modern World.* Oxford University Press.

Stavroyiannis, S., & Babalos, V. (2015). On the time varying nature of herding behaviour: Evidence from major European indices. *Global Business and Economics Review*, 17(03), 298–309. DOI: 10.1504/GBER.2015.070307

Stephens, C. P., & Weisbach, M. S. (2008). Stock repurchases in the 1980s and 1990s: What did we learn? *The Journal of Finance*, 53(6), 2071–2092.

Stiebel, J. H. (2024). Beyond the Individual: Investigating the Interdependence of Speculative Bubbles and Herding in Financial Markets. Available at *SSRN* 4787676. DOI: 10.2139/ssrn.4787676

Stone, D. (2012). Cultivating Financial Mindfulness: A Dual-Process Theory. In *Consumer Knowledge and Financial Decisions* (pp. 15–28). DOI: 10.1007/978-1-4614-0475-0

Subedi, D. P., & Bhandari, D. R. (2024). IMPACT OF PSYCHOLOGICAL FACTORS ON INVESTMENT DECISIONS IN NEPALESE SHARE MARKET: A MEDIATING ROLE OF FINANCIAL LITERACY. *Investment Management and Financial Innovations*, 21(03), 317–329. DOI: 10.21511/imfi.21(3).2024.26

Sunstein, C. R. (2005). The Availability Heuristic, Intuitive Cost-Benefit Analysis, and Climate Change *Chicago John M. Olin Law and Economics Working Paper no. 263*

Su, Q., & Deng, Y. (2024). Tax Avoidance News, Investor Behavior, and Stock Market Performance. *Finance Research Letters*, 67, 105834. DOI: 10.1016/j.frl.2024.105834

Suresh, G., & Loang, O. K. (2024). The Rationality Conundrum: Exploring Herd Mentality among Individual Investors in the Indian Stock Market. *Indian Journal of Finance*, 18(6), 26–45. DOI: 10.17010/ijf/2024/v18i6/173967

Taffler, R. J., Agarwal, V., & Obring, M. (2024). Narrative Emotions and Market Crises. *Journal of Behavioral Finance*, ●●●, 1–21. DOI: 10.1080/15427560.2024.2365723

Takahashi, H., & Nobuyuki, L. (2004). Stock price behavior surrounding stock repurchase announcements: Evidence from Japan. *Pacific-Basin Finance Journal*, 12(3), 271–290. DOI: 10.1016/j.pacfin.2003.10.002

Talbi, M., Ferchichi, M., Ismaalia, F., & Samil, S. (2024). Resilience Amidst Turbulence: Unraveling COVID-19's Impact on Financial Stability through Price Dynamics and Investor Behavior in GCC Markets. *International Journal of Economics and Finance*, 16(4), 22. DOI: 10.5539/ijef.v16n4p22

Tauseef, S. (2023). Herd behaviour in an emerging market: An evidence of calendar and size effects. *Journal of Asia Business Studies*, 17(3), 639–655. DOI: 10.1108/JABS-10-2021-0430

Tekçe, B., Yılmaz, N., & Bildik, R. (2016). What factors affect behavioral biases? Evidence from Turkish individual stock investors. *Research in International Business and Finance*, 37, 515–526. DOI: 10.1016/j.ribaf.2015.11.017

Teti, E., & Maroni, D. (2021). The new great bubble in the technology industry? *Technology Analysis and Strategic Management*, 33(05), 520–534. DOI: 10.1080/09537325.2020.1828577

Tetlock, P. C. (2010). Does public financial news resolve asymmetric information? *Review of Financial Studies*, 23(12), 3520–3557. DOI: 10.1093/rfs/hhq052

Thompson, E. A. (2007, January). The tulipmania: Fact or artifact? *Public Choice*, 130(1-2), 99–114. DOI: 10.1007/s11127-006-9074-4

Tian, W. (2016). *Commercial banking risk management: Regulation in the wake of the financial crisis*. Palgrave Macmillan., DOI: 10.1057/978-1-137-59442-6

Tong, H., & Wei, S. (2008) Real Effects of the Subprime Mortgage Crisis: Is it a Demand or a Finance Shock? NBER Working Papers, 14205.

Tran, N. T. (2024). A systematic review of the monetary policy and herd behavior. Journal of Management, Economics, & Industrial Organization (JOMEINO), 8(1).

Tran, M., Pham-Hi, D., & Bui, M. (2023). Optimizing Automated Trading Systems with Deep Reinforcement Learning. *Algorithms*, 16(1), 23. DOI: 10.3390/a16010023

Trichilli, Y., Gaadane, S., Boujelbène Abbes, M., & Masmoudi, A. (2024, June 03). Impact of the confirmation bias on returns, expectations and hedging of optimistic and pessimistic traders before and during COVID-19 pandemic. *EuroMed Journal of Business*, 19(02), 338–365. DOI: 10.1108/EMJB-03-2022-0046

Trisno, B., & Vidayana. (2023). Understanding herding behavior among Indonesian stock market investors. *5th International Conference of Biospheric Harmony Advanced Research, ICOBAR 2023. 426*. Jakarta: EDP Sciences. DOI: 10.1051/e3sconf/202342601088

Tsetsekos, G. P. (1993). Valuation effects of open market stock repurchases for financially weak firms. *Review of Financial Economics*, 2(2), 29–42. DOI: 10.1002/j.1873-5924.1993.tb00563.x

Tuominen, N. (2017) *A Basic Theory of Rational Herd Behavior and Informational Cascades Does It Apply to Financial Markets,* Bachelor's Thesis in Economics, Aalto University's School of Business.

Tversky A. and Kahneman D. (1986). Rational Choice and the Framing of Decisions *The Journal of Business*, vol. 39, no. 4, part. 2, 251-278.

Tversky, A., & Kahneman, D. (1973). Availability: A Heuristic for Judging Frequency and Probability. *Cognitive Psychology*, 5(2), 207–232. DOI: 10.1016/0010-0285(73)90033-9

Tversky, A., & Kahneman, D. (1974). Judgement Under Uncertainity: Heuristics and Biases. *Science*, 185(4157), 1124–1131. DOI: 10.1126/science.185.4157.1124 PMID: 17835457

Tversky, A., & Kahneman, D. (1981). The Framing of Decisions and the Psychology of Choice. *Science*, 211(4481), 453–458. DOI: 10.1126/science.7455683 PMID: 7455683

Ukpong, I. (2023). Determinants of industry herding (Doctoral dissertation, Anglia Ruskin Research Online (ARRO)).

Ulibarri, C. A., Anselmo, P. C., Hovespian, K., Tolk, J., & Florescu, I. (2009). Noise-trader risk' and Bayesian market making in FX derivatives: Rolling loaded dice? *International Journal of Finance & Economics*, 14(03), 268–279. DOI: 10.1002/ijfe.373

Van Rooij, M., Lusardi, A., & Alessie, R. (2011). Financial literacy and stock market participation. *Journal of Financial Economics*, 101(2), 449–472. DOI: 10.1016/j.jfineco.2011.03.006

Vargo, S. L., Peters, L., Kjellberg, H., Koskela-Huotari, K., Nenonen, S., Polese, F., Sarno, D., & Vaughan, C. (2023). Emergence in marketing: An institutional and ecosystem framework. *Journal of the Academy of Marketing Science*, 51(1), 2–22. DOI: 10.1007/s11747-022-00849-8

Va că-Zamfir, D., & Slave, C. (2018). Tulip-the flower that conquered Europe. *18th International Multidisciplinary Scientific Geoconference, SGEM 2018Albena. 18*, pp. 1003-1010. International Multidisciplinary Scientific Geoconference. Retrieved Sep 15, 2024, from https://www.scopus.com/record/display.uri?eid=2-s2.0-85058814075&origin=scopusAI

Va că-Zamfir, D., & Slave, C. (2018). *Tulip-the flower that conquered Europe. 18th International Multidisciplinary Scientific Geoconference, SGEM 2018. 18.* International Multidisciplinary Scientific Geoconference., DOI: 10.5593/sgem2018/5.1/S20.129

Venkatraman, V., & Beard, E. (2020, Jan 01). Neural Correlates of Decision Variables and Strategic Preferences. In *Psychological Perspectives on Financial Decision Making* (pp. 21–38). Springer International Publishing., DOI: 10.1007/978-3-030-45500-2_2

Vermaelen, T. (1981). Common stock repurchases and market signaling. *Journal of Financial Economics*, 9(2), 139–183. DOI: 10.1016/0304-405X(81)90011-8

Verma, S., Rao, P., & Kumar, S. (2024). Is investing inherently emotionally arousing process? Fund manager perspective. *Qualitative Research in Financial Markets*, 16(2), 380–400. DOI: 10.1108/QRFM-09-2022-0153

Vidani, J. (2024). Why 90% of Stock Market Traders are in Loss? *Available atSSRN 4849875.*

Vukovic, D. B., Kurbonov, O. O., Maiti, M., Özer, M., & Radovanovic, M. (2024). Outperforming the market: A comparison of Star and NonStar analysts' investment strategies and recommendations. *Humanities & Social Sciences Communications*, 11(1), 1–15. DOI: 10.1057/s41599-023-02527-8

Vuković, M., & Pivac, S. (2024, January 30). The impact of behavioral factors on investment decisions and investment performance in Croatian stock market. *Managerial Finance*, 50(02), 349–366. DOI: 10.1108/MF-01-2023-0068

Walsh, P. (2012, April). The bubble on the periphery: Scotland and the South Sea bubble. *The Scottish Historical Review*, 91(01), 106–124. DOI: 10.3366/shr.2012.0073

Wang, D. (2008). *Herd behavior towards the market index: Evidence from 21 financial markets.*

Wang, L. (2019). Research on financial risk of software and information technology service industry enterprises. Finance and Accounting Study, No. 228(19), 84+86.

Wang, Q. (2018). Research on the market effect of stock buyback of listed companies and its influencing factors [Doctoral dissertation, Xi'an University of Science and Technology].

Wang, J., & Liu, K. (2019). Understanding WeChat Users' Herd Behavior in Forwarding Health Information: An Empirical Study in China. *7th International Conference for Smart Health, ICSH 2019. 11924 LNCS*, pp. 177-188. Shenzhen: Springer. DOI: 10.1007/978-3-030-34482-5_16

Wang, W. (2002). Information connotation and market identification of state-owned legal person share repurchase: An empirical study on the repurchase of state-owned legal person shares by Yuntianhua and Shenneng companies. *Management World (Monthly)*, 2002(6), 109–117.

Wang, X., Kim, M. H., & Suardi, S. (2022, August). Herding and China's market-wide circuit breaker. *Journal of Banking & Finance*, 141, 106533. Advance online publication. DOI: 10.1016/j.jbankfin.2022.106533

Wang, Y. (2023). The Impact of Information Asymmetry on Investment Behavior in the Stock Market. Highlights in Business. *Economics and Management*, 19, 165–170.

Wansley, J. W., Lane, W. R., & Sarkar, S. (1989). Managements' View on Share Repurchase and Tender Offer Premiums. *Financial Management*, 18(3), 97–110. DOI: 10.2307/3665652

Wen, J., Okolo, C. V., Ugwuoke, I. C., & Kolani, K. (2022). Research on influencing factors of renewable energy, energy efficiency, on technological innovation. Does trade, investment and human capital development matter? *Energy Policy*, 160, 112718. DOI: 10.1016/j.enpol.2021.112718

Westphal, R., & Sornette, D. (2023, September 29). How Market Intervention can Prevent Bubbles and Crashes: An Agent Based Modelling Approach. *Computational Economics*. Advance online publication. DOI: 10.1007/s10614-023-10462-8

Wheale, P. R., & Amin, L. H. (2003). Bursting the dot.com "Bubble': A Case Study in Investor Behaviour. *Technology Analysis and Strategic Management*, 15(1), 117–136. DOI: 10.1080/0953732032000046097

Whitehouse, H. (2002). Diversification too narrowly defined. *The CPA Journal*, 72(5), 18.

Wikipedia. (2022). *The Crowd: A Study of the Popular Mind*. Retrieved Sep 04, 2024, from https://en.wikipedia.org/wiki: https://en.wikipedia.org/wiki/The_Crowd:_A_Study_of_the_Popular_Mind

Wilinski, A., Sochanowski, M., & Nowicki, W. (2022). An investment strategy based on the first derivative of the moving averages difference with parameters adapted by machine learning. *Data Science in Finance and Economics*, 2(2), 96–116. DOI: 10.3934/DSFE.2022005

Williams, O. J., & Satchell, S. E. (2011, Aug). Social welfare issues of financial literacy and their implications for regulation. *Journal of Regulatory Economics, 40*(01), 01-40. DOI: 10.1007/s11149-011-9151-6

Williams, T. (2007, April). Empowerment of whom and for what? Financial literacy education and the new regulation of consumer financial services. *Law & Policy*, 29(02), 226–256. DOI: 10.1111/j.1467-9930.2007.00254.x

Wu, Y. (2018). Research on the short-term market effect of stock repurchase announcement of A-share listed companies and its influencing factors [Doctoral dissertation, East China University of Politics and Law].

Wu, B., Min, F., & Wen, F. (2023). The stress contagion among financial markets and its determinants. *European Journal of Finance*, 29(11), 1267–1302. DOI: 10.1080/1351847X.2022.2111222

Wyer, R. S.Jr, & Carlston, D. E. (2018). *Social cognition, inference, and attribution.* Psychology Press. DOI: 10.4324/9780203781593

Wynes, M. J. (2021). Anger, Fear, and Investor's Information Search Behavior. *Journal of Behavioral Finance*, 22(04), 403–419. DOI: 10.1080/15427560.2020.1786386

Xia, Y., & Madni, G. R. (2024). Unleashing the behavioral factors affecting the decision making of Chinese investors in stock markets. *PLoS One*, 19(2), e0298797. DOI: 10.1371/journal.pone.0298797 PMID: 38349946

Xie, H.-B., Chen, C., Bu, H., & Wang, S.-Y. (2011, April). Testing market responses under extreme risks. *Xitong Gongcheng Lilun yu Shijian/System Engineering. Theory into Practice*, 31(04), 650–655. Retrieved September 14, 2024, from https://www.scopus.com/record/display.uri?eid=2-s2.0-79957562308&origin=scopusAI

Xie, J., Fang, Y., Gao, B., & Tan, C. (2023, January). Availability heuristic and expected returns. *Finance Research Letters*, 51, 103443. Advance online publication. DOI: 10.1016/j.frl.2022.103443

Xie, Z., Qu, L., Lin, R., & Guo, Q. (2022). Relationships between fluctuations of environmental regulation, technological innovation, and economic growth: A multinational perspective. *Journal of Enterprise Information Management*, 35(4/5), 1267–1287. DOI: 10.1108/JEIM-02-2021-0104

Xiong, H. (2022). Analysis of the reasons for share repurchase—Taking Gree Electric as an example. *China Management Informatization*, 25(03), 25–28.

Xu, G., & Chi, M. K. (2003). Stock repurchases and firm value: A theoretical and empirical analysis. *Management Science*, 49(4), 60–64.

Yang, S. (2024, Aug 01). Pandemic, policy, and markets: insights and learning from COVID-19's impact on global stock behavior. *Empirical Economics*, 01-29. DOI: 10.1007/s00181-024-02648-2

Yang, X. (2012). Research on share buyback behavior of listed companies based on long-term market effect analysis [Doctoral dissertation, Chang'an University].

Yang, H., Tian, C., & Shen, H. (2022). Dual effects of share repurchase to maintain market value and incentivize employees: A case study based on Midea Group. *China Management Accounting*, (01), 98–114.

Yang, N.-T., Chu, H.-H., Ko, K.-C., & Lee, S.-W. (2018, April). Continuing overreaction and momentum in a market with price limits. *Pacific-Basin Finance Journal*, 48, 56–71. DOI: 10.1016/j.pacfin.2018.01.005

Yang, W., & Loang, O. K. (2024). Systematic Literature Review: Behavioural Biases as the Determinants of Herding. *Technology-Driven Business Innovation: Unleashing the Digital Advantage*, 1, 79–92. DOI: 10.1007/978-3-031-51997-0_7

Yang, W., & Loang, O. K. (2024). Unpacking Financial Herding Behaviour: A Conceptual Study of Youth and Working Adults in Chongqing, China. In *Technology-Driven Business Innovation: Unleashing the Digital Advantage* (Vol. 1, pp. 67–78). Springer Nature Switzerland. DOI: 10.1007/978-3-031-51997-0_6

Yang, X., Zhu, Y., & Cheng, T. Y. (2020, February). How the individual investors took on big data: The effect of panic from the internet stock message boards on stock price crash. *Pacific-Basin Finance Journal*, 59, 101245. Advance online publication. DOI: 10.1016/j.pacfin.2019.101245

Ye, J., Li, D., & Cao, Y. (2020, January 01). Investor irrational selection bias in stock market based on cognitive psychology: Evidence from herding behaviour. *Revista Argentina de Clínica Psicológica*, 29(01), 90–98. DOI: 10.24205/03276716.2020.13

Yu, L. (2010). Research on the market effect of stock repurchase of listed companies in China [Doctoral dissertation, Southwest University of Finance and Economics].

Yuen, K. F., Wang, X., Ma, F., & Li, K. X. (2020, May 02). The psychological causes of panic buying following a health crisis. *International Journal of Environmental Research and Public Health*, 17(10), 3513. Advance online publication. DOI: 10.3390/ijerph17103513 PMID: 32443427

Yu, R., & Zhou, X. (2007, May). Neuroeconomics: Opening the "black box" behind the economic behavior. *Chinese Science Bulletin*, 52(09), 1153–1161. DOI: 10.1007/s11434-007-0193-1

Zaimovic, A., Arnaut-Berilo, A., & Mustafic, A. (2017, April 01). Portfolio Diversification in the South-East European Equity Markets. *South East European Journal of Economics and Business*, 12(01), 126–235. DOI: 10.1515/jeb-2017-0010

Zhang, Y. (2020). Research on the market effect of stock repurchase announcements of listed companies in China [Doctoral dissertation, Shanghai International Studies University].

Zhang, K., & Long, D. (2021). Individual and Institutional Investor: Who is More Rational. *2nd Asia-Pacific Conference on Image Processing, Electronics and Computers, IPEC 2021* (pp. 431-434). Dalian: Association for Computing Machinery. DOI: 10.1145/3452446.3452555

Zhang, R. (2018). Decision-making neuroscience-based research on stock herd and anti-herd behavior. *NeuroQuantology : An Interdisciplinary Journal of Neuroscience and Quantum Physics*, 16(06), 200–204. DOI: 10.14704/nq.2018.16.6.1625

Zhang, R., Song, X., & Yin, W.. (2021). Analysis of motivation and effectiveness of stock repurchase in listed companies—Taking Gree Electric Appliances as an example. *Value Engineering*, 40(24), 3. DOI: 10.3969/j.issn.1006-4311.2021.24.019

Zhou, L., & Yang, C. (2020, July 01). Investor sentiment, investor crowded-trade behavior, and limited arbitrage in the cross section of stock returns. *Empirical Economics*, 59(01), 437–460. DOI: 10.1007/s00181-019-01630-7

Zhou, M. (2007). Analysis of negative financial effects of corporate share buyback. *Science and Industry*, 7(1), 4. DOI: 10.3969/j.issn.1671-1807.2007.01.019

Zhou, S., & Liu, X. (2022, December). Internet postings and investor herd behavior: Evidence from China's open-end fund market. *Humanities & Social Sciences Communications*, 09(01), 441. Advance online publication. DOI: 10.1057/s41599-022-01462-4

Zhu, X., Li, S., Srinivasan, K., & Lash, M. T. (2024). Impact of the COVID-19 pandemic on the stock market and investor online word of mouth. *Decision Support Systems*, 176, 114074. DOI: 10.1016/j.dss.2023.114074

About the Contributors

Ooi Kok Loang is a renowned expert in behavioral finance and capital markets, currently serving at the University of Malaya (UM) in the Department of Finance, Faculty of Business and Economics. He holds a Master's degree in Finance and a PhD in Behavioral Finance from Universiti Sains Malaysia (USM), and a Master's degree in Law from the International Islamic University Malaysia (IIUM). Additionally, he is a US Certified Internal Auditor (CIA) with professional experience as an auditor at KPMG. Dr. Ooi has published multiple articles in high-impact SSCI and top-tier Scopus journals and serves as a reviewer in the field of behavioral finance. His academic contributions are complemented by his tenure as Deputy Dean at a prestigious private university and his active involvement in research and professional organizations, making him a leading figure in the study and application of behavioral finance.

***

Asheetu Bhatia Sarin is an Assistant Professor (Management) at Vivekananda Institute of Professional Studies-Technical campus affiliated to GGSIPU, Delhi. She is having around 11+ years of teaching experience in the field of Commerce and Management. She has done Ph.D. in Behavioral Finance, did her post-graduation (MBA) from ICFAI Business School in Finance and Marketing, and earned her graduate degree in B.Com (H) from Delhi University. She is a lifetime member of the Indian Commerce Association and has to her credit many national and International publications.

Lakshmi Bhooshetty is an accomplished Assistant Professor with over a decade of experience teaching accounting subjects. She is a certified US Certified Management Accountant (CMA), demonstrating her expertise in financial planning, analysis, and control. Known for her productivity-driven mindset and leadership skills, Dr. Bhooshetty has served as a program coordinator, enhancing her organizational abilities. Her research primarily focuses on Human Resource topics, with a recent publication in Management Review Quarterly (Springer Nature) titled "Rejuvenating Human Resource Accounting Research: A Review Using Bibliometric Analysis." This sole-authored paper explores the intellectual structure of Human Resource Accounting, identifying research gaps and future trajectories. Dr. Bhooshetty's expertise spans Human Resource Management, Intellectual Capital, Human Capital, and Voluntary Disclosure. She continues to blend her teaching experience with research pursuits, aiming to make impactful contributions in both academic and business settings.

Duygu Çeri has a bachelor's degree in Business Administration and a PhD in Finance. She worked as a research assistant at Anadolu University between 2008-2018. Since 2018, she has been working as an assistant professor at Sinop University. Her research areas are behavioural finance, financial management, entrepreneurship, innovation and high-tech enterprises.

Manjiri Gadekar is a fellow member of Institute of Chartered accountants of India and is Assistant Professor at Dr. Vishwanath Karad MIT World Peace University. She has an industry experience of six years and academic experience of 8 years. Her research areas include Sustainability, Digital Finance, Blockchain Technology, and Behavioural Finance. She actively participates in Management Development Programs, providing finance training to non-finance professionals. She also has expertise in direct and indirect taxation and has conducted numerous seminars on India and US taxation.

Sushil Gupta is an Alumnus of IIM Ahmedabad having 20 years of experience in Industry & Academia. He has a rich experience of 10 years in the area of Financial Advisory, Asset Management and Sales/business development of Financial Services and 10 years in Teaching and Research. He has authored multiple research papers on Mutual Fund, Micro Finance and Family Office. He has completed the Ph.D. in Management (Finance) from Amity University, Uttar Pradesh in 2020 and qualified for the National Eligibility Test (UGC NET, JUNE-2012) in Management. He has written 10 Scopus and 6 ABDC- C & B Category research papers. And also awarded with the 'NSE Certified Market Professional (NCMP)- Level 1' Certification by National Stock Exchange. His areas of interest are Mutual Fund, Financial Derivatives, Financial planning & Wealth management, Banking and Financial Services.

Manjusha J is a dedicated academic and researcher pursuing her Ph.D. in Finance at Christ University, Bangalore, with a focus on behavioral finance. Her doctoral research explores the "Impact of Financial Mindfulness on Portfolio Diversification" among Indian investors. She holds a Master's degree in Commerce with a specialization in Accounting and Taxation and is NET qualified. As a Teaching Associate at Christ University, she educates undergraduate students in Commerce, Accounting, and Taxation. Manjusha's research interests include financial mindfulness, financial anxiety, and risk tolerance in portfolio diversification. She is passionate about contributing to academia and society, aiming to unravel the complexities of economic decision-making and psychological influences on financial behavior, while shaping future professionals in finance and commerce.

Christian Kaunert is Professor of International Security at Dublin City University, Ireland. He is also Professor of Policing and Security, as well as Director of the International Centre for Policing and Security at the University of South Wales. In addition, he is Jean Monnet Chair, Director of the Jean Monnet Centre of Excellence and Director of the Jean Monnet Network on EU Counter-Terrorism.1b5d2a21-e5b3-45d9-bba0-d041a4516762)

Eren Kırmızıaltın has PhD in economics. He worked at Gazi University in Türkiye between 2009-2017. Since 2023, he has been working at Sinop University in Türkiye. He has publications in the fields of Behavioural Economics, Heterodox Economics, Development Economics, and Economic Sociology.

Varsha Nerlekar is an Associate Professor in Finance at the School of Management (PG) MIT World Peace University in Pune, India. With over 20 years of teaching and industry experience, her research interests include Sustainability, Public Finance, Financial Technologies, Behavioural Finance, and Investments. She received her Ph.D. in Management from Nagpur University, and her postgraduate degree from Indira Institute of Management, Pune. Dr. Nerlekar has published more than 20 research papers and case studies in national and international journals, and is a member of the Board of Studies for reputed institutes such as Symbiosis College of Commerce. She has also conducted Faculty Development Programs and Management Development Programs for various institutions and corporates.

Anjali Sane is an accomplished teacher with over 20 years of experience in the areas of Economics and Banking, Dr. Anjali Sane is also a capable administrator. In addition to academic administration, her research areas include Managerial Economics, Micro and Macro Economics, Financial Literacy and various areas in international business. A dedicated and sincere teacher, she is known for use of practical examples and case studies to supplement classroom learning. Apart from pursuing research in her domain areas, she is also involved in interdisciplinary areas of research such as higher education, sustainable consumption and so on. She has completed Minor Research Project in the area of Financial Literacy with grant from Board of College and University Development (BCUD), Savitribai Phule Pune University. Dr. Anjali Sane prefers to use a combination of quantitative and qualitative research tools while using exploratory research methodology. She has published more than 20 research papers in peer reviewed management journals of repute as well as in conference proceedings of national and international seminars and conferences. She has co-authored 3 books on Business Economics (Micro), 1 book each on Analysis of Financial Statements and Business Economics (Macro). Dr. Anjali Sane has been awarded with the "Ideal Teacher Award" by MAEER's MIT Group of Institutions and also as the "Super Achiever in the field of Education" from Kaveri Group of Institutions, Pune. She was also recognized as Research fellow at Centre for International Trade and Business in Asia (CITBA) at James Cook University, Australia. She has also received the "Best Paper" award for during the International Conference on Innovation in Business, Trade and Commerce in March 2022 and March 2023.

Partap Singh is committed to teaching and research in Finance and Investment domain since last 16 years+. His qualification is PhD (Commerce), M.Com, MBA. He has rich work experience in the field of Teaching, administration and research as well. He held various responsibilities like Editor, Co-editor, and Editorial Board member, Associate Editor in number of national and international journals. He has been regularly been receiving offers for writing books from the top publishing houses of India and received many letter of thanks& compliments for giving valuable suggestions and commendable views concerning improvement of many leading Publications/Books. He has written and published 5 books namely Financial Management, Risk Management, working capital Mana

Bhupinder Singh working as Professor at Sharda University, India. Also, Honorary Professor in University of South Wales UK and Santo Tomas University Tunja, Colombia. His areas of publications as Smart Healthcare, Medicines, fuzzy logics, artificial intelligence, robotics, machine learning, deep learning, federated learning, IoT, PV Glasses, metaverse and many more. He has 3 books, 139 paper publications, 163 paper presentations in international/national conferences and seminars, participated in more than 40 workshops/FDP's/QIP's, 25 courses from international universities of repute, organized more than 59 events with international and national academicians and industry people's, editor-in-chief and co-editor in journals, developed new courses. He has given talks at international universities, resource person in international conferences such as in Nanyang Technological University Singapore, Tashkent State University of Law Uzbekistan; KIMEP University Kazakhstan, All'ah meh Tabatabi University Iran, the Iranian Association of International Criminal law, Iran and Hague Center for International Law and Investment, The Netherlands, Northumbria University Newcastle UK,

Index

A

Artificial Intelligence 1, 2, 5, 9, 10, 11, 12, 13, 14, 15, 16, 18, 19, 20, 96, 139, 145, 146, 152, 153, 154, 157, 160, 166, 167, 170, 171, 205, 209, 240, 307
availability cascade 23, 24, 25, 26, 27, 28, 35, 36, 37, 38, 39, 40, 41, 43
Average Abnormal Return 192
Average Cumulative Abnormal Return 189, 192

B

Bandwagon Effect 16, 48, 80, 241, 242
Behavioral bias 43, 55, 59, 62, 71

C

Cognitive Biases 39, 40, 41, 131, 132, 163, 222, 232, 245, 246, 248, 263, 277, 291, 292, 293, 294, 295, 296, 297, 299, 300, 301, 302, 303, 304, 305, 306, 307
cognitive factors 23, 24, 29, 32, 35, 37, 41, 47, 222
Collective Intelligence 291, 292, 294, 296, 300, 309
CSAD 267, 268, 269, 285
CSSD 267, 268, 269, 285

D

Directional Herding 269, 270, 271, 272
Dot-com Bubble 38, 39, 43, 44, 50, 129, 146, 158, 226, 227, 229, 243, 256, 259, 269, 272, 273, 274, 276, 280, 286

E

Economic Indicators 123, 124, 126, 127, 128, 129, 130, 131, 132, 133, 135, 136, 137, 138, 139, 241, 271, 272

Emotional Contagion 24, 29, 30, 36, 39, 43, 44, 79, 80, 81, 82, 83, 84, 85, 86, 87, 88, 89, 90, 91, 92, 93, 94, 95, 96, 228, 229, 230, 249
Event Study 173, 175, 176, 181, 182, 187, 189, 192, 208

F

Fear and Greed 79, 80, 81, 82, 83, 84, 85, 87, 88, 89, 90, 91, 93, 94, 95, 244, 262, 263, 264
Financial decision-making 15, 54, 66, 69, 82, 85, 86, 104, 162, 249, 293
Financial Literacy 39, 41, 64, 66, 70, 72, 73, 74, 75, 84, 89, 95, 97, 98, 99, 117, 123, 138, 139, 142, 143, 235, 236, 237, 242, 245, 246, 252, 253, 277, 282, 298, 303, 307, 309, 310
Financial Markets 1, 2, 3, 4, 5, 6, 9, 11, 18, 23, 24, 28, 29, 33, 34, 35, 37, 40, 41, 42, 46, 49, 53, 55, 56, 57, 61, 70, 71, 72, 75, 76, 79, 80, 81, 82, 83, 84, 85, 86, 87, 88, 89, 90, 91, 92, 94, 95, 97, 99, 101, 103, 105, 106, 107, 108, 109, 111, 112, 113, 114, 115, 116, 118, 119, 120, 123, 124, 125, 127, 128, 129, 130, 131, 132, 133, 134, 135, 136, 137, 138, 140, 142, 143, 145, 146, 147, 148, 151, 155, 160, 162, 163, 164, 166, 167, 168, 169, 171, 225, 227, 229, 230, 231, 232, 234, 235, 242, 243, 244, 255, 256, 257, 258, 259, 260, 261, 262, 263, 264, 266, 267, 269, 271, 273, 276, 280, 282, 283, 284, 286, 287, 291, 292, 293, 294, 295, 296, 299, 300, 303, 304, 305, 306, 308
Financial mindfulness 53, 54, 56, 63, 64, 65, 66, 67, 68, 69, 71, 72, 73, 76

G

Global Financial Crisis 124, 226, 247, 251, 259

H

herd behavior 2, 23, 24, 25, 28, 29, 30, 31, 32, 34, 35, 36, 37, 38, 39, 40, 41, 44, 46, 47, 49, 50, 57, 68, 70, 71, 73, 75, 76, 97, 98, 118, 140, 143, 158, 159, 160, 162, 163, 164, 165, 168, 169, 223, 229, 234, 258, 259, 261, 264, 275, 278, 279, 282, 288, 289, 308, 309

Herding and Market Overreaction 1, 4, 5

Herding behavior 1, 2, 3, 4, 5, 6, 8, 11, 17, 23, 24, 35, 36, 37, 39, 40, 49, 53, 54, 55, 56, 57, 58, 59, 61, 62, 69, 70, 72, 74, 86, 87, 91, 94, 99, 102, 103, 104, 105, 106, 107, 108, 109, 110, 111, 112, 113, 114, 115, 118, 121, 123, 124, 125, 126, 127, 128, 129, 130, 131, 132, 133, 134, 135, 136, 137, 138, 139, 142, 143, 144, 145, 146, 147, 149, 150, 151, 152, 157, 158, 160, 161, 162, 165, 166, 167, 168, 171, 222, 225, 235, 236, 237, 238, 241, 242, 246, 249, 252, 254, 255, 256, 257, 258, 259, 260, 262, 263, 265, 266, 267, 268, 269, 271, 272, 273, 274, 275, 276, 277, 278, 279, 280, 281, 282, 283, 284, 285, 287, 288, 289, 291, 292, 293, 294, 295, 296, 297, 298, 299, 300, 301, 303, 304, 305, 306, 307, 308, 309, 310

Herd Mentality 11, 99, 113, 120, 138, 143, 222, 225, 255, 256, 257, 259, 266, 310

Historical Market Events 123, 127, 128, 129, 131, 132, 133, 135, 138, 139

I

Informational Herding 269, 270

Information Cascade 28, 29, 32, 266

Institutional Investor Activity 101, 102, 104, 105, 108, 109, 111, 112, 114, 115, 116

investment decision making 18, 280

Investor psychology 59, 82, 124, 126, 141, 247, 256

Investor Sentiment 17, 84, 85, 86, 98, 101, 102, 105, 106, 107, 108, 109, 110, 112, 113, 114, 115, 116, 118, 119, 120, 130, 138, 159, 166, 225, 228, 243, 247, 249, 250, 254, 272, 283, 298

Irrational Exuberance 120, 143, 226, 227, 238, 241, 242, 243, 244, 250, 252, 303, 306

L

Listed Companies 173, 174, 175, 176, 177, 178, 179, 180, 181, 182, 183, 184, 185, 186, 187, 188, 189, 192, 194, 195, 196, 198, 201, 203, 208, 209, 210, 211, 212, 214, 215, 216, 217, 218, 219

M

Market bubbles and Crashes 37, 41, 89, 128, 163, 164, 165, 272, 297, 300, 306

Market inefficiency 58

Market News and Rumors 79, 82, 83, 88, 94, 95

Market Overreaction 1, 4, 5, 6, 8, 13, 23, 24, 25, 79, 80, 82, 83, 85, 87, 88, 90, 92, 93, 94, 95, 96, 221, 222, 223, 224, 225, 226, 228, 229, 230, 231, 232, 241, 243, 244, 245, 246, 251, 252

Market Sentiment 80, 84, 124, 147, 160, 163, 166, 179, 222, 225, 229, 238, 246, 250, 279, 291, 292, 293, 294, 295, 296, 297, 298, 299, 300, 301, 303, 304, 305, 306, 307

Market Volatility 38, 61, 79, 82, 83, 84, 85, 86, 87, 88, 90, 91, 92, 93, 94, 101, 102, 103, 104, 105, 107, 108, 109, 110, 112, 113, 114, 115, 116, 119, 141, 142, 149, 157, 159, 161, 163, 168, 169, 201, 222, 232, 233, 234, 236, 241, 245, 256, 280, 296, 306

Media Coverage Intensity 101, 103, 105, 109, 112, 114, 116

Misinformation 2, 158

N

Noise Trader Models 266

P

Portfolio diversification 40, 62, 63, 72, 73, 289

psychological factors 29, 39, 49, 61, 86, 95, 110, 111, 118, 146, 222, 227, 241, 252, 298

R

Regulatory Announcements 101, 104, 105, 108, 109, 111, 112, 113, 114, 116, 117

Regulatory Changes 123, 124, 125, 127, 128, 129, 131, 132, 133, 135, 136, 137, 138, 139

Risk Aversion 228, 239

Risk Management 2, 10, 12, 15, 106, 128, 146, 149, 151, 157, 158, 168, 169, 170, 222, 227, 245, 276, 277, 288, 296

S

Share Price 173, 175, 176, 178, 179, 180, 181, 183, 184, 185, 186, 187, 188, 189, 192, 197, 204, 206, 207, 208, 209, 211, 212

Share Repurchase 173, 174, 175, 176, 177, 178, 179, 180, 181, 182, 183, 184, 185, 186, 187, 188, 189, 190, 191, 192, 193, 195, 197, 198, 201, 202, 204, 205, 206, 207, 208, 209, 211, 214, 215, 216, 217, 218, 219

Stock Market 17, 18, 21, 57, 73, 98, 99, 118, 119, 120, 124, 140, 142, 143, 173, 174, 179, 234, 247, 249, 250, 251, 253, 254, 259, 264, 282, 283, 284, 285, 287, 288, 289, 309, 310

T

The Dot-com Bubble 38, 39, 43, 44, 50, 129, 146, 158, 226, 227, 229, 243, 256, 259, 269, 272, 273, 274, 276, 280, 286

The South Sea Bubble 3, 124, 258, 269, 288

Tulip Mania 124, 226, 227, 258, 269

www.ingramcontent.com/pod-product-compliance
Ingram Content Group UK Ltd.
Pitfield, Milton Keynes, MK11 3LW, UK
UKHW012123171224
452514UK00007B/40